ARTHUR R. ASHE, JR.

A HARD ROAD TO GLORY

BASKETBALL

The African-American Athlete in Basketball

Other titles in the *Hard Road to Glory* series

ARTHUR R. ASHE, JR.

A HARD ROAD TO GLORY

BASKETBALL

The African-American Athlete in Basketball

WITH THE ASSISTANCE OF
KIP BRANCH, OCANIA CHALK, AND FRANCIS HARRIS

Amistad

NEW YORK, NEW YORK

"Views of Sport: Taking the Hard Road With Black Athletes" by Arthur R.
Ashe, Jr., © 1988 by The New York Times Company. Reprinted by
permission.

Amistad Press, Inc.
1271 Avenue of the Americas
New York, New York 10020

Distributed by:
Penguin USA
375 Hudson Street
New York, New York 10014

Produced by March Tenth, Inc.

   2   3   4   5   6   7   8   9   10

Library of Congress Cataloging-in-Publication Data
Ashe, Arthur.
     A hard road to glory—basketball : the African-American athlete in
  basketball / Arthur R. Ashe, Jr.; with the assistance of Kip
  Branch, Ocania Chalk, and Francis Harris.
       p.   cm.
     "The text of this book was taken from the three-volume set of A
  hard road to glory and combined into a compendium on basketball"—
  CIP data sheet.
     Includes bibliographical references and index.
     ISBN 1-56743-037-6 : $9.95
     1. Basketball—United States—History.   2. Afro-American
  basketball players—Statistics.   I. Ashe, Arthur.   Hard road to
  glory.   II. Title.
  GV885.7A84   1993
  796.323'0973—dc20   93-37948
                                                              CIP

Contents

To my wife, Jeanne, and my daughter, Camera

Publisher's Statement

The untimely passing of Arthur Ashe on February 6, 1993, requires telling the story of how *A Hard Road to Glory* came to be. It is a story that echoes its title, a tale that takes place in the publishing world and yet, not surprisingly, contains similar elements to those found in the world of sports: extraordinary individual effort, unified teamwork, setbacks, defeats, and eventual victory. It is only a partial testimony to a courageous man whom I was proud to have as a colleague and a friend.

Ten years earlier, in February 1983, while I was executive director of Howard University Press in Washington, DC, I received a telephone call from Arthur Ashe. He had heard of my interest in seeing that a work on the history of the Black athlete be published. He had expressed a similar desire to Marie Brown, a literary agent, who had referred him to me. He asked me when I planned to visit New York City again, and I told him it just so happened that I had to be there the next day.

That was not completely true. However, this subject was of such burning interest to me and I was so excited that a person of Arthur's stature was interested in writing such a book that I felt I should move expeditiously.

The following day I met him at his apartment on East 72nd Street, where we had a brief discussion. Then we went to his agent, Fifi Oscard, and met with her and Kevin McShane of the Oscard Agency. Arthur presented a general outline of the book that became the basis of our discussion, which in turn led to the negotiation of a contract.

On April 5, 1983, with the approval of the Executive Committee of the Commission on Management and Operations of Howard University Press, we formally executed a contract for a book that was tentatively titled *A History of the Black Athlete in America.* In May 1983 Arthur came to Washington, where we held a press conference and a ceremonial signing of the contract at the Palm Restaurant. I felt ecstatic that we were making the kind of history that would influence generations.

It should be noted that Arthur came to Howard University Press because, of the more than twenty commercial publishers in New York that he had approached, not one had seen the value or viability of a book on the history of Black athletes.

As he was soon to learn, however, Arthur and I had much more in common. We shared similar backgrounds of growing up in Virginia: He was from Richmond and I am from Portsmouth. We both attended schools (Maggie L. Walker High School and I. C. Norcom High School) that although segregated had outstanding teachers who nurtured Black students, instilled in them the desire to achieve, and provided important contacts to do so in the wider world. We were proud to be working together.

In June 1983, Arthur underwent double-bypass heart surgery. Miraculously, in a matter of weeks he was back at work on this project. His commitment went far beyond intellectual curiosity and enthusiasm. By this time Arthur had already assembled the nucleus of his research team, which included Ocania Chalk, Kip Branch, Derilene McCloud, and Sandra Jamison. (Rod Howard later replaced Ms. Jamison.) My son Francis Harris was to join this team in September 1983. (Doug Smith, of USA Today, assisted in this edition.)

In December 1985, I resigned from my position at Howard University Press, effective June 1986. I then began the preliminary stages of forming Amistad Press, Inc. as an independent publishing house managed and controlled by African Americans. After fifteen years at a university press, which had followed fifteen years with commercial publishers in New York, I was ready to move on to the professional challenge of my life.

There were still, however, some loose ends at Howard. Sensing a lack of scholarly and administrative support, Arthur asked university officials in January 1986 if they still had a commitment to publish his book. Within twenty-four hours of his question he was informed by an officer of the university that they had no further interest in his work. They were agreeable to his finding another publisher, and on February 21, 1986, Howard University released Arthur from his contract. By this time he had compiled about 75 percent of the material found in the present volumes. It was inconceivable that the project should stop at this point. We had come too far.

Arthur and I agreed that he would explore opportunities with other publishing houses

for his work while I was attempting to raise capital to launch Amistad Press. In May 1986, I met Lynne Lumsden and Jon Harden, who had recently purchased Dodd, Mead and Company, Inc., a venerable New York firm with a reputation for publishing influential African-American authors. We began negotiations for a joint venture in book publishing. By the middle of June 1986, we had settled on the legal parameters for this relationship. On July 1, 1986, Amistad Press, Inc. was incorporated in the State of New York. On August 22, 1986, Arthur Ashe signed a contract with Dodd, Mead and Amistad Press to publish A Hard Road to Glory: A History of the African-American Athlete. He had decided on this evocative title, and we all agreed that the work, based on original and extensive research, would necessarily consist of several volumes.

The entire team was working well. We had negotiated another critical turn in the development of this project, and we were feeling elated, for we had finally found a supportive atmosphere in the private sector. We shared an enthusiasm and a commitment to see this work through to its successful publication.

We planned to publish the work in the fall of 1987. To this end, Arthur appeared on the Author's Breakfast Program of the annual meeting of the American Booksellers Association, which was held in Washington, DC, at the end of May.

A Hard Road to Glory was announced with great fanfare and extensive promotional material, and it was received with equally positive interest.

In November 1987, while we were furiously engaged in the tasks of copyediting, proofreading, and typesetting, we learned that Dodd, Mead was experiencing financial difficulty. By February 1988, when it was confirmed that Dodd, Mead would not be able to proceed with this project, Amistad was offered the opportunity to purchase the Dodd,

Mead interest in the contracts that we owned jointly, including that of *A Hard Road to Glory*. I accepted with great pleasure and some trepidation. We still had to find a way to get the books out.

I initiated discussions with several publishing houses to explore their interests in a joint venture relationship similar to the one that Amistad had had with Dodd, Mead. In the spring of 1988 discussions began with Larry Kirshbaum, president of Warner Books. Simultaneously, through the efforts of Clarence Avant, I met Martin D. Payson, who at the time was general counsel of Warner Communications, Inc., which owned Warner Books. Marty Payson, who worked closely with Warner Communications's chairman, Steve Ross, became enthralled with the idea of *A Hard Road to Glory* and thought it would be a significant project for Warner Books and Warner Communications. A joint venture between Amistad Press and Warner Books began in April 1988. We then set a new publication date for November. Our spirits were lifted again.

While completing the final stages of reviewing galleys and sample page proofs, Arthur began having trouble using his right hand. Ultimately, he underwent brain surgery. As a result of this operation, he learned that he had been infected with HIV, the virus which was to take his life.

The publication of *A Hard Road to Glory* was a major achievement for a man who had had many triumphs. Arthur was intimately involved in the work at every stage of its development, from proposal to manuscript to bound books. He had been released from the hospital only a few days before the books arrived from the printer in October 1988. He asked his wife, Jeanne, to drive him from their home in Mt. Kisco, New York, to my apartment in Manhattan, where he saw the finished copies for the first time.

The first books had come from the bindery on a Friday and were sent directly to my home so that I would not have to wait until Monday to see them. I had received the books on Saturday, when I telephoned Arthur. His first reaction upon seeing them was similar to mine: He simply stared at them. We both looked at each other and smiled continuously. Because their daughter, Camera, was asleep, Jeanne had remained in the car and waited until my wife, Sammie, and I came back with Arthur and his first set of books. I think we were all nearly speechless because we realized what a tremendous ordeal and success we had experienced together.

This edition of *A Hard Road to Glory* names a single publisher of the work, Amistad Press, Inc. My wife and I started this company with our own personal financial resources. We were able to keep the company going in lean early years because Arthur became the first outside investor and supported us in attracting other investors. He personally guaranteed a bank loan that had been difficult to obtain, since the company had not yet published any books. Fortunately, we paid off that loan many years ago. Through Arthur's efforts we were able not only to publish his work, but we were also able to bring other important works to the public. We are on the road to achieving the goals for which Amistad Press was founded.

Present and future generations of writers will owe a great debt to a great man, Arthur R. Ashe, Jr., for helping make it possible for them to have a platform from which to present their creativity to the world.

Charles F. Harris
President and Publisher
Amistad Press, Inc.
March 1993

Views of Sport:

Taking the Hard Road With Black Athletes

by Arthur R. Ashe, Jr.

My three-volume book, *A Hard Road to Glory: A History of the African-American Athlete,* began almost as an afterthought to a seminar class I was asked to give on the historical and sociological role of the African-American athlete. Though I had never seen it, I assumed some esteemed black historian, sociologist or sports reporter had compiled the entire story of the black athlete in one volume. A search found only "The Negro in Sports," by Edwin B. Henderson, written in 1938 and slightly updated in 1948.

After three months of preliminary research, three inhibiting factors emerged for anyone wishing to put it all together: it would take more money than any reasonable publisher's advance would cover; black historians never deemed sports serious enough for their scarce time; and these same historians had underestimated the socio-historical impact of the black athlete in black American life. But the truth is that the psychic value of success in sports was and is higher in the black community than among any other American subculture.

This high psychic reward is not a contemporary phenomenon. Just after the Civil War when sports clubs were formed and rules were written, athletes became the most well known and among the richest of black Americans. Isaac Murphy, perhaps the greatest American jockey of the 19th century, earned more than $25,000. A black newspaper, the Baltimore Afro-American, complained in an editorial in 1902 that Joe Gans, the black world lightweight boxing champion, got more publicity than Booker T. Washington. It is no different today; Mike Tyson is better known around the world than Jesse Jackson.

In spite of the obstacles, I decided to proceed with the book because I became obsessed with so many unanswered questions. How did black America manage to create such a favorable environment for its athletes? Why did so many blacks excel so early on with so little training, poor facilities and mediocre coaching? Why did the civil rights organizations of the time complain so little about the discrimination against black athletes? And why were white athletes so afraid of competing on an equal basis with blacks? I just had to have my own answers to these and other puzzling sets of facts.

For 120 years, white America has gone to extraordinary lengths to discredit and discourage black participation in sports because black athletes have been so accomplished. The saddest case is that of the black jockeys. When the first Kentucky Derby was

A HARD ROAD TO GLORY

run in 1875, 15 thoroughbreds were entered and 14 of their riders were black. Black domination of horse racing then was analogous to the domination of the National Basketball Association today. Subsequently, the Jockey Club was formed in the early 1890's to regulate and license all jockeys. Then one by one the blacks were denied their license renewals. By 1911 they had all but disappeared.

This example appears in Volume I, which covers the years 1619–1918. It is the slimmest of the three volumes but took the most time, effort and cross-referencing of facts. Starting with official record books of all the sports, I sought to find out who was black, where he (there was no appreciable female involvement until World War I) came from, and where he learned his skills. I encountered two major obstacles: no American or world record was recognized unless it was under the auspices of a white college or the Amateur Athletic Union (simply put, no records set at black colleges or black club events counted to national or international governing bodies); and some early black newspapers published accounts that were frequently, if unintentionally, just plain wrong.

In the 27 years between the end of the two World Wars (the period covered by Volume II), the foundation for the quantum leaps made by black athletes after 1950 was laid. Again there were several cogent factors that influenced both the pace and progress of the black athlete. The one institution that provided minimum competition and facilities was the black college. But many of these schools still had white presidents and the small cadre of black presidents were hesitant to spend money on athletics for fear of alienating white donors who may have preferred an emphasis on academics.

A very positive factor was the formation of the black college conferences. But to white America, these conferences were nearly nonentities. They never got to see Alfred (Jazz) Bird of Lincoln University in Pennsylvania, or Ben Stevenson of Tuskegee Institute, who is by consensus the greatest black college football player before World War II. They never saw Ora Washington of Philadelphia, who may have been the best female athlete ever. Of course everyone knew and saw Jack Johnson, Jesse Owens and Joe Louis. They were, and still are, household names.

There were other famous names who because of their own naivete, bitterness and ignorance suffered indignities that brought me and my staff to tears of sadness and tears of rage. In 1805, for example, according to an account in The Times of London, Tom Molineaux, a black American from Richmond, Va., actually won the English (and world) heavyweight boxing title in the 27th round against Tom Cribb, but the paper quotes the English referee as saying to the prostrate Cribb, "Get up Tom, don't let the nigger win." Cribb was given four extra minutes to recover and eventually won.

. . .

There were times, to be sure, when white America got a glimpse of our premiere black athletes. The first black All-American football player, William H. Lewis, surfaced in 1892. Lewis was followed 25 years later by Paul Robeson and Fritz Pollard. But the most heralded confrontations took place on the baseball diamond when black teams played white major league all-star aggregations. The black squads won almost 75 percent of the time. The same for basketball. In the late 1920's and 1930's the original Celtics refused to join the whites-only professional leagues so they could continue to play against two black teams: the New York Rens and the Harlem Globetrotters.

Between 1945 and 1950, the athletic establishment was upended when all the major sports were integrated, in some places. What the black athlete did in the next 38 years is nothing less than stupendous. In particular, he (and she) brought speed to every activity. With fewer and fewer exceptions, whites were not to be seen in the sprints on the tracks or in the backfield on the gridiron.

Which brings us to the primary unanswered question of the project. Do black Americans have some genetic edge in physical activities involving running and jumping? My reply is that nature, our unique history in America, and our exclusion from other occupations have produced the psychic addiction to success in sports and entertainment. Once the momentum was established, continuing success became a matter of cultural pride. And yes, we do feel certain positions in sports belong to us. Quick, name a white halfback in the National Football League? Who was the last white sprinter to run 100 meters under 10 seconds?

Records aside, black athletes have had a major impact on black American history. In the early 1940's, for example, the black labor leader A. Phillip Randolph made the integration of major league baseball a test of the nation's intentions regarding discrimination in employment. The phrase "If he's [a black man] good enough for the Navy, he's good enough for the majors" became an oft-heard slogan for many. And when the opportunity finally came, it seemed almost predictable that black America would produce a Jim Brown, a Wilt Chamberlain, an Althea Gibson, a Bill Russell, a Gale Sayers, a Muhammed Ali, a Lee Evans, a Carl Lewis, and yes, a Tommie Smith and a John Carlos.

Proportionately, the black athlete has been more successful than any other group in any other endeavor in American life. And he and she did it despite legal and social discrimination that would have dampened the ardor of most participants. The relative domination of blacks in American sports will continue into the foreseeable future. Enough momentum has been attained to insure maximum sacrifice for athletic glory. Now is the time for our esteemed sports historians to take another hard look at our early athletic life, and revise what is at present an incomplete version of what really took place.

This essay first appeared in the New York Times *on Sunday, November 13, 1988, one day before* A Hard Road to Glory *was first published. We reprint it here as Arthur Ashe's reflections on the necessity and significance of this work.*

Foreword

Basketball truly is an American sport. It was invented by Dr. James Naismith at the Springfield, Massachusetts YMCA in 1891.

It's impossible to overemphasize the impact that Black athletes have had on basketball. We have been a part of the game since 1904, when Dr. Edwin B. Henderson learned it while attending a summer institute at Harvard, his alma mater. Dr. Henderson was the director of physical education for the Colored Schools in Washington, D.C., and helped organize a network of basketball teams in Baltimore, New York City, Newark, Philadelphia, and Washington, D.C., through YMCAs and schools. From small beginnings at a Washington, D.C., YMCA eighty years ago, Black athletes have moved on to dominate the sport at the prep, college, and professional levels. The opportunity to show our skills didn't come easily. It was won by the vision and hard work of Black pioneers who gave today's stars the opportunity to show, and to market, their skills.

Black colleges began playing the game in 1909 or 1910, when Howard University started a team as an outgrowth of the YMCA team. The development of the game was delayed by a lack of indoor facilities, but teams learned to improvise, and played in any arena they could find—even if it didn't meet court specifications.

Professional basketball started for Blacks in 1923 when Bob Douglas organized a club team, the New York Renaissance. The team played college and semi-pro teams. In 1928, they beat the New York Knickerbockers to win the world title.

Although there were a few Black players in the White schools of the North and West, for the most part, Black athletes developed and honed their talents at Black colleges against other Black players. The quality of their play can be seen in the fact that in 1950, two of the three Black players signed to the NBA were from Black colleges: Earl Lloyd of West Virginia State (Washington Capitols) and Nathaniel "Sweetwater" Clifton from Xavier (New York Knickerbockers). The first Black player drafted that year, Harold Hunter, was from North Carolina College. Still, Black coaches had to form a pressure group to get their teams into a national tournament.

In 1957, the National Athletic Steering Committee, composed of representatives from the all-Black Midwestern; Southern Intercollegiate; Southwestern athletic conferences; and the Central Intercollegiate Athletic Association (CIAA) got the National Association of Intercollegiate Athletics (NAIA) to admit *one* Black school to their national tournament. The representative was chosen through competition in an all-Black District 29. Black schools could not compete in any other district, regardless of their location.

Tennessee State, under the guidance of Coach Johnny Mclendon, a pioneer Black coach who had studied under Naismith (the inventor of the game) won the NAIA championship at the Kansas City tournament in 1957, beating Southeast Oklahoma, 92–73. Tennessee State won the championship for the next two years. Central State won in 1965 and 1968. Kentucky State, like Tennessee, also won three NAIA championships.

The National Collegiate Athletic Association (NCAA) followed the NAIA lead of allowing Black college teams to participate in it's National Tournament, and in 1967, Winston-Salem State became the first Black school to win the Division II title. Other Black colleges to win the title were: Morgan State (1974), Cheyney University (1978), Virginia Union (1980, 1992), District of Columbia (1982), and North Carolina Central (1989). Black colleges also have highly successful post-season tournaments of their own. Most notable is the CIAA, which grosses $1 million a year and attracts capacity crowds.

As segregation broke down, more Black players had a chance to compete at White schools. At first, there was an unwritten quota system, and coaches did not play more than one Black player at a time. But, as the athletes' skills became apparent, coaches realized that playing more Black players would help them to win. The quotas vanished. Now, many "White" schools have all-Black starting lineups.

In the early days, Black players did a lot to promote better race relations in the South;

Players such as Earl Monroe at Winston-Salem State, Henry Logan at Western Carolina, Gene Littles at High Point, and David Thompson at North Carolina State drew fans of both races to the coliseum, where they sat together and cheered their teams.

At first, Black coaches were hired by White colleges as assistants to *recruit* and *police* Black athletes. But, as with the players, it soon became apparent that the coaches could, and should, be doing a lot more.

John Thompson took a weak Georgetown program and turned it into a winning one, producing a national championship team. He also insisted that his players pay attention to their academic work and graduate. Soon, other Black coaches followed Thompson to become head coaches at majority White universities.

Some people are concerned aout the impact of Proposition 48 on Black athletes. I am not. This proposition states that to be eligible for varsity sports, a freshman must have scored 700 on the SAT College Entrance Exam or fifteen on the ACT Exams, and have a "C" average in eleven core subjects. I truly believe that as high schools offer the required courses, young Black men and women will take them, pass them, and continue on to star in college. Proposition 48 also enhances their chances of getting their degrees, giving them the opportunity to be equally successful after college.

The NBA has been dominated by the Black athlete. When the United States organized its "Dream Team" for the 1992 Olympics, it was predominately Black.

Black athletes are role models for youngsters. Men who have been successful at the college and professional level show young people that there is opportunity for them, if they are willing to work diligently. The road to glory is a hard one, as Arthur Ashe, Jr. documents in this excellent book. Ashe also documents that there is a tradition of not only surviving, but prevailing. For those who might have forgotten, this volume is a reminder, a testament.

Clarence "Big House" Gaines
October 1993

Clarence Gaines was basketball coach at Winston-Salem State University until he resigned in 1992, having spent 46 years there as coach. During that time he developed such legendary players as Cleo Hill and Earl Monroe. Coach Gaines was the first Black coach to win an NCAA Division II basketball title and has 822 wins, second only to Kentucky's Adolph Rupp.

Foreword

TO

A Hard Road to Glory:
A History of the African-American Athlete, Volumes 1–3

This book began in a classroom at Florida Memorial College in Miami, Florida, in 1981. I was asked to teach a course, The Black Athlete in Contemporary Society, by Jefferson Rogers of the school's Center for Community Change. When I tried to find a book detailing what has surely been the African-American's most startling saga of successes, I found that the last attempt had been made exactly twenty years before.

I then felt compelled to write this story, for I literally grew up on a sports field. My father was the caretaker of the largest public park for blacks in Richmond, Virginia. Set out in a fanlike pattern at Brookfield Playground was an Olympic-size pool, a basketball court, four tennis courts, three baseball diamonds, and two football fields. Our five-room home was actually on these premises. Little wonder I later became a professional athlete.

My boyhood idol was Jackie Robinson, as was the case with every black kid in America in the late 1940s and early 1950s. But I had no appreciation of what he went through or, more importantly, what others like him had endured. I had never heard of Jack Johnson, Marshall Taylor, Isaac Murphy, or Howard P. Drew—icons in athletics but seldom heralded in the post-World War II period.

These and others have been the most accomplished figures in the African-American subculture. They were vastly better known in their times than people such as Booker T. Washington, William E.B. Du Bois, or Marcus Garvey. They inspired idolatry bordering on deification, and thousands more wanted to follow. Indeed, in the pretelevision days of radio, Joe Louis's bouts occasioned impromptu celebration because, between 1934 and 1949, Louis lost only once.

But if contemporary black athletes' exploits are more well known, few fully appreciate their true Hard Road to Glory. Discrimination, vilification, incarceration, dissipation, ruination, and ultimate despair have dogged the steps of the mightiest of these heroes. And, only a handful in the last 179 years have been able to live out their post-athletic lives in peace and prosperity.

This book traces the development of African-American athletes from their ancestral African homelands in the seventeenth century through the present era. Their exploits are explored in a historical context, as all African-American successes were constrained by discriminatory laws, customs, and traditions.

As I began to complete my research, I realized that the subject was more extensive than I had thought. All of the material would not fit into one volume. Therefore, I have divided the work as follows:

Volume I covers the emergence of sports as adjuncts to daily life from the time of ancient civilizations like Egypt through World War I. Wars tend to compartmentalize eras and this story is no different. Major successes of African-Americans occurred in the nineteenth century, for example, which are simply glossed over in most examinations of the period.

Volume II examines black athletics during that vital twenty-year period between the World Wars. No greater contrast exists than that between the 1920s—the Golden Decade of Sports—and the Depression-plagued 1930s. The infrastructure of American athletics as we know it today was set during these crucial years, and the civil rights apparatus that would lead to integration in the post–World War II era was formalized. Popular African-American literature and its press augmented the already cosmic fame of athletes such as Jesse Owens and Joe Louis, who were the first black athletes to be admired by all Americans.

Volume III is set between World War II and the present. It begins with an unprecedented five-year period—1946 through 1950—in which football, baseball, basketball, tennis, golf, and bowling became integrated. These breakthroughs, coupled with the already heady showings in track and boxing, provided enough incentive for African-Americans to embark on nothing less than an all-out effort for athletic fame and fortune.

The reference sections in each volume document the major successes of these gladiators. These records are proof positive of effort and dedication on the playing field. More importantly, they are proof of what the African-American can do when allowed to compete equally in a framework governed by a set of rules.

Each volume is divided into individual sport histories. Primary source materials were not to be found in the local public library and not even in New York City's Fifth Avenue Public Library. Chroniclers of America's early sports heroes simply left out most of their darker brothers and sisters except when they participated in white-controlled events. Much had to be gleaned, therefore, from the basements, attics, and closets of African-Americans themselves.

Interviews were invaluable in cross-referencing dubious written records. Where discrepancies occurred, I have stated so; but I have tried to reach the most logical conclusion. Some unintentional errors are inevitable. The author welcomes confirmed corrections and additions. If validated, they will be included in the next edition of this work.

Today, thousands of young African-Americans continue to seek their places in the sun through athletics. For some African-Americans the dream has bordered on a pathological obsession. But unless matters change, the majority may end up like their predecessors. Perhaps this history will ease the journey with sober reflections of how difficult and improbable the Hard Road really is. In no way, however, do I care to dissuade any young athlete from dreaming of athletic glory. Surely every American at some time has done so.

A word about nomenclature. Sociologists have referred to nearly all immigrant groups in hyphenated form: Irish-Americans, Italian-Americans, and Jewish-Americans. African-Americans are no different, and this term is correct. Throughout this book, I shall, however, use the modern designation "*black*" to refer to African-Americans. The appellations *Negro* and *colored* may also appear, but usually in quotes and only when I thought such usage may be more appropriate in a particular context.

November 1988

Acknowledgments

A Hard Road to Glory would have been impossible without the help, assistance, contributions, and encouragement of many people. Initial moral support came from Reverend Jefferson Rogers, formerly of Florida Memorial College; Professor Henry Louis "Skip" Gates of Cornell University; Howard Cosell; Marie Brown; my editor, Charles F. Harris; and my literary agent, Fifi Oscard. All made me believe it could be done. An inspiring letter urging me to press on also came from Professor John Hope Franklin of Duke University, who advised that this body of work was needed to fill a gap in African-American history.

My staff has been loyal and faithful to the end these past four years. I have been more than ably assisted by Kip Branch, who has stood by me from the first day; and by Ocania Chalk, whose two previous books on black collegiate athletes and other black athletic pioneers provided so much of the core material for *A Hard Road to Glory*. To my personal assistant, Derilene McCloud, go special thanks for coordinating, typing, filing, phoning, and organizing the information and interviews, as well as keeping my day-to-day affairs in order. Sandra Jamison's skills in library science were invaluable in the beginning. Her successor, Rod Howard, is now a virtual walking encyclopedia of information about black athletes, especially those in college. To Francis Harris, who almost single-handedly constructed the reference sections, I am truly grateful. And to Deborah McRae, who sat through hundreds of hours of typing—her assistance is not forgotten.

Institutions have been very helpful and forthcoming. The people at the New York Public Annex went out of their way to search for books. *The New York Times* provided access to back issues. The Norfolk, Virginia, Public Library was kind and considerate. This book could not have been done without the kind help of the Schomburg Library for Research in Black Culture in Harlem, New York. Its photography curator, Deborah Willis Thomas, found many photographs for me, and Ernest Kaiser followed my work with interest.

The Enoch Pratt Free Library in Baltimore, Maryland; the Moorland-Spingarn Library at Howard University in Washington, D.C.; and the Library of Congress not only assisted but were encouraging and courteous. The offices of the Central Intercollegiate Athletic Association, the Southern Intercollegiate Athletic Conference, the Mideastern Athletic Conference, and the Southwestern Athletic Conference dug deep to find information on past black college sports. The National Collegiate Athletic Association and the National Association for Intercollegiate Athletics were quick with information about past and present athletes. The home offices of major league baseball, the National Basketball Association, the National Football League, and their archivists and Halls of Fame were eager to provide assistance. Joe Corrigan went out of his way to lend a hand.

The staffs at Tuskegee University and Tennessee State University were particularly kind. Wallace Jackson at Alabama A&M was helpful with information on the Southern Intercollegiate Athletic Conference. Alvin Hollins at Florida A&M University was eager to assist. Lynn Abraham of New York City found a rare set of boxing books for me. Lou Robinson of Claremont, California, came through in a pinch with information on black Olympians, and Margaret Gordon of the American Tennis Association offered her assistance.

Many people offered to be interviewed for this project—especially Eyre Saitch, Nell Jackson, Dr. Reginald Weir and Ric Roberts—and I am truly grateful for their recollections. (Eyre Saitch and Ric Roberts have since passed away.) Others who agreed to sit and talk with Kip Branch, Ocania Chalk, or me include William "Pop" Gates, Elgin Baylor, Oscar Robertson, Anita DeFranz, Nikki Franke, Peter Westbrook, Paul Robeson, Jr., Afro-American sportswriter Sam Lacy, A.S. "Doc" Young, Frederick "Fritz" Pollard, Jr., Mel Glover, Calvin Peete, Oscar Johnson, Althea Gibson, Mrs. Ted Paige, Charles Sifford, Howard Gentry, Milt Campbell, Otis Troupe, Beau Jack, Coach and Mrs. Jake Gaither, Lynn Swann, Franco Harris, Dr. Richard Long of Atlanta

University, Dr. Leonard Jeffries of the City College of New York, Dr. Elliot Skinner of Columbia University, and Dr. Ben Jochannon.

Dr. Maulana Karenga of Los Angeles and Dr. William J. Baker of the University of Maine offered material and guidance on African sports. Dr. Ofuatey Kodjo of Queens College in New York City helped edit this same information. Norris Horton of the United Golfers Association provided records, and Margaret Lee of the National Bowling Association answered every inquiry with interest. To Nick Seitz of *Golf Digest* and *Tennis*, I offer thanks for his efforts. Professors Barbara Cooke, Patsy B. Perry, Kenneth Chambers, Floyd Ferebee, and Tom Scheft of North Carolina Central University were kind enough to read parts of the manuscript, as did Mr. and Mrs. Donald Baker. Professor Eugene Beecher of Wilson College, an unabashed sports fan, shuttled many clippings our way.

To the dozens of people who heard about my book on Bob Law's *Night Talk* radio show and sent unsolicited but extremely valuable information, I cannot thank you enough. And to the hundreds of unsung African-American athletes who played under conditions of segregation and whose skills and talents were never known to the general public, I salute you and hope this body of work in some measure vindicates and redresses that gross miscarriage of our American ideals.

Finally, to my wife Jeanne Moutoussamy-Ashe, I owe gratitude and tremendous appreciation for her understanding, patience, tolerance, and sacrifice of time so I could complete this book.

Arthur R. Ashe, Jr.
1988

CHAPTER 1

The Beginnings to 1918

The Springfield YMCA

The game of basketball had to be invented sooner or later. In the late 1800s the nation's athletic calendar was filled in three of the four seasons: baseball in the summer; football in the fall; and track and field in the spring. A winter game was needed to keep the competitive juices flowing, and basketball was the answer.

James Naismith, a Canadian YMCA training instructor in Springfield, Massachusetts, hit upon the idea in 1891 of tossing a soccer-size ball through an elevated opening. He asked a janitor, so the story goes, for some containers that he could affix to the wall. The workman replied with peach baskets—with the bottoms intact. Soon the bottoms were removed and the baskets refined, and the sport was on its way. No indoor game ever caught on as fast, and the YMCA spread its virtues the world over.

Naismith's fellow instructors did not like his invention because too few people could play. The initial scoring system called for three points for a basket and three points for a free throw. In just five years it was changed to two points for a basket and one point for a free throw. This did not change until the introduction of the three-point basket in the 1980s. In 1897 the team size was set at five, and that too has remained. This simplicity was central to the sports early appeal.

The influential *New York Times* on May 7, 1894, merely echoed the obvious in reporting that "Basketball is about the youngest of the athletic games, but it has gained great popularity...played with more enthusiasm than any other sport in the gymnasiums in this city." Girls played, too, according to a special set of rules formulated by Senda Berenson of Smith College. Other schools and clubs quickly added it to their roster of activities.

As with the other sports, it was not long—1896—before the first professional game was played at the Masonic Temple in Trenton, New Jersey. The professional National Basketball League (NBL) was formed in 1898. In 1897 the Amateur Athletic Union began competitions, and the final seal of approval came with an introduction at the 1904 Olympic Games. This first Olympic event was won by a team composed almost entirely of members of the Buffalo (New York) German YMCA.

First Black Participation

Black players began with the YMCAs and schools of the Ivy League. YMCA College

1

Student Associations at Clafflin, Straight, Tougaloo, Spelman, Alabama A&M, and Howard Universities introduced the game, and other Colored YMCAs with gymnasiums embraced it wholeheartedly. YMCAs and YWCAs formed the first black teams and continued to be the focal point for a decade until clubs offered stronger competition.

One gentleman who helped bridge the decade 1895–1905 was Edwin B. Henderson. He attended Harvard University as this century began and returned to his native Washington, D.C., to organize local teams in the public school system. He immediately included it in his Interscholastic Athletic Association (ISAA) program formed in 1905. At the same time the first club team was organized in Brooklyn, New York, calling themselves the Smart Set Club. They built their athletic programs around basketball and track. Within a year the St. Christopher Athletic Club and the Marathone Athletic Club joined Smart Set in forming the Olympian Athletic League (OAL), which became the first black club league outside the YMCA family.

In 1907 Smart Set won the first OAL title with the following members: Charles Scrotton, Chester Moore, Robert Lattimore, Robert Barnard, Harry Brown, Alfred Groves, George Trice, and manager George Lattimore. One year later, the OAL added the Alpha Physical Culture Club, the St. Cyprian Athletic Club, and the Jersey City YMCA to its membership. In spite of its distinct northeastern location, the OAL was a solid beginning for a sport eventually dominated by black players.

Similar clubs formed in the Wash- ington, D.C., vicinity with Henderson's assistance, and interregional competition began on December 18, 1908, when that city's Crescent Athletic Club lost to Smart Set in "the first athletic contest between colored athletes of New York and Washington."[1] The success of this game was not lost on the segregated black public schools in Washington, D.C., and other cities.

Schools and clubs in Baltimore, Philadelphia, St. Louis, Wilmington (Delaware), and northern New Jersey soon had clubs of players. Philadelphia was a special case as its schools were integrated. As Henderson noted, their "colored athletes are thrown into competition with the whites."[2] Its clubs, however, were segregated. The Wissahickon School Club and the Stentonworth Athletic Club were the first black groups to form in that city.

With the exception of St. Louis and towns where black colleges were positioned, the sport in southern black communities was almost nonexistent before 1910. Warm weather the year round lessened the impetus for a winter game. There were no gymnasiums, equipment was poor, coaching was out of an A. G. Spaulding manual. The YMCAs had too few indoor facilities. Yet the YMCAs' outdoor play areas offered the only hope for a time.

The best YMCA squad was the Twelfth Street Branch in Washington, D.C., which was so good that when Howard University began varsity play in 1911, it inherited the YMCA team almost intact. Its members were Lewis S. Johnson, Hudson J. Oliver, Arthur L. Curtis, Henry T. Nixon, J. L. Chestnut, Robert Anderson, Maurice Clifford, Edward B. Gray, and Edwin B.

Henderson. They were undefeated in 1909–10 and had wins over school and club teams from Washington, D.C., to New York City. At Brooklyn's Manhattan Casino in 1910 they defeated Smart Set before 3,000 fans. In Alabama, Tuskegee's first game was also against a YMCA team from Columbus, Georgia, in 1908, which they crushed 33-0.

These YMCA teams remained central to the success of basketball among blacks. School attendance was not required for blacks in the south, and only a small minority of those between 15 and 20 years of age attended. Consequently, if the YMCAs did not have teams, there would have been no play at all. In addition, their strict code of amateurism kept most players from trying to form professional associations. But that too changed before World War I.

The Early Club Teams

After the YMCAs initial influence came the clubs that sprang up in the major cities in the Northeast. Because of the YMCAs amateur tradition, it could not hope to keep the best players permanently. Likewise, school teams were hampered by the availability of its students. Like other sports—baseball, track, and football—club fives (basketball teams are sometimes called fives) filled a vacuum in the black basketball world. Their quality of play was superior, and their Friday and Saturday night games—followed by a dance—became a staple in the social calendar.

Clubs like Smart Set and Wissahickon blossomed because of natural constituencies and access to facilities and coaching.

Smart Set and Alpha Physical Culture also fielded girls' teams. Dora Cole and her sisters dominated the first Smart Set team and soon had imitators who played their games in blousy knee-length bloomers and long-sleeved shirts. Most girls' games were played with six players on a side, and there was a limit to the number of bounces a girl could take before being forced to pass or shoot. The idea of performing in short pants—or for money—was simply out of the question for women.

Not so for the second wave of clubs that began operating around 1910. Two of the earliest were the Incorporators of New York City and the Monticello Delaney Rifles of Pittsburgh, Pennsylvania. Will Madden, who ran the St. Christopher five, formed the semiprofessional Incorporators in 1911, and they were the best team in the area until World War I. Their main rivals were the Independents and the Scholastics. They had no reservations whatever about the propriety of playing for pay. Monticello agreed.

Nearly every black team was aware of the inaugural World Professional Championship held in 1905 between Company E of Schenectady, New York, and the Kansas City Blue Diamonds. Cumberland Posey of Pittsburgh, the Monticello organizer, wanted to do the same. He formed his team in 1909 and set out to put the skills he learned while on Penn State's varsity to good use. Oddly enough, Posey left the Penn State squad because his grades made him ineligible for games.

Posey's premier team consisted of his brother Seward; Baker, the coach; Mahoney, the manager; Dorsey; Brown; Clark; Hall;

and Richmond. The second year he added the Bell brothers and Norris. (First names could not be found for most of Posey's team.) Their play was so spectacular that the New York *Age* of March 14, 1912, said, "[T]he colored basketball world will be forced to recognize Monticello as one of the fastest colored quints. The Monticello team is open to meet all comers. It has not met defeat in two years, playing all white teams."

Posey was an anomaly among black sports figures in the pre–World War I era. He was a scion of a solid, stable, upper-class black family. His father was the first black man granted a chief engineer's license to operate a steamboat on the Mississippi River. Few prosperous blacks bothered with sports beyond their school days then.

Club owners like Posey were more market-oriented than product-oriented. There was evident public demand for quality basketball, and they meant to supply it. Some of these teams even played against all-black army squads like the 10th Cavalry Regiment, billed as "The Championship Team of the United States Army." The January 10, 1911, New York *Age* reported a loss by this squad to a black all-star team, saying, "The boys in blue proved as tricky as the horses they ride, and whenever an all star player attempted to tackle a cavalryman by jumping on his back he was usually given a quick excursion through the air. Medical aid and sticking plaster were called into use several times...but no one was seriously injured." Sounds rather exciting.

Professional teams like Monticello

and the Incorporators were bound to cause dissension, and they did. The black elite wanted to see a sharper line of demarcation from amateur play, but the play-for-pay fives were more entertaining than school squads or those from social clubs. Possibly the fear was loss of control, as may be inferred from this quote in a black periodical, *The Competitor Magazine*, of 1914: "There is...a place for the professional in basketball, but let him promote his own following....There can be no middle ground...the duty of each is plain."[3] The formation of the Colored Intercollegiate Athletic Association (CIAA) in 1912 and the Southern Intercollegiate Athletic Conference (SIAC)—two black college conferences—helped address the amateur-vs-professional issue.

In 1913, the same year, that the SIAC was formed, Posey organized a new team that featured the first truly famous players. He called his new quintet The Loendi Big Five, and they played their home games at Pittsburgh's Labor Temple. The members were Posey, James "Stretch" Sessoms, William T. Young, William "Big Greasy" Betts, and James "Pappy" Ricks. They dominated the black basketball world until the coming of the New York Renaissance and Harlem Globetrotters squads a decade later. Loendi was the best-known black team in any sport in the Ohio Valley until the Homestead Grays baseball team formed.

The Loendi Five played very physical basketball that fit the image of their steel-making hometown. For instance, most teams stalled when they had a sizable lead near the end of games because there was then no rule requiring the offense to move the ball beyond the midcourt line in ten seconds. Not Loendi. Posey realized that boredom meant lower profits, so his team was aggressive. Most of their results were carried in the white press, especially when they played the all-Jewish Coffey Club. Crowds of five thousand at the Labor Temple were not uncommon.

Sometimes the aggression got a little out of hand because the spectators were so close. Basketball players got their familiar nickname "cagers" because in these early days the teams were separated from the spectators by floor-to-ceiling netting, which made it look like they were playing in a cage. In one game between the Incorporators and Orange (New Jersey), the Incorporators' captain "was struck on the nose by one of the Orange rooters and incapacitated for the rest of the game."[4] The paper did not say which team won that night.

By World War I the black press began trying to anoint a Colored World Champion for basketball as baseball and boxing had (though in boxing, a white paper, *The Police Gazette*, named the Colored Champion). But depending on which paper was believed, the Loendi Big Five won most nods before and during the war. *The Competitor Magazine* thought Loendi so good that it told its readers it was hardly possible to pick a basketball team from all the colored players of the country that would have a ghost of a chance to beat that Pittsburgh five. It was probably correct.

Loendi's success inevitably spawned imitators. Soon the black papers were trumpeting the wins and losses of semiprofessional squads like Homestead Steel, the Spartans, Edgar Thompson Steel, the Vandals (Atlantic City), Athenian (Baltimore), and the Borough Athletic Club of Brooklyn. Most of their players were making around twenty-five dollars per game and working at their regular jobs. Within a decade their successors had quit their jobs and played basketball full time.

White College Stars

While black colleges struggled with their meager athletic facilities, some white schools fielded respectable squads, and black players were sprinkled here and there. But neither the enthusiasm nor the presence was like that of football, and no All-America lists were published. Samuel Ransom of Beloit College (1904–08) seems to have been among the earliest players.

Though no specific names could be found, other blacks must have been playing since this quote appeared in the December 24, 1904 Indianapolis *Freeman*: "For drawing the color line a basketball team in Massachusetts was fined $100 by the president of the New England League." The New England League was composed of Dartmouth, Holy Cross, Williams, Amherst, and Trinity, so some guesses could be made to determine the culprit.

Other blacks documented before World War I include Wilbur Wood at Nebraska in 1907–10; Fenwich H. Watkins at the University of Vermont in 1907–09; Cumberland Posey at Penn State in 1909; William Kindle at Springfield College in 1911; Cleveland Abbott at South Dakota

State in 1913; and Sol Butler at Dubuque (Iowa) in 1916.

After the war participation in basketball became a cause célèbre at some schools. Blacks were allowed on football teams but not on basketball teams at the same institution. Racism was becoming more selective, but protestors demanded explanations just the same.

Notes

1. *ISAA Handbook* (1910), p. 67.
2. Ibid., p. 41.
3. Quoted in Chalk, op. cit., p. 79.
4. New York *Age*, January 14, 1915.

CHAPTER 2

1919–1945

Though basketball grew rapidly after its invention in 1891, it was hampered for the first forty years by poor facilities. This winter game was played in makeshift halls with poor indoor lighting. The gymnasiums in the first quarter of this century were just not built with spectator basketball in mind. Court sizes were standardized, but most teams took what they could get, or settled for what was most convenient. So small were the playing arenas that floor-to-ceiling nets had to be strung up to keep the fans from the players—hence the term "cagers" used to describe basketball performers.

Basketball was also limited by the normal six-day work week. Saturday and Sunday night games were the most popular but they ran counter to many states' "blue laws" which forced some Sunday night games to begin at midnight. Then there were, of course, the vast distances between the good teams. With only five players to a squad, it was so easy to form a team that good ones were rare. By far, most of the talent emerged from the northern ghettos—of Chicago and New York City in particular.

Down South the game was still subject to the tourist season. The winters were warm and when wealthy northerners headed for the local resorts in Arkansas, Florida, Louisiana, Mississippi, and the Car-olinas, many would-be basketball players were carrying luggage and waiting on ta-bles. It is no wonder then that energetic and resourceful clubs fielded the strongest teams. Since these aggregations grew out of organizations that featured more than just basketball—like Brooklyn's Smart Set Club—their teams proved more cohesive and entertaining than those from schools.

Between the two World Wars, the white club teams tried to form leagues similar to those in major league baseball but without success. It was only after the Second World War, when black players were finally accepted into these profes-sional league ranks, that the leagues them-selves matured. Within a few short years of this breakthrough in 1946, the sport fea-tured, by common consensus, the very best athletes in the entire world.

The Great Club Teams

World War I forced many women to work in the northern urban factories and the very image of the American woman underwent subtle changes. Victorian at-titudes toward female manners, dress, be-havior, and sports changed from strict adherence to established norms to one of modified permissiveness. Females were

7

even allowed the opportunity to vote in 1920. Two black female basketball teams emerged in the first fifteen years following the war that featured two of our nation's best-ever athletes.

The first of the two teams was the Chicago Romas, organized by Edward "Sol" Butler, formerly of Dubuque College and Seminary. Their starting lineup included Isadore Channels, Corinne Robinson, Mignon Burns, Lillian Ross, Virginia Willis, and Lula Porter. Channels was the star and, in addition, was a four-time winner of the American Tennis Association (ATA) Women's Singles title. (The ATA was the black counterpart to the white United States Lawn Tennis Association.) The Romas dominated ladies' basketball in the Chicago and Midwest regions.

The second dominant team was the *Philadelphia Tribune* squad, that was sponsored by the black newspaper of the same name. Black and white papers frequently sponsored sports events and/or teams to enhance their image and increase sales. The *Tribune* must have done a bit of both because the team, which was begun in 1931, seldom lost. Coincidentally, the *Tribune's* leading player was another tennis star, Ora Washington, who won an unprecedented eight ATA Singles titles during her career. Washington, a center, also later played for the Germantown Hornets of Philadelphia.

The *Tribune* squad, as well as the YWCA and other club teams, played the typical six-players-per-team style which had separate threesomes for offense and defense at opposite ends of the court. This was done so as to minimize the "strain" on the players. It was still fervently, but erroneously, believed that women had innately delicate natures and too much exercise would damage their equilibrium. Hence, women never played full-court basketball until well into the 1960s. Frequently though, the *Tribune* team did use men's rules and the results were usually the same. Miss Washington's teammates included Gladys Walker, Virginia Woods, Lavinia Moore, Myrtle Wilson, Rose Wilson, Marie Leach, Florence Campbell, and Sarah Latimere. They were named by most black papers as national champions during most of the 1930s.

In 1938 the Tribunes toured the South in February and March, giving clinics, offering advice and encouragement, and demonstrating for crowds the high quality basketball of which women were potentially capable. The Philadelphia Tribune was black America's first premier female sports team. When it disbanded in 1940, its fame was superseded only by the women's track team at Tuskegee, which was the AAU national champion.

The two stellar men's squads—the New York Renaissance Big Five and the Harlem Globetrotters—came from New York City and Chicago, respectively. This came as no surprise since these cities' public school, club, YMCA, church, American Legion, and college teams were nationally recognized. It so happened that the rise and subsequent demise of these squads as basketball powerhouses fell almost neatly between the two World Wars.

The New York Renaissance, better known as the Rens, began as the Spartan Braves of Brooklyn. The Spartan Braves became the Spartan Five that later still became the Rens in 1923. The Braves had joined New York City's Metropolitan Basketball Association (MBA) but the MBA in 1922 ordered the Braves to suspend Frank Forbes and Leon Monde for a violation. The Spartans refused and were fined. The following year—the same year the YMCA held its first national event—the Braves' owner, Robert J. Douglas, took Forbes and added four others to form the Rens. It was the first full-salaried, black professional basketball team.

Full credit must go to Douglas who is now referred to as the father of black basketball. His keen eye for talent and sound business acumen enabled his squad to survive until the late 1940s. He was born on the Caribbean island of St. Kitts in 1885, and had brought with him to America those traits of perserverance and hard work that so typified the black West Indian immigrants. A. S. "Doc" Young went so far as to say that "Never before, or since, in American sports history has an all-Negro team operated by Negroes earned the national acclaim that accrued to the Rens."[1]

The Rens first starting five were captain Hilton Slocum, Frank Forbes, Hy Monte, Zack Anderson, and Harold Mayers. The team got its name from Harlem's Renaissance Ballroom on 135th Street and 7th Avenue. To show they were to be taken seriously, the Rens won their debut game, 28 to 22, against the Collegiate Big Five on November 3, 1923. They finished the season with a 15–8 record.

The Rens soon had little difficulty finding opponents. Their main black rivals were the Harlem Globetrotters, the Chicago Hottentots with Joe Lillard, the Chicago Collegians, the Chicago Studebakers, and the Savoy Big Five. Other opponents included the Celtics, the Philadelphia Sphas, the Detroit Eagles, and the Akron Firestones. The most intense games were those against the Globetrotters and the Celtics. In the past such rivalries often led to violence on the court between teams. Before the rules changes of the 1930s and 1940s, play was often plodding. There was a jump ball after every basket, and everyone clogged the middle.

There was also heavy betting, poor officiating, and selfishness. Douglas saw this shortcoming early and insisted his players perform more like a team, with strict adherence to discipline and the good of the team over that of the individual. Things had gotten so out of hand earlier that the *Chicago Defender* editorialized for a change. "The first thing to be done to help make this game one of the cleanest and best played and liked of games," it said, "is to cut out some of the rough stuff....Another big fault is gallery playing and what might be termed as clique playing. Players...sent into the game have been refused the opportunity to handle the ball....The biggest and most important of all things is choice of referees."[2]

The *New York Age* was just as adamant. "...some teams began to fight among themselves. By the end of the 1921 season, basketball in this city was in an unhealthy condition, although from outward appearances, the game was never more popular, or the clubs more prosperous."[3] The Rens tried to compensate with teamwork. Noted the late Rens player Eyre "Bruiser" Saitch, "We didn't even have a coach! We didn't have positions; we played the man."[4] He further claimed that after playing together so often, it was just easier for the same five players to adjust to one another. A man's position on the team in those days mattered less than now. A center—now the tallest player on a team—was so named in the 1920s only because he was used to jump-center at the beginning of a play. After that, positions made little difference.

Saitch did, however, deplore the necessity to combine the social with the athletic. A highly skilled athlete, he wanted to see the game stand on its own but that never came to pass in the 1920s. "We had to have a dance afterwards or nobody would come to the damn thing...the Renaissance [Ballroom] was right across the street from The Red Rooster [nightclub]....If you didn't get there by seven o'clock, you didn't get in the damn door. The big game didn't start until 10 o'clock."[5] Such was the case in the socio-athletic milieu of the nation's black cultural capital during the Harlem Renaissance period of the 1920s.

How much did players make back then? Saitch mentions salaries of between $800 to $1,000 per month and noted that "a loaf of bread was only a nickel and the best apartment was $60 a month."[6] But they more than earned their pay since they were on the road 75 percent of the time. Of particular importance was their annual swing through the South in the early spring to play against some black college teams.

William "Pops" Gates recalled that "We'd tour the South and play the Negro colleges, sometimes playing three teams in the same day. In Atlanta, we'd play Morehouse, Morris Brown, and Clark twenty-minute periods each."[7] Saitch added that "We played in some areas where they didn't have backboards; just a net attached to an iron pipe."[8]

Unfortunately, this was often seen as out-of-bounds for a professional team and much worse for the colleges. Fay Young of the *Chicago Defender* was against college-versus-professional games. However, the colleges needed all the help they could get. But it was 1930 before any school had a twenty-game schedule per season, and facilities were poor. Otis Troupe, the Morgan State star, said he and his teammates "...had to go into town to practice at the New Albert Casino one or two nights a week."[9] Imagine trying to field a quality team with twice-a-week practices! The farther South a school was located, the more likely its schedule and practice time was to be interrupted by the tourist season. But these college-versus-professional games were scheduled anyway, despite conference rules against it. The demand for such matchups was high, the experience was invaluable for the collegians, and the schools needed the revenue. The professionals simply used this time to work on new plays, get into condition, and integrate new players into the lineup. Indeed, new players did come in and out of the team.

In addition to the original five, some other players of the late 1920s, the 1930s, and early 1940s included William "Wee Willie" Smith, Charles "Tarzan" Cooper, Eyre "Bruiser" Saitch, Clarence "Fats" Jenkins, George Fiall, James "Pappy" Ricks, Clix Garcia, Walter Saunders, and Bill Yancey. Later Rens included Johnny Isaacs, William "Pops" Gates, Clarence "Puggy" Bell, Zack Clayton, Johnny "Casey" Holt, Al Johnson, and for a very short time, Wilmeth Sidat-Singh. Nearly all came from New York City schools, clubs, and public parks before 1930.

Ricks had been a star for Loendi before joining the Rens in 1924, After that year, Loendi lost much of its initial strength. This was confirmed somewhat in the February 23, 1924, edition of the *Pittsburgh Courier*: "Loendi has lost more games this season than any other season...one or more players...neglect their defense entirely in efforts to score more field goals continuously."[10] In Ricks' second year, the Rens tied a heated six-game series, 3–3, against the all-white Original Celtics (then so-called because other teams also used the name "Celtics"), the acknowledged world professional champions, with its star Joe Lapchick. These games secured the reputation of the Harlem-based team and earned it a tremendous following.

In 1925, the American Basketball League (ABL) was organized without inviting any black teams to join. The Original Celtics themselves refused to join partly because ABA rules may have disallowed games against black fives. This snub of blacks came in the same year the National Football League began to ease its black players from its member teams. But, like the best white major league baseball squads, the best white professional teams actually sought out confrontations against the premier black aggregations. These interracial games virtually guaranteed a jammed box office.

In 1927, the Rens were joined by another black team, the Harlem Globetrotters, that would in time rival it in fame though not in the record books. Some players like Zachary Clayton wore the uniforms of both teams. Though the Rens now had company, the addition of the Globetrotters enhanced all of black basketball; fans took it more seriously and a sort of intra-racial rivalry began.

In the latter part of the 1920s the Rens were playing 150 games per year against club, YMCA, and college fives. They would appear for a guarantee plus expenses. Robert Douglas' Rens team was booked as much as an entire season in advance for certain games. In one of these highly publicized contests against Morgan State on March 18, 1927, the Rens won 26–22 at their home base, the Renaissance Casino. As usual, the post-game dance began right after the game in the same hall. On March 20, 1929, Morgan State finally defeated the Rens 41–40.

The Celtics rivalry, too, continued to blaze. In 1928, the Rens won even though Lapchick and Nat Holman were in uniform for the Celtics. But the following year the Celtics won 38–31, in front of 10,000 fans. Tarzan Cooper had ten points for the Rens. Lest these scores seem low by today's standards, there was a jump ball after every basket, players continued clogging the middle, and there was no rule requiring teams or players to advance the ball beyond the mid-court stripe in any length of time. A "fast break" was unheard of and was not even considered a part of the language of the sport.

Partly because of the low scores and the spectator demand for a faster pace, the rules were revolutionized during a twelve-year period beginning in 1932. The ABL had disbanded the year before and the need for adjustments was obvious and clear. The first rule to be changed struck at the very heart of the pace of play. Teams had to advance the ball past the aforementioned mid-court stripe within ten seconds toward their own end of the court. In addition, no player with the ball could stand in the foul lane more than three consecutive seconds. These changes forced teams with large leads to play more aggressively and to emphasize teamwork more than brute strength. Scores immediately increased almost 50 percent in some instances.

In 1936, the three-second rule was further amended to disallow *any* players on offense to stand in the foul lane more than three consecutive seconds. Blacks particularly liked this innovation because the fancy passing that ensued was entertaining as well as productive. Now, all ten players were constantly in motion, juggling for position and looking for fakes and picks. The fans loved it and an added premium was placed on compatibility.

A year later in 1937, the center jump after each basket was eliminated, and players on defense could no longer interfere with the ball while it was above the rim of the basket. The immediate result was the introduction of what was then termed the "race horse" maneuver, which is known today as the "fast break." Teams henceforth had to have backcourt players who were not only adept ball handlers but they had to be quick to exploit a weak defense. Black players turned out to be among the quickest ever seen. (Coincident with that year's rule change came the new National Basketball League [NBL], which also declined to invite black squads to join. Black teams like the Globetrotters and the Rens had now been snubbed twice.)

Saitch had this to say about the elimination of the center jump. "In those days...we played by halves and then changed to fifteen-minute quarters...the referees only called flagrant fouls...with no jump ball, we just outran everybody...."[11]

In 1944, "goal tending," which forbade players on defense from interfering with the ball once it was on its way in its *downward* path after a shot, was made illegal. Defenders had to then block shots in the ball's upward path only. All these changes over a dozen seasons resulted in increased demand for the sport among public schools, clubs, churches, fraternal leagues, YMCAs, YWCAs, industrial leagues, colleges, and the professionals.

Just before the first series of rules changes in 1932, the Rens won their first world professional championship from the Celtics 37–34 on March 30. On April 3 they beat them again 30–23—with a team that included Lapchick and Henry "Dutch" Dehnert. The reigning world champions then made a six-state sweep that included stops in Pennsylvania, Maryland, Washington, D.C., North Carolina, Georgia, Alabama, and Tennessee. Douglas believed such a tour could not only enhance the image of his team but help to improve the quality of the game itself among blacks. He knew about the "iron pipe" baskets and the lack of coaching, but he also thought that first-hand experience with the world champions would be a tremendous morale boost to any fledgling team. He was correct, of course.

For the record, that world championship squad incuded Saitch, Cooper, Jenkins, Slocum, Yancey, Holt, Smith, and Ricks—one of the best teams before World War II.

The following season, 1932–33, was marked by an eighty-eight game winning streak that was finally broken by, of all teams, the Celtics, on April 3, 1933. Two years after that, another memorable encounter involved a win over the New York Celtics by one point when the Rens, featuring Johnny Isaacs, controlled the ball for the last six minutes of play. Crowds in this mid-Depression era sometimes reached 15,000 a true testament to the popularity of this famous five from New York City. Douglas' team was in its prime.

But there was a price to pay for this fame that attended anyone who was black, even someone like Bill "Bojangles" Robinson, the black actor/dancer. As in the Negro leagues for baseball, Saitch said he and his teammates sometimes "...slept in jails because they wouldn't put us up in hotels...standard equipment for us was a flint gun; we'd spray all the bedbugs before we went out to play and they'd be dead when we got back....We sometimes had over a thousand damn dollars in our pockets and we couldn't get a good goddamn meal. Our per diem was $2.50 a day. 'Fats' Jenkins was so tight that he'd save the tea balls and later ask for a cup of hot water. Man, he was tight [laughter]!"[12]

Nineteen thirty-nine was the Rens' last good year. They were then coached by Eric Illidge and they won the world professional title again at Chicago Stadium. The Globetrotters went down 27–23 in the semifinals and the Oshkosh All-Stars succumbed 34–25 in the finals. Each Rens player received $1,000 for his efforts. In 1943—during the war—the Rens changed their name to the Washington Bears and won the world professional title in 1943,

before 12,000 of their faithful in Chicago Stadium. Zack Clayton, a Bears player, had then played on three world championship teams; for the Rens, the Globetrotters, and the Bears.

At war's end, the Bears changed their name back again to the Rens but took the name Dayton Rens in 1948, and joined the National Basketball League as a replacement for the Detroit Vagabonds, an all-white team. Still owned by Douglas, the Dayton Rens had a 16–43 season and played their last game against the Denver Nuggets on March 21, 1949, at Rockford, Illinois. The Rens' lifetime record was an astounding 2,318 wins and 381 losses. They were the first black team to win a world professional title in any sport and led the way for the post-World War II surge of blacks who eventually dominated the sport at every level.

The Rens' alter ego, the Harlem Globetrotters, were also formed from earlier fives that needed an overhaul. The Savoy Big Five of Chicago—managed by Dick Hudson, and formerly named the Giles Post (Negro American Legion) team—featured the football star Joe Lillard. A Jewish businessman, Abe Saperstein, thought he detected more potential if the marketing of the team were improved. The Rens had provided enough evidence to convince him that in the face of continuing prejudice, another all-black team had appeal. Saperstein, only five feet three and a half inches tall, decided to assume complete control of the Savoy squad and called his new team the Harlem Globetrotters, although they were based in Chicago. Though he did not know it, he had created what eventually became the most well-known team in sports history.

A.S. "Doc" Young said, "In all the history of American sports, no team has made a greater impact on the international scene than the Harlem Globetrotters professional basketball team...who are more personally familiar to fans in the remotest crannies of the world than the New York Yankees...or the Boston Celtics."[13] This was true in 1962 when Young wrote it, and even more true today in the mid-1980s.

Saperstein's starting five were Walter "Toots" Wright, Byron "Fat" Long, Willis "Kid" Oliver, Andy Washington, and Al "Runt" Pullins. In 1929, he replaced Washington with Inman Jackson, who became the first Globetrotter clown. Jackson played for fourteen years and made people laugh. But the Globbies could be and were a serious team as well. Even the name Globetrotters was just a dream at first. "...When the Globetrotters came into being, the possibility that the team would someday justify the 'Globetrotters' part of its title seemed as remote as some far distant planet."[14]

Saperstein's choice was based on hard business practices. No black teams belonged to the ABL, and they were not about to, for that would give them access to Madison Square Garden and other sports palaces on a regular basis. Black-versus-black games had little appeal unless the squads were truly superior; so the Globetrotters became a well-paid troupe of players who put on a good show and played well. They are also the oldest current black professional team in existence and still going strong. In the beginning, though, they were compared with the Rens and in fact its rivalry began in the early 1930s. By the late 1930s the Globbies were in the Chicago Herald American's world professional tournament, finishing third in 1939.

By 1940, the Globetrotters were better than the Rens; they won the professional title over their black rivals 37–36 in the semi-finals and over the Chicago Bruins in the final game. Not taking their success for granted, the Globbies organized their first fall training camp in 1940. The sport was by then more intense, more competitive, and required better conditioning and coordinated teamwork. This meticulous preparation paid off as they won the International Cup Tournament in Mexico City, in 1943, over stiffening competition.

Both the Globetrotters and the Rens suffered from the lack of a black league. Seating facilities remained small well into the war years, though by 1942 some black college fives had national followings. Distances between the quality teams remained vast and there were no super highways for cars. The turnpikes were not yet built, let alone the modern interstates. A trip that averaged forty miles per hour in a car was considered swift.

As the Globetrotters came into their own relatively late and during the war, they played many colleges as morale boosting experiences with diminished resistance from the press, but with problems from the college conferences. (Virginia Union University had their CIAA title taken away in the

1940–41 season because they played the Globetrotters.) A game against the University of Washington in 1943 for the Servicemen's Fund drew over 10,000 fans, though the author wonders how much of that went to black servicemen. These displays of patriotism were not enough to elicit an invitation to join the Basketball Association of America (BAA) that was formed in 1946.

Another theory much believed by the black press was that, being white, Saperstein made an arrangement with the owners of the white teams to keep blacks out so that his Globetrotters could always have the pick of the best blacks. This would accomplish two ends: ensure that the Globetrotters always had quality black players; and, with no black players in the white leagues, the white players would never complain. This was never proven one way or the other. Nevertheless it was believed by many black players and fans.

With the integration of the professional leagues, the Globetrotters in 1949 switched entirely to entertaining rather than trying to find a place as a serious team. This again was a sound business decision if albeit, a sad athletic one. Major league baseball did not allow any Negro league teams to enter their domain and the basketball leagues thought along the same lines. Black players? yes; black teams? no. Black America had to look toward its college squads to find all-black teams to follow. But they, too, had a rocky transition after the First World War.

Black College Basketball

Basketball at black colleges after World War I was little more than a diversion at best and, in most places, an afterthought. Howard University stopped the sport for a while in 1919. Except for the CIAA, other conferences either did not exist or did not play for a title. The facilities were just not there at the majority of schools and spectator seating was usually standing-room-only. Coaches were more attuned to football and baseball and they were not hired full-time; they had to teach academic subjects as well. The segregated and poorly outfitted black public schools in the South—where all but a handful of the colleges were located—had either no facilities or makeshift dirt courts.

Competition was usually of the intramural variety or against other colleges or YMCAs. Even less attention was paid to competition for women; if at all. Then there was the need of players to leave college to work during planting and harvesting seasons and to fill the choice jobs (for blacks) in the resort hotels in the winter. Most schools just closed during these times. It was no surprise then that the decade of the 1920s was spent building both interest and courts.

Hampton probably had the best team around in 1920 since it had an indoor gymnasium. It could draw upon local Virginia high school players that were reasonably competent in athletic ability. The state also had St. Paul's, Virginia Normal and Industrial, Virginia Union, and Howard University located virtually within a three-hour train ride. In the West, the SWAC conference had formed in 1920, but did not host a title competition until 1928. The sport could only improve in importance.

In 1925, Morehouse won the first tournament played (outdoors) among black colleges in the South. They defeated Atlanta

University 37–13 and followed this victory with a 9–0 undefeated season in 1926. But nine games were hardly enough to build a quality team and test its compatibility, and frankly, nothing of grand importance except pride was hanging in the balance. There were no athletic scholarships, no professional leagues save local groups up North, and no high expectations. The primary benefit was merely the chance to garner some favorable publicity for the college.

Some thought the schools took this approach too far when games were scheduled against professional teams. There were definite conference rules forbidding these contests, but administrators just winked and proceeded as if they had not noticed. Conference cohesion was sorely tested in the mid-1920s as a result, when schools such as Howard railed against losing their perceived independence. After all, Howard was black America's most famous college.

In any event, some standards were set. Horace "Itty" Dalton, of Clark College, scored 336 points in 1927; quite a feat, but it included games against all opponents— collegiate and otherwise. In 1928, the Southern Intercollegiate Athletic Conference (SIAC) was formed and immediately embraced basketball. Schoolboy teams looked up to these squads. There was even an attempt to establish a high school league in Virginia in 1928. The Deep South was catching up.

The westernmost colleges joined the ranks of basketball fives in 1928, when Sam Houston in Texas won the first Southwest Athletic Conference (SWAC) title. Two years later, every section of the country that had black colleges had at least two or three schools that played varsity basketball. But

they all took a back seat to the teams from Morgan State College in Baltimore. Morgan State teams in the late 1920s and early 1930s could, on any given day, defeat any squad, amateur or professional.

From 1927 until 1934, Morgan never lost a home-court game until Howard stopped the streak. Its 41-40 victory over the professional Rens squad in 1929 was the greatest college victory of the decade. For a time, only Virginia Seminary could give coach Eddie Hurt's team any competition. With Morgan State in the CIAA, it assured a conference of premier standing among the others. Morgan State's conference mate, Howard University, played and won a game, 32–26, against Lincoln University (Penn.) in New York City, in 1930. Both teams had tremendous followings at the game due to their football rivalry.

As the decade of the 1930s began, facilities remained a problem. Few schools could justify the expense of building special gymnasiums just for basketball. Scores were low because of rules that did not penalize stalling; conferences were imbalanced; and the sport lacked a tradition akin to that for baseball or football. Baseball had a traditional Easter Monday game; football a Thanksgiving Day game; but basketball was bereft of national social importance. Where would a school's alumni sit even if they came to see a big game?

General purpose gymnasiums could be found at Talladega, Tennessee A&I, Morehouse, Hampton, and Howard; exceptions all. Even mighty Morgan State lacked its own on-campus site. The farther south a school's location, the more likely that school played its games outdoors. Black high schools in the South had no gymnasiums at all; sports facilities were outdoors. The best of these secondary school teams were found in the Midwest and on the East Coast; in Indiana, Kentucky, and the Carolinas; in Chicago, Philadelphia, New York City, Wilmington (Delaware), Baltimore, and Washington, D.C. School teams with regional reputations were DeWitt Clinton in New York; Dunbar and Armstrong in Washington, D.C.; Wendell Phillips in Chicago; and Roosevelt in Gary, Indiana. There were attempts to organize national tournaments for high school teams but the cost was prohibitive and a venue could never be agreed upon. No thought whatever was given to such competition for girls.

Into these circumstances appeared a few college teams that competed for column space in the black press. (There were no radio or television broadcasts.) Morgan State fielded outstanding teams until the mid-1930s. They were CIAA champions from 1931 to 1934 then tied for the title with Virginia State in 1937–38. Morgan's lineup included big names from the gridiron, plus others: Edward "Lanky" Jones, Pinky Clark, Cutie Brown, Babe Jones, Skippy Gibson, Otis Troupe, Tom "Big Tank" Conrad, and Howard "Brutus" Wilson. Troupe, Conrad, and Wilson also played football. Jones was later instrumental in assisting former Lincoln University (Pa.) football star, Dr. Robert W. Johnson, with his junior tennis program that produced Arthur Ashe.

Wiley College enjoyed the first serious winning streak in the SIAC, a thirty-three-game record that ended in 1936. Under coach F.T. Long, it featured such players as Stretch Byrd, Crab Neely, John Aikens, Bill Spiller, Chuck Johnson, and Fess Widemon. The SIAC and the South Central Athletic Conference (SCAC) began title awards in 1934.

Xavier University in New Orleans had some of the best teams before the Second World War during the 1935-38 period. Their stars were Cleveland Bray, Leroy Rhodes, Tilford Cole, Charlie Gant, and William McQuitter. At one time this fivesome had a record of sixty-seven wins and two losses. One loss was to LeMoyne, 33–32, in 1935, and the other to Clark, 27–26, in 1937. The unique feature of this team was that the five stars all came from Chicago's Wendell Phillips High School. On two occasions it played the Rens, losing 38–37 and 24–20, before the largest crowd to see black college basketball in the South. Though not a part of this illustrious team, Frank "Blotto" Crozier, in 1939, set a new single–season scoring record of 343 points.

Virginia Union fielded its famous "dream team" in the 1939–40 season. It had won the CIAA title in 1939, and the press believed the squad of Mel Glover, Gerald "Pickles" Frazier, Obie Knight, Kavanzo Hyde, and Wylie "Soupy" Campbell were the pick of the year. Other members were Howard Jones, Wendell Williams, Alvin Storres, Floyd Atkins, Lewis White, Vincent Tinsley, and Norman Hines. Mel Glover claims that Virginia Union actually won the CIAA title in both the 1940 and 1941 seasons, but the conference officials would not acknowledge it because the school played against the Globetrotters. "We are still mad about that," noted Glover, "because other schools did it too but we were pretty good and they wanted to make an example out of us."[15] It seemed as if the college game had sprouted new talent all at once but, in reality, it was only maturing. On the cusp of its growth during the Depression, basketball had a deepening constituency.

Part of this effort resulted in the first games against white schools. Under the direction of its athletic director, Charles H. Williams of Hampton, that school played Brooklyn College in 1938, losing 46–31, at Brooklyn. Virginia Union and Kentucky State followed in 1939 with games against Long Island University. (Back in 1934, Ned Irish had begun his soon-to-be-famous college doubleheaders at Madison Square Garden but black teams were never invited.) In 1940, Glover and Campbell starred for Virginia Union, as it defeated Brooklyn College 54–38 before 3,500 fans. The black press campaigned for this game to be played in Madison Square Garden, but it did not materialize.

Clark College also had a notable team in 1939. A decade earlier it had been behind its other Atlanta University sister schools, Morris Brown and Morehouse, but with the stellar play of Abbey Henderson, Sonny Younger, Hank DeZowie, Joe Johnson, Dale Pemberton, and the incomparable William "Pops" Gates, Clark was the best in the Southeast.

North Carolina College (now North Carolina Central) won the CIAA title in 1940–1941 and was 14–0. It also played Brooklyn College that same year, winning 37–34. Langston University in Oklahoma had a fifty-game winning streak that began in 1942. South Carolina State had Henry "Mice" Holden who scored fifty points against Delaware State and 458 points for the season in 1942. Under coach Ollie

Dawson, Holden's teammates included Ezra Moore, Charles Penn, William "Ducky" Copeland, Luther "Pepsi-Cola" Bligen, Curtis Torrey, Walter "Dynamite" Palmer, Curtis Moreland, and Morris Esmond.

With all this talent, a national tournament was suggested and planned to be held in Cincinnati, but it was a financial disaster. At least it was tried. By the end of World War II, the college game in the South was much less susceptible to the resort season and plantings and harvestings. Farm machinery had improved the productivity of the average farmer and he was less dependent on black labor to work the fields and pick the crops. Thus, basketball benefitted black colleges and high schools.

The most compelling and positive force for change, though, was the imminent integration of the professional leagues. Along with baseball and football, basketball—by 1950—brought three blacks into its professional ranks and two of them were products of black colleges. This was proof enough that these institutions had arrived as sports powers.

Blacks at White Colleges

The basketball policy of the various white athletic conferences was mixed toward blacks between the two World Wars. The Ivy League and other schools that competed in the Intercollegiate Amateur Athletic Association of America (ICAAAA) competitions were generally receptive. There was a history of black participation dating back to William T.S. Jackson and John B. Taylor in track; and baseball and football had already bestowed national honors on their token darker brethren. Jim Crow laws and white racist customs in the South, however, kept all blacks out of white colleges there. Princeton University, in New Jersey, had a "whites only" policy until 1944. Black cagers simply had to weave their way through a maze of obstacles if they wanted to play.

John Howard Johnson was Columbia University's first black player and as the following report shows, he was not afraid to defend himself. "Johnson, Columbia's Negro center, and Peck, a Quaker [University of Pennsylvania] guard, lost their heads and exchanged blows under the Columbia basket."[16] Peck seemed to have taken on more than he could handle since Johnson was a much larger center. Johnson graduated in 1921.

Ralph Bunche, the future Nobel Peace Prize recipient, was a standout at UCLA in the mid–1920s, though he stood only five feet ten inches. The tallest players in this era were around six feet five inches as in the case of famed Celtic star, Joe Lapchick. Charles Drew, who later received acclaim for his work on blood plasma, played at Amherst in 1923. He won his school's Ashley Trophy as the best all-around athlete.

George Gregory, a graduate of New York City's DeWitt Clinton High School, was elected Columbia's captain in 1930. He was also named to the Helms Foundation All-America team in 1931, alongside the soon-to-be legendary UCLA coach, John Wooden. In his three-year career, Gregory scored 509 points in sixty-two games. James D. and Samuel E. Barnes were the first black siblings to play at Oberlin in Ohio, where there was a long tradition of black participation. As at black colleges, competition for women was strictly intramural and informal almost everywhere.

Most black sports enthusiasts had hoped the records of George Gregory and others would help counter the wave of re-segregation taking place in American athletics in the latter half of the 1920s. However, the controversial legacy of the black former heavyweight champion Jack Johnson had caused Harry Wills, another black heavyweight, to be denied his rightful title opportunity. The National Football League had begun to freeze out its black players; in 1933 they banned all of them for thirteen years. Major league baseball gave no hint of integrating, and black jockeys had been systematically driven off the tracks by the eve of World War I. Northern white college basketball's odd-league-out was the Big Ten. While it showcased black football talent, it refused to allow black basketball players until after World War II.

In January 1934, the University of Michigan—a Big Ten school—caused an uproar when it dismissed Franklin Lett from its freshman squad. Lett had been informed by coach F.C. Cappon that "There has never been a colored boy to play basketball in the Big Ten. It has been a mutual agreement between the coaches not to use a colored boy in basketball."[17] In a letter to Cappon, Roy Wilkins, the young assistant secretary of the National Association for the Advancement of Colored People, angrily replied that Cappon's remarks were an insult to young Lett personally and to blacks in general.

Two weeks later, the January 27 *Afro-American* newspaper reported that "...an alleged agreement between the Big Ten coaches to keep colored players off basketball teams...was broken this week when...Michigan was forced to place Franklin Lett, star athlete, back on the freshman squad."[18] Lett, however, never played varsity basketball for Michigan. Two years before, Michigan track star Eddie Tolan won two gold medals at the Los Angeles Olympic Games. Michigan's and the Big Ten's treatment of black basketball players was patently unfair and discriminatory. As if to verify the University of Michigan's racist policies, all-white college basketball doubleheaders at New York City's Madison Square Garden were begun the same year.

Some white schools *did* continue to use black players and a partial listing includes Horace Johnson at Dakota College from 1936 to 1938; Bobby Yancey and Ben Franklin at Boston University in 1937; and Lawrence Bleach at Detroit University in 1937. Of particular interest was William "Dolly" King at Long Island University. King was a graduate of Brooklyn's Alexander Hamilton High, where he lettered in three sports (basketball, baseball, and football), for three years. King was the first black player in the National AAU tournament, in 1937. On November 29, 1939, he performed a unique double by playing in a football and a basketball game on the same day. After his college years, King played professionally for the Scranton Miners, the Rens, the Washington Bears, and in 1946 for the Rochester Royals, a National Basketball League squad.

Frank "Doc" Kelker played at Western Reserve from 1936 to 1938. Kelker graduated Phi Beta Kappa after three varsity seasons. Wilmeth Sidat-Singh, the adopted son of Dr. Samuel Sidat-Singh, starred at Syracuse University after attending DeWitt Clinton High in New York City. As had happened on his school's football team, Sidat-Singh was left off the team in a game against Navy. His 1939 squad was 14–0. He joined the Syracuse Reds after graduation and played for the Rochester Seagrams in 1940, in the World Professional Tournament. After attending Tuskegee's (Alabama) Army Air Corps Flying School, he became a member of the all-black 332nd Fighter Group stationed at Selfridge Field, Michigan. He was unfortunately killed on June 9, 1943, when his military plane caught fire and crashed in Lake Huron.

Another in the news was Jackie Robinson at UCLA in 1939–40. He won the Pacific Coast Conference-Southern Division scoring title in his first year with 148 points in twelve games. The following season he won the title again with 133 points in twelve games. Back East, Jim Coward was at Brooklyn College; Ed Younger at Long Island University; Tom Wood and Norman Skinner at Columbia; Jay Swift at Yale; Sonny Jameson at City College of New York; Dick Culberson at Iowa; Dick Wilkins scored 345 points in 1944 at the University of Oregon; and Art White became Princeton's first black player in 1944.

These players seldom had the impact of their black football brothers. No basketball player garnered the publicity accorded Cornell's All-America football star Jerome Holland, for example. Seldom did a white school play more than one black player at the same time, and there were few black substitutes. All of them were tokens since there were always more blacks qualified to play than were allowed on varsity fives.

The racial logjam was finally broken during the five years from 1946 to 1950. Joe Louis, Jackie Robinson, Althea Gibson, and Jesse Owens left such positive impressions upon their respective sports that the entire American sports establishment felt freer to experiment. Old groundless fears were proven to be just that—groundless. But most important, the world found out just how good black athletes were and how eager they were to compete. As for basketball, the best was yet to come.

Notes

1. A.S. "Doc" Young, *Negro Firsts in Sports* (Chicago: Johnson Publications, 1963), p. 81.
2. *Chicago Defender*, 18 January 1921.
3. *New York Age*, 8 April 1922.
4. Eyre Saitch interview with author, 7 April 1984, New York City.
5. Ibid.
6. Ibid.
7. William "Pops" Gates telephone interview with author, 24 April 1985.
8. Eyre Saitch interview with author, 7 May 1984, New York City.
9. Ocania Chalk, *Black College Sports* (New York: Dodd, Mead & Co., 1976), p. 28.
10. *Pittsburgh Courier*, 23 February 1924.
11. Eyre Saitch interview with author, 7 May 1984, New York City.
12. Ibid.
13. Young, *Negro Firsts in Sports*, p. 230.
14. Ibid., p. 78.
15. Mel Glover interview with author, 17 March 1987, New York City.
16. *New York Times*, 26 January 1919.
17. *Pittsburgh Courier*, 13 January 1934.
18. *Baltimore Afro-American*, 27 January 1934.

CHAPTER 3

ͻINCE 1946

><><><><><><><><><><><><><><><><><><><><><><><><><><><><

After the Second World War, black basketball players were not as fortunate as their baseball brethren. In 1946, Jackie Robinson was playing for the Montreal Royals in the International League and followed that with an historic berth in the Brooklyn Dodgers' lineup in 1947. Nineteen forty-six for William "Pop" Gates and William "Dolly" King was quite different; both were playing in a white professional basketball league, but lasted only one season. Gates believes it was due to a racial incident involving Chick Meehan.

Gates was playing a game for the Tri-Cities Blackhawks against Meehan and the Syracuse Nationals; both teams were in the Basketball Association of America (BAA). As Gates relates the story: Meehan ". . . threw me down one time, and I said 'Chick, don't do that no more!' Well, he threw me down again, so I deliberately placed myself in the pivot. When he tried again, I threw *him* down and he got up whaling. So I got mine [punch] in first before he got his in. I made him bleed. That's the reason Dolly and I only played one season."[1]

Life in the BAA was difficult that season for Gates and King. They encountered the same housing problems the Negro League baseball players had, and solved them in the same manner: they coped. Most of the time they looked for a "Colored" YMCA, and sometimes they managed to stay with their white teammates. Gates mentions the Claypool Hotel in Indianapolis, Indiana, the Seneca Hotel in Rochester, New York, and a few others as being accommodating to black ballplayers.

This treatment of Gates and King should be, but is not surprising in comparison to the famous Harlem Globetrotters, whose housing was pre-arranged by Abe Saperstein, and who had a very successful season between 1947–48. That season included a 52-game winning streak, a victory in the Cuba Invitational, a victory over the Minneapolis Lakers and their star center George Mikan, and two movies, entitled The *Globetrotters Story* and *Go Man Go*. In the win over the Lakers at Chicago Stadium on February 20, 1948, Ermer Robinson drilled a 20-foot set shot after a pass from Marques Haynes at the buzzer.

The following year, the Globetrotters began the transformation from a serious team to one that entertained with fancy passes, trick shooting, and hilarious routines. They toured with an all-star squad of collegians and by 1951, the change was nearly complete, when they made their first round-the-world tour, playing 108 games in their twenty-fifth season. They still hoid the attendance record of 75,000 in the Berlin Olympic Stadium and

50,041 in Rio de Janeiro, Brazil. As of the end of 1992, over 100 million people have watched the Globetrotters in action. They remain the world's best-known sports team.

In the late 1940s, the Globetrotters' success did not rub off on most other black teams. Except for the New York Renaissance squad, other all-black professional teams, like the Chicago Collegians and the Chicago Studebakers, struggled. Without a league, Collegians teammates Al Johnson, Ages Bray, Victor Kraft, Hank Blackburn, Anthony Payton, Bill Kelly, and Bob Farrell had nowhere else to go. The two competing white leagues had their own problems, and they finally decided that a merger was part of the answer but signing black players was another matter.

The *New York Age* announced the breakthrough in its October 9, 1948, edition: "Color Line Is Broken in Basketball Assn. of America: Six Join Chicago Stags."[2] Those six black pioneers were Henry Blackburn, Leon Wright, Irving Ward, George Raby, Arthur Wilson, and Leonard Jordan. Though none of them played in the National Basketball Association (NBA), they nevertheless widened the door opened by William "Pop" Gates and William "Dolly" King. The professional game has not been the same since then.

A GROWING BLACK TRADITION

The tradition inherited by black basketball players after World War II was perhaps the most fruitful of the major team sports. Unlike baseball and football, basketball tradition had included an all-black team generally recognized as the best in the world. This squad, the New York Renaissance, was unsurpassed in consistency and teamwork and, at its height in the late 1930s, thrilled many audiences. The Harlem Globetrotters also enjoyed a national reputation. However, both the Renaissance and Globetrotters teams owed a debt

to the pioneer work of Dr. Edwin B. Henderson and Cumberland Posey. Henderson was instrumental in the early 1900s in developing the sport among blacks along the Washington, D.C.–New York City corridor from his base as Director of Physical Education for the Colored Schools of the nation's capital and its local Colored YMCA.

After World War II, interest in the sport increased considerably. In particular, the northern urban areas became magnets for the best public school, college, and club players, most of whom played indoors in gyms and armories. More high schools fielded teams that improved the selection pools of college coaches, yet the sport that is today so identified with black America developed most of its best talent on the public courts, which began to organize its play.

One of the prime innovators in the organization of public parks basketball competition was Holcombe Rucker, who began his summer leagues in 1946. From this New York City tournament came dozens of future professional players. Similar programs, like the Baker League of Philadelphia, sprang up in other urban areas from Baltimore to Los Angeles. These leagues have grown in sophistication to include academic counseling along with on-court play.

Uniqueness for Blacks: Basketball was an ideal athletic pursuit for the masses of black Americans in the immediate post–World War II period. Equipment requirements were minimal—just a basketball, some "gym shoes," and a court. Public courts were usually within walking distance of any black residential area in the northern cities. Most public courts used by blacks in the segregated South were found in school yards and Colored YMCAs and YWCAs.

Little coaching was needed to master basketball's basic offensive moves, and the small size of teams enabled most pickup squads to literally teach themselves. The sport was also less tradition-bound than baseball or football, so rule changes could be made more quickly to enhance its spectator appeal. Additionally, girls were encouraged to play since, in basketball's ideal form, there was supposedly little violent body contact. YWCAs, churches, clubs, and black newspaper-sponsored squads played in women's leagues.

The foregoing factors enabled black American communities to utilize their own resources to produce superior players. In the process, the players themselves built on the legacy of outstanding past performances from former Globetrotters and Renaissance players like Hilton Slocum, Eyre Saitch, William "Pop" Gates, "Fats" Jenkins, and William "Dolly" King. A distinctive "black" style of play developed that featured speed, uncommon jumping ability, and innovative passing skills. Though this style was frequently at odds with white coaches' philosophies of the late 1940s, it produced results and was extremely exciting to watch. Thus, it was only a matter of time before the professional leagues admitted black players.

The Basketball Association of America Admits Blacks: In 1946, owners of some of the nation's largest northern indoor arenas sensed the increased popularity of basketball and formed the Basketball Association of America (BAA). Their main objective was to fill their empty arena dates with professional basketball games, though college and AAU basketball had a larger following. After much discussion and with an eye on the progress of Jackie Robinson in professional baseball, these proprietors decided to admit black players. In spite of the clash in 1946 involving "Pop" Gates and Chick Meehan, black participation was inevitable, due in large measure to Don Barksdale's play as the first black player on an Olympic team in 1948.

Within thirty years, black players, both men and women, would dominate what is now referred to as "the city game" at all levels of play.

THE AMATEURS

The Olympians: Since the YMCA gave birth to basketball and the organization was international in scope, it spread the hoop gospel quickly around the world. Inevitably basketball became an Olympic event. In the 1904 Games basketball was a demonstration sport, but at the 1936 Berlin Olympics its official debut was made on a dirt court turned muddy by rain. Twelve years later, at the 1948 London Olympics, Don Barksdale, an All-American from UCLA, earned a gold medal as part of the United States team. Barksdale, who was 6-feet 5-inches, had played in the American Amateur Basketball League and had been named by California sportswriters to the all-time Pacific Coast Conference Team. Blacks would star, and in some cases dominate, in all succeeding Olympics competitions.

Though there was a strong black contingent of track athletes on the American Olympics squad in 1952, there were no basketball players. The United States defeated the previously undefeated Soviet Union squad 86–58. At the 1956 Games in Melbourne, Australia, Bill Russell and K.C. Jones starred, as the American team continued undefeated. To ensure that Russell, who was the most popular choice ever for All-American, would be present, President Dwight D. Eisenhower personally appealed to the University of San Francisco star: "We need you for our next Olympics team," Eisenhower told Russell. "I certainly hope we'll have you."[3] Russell replied, "I promise . . . I'll be on that Olympic team if I can make it." At the time, Russell characterized his participation on the Olympic team as his proudest moment. Later in his career, Russell would become very critical of his own country's racial policies.

The 1960 Olympic team featured the inimitable Oscar Robertson and Jerry West, a white player from West Virginia. The team averaged over a hundred points per game under coach Pete Newell (who figured prominently in future incidents involving black players).

The 1964 squad included five black players, all of whom continued to be selected from midwestern and western colleges. Walt Hazzard, of John Wooden's UCLA NCAA-winning team, became the playmaker.

The 1968 competition was the first to feature important no-shows. Of the proposed boycott of the Mexico City Games by black track and field athletes, some basketball players were supportive. Among those who were unavailable were: Bob Lanier, Elvin Hayes, Wes Unseld, Mike Warren, Lucius Allen, and Lew Alcindor (now Kareem Abdul-Jabbar). Coach Hank Iba called these missing black players "bad citizens."[4]

However, Spencer Haywood of the University of Detroit and Jo Jo White of the University of Kansas were not only eager to participate in the Olympics but were unafraid to speak about it. Said Haywood at the time, "I wake up in the morning thinking Olympics, I dream Olympics, I wrote to my mother about the Olympics."[5] Bill Russell had counselled Haywood about his views. White was also adamant in his feelings, saying "I make up my own mind and I've decided to play. I don't care if I'm the only one [black player]. They can go ahead and boycott. I'm playing."[6] Publicly at least, Coach Iba made matters a little worse by saying, "I don't think the Negroes playing for us will be bothered by the boycott."[7]

When the Olympics were over, Haywood's elation was undiminished. "When we won the final and took the victory stand and they draped those gold medals around our necks and played the national anthem, it sent shivers down my spine."[8] Nevertheless, the five black players on this 1968 team were criticized in some quarters of the black community.

In 1972, the American basketball squad lost its first game after sixty-three consecutive wins. The loss was to the Soviets on a controversial decision by the referee to set the clock back three seconds at the expiration of play. The Soviets were able to inbound the ball and get it downcourt for a quick layup before the three extra seconds had elapsed. The Americans refused to accept the 51–50 loss and did not show up to receive their silver medals.

The 1976 squad featured the second and third black twosomes from the same schools—Walter Davis and Phil Ford from the University of North Carolina at Chapel Hill, and Scott May and Quinn Buckner from Indiana University. There were still no representatives from predominantly white colleges in the deep South or from black colleges.

The 1980 overall Olympic black contingent was the largest ever, but they did not get a chance to play because of President Jimmy Carter's decision to boycott the Moscow Games.

In 1984 at Los Angeles, the University of North Carolina at Chapel Hill produced its fifth and sixth black Olympians in Michael Jordan and Sam Perkins. For the first time ever, one of the players, Patrick Ewing, was selected from a team with a black coach—John Thompson of the Georgetown Hoyas. Thompson had been an Olympic team assistant coach in 1976. George Raveling was appointed as an assistant coach for the 1984 squad.

At the 1988 Seoul Games, the Americans met the Soviets in the semifinals in a rematch, 16 years after the 1972 Munich final. The USA squad, coached by Georgetown's John Thompson and led by David Robinson, Hersey Hawkins, and Stacey Augmon, didn't extract the sweet revenge the nation craved. The seasoned Soviet squad withstood every challenge, defeating the US 82–76. Thus, the U.S. failed to win the basketball gold medal for only the second time since 1936.

It was generally believed that the humiliating loss led to the decision that allowed U.S. professionals to play at the 1992 Barcelona Games. But Dave Gavitt, then-senior vice-president of the NBA's Boston Celtics and president of USA Basketball, in an article in *USA Today* in July 1992 said U.S. pros made their Olympic debut in Barcelona because the world, not the U.S., demanded their presence.

"Professionals have been involved in the Olympics for a long time in every country's team except the U.S.A.'s," Gavitt said. "Ironically, our decision was made for us by the rest of the nations of FIBA, basketball's international governing body. They did so by voting 59–13 in favor of making all basketball players eligible at a special meeting in Munich in April 1989. I know because I cast a "no" vote for the USA at that meeting."

Birth of the Dream Team: Top pros, such as Patrick Ewing and Michael Jordan, teammates on the USA's '84 gold medal team, initially were lukewarm about U.S. pros invading Olympic basketball. But their minds were changed by passionate pleas from Magic Johnson, who became the spiritual point-guard in the drive to assemble unquestionably the world's greatest players on what was appropriately dubbed The Dream Team.

Johnson stunned the sportsworld in November 1991 announcing his retirement from the NBA because he had contracted the AIDS virus. But Johnson vowed to play in Barcelona, health permitting.

"I desire that gold medal more than anything," Johnson said. "The library would be complete then. It can be closed because I will have won everything from Pop Warner on

up. This might even be bigger than winning the NBA title because it's worldwide."

The Dream Team swept through the Olympic competition with the efficiency of a finely-tuned juggernaut. The Dream Team won eight Olympic games by an average of 43.8 points, defeating Croatia 117–85 in the gold medal finale. The squad averaged 16.4 more assists and 13.5 more rebounds and forced 6.7 more turnovers a game than its opponents.

"We owe so much of this Dream Team experience to Magic," Michael Jordan said. "Chuck [Daly] did it as a coach, but Magic did it as a player. He kept everyone's ego in check and he always made sure the chemistry was what it's supposed to be. He united the team and molded it. Some of us were local leaders and some of us were physical leaders. Magic was both." (*USA TODAY*, July 10, 1992.)

But the Dream Team also drew its share of criticism. Some critics, including USOC president LeRoy Walker, raised questions about whether NBA pros should play in Olympic competition. "I'm not saying I don't want a Dream Team in Atlanta (site of 1996 Olympics)," Walker said. "I'm saying I don't want it in Atlanta under the same circumstances. So it's not that I don't want the NBA in the Olympics."

Dream Team: Magic Johnson, Michael Jordan, Larry Bird, Charles Barkley, Patrick Ewing, John Stockton, David Robinson, Christian Laettner, Chris Mullen, Scottie Pippen, Karl Malone, and Clyde Drexler.

Dream Team Results: Game 1, defeated Angola 116–48; Game 2, defeated Croatia 113–70; Game 3, defeated Germany 111–68; Game 4, defeated Brazil 127–83; Game 5, defeated Spain 122–81; Game 6, defeated Puerto Rico 115–77; Game 7 defeated Lithuania 127–76; Game 8, defeated Croatia 117–85.

The record of black achievement in Olympic competition is an enviable one. Were Edwin B. Henderson, Cumberland Posey and

Robert Douglas alive today, they would be justly proud of these accomplishments.

The Female Olympians: The United States fielded strong teams during the inaugural women's competition in 1976 and at the 1984 Games. The list of black female Olympians appears in the Reference section.

In the mid-1970s, women's basketball was just beginning to emerge as a possible professional sport. At the 1976 Games, the Soviet Union won the gold medal and the United States defeated Bulgaria 95–79 for the silver medal. The eight-year interim between the 1976 and 1984 Games was a period of unparalleled growth for women's basketball in America, and the squad at Los Angeles was the most highly-touted assemblage ever seen on one team.

Though the 1984 team was well balanced, the stars were Cheryl Miller, Lynette Woodard, and Pam McGee; Miller was hailed as the best women's player in the history of the sport. Born and raised in Riverside, California, she came from a middle-class family that featured two other outstanding athletes. (Her brother, Reggie, played for UCLA, and another brother, Darrell, played professional baseball for the California Angels.)

Miller, who is 6-feet 3-inches, once scored 105 points in one game while at Polytechnic High in Riverside. She was also a member of two NCAA championship teams at the University of Southern California. Said former All-American Nancy Lieberman of Miller: ". . . Cheryl has revolutionized the game . . . she learned to do that the same way I did—we had to play like the guys . . . I think Cheryl is the best thing that could have happened to the game."[9]

McGee is one-half of a basketball playing set of twins. Her sister, Paula, did not make the cut for the Olympic team, yet she was present throughout to lend moral support. In a touching and heartwarming moment following her gold medal performance against the Koreans, Pam presented her gold medal to Paula, who was already in tears over the medal ceremony. The scene was one of the most touching memories of the 1984 Olympic Games.

Lynette Woodard later made history in accepting an offer to become the first female member of the Harlem Globetrotters. She had been the all-time leading scorer at the University of Kansas (topping even the totals set by Wilt Chamberlain). She was also the NCAA's top career scorer, for women's basketball, with 3,649 points—an average of 26.3 points per game.

At the 1988 Seoul Games, the American women's team grabbed the gold again, defeating Yugoslavia 77–70 in the final. The U.S. squad was led by playmaker Teresa Edwards, who averaged 16.6 points a game, and Georgia teammate Katrina McClain, who led the U.S. squad in scoring with 17.6 points a game and rebounding with 10.4 per game.

But USA women fell short at the '92 Barcelona Games, losing to the Unified Team 79–73 in the semifinals. The loss snapped a 15-game Olympic winning streak by the USA women, who won the bronze medal, defeating Cuba 88–74.

The Black Colleges

The black colleges were primary beneficiaries of a continuing interest in basketball immediately following World War II. Athletically gifted black GIs returned home and headed for college, where tuition was paid for with G.I. Bill benefits. As was the case at predominantly white colleges, the sport became a coach-dominated game. Unlike his white counterpart, the black coach was most probably a teacher, as well.

The dominant powers in the early 1950s included North Carolina College (now known as North Carolina Central University), coached by Johnny B. McLendon; Virginia Union, coached by Tom Harris; Winston-Salem, coached by Clarence "Big House" Gaines; Morris Brown, coached by H.B. Thompson; and Florida A & M, coached by Ed Oglesby. The major schools were compressed into three conferences—the Central Intercollegiate Athletic Association (CIAA), the Southern Intercollegiate Athletic Conference (SIAC), and the Southwestern Athletic Conference (SWAC). A fourth conference, the Mid-east Athletic Conference (MEAC), would be added in the 1970s.

In April 1989, North Carolina Central joined a handful of black colleges to win NCAA titles, defeating Southeast Missouri State 73–46 in the NCAA-II final in Springfield, Massachusetts. None of these schools had large gymnasiums, and their small budgets limited recruiting efforts to high school players within a day's drive. These efforts were augmented by word-of-mouth recruiting and the judicious use of former alumni. Though all but five black schools were located in southern or border states, it was not unusual for a southern team to have a starting five from Detroit, Chicago, or New York City. The mass migration of blacks from the South to northern factories during World War II had helped spread the word about black colleges.

The coaches who were able to consistently field conference-winning teams were in many cases better known than some of their star players. None was better known than Johnny B. McLendon.

Johnny B. McLendon: He received his early training from the master himself—James Naismith, the Canadian YMCA instructor who invented the sport and later taught at the University of Kansas that McLendon attended. McLendon first earned fame at Tennessee State after joining the staff in 1954. Tennessee State president Walter Davis was an avid sports fan, and he truly believed that

a winning team could only help to spread the word about his school.

Tennessee State became the first black college team invited to play in the National Association of Intercollegiate Athletics (NAIA) tourney in 1954. In March 1957, they won their first NAIA title at Kansas City. They defeated Southeast Oklahoma State by the score of 92–73 before eight-thousand fans, and became the first black college to win a national basketball title. The starting five on this historic team were Ron Hamilton, captain; John Barnhill; Henry Carlton; Jim Satterwhite; and Dick "Skull" Barnett. On the Eastern Airlines flight back to Nashville, a bomb threat was reported, but an investigation turned nothing up.

McLendon was hailed as the finest coach in black intercollegiate athletics. No black school before 1957 had ever won a national title against a white school in any sport. Tennessee State repeated as NAIA champions in 1958 and 1959. The 1958 victory was gained over Western Illinois 85–73, and Dick Barnett was named Most Valuable Player. The 1959 win came over Pacific Lutheran 97–87 and contributed to Barnett being a three-time NAIA All-American, who finished his collegiate career with 3,209 points.

In 1961, McLendon shocked Tennessee State's administrators by resigning to become the first black professional basketball coach of the Cleveland Pipers of the new American Basketball League (ABL). The prime force behind the ABL was Abe Saperstein, the owner of the Harlem Globetrotters. In January 1962, McLendon submitted his resignation to Pipers' president George Steinbrenner. Steinbrenner had withheld salary checks to players because he was supposedly irritated over their play. McLendon stood up for his players, saying, "I cannot stand by and see a good group of young athletes intimidated."[10] Later, when Ralph Wilson bought the Pipers from Steinbrenner, McLendon was brought back.

Years later, Steinbrenner was again involved in a feud with another black, Reggie Jackson, when Steinbrenner became the principal owner of the New York Yankees baseball team in the 1970s.

Clarence "Big House" Gaines: He completed his 46th year as Winston-Salem State University coach in the spring of 1992, placing him second to Kentucky's Adolph Rupp for most career victories. (Gaines' record: 822–430; Rupp's record—875–190 in 41 seasons.) Just as Johnny B. McLendon was closely associated with Dick Barnett, Gaines was instrumental in the development of Earl Monroe, who played for Winston-Salem in 1967, the year Gaines became the first black coach to win an NCAA Division II title.

Dave Whitney: He enjoyed tremendous success as the coach at Mississippi's Alcorn State University. He won eight SWAC titles between 1969 and 1984, the period when predominantly white southern colleges began recruiting black athletes.

The mid-1970s was a particularly difficult transition period for black colleges. Bobby Vaughn, the CIAA's president, noted in 1976 that: "The competition for the good players is much greater. We're so far behind in finances, just like everything else."[11]

"Big House" Gaines, remarking on the paradoxical situation of black colleges, said, "The only thing that keeps us on an even keel is so many kids are playing basketball that the supply is greater than the demand . . . I'm not playing the University of Indiana with all those seven footers."[12] First Gaines and then Whitney realized that they could no longer rely on recruiting exclusively the best black talent. Through the 1984–85 season, Whitney's teams earned 416 victories in twenty-one years. Later, he was appointed as a member of the Olympic Trials coaching staff, and guided Alcorn State to four NCAA Playoff

Tournaments, and two National Invitation Tournament (NIT) berths.

Conference Champions: Though most black NBA players played at white schools, the black colleges maintained their interest in basketball and a fourth major conference, the MEAC, was formed in the early 1970s in response to increased demand. The list appears in the Reference section.

National Champions: A surprising number of black schools have won NAIA, NCAA II, and NCAA III national titles. The list appears in the Reference section.

Black Women Score Victories: Black females had traditionally concentrated on track and field as their major athletic outlet. When men's basketball became a revenue-producing sport, few black college athletic directors were willing to give "equal time" to women's games which were events usually open to the public free of charge. Title IX of the Education Amendments Act of 1972 changed that, and all universities receiving federal funds had to provide varsity sports for women who wanted them. Cheryl Miller, the University of Southern California star, told *Sports Illustrated*: "Without Title IX I wouldn't be here."[13]

Three black schools won national women's titles between 1979 and 1988: South Carolina State, coached by Willie Simon, won the Association for Intercollegiate Women's Athletics II title (AIAW II) in 1979; Virginia Union, coached by Louis Hearn, won the NCAA II title in 1983 and Hampton University, coached by James Sweat, won the NCAA II title in 1988.

Vivian Stringer: She began a remarkable coaching career in 1971 at Cheney State in Pennsylvania, where she compiled a 251–51 record in 11 years. She coached Cheney State to the final of the first women's championship in 1982, losing to Louisiana Tech, 76–62.

Stringer, who played at Slippery Rock State College, took control of the Iowa Hawkeyes' dismal program in 1983 and quickly became the only Division I coach to lead two schools to a No. 2 or better ranking. In 1992, she ranked fifth in the nation for most wins by an active coach (461) and ranked third in the nation with a career winning percentage of 812 (461–107). She was selected NCAA Coach of the Year (1982), NCAA District V Coach of the Year (1985, 1988), and Big Ten Coach of the Year in 1991. More impressively, in her first 14 years of coaching, 97 percent of Stringer's players graduated.

By the late 1970s, women's basketball was a serious endeavor among its participants and bore little resemblance to the genteel game played right after World War II. As Luisa Harris of Delta State soberly noted, "You have to get rough with the sport. You have to be tough."[14]

The White-College Experience

Some white-college conferences including the Ivy League and schools in the Midwest, the Middle Atlantic, and on the Pacific coast continued allowing blacks on their basketball teams, but southern and southwestern schools, and the Big Ten Conference, did not. This situation existed when the college game was more popular than the professional version. Ed "Ned" Irish had begun his college basketball doubleheaders at Madison Square Garden in 1936, and they were extremely popular. However, by 1950, the idea began to take hold that "if blacks were good enough to fight in World War II, they were good enough to play anywhere in America." Unfortunately, some black basketballers were named in some of the most damaging scandals to beset the college game.

Blacks eventually dominated all college basketball, but they have suffered through periods of blatant exploitation and are frequent victims of illegal schemes involving gambling, point shaving, receiving unaccounted sums of money, recruiting violations, and broken promises. Contributing factors include the low socioeconomic class of the players, their relative lack of sophistication, their lack of knowledge of the rules, their naiveté, and temptation.

The first recorded incident occurred in 1951. Arthur Daley, the *New York Times'* esteemed sports columnist, described the atmosphere. ". . . The gambling craze has swept the country," he wrote, "with the avariciousness of a prairie fire . . . The satanic gimmick is the point spread."[15] Bettors on athletic contests used to wager using "odds," but by this time they began using the "point spreads" that are common today.

Manhattan College (New York City) players Hank Poppe and Jack Byrnes, both white, confessed to District Attorney Frank Hogan that they "shaved" points in five games in return for money. Junius Kellog, a black player from Portsmouth, Virginia, reported his bribe offer to Manhattan coach Kenny Norton. His actions were lauded in the biggest sports scandal since the "fixed" World Series games of 1919. The *Pittsburgh Courier's* Wendell Smith said, "Junie Kellog rates a special salute from the entire sporting world."[16]

Further investigation showed that between 1947 and 1950, eighty-six games in New York City and twenty-two other cities were fixed by thirty-two players at seven schools. Even the University of Kentucky, referred to in the black community as the "Blue Grass Bigots," lost their National Invitation Tournament title of 1949 due to point shaving.

In 1961, there was another fixing scandal involving a total of forty-seven players. This time, Connie Hawkins, an eighteen-year-old black freshman at Iowa, was falsely implicated. Hawkins was a much-lauded player from Brooklyn's Bedford-Stuyvesant neighborhood and Kareem Abdul-Jabbar (formerly Lew Alcindor) once said of him: "I've seen the best in the NBA, but I've never seen anybody better than Hawkins."[17]

Hawkins was wrongfully accused by Dave Budin, a former Brooklyn College player and public-school teacher, of acting as an intermediary in fixing games. Budin's partner in the illegal scheme was Jack Molinas, who masterminded the fixed games and was prosecuted by District Attorney Frank Hogan. Though he was never charged or prosecuted, Hawkins was blackballed by the NBA and sued the organization for $6 million. This 6-foot 8-inch star finally began to play professionally in the American Basketball League with the Pittsburgh Pipers in 1967. Hawkins and the NBA finally settled out of court for $1 million. His lawyers had been so sure of Hawkins's innocence that they spent $35,000 of their own money to defend him.

Pressure intensified on black athletes as they helped to win games and to fill arenas. In response to the increasing competitiveness of the college game, the rules were amended in 1972 to make freshman student-athletes eligible for varsity competition. This meant that eighteen-year-old black players, most of whom came from low socioeconomic backgrounds, without proper social or legal counseling, would be even more vulnerable on and off the court. In 1975, Moses Malone of Petersburg, Virginia, became the first player—white or black—to go directly from high school to the professional basketball ranks.

By 1976, roughly 1,250 colleges had varsity teams, and recruiting was the key to a winning program. Naive black families were now promised unheard of, and illegal amounts of money, and favors in return for their sons' (and later their daughters') promise to attend certain schools. Hundreds of promises were broken when the players' eligibility was used up. Less than ten percent graduated (most would not have been admitted to college in the first place without the benefit of "special exemption" rules). But the presence of two competing leagues; the NBA and the ABA, increased the number of available jobs.

In some cases, illusions began in high school. Billy Harris, a black high school star in Chicago in 1969, tells of his treatment before his demise. "An athlete is not part of the [high school] student population . . . Hey man, I got paid. In high school, I got free lunches, clothes. I went to the prom in a limo. I had money."[18] Harris eventually went to Northern Illinois, was drafted by the Chicago Bulls in the seventh round, and was eventually cut.

Current NBA star Isiah Thomas' brother Gregory at one time accused Indiana's coach Bobby Knight of wanting to exploit his brother during a recruiting interview. The exploitation of blacks by whites is a common belief held by the black community at large. The fiery Bobby Knight, who prided himself on his professional integrity, lashed back and plainly told Gregory, "You're an asshole and you're a failure, and the worst thing about you is that you want Isiah to fail the way you did . . . I'm getting out of here. I'm sorry we lost you."[19] In the end, Thomas did go to Indiana, and is now one of the NBA's premier performers. The altercation between Knight and Gregory Thomas displayed the overall tension of the recruiting process in the mid-1970s.

There were also many incidents of college coaches and assistant coaches having altered the academic records of high school and junior-college athletes to make them eligible. One coach who was caught was Manny Goldstein, an assistant at the University of New Mexico, who admitted doctoring the records of Craig Gilbert, an Oxnard Junior College transfer student. Goldstein later resigned, and the head coach, Norm Ellenberger, was fired.

Arizona State University also admitted doing a similar thing. Many black athletes spent a year or two at a junior college before transferring to a major NCAA Division I school because their grades or SAT/ACT test scores were low.

Some black student-athletes were passed right through the college system as though they were in public schools, lacking even the ability to read or write. The most widely noted example is Kevin Ross, who attended Creighton University by way of Wyandotte High School in Kansas City, Kansas. Ross shocked the sports world by enrolling in Westside Prep in Chicago *after* his senior year at Creighton. "I went to school for sixteen years, and then four years at college. When I got out, I couldn't even read a menu or a street sign,"[20] Ross said. Billy Ray Bates, who played for the Portland Trailblazers, said he had a similar problem. John "Hot Rod" Williams, the Tulane University player who was charged in 1984 with accepting illegal payments while in school, and who was later tried and found innocent, said of his college-entrance SAT exam: "I couldn't even read the English part."[21]

Illegal Payments: As the Billy Harris case shows, money and other favors are used freely to corrupt and coerce white and black athletes. The more important the athlete, the bigger the payoff. Wilt Chamberlain, for instance, wrote in his controversial book, *Wilt*, that in the mid-1950s "I guess I got about $15,000 or $20,000 while I was there [University of Kansas] . . . I never kept any records."[22] The NCAA later put Kansas on probation, but this was after Chamberlain's departure, and before his disclosure.

Basketball players were more likely to receive these payments, since one good player could easily make a difference. Booster clubs that were loosely associated with the school, but nevertheless zealous in their support,

supplied cars, money, girls, and jobs to some players. If a player did not perform up to expectations, these fringe benefits sometimes disappeared. Black players were expected to be grateful and not make waves—like demanding that white fraternities admit them or dating white coeds.

A highly publicized scandal in 1984 involved the academically troubled John "Hot Rod" Williams. Williams, of Sorrento, Louisiana, came from a broken home—he never knew his mother and saw his father once a year—but he was the Metro Conference's Player of the Year in 1984. In 1985, he and David Dominique, also black, were tried for sports bribery (point shaving) in New Orleans. Both were freed when after trials in both state and federal courts, the prosecutors failed to prove their cases.

At Memphis State, some players were allegedly getting as much as $1,500 per month in illegal payments. Keith Lee, their star black player, was supposedly promised money for his mother by coach Dana Kirk, according to *Sports Illustrated* sources. A check of the records showed that only 4 of 38 Memphis State players graduated between 1973 and 1984, none of them black. To make matters worse, a Tennessee government audit showed that, between 1980 and 1984, 109 Memphis State basketball and football players received federal grants that were legally reserved for needy, academically eligible students. Blacks, therefore, lost out in two ways: they were illegally used to field winning teams and never graduated; plus their fees were paid from funds earmarked for scholastically eligible, but destitute students—many of whom were also black.

The Spencer Haywood Case: One of the most controversial cases in all of college sports involved a poor black youngster from Silver City, Mississippi. Spencer Haywood, a 6-foot 9-inch, 215-pounder who moved to Chicago and eventually attended the University of Detroit, was the hero of the 1968 Olympic basketball team, who did not want to wait to turn professional. In 1969, the NBA had a rule against signing college players before they had used up four years of eligibility; the ABA, however, was not so strict.

At age nineteen, Haywood signed three separate contracts with the ABA's Denver Rockets without benefit of legal counsel. The first, in August 1969, called for $450,000 for three years, and was also signed by his friend and adviser, Will Robinson, who is also black. Two months later, Haywood signed another contract with the Rockets for $500,000 for three years plus $3,000 per year for ten years to be invested. Finally, in April 1970, he signed a third contract with the Rockets for $1.9 million for six years, and the rival NBA showed interest.

Haywood realized that he would be more valuable in the NBA, and with the assistance of a lawyer, Al Ross, tried to invalidate his Rockets agreement, even though he had been designated ABA MVP and Rookie of the Year. Sam Schulman, owner of the NBA's Seattle Supersonics, asked permission to sign Haywood. By a vote of fifteen to two, Schulman's request was denied by the NBA. Schulman signed Haywood anyway to a $1.5 million contract for six years, plus payments of $100,000 per year for fifteen years. The Rockets then petitioned for and received a temporary injunction against Schulman.

On March 30, 1971, in Los Angeles, Judge Warren Ferguson in a summary judgment ruled the four-year college stay illegal and that Haywood could play for Seattle pending a final resolution. College administrators and most white sportswriters were brutal in their denunciation of Haywood. College officials feared for their programs, and Roger Stanton, a Detroit reporter, may have spoken for many when he said, "He [Haywood] is ungrateful, misguided, uneducated and irresponsible . . .

In his greed for wealth, he has stopped at nothing."[23] But Haywood was a better athlete than student at the time.

Now the NBA and ABA tried to limit the pregraduation signings to "hardship" cases, but that was eventually scuttled. Henceforth, college players could turn professional any time they chose.

Considerations and Temptations: Not all college coaches were devious and deceitful. Some were just indifferent. NBA Hall of Fame inductee Elgin Baylor recalled that in the early 1950s, "White colleges did not explore black high schools . . . [they] didn't know anything about us. I went to the College of Idaho for the first year on a football scholarship."[24]

At the NCAA Western Regionals in Dallas in 1957, a cross was burned on a vacant lot across from where Wilt Chamberlain and his Kansas teammates stayed. Oscar Robertson, another NBA Hall of Fame inductee, was the lone black on the University of Cincinnati squad, and he had to stay at a black college, Texas Southern University, when his team played in Houston in 1959. Life for a black on a white college campus was (and still is) a lonely existence since there were (and still are) only a few other blacks. Nearly a decade later when blacks were protesting, they were accused of not being thankful for their "coveted" positions.

Texas Western University (now University of Texas at El Paso) won the 1966 NCAA title with an all-black starting five. They beat Kentucky 72–65 in the finals. The school had only 250 black students among a population of 10,000, and it was supported, in part, by black tax dollars. Yet, school athletic officials referred to blacks as "niggers" and expressed amazement when black students sought improved conditions.

Texas Western's Assistant Athletic Director, Jim Bowden, was quoted as saying, angrily, "This was the first institution in Texas—

right here!—that had a colored athlete and George McCarty, our athletic director, was the coach who recruited him . . . McCarty's done more for 'em than this damn guy Harry Edwards that's coming in here to speak. George McCarty's done more for the nigger than Harry Edwards'll ever do if he lives to be 100."[25]

The black social revolution of the mid-1960s *forced* black athletes on white campuses to be more assertive. When University of California coach Rene Herrerias dismissed Bob Presley for not cutting his Afro hairstyle, a faculty committee discussed the matter and Herrerias was replaced. John Wooden, UCLA's coach of ten NCAA titles, was tolerant of the new black assertiveness, though he did tell a reporter that "I feel it's outside influences trying to use the Negro athletes."[26]

In 1968, Notre Dame fielded its first all-black starting five with Austin Carr, Sid Catlett, Colis Jones, Bob Whitmore, and Dwight Murphy. When they were greeted with boos from their own fans, they demanded an apology before they would play again. However, it is important to remember that in 1956, Notre Dame had joined with the University of Dayton and St. Louis University in withdrawing from the Sugar Bowl tournament in New Orleans, because a Louisiana law forbade interracial sports.

For some whites, racial progress had been too fast, especially in the period from 1966 to 1970. The on-court results were obvious. According to a report on 246 integrated college teams in 1970, approximately two-thirds of all blacks were starters, "regardless of region, size, and type of school."[27] Furthermore, between 1958 and 1970, blacks were only 29 percent of the total of players, but accounted for nearly half the points scored.

General Gripes: During the late 1960s there were enough black athletes on white-college campuses to press for reforms. Along

with the football and track athletes, black basketball players complained about off-campus housing, low academic expectations from coaches, sarcastic and racial slurs from coaches, a belief that coaches assumed blacks could play in more pain than whites, a lack of black cheerleaders, the scarcity of black faculty and advisers, and a quota system that favored whites at the expense of more talented blacks. Stu Inman, who later became an assistant coach with the Portland Trailblazers, was told in 1960 at the University of Idaho, "Stu, out here we only play three of them [blacks] at a time."[28] Inman left the school.

To be sure, black athletes must shoulder *some* of the blame for their predicament. The overwhelming majority of black basketball players had visions of a professional career when they entered college. Most were academically unprepared and would never have been admitted under ordinary circumstances. By the mid-1970s, there had been enough stories in the press about black exploitation to warn even the most cynical among them. During the recruiting period of Moses Malone, one quote from Lefty Driesell, the University of Maryland's coach, was obviously in part jest, but much publicized. Driesell said of Malone, "I don't care if you never go to class. Hell, don't go to class. They'll kick you out after seven months, but in the meantime we'll have had a pretty good basketball team."[29]

Proposition 48: "By 1980, the NBA had only a 20 percent graduation rate among its players, black and white. The average salary was $185,000. There were roughly 15,000 players in NCAA-affiliated schools and another 700,000 on high school squads."[30] Blacks, however, had the lowest high school test grades and SAT/ACT scores. Those who went to college seldom graduated. At the University of Georgia, for example, only 4 percent of blacks graduated between 1974 and 1984, as opposed to 63 percent of whites. The American Council on Education, made up of college presidents, felt they had to do something about this exploitation of black athletes.

What emerged, in 1983, was NCAA Proposition 48, that sought to impose mandatory academic minimums for all scholarship athletes. To be eligible for college varsity competition, a player had to have a C average in high school courses that normally led to graduation, plus either a combined score of 700 on the SAT exam, or 15 on the ACT exam. Once in college, the student-athlete had to maintain a "C" or 2.0 grade average to remain athletically eligible.

While white-college officials and coaches realized that the proposal was probably a good idea, reaction among black-college administrators was surprisingly mixed. Some, like Southern University's Jesse Stoner, thought it was a plan to rid collegiate athletics of superior black athletes. Reverend Jesse Jackson, one of the most prominent black leaders, thought the plan was motivated by some who felt black athletes were just "too good." Others, led by Hampton University president William Harvey and black sociologist Harry Edwards, thought the proposal was long overdue. Scheduled for implementation in August 1986, the proposal was amended, and is now in use.

Proposition 42: While Proposition 48 stirred discussion and concern, the NCAA's followup proposal—Proposition 42—drew vigorous protests from several black coaches, including Georgetown's John Thompson and Temple's John Chaney.

Proposition 42, which would have become effective in 1990, would have denied financial help for athletes who did not score at least 700 (of a possible 1600) on the Scholastic Aptitude Test (SAT) or 15 (of possible 36) on the American College Test and fail to earn at least a 2.0 grade point average in 11 defined subjects.

Thompson dramatically showed his distain for Proposition 42 by walking off the court before the tipoff of a home game against Boston College, as a crowd of 15,379 gave him a standing ovation.

Chaney called Proposition 42, "racist and absurd." Harry Edwards, a sociologist at the University of California at Berkeley, described it as "an elitist racist travesty."

Those opposing Proposition 42 argued that black athletes—particularly those from underprivileged environments—rarely receive adequate academic assistance at the high school level. An NCAA study revealed that 90 percent of Proposition students became eligible after freshman year. Proposition 42 would deny them an opportunity altogether, the critics contended.

Former tennis pro Arthur Ashe seemed to be the lone prominent black favoring the proposal. In a *New York Times* op-ed column, Ashe said, "We need to address the deep-seated cynicism of coddled, black public school athletes, many of whom are carried through school with inflated grades and peer group status that borders on deification. High school coaches need to be held accountable for the academic preparation of their would-be Michael Jordans.

"The critics of Proposition 42 seriously underestimate the psychic value that black athletes place on their athletic success and how that could be used to motivate them academically. . . . Proposition 42—or something like it—would motivate high school coaches and their best players to take education seriously."

But the protests and media attention forced the NCAA to reconsider Proposition 42. At its annual meeting in January 1992, the NCAA voted to require freshmen to achieve a 2.5 grade-point average in 13 high-school core courses by 1995, instead of the 2.0 in 11 courses required by Proposition 48.

An Outstanding Record: Despite the problems, no one could say the black athlete did not measure up on the court. From the 1954–55 season when Bill Russell and K.C. Jones led the University of San Francisco to the NCAA Championship, to the 1983–84 championship season at Georgetown, blacks have continued to play a major part in college basketball. Along the way, some coaches have proven their respect for black athletes: Dean Smith at North Carolina; Bobby Knight at Indiana; John Wooden at UCLA; Al Maguire, formerly of Marquette, and Denny Crum at Louisville; among others. And John Thompson, the black head coach of the Georgetown "Hoyas," deserves special mention.

The son of a hardworking tile factory worker and a domestic, Thompson attended John Carroll High School in Washington, D.C., and later Providence College. After two years with the Boston Celtics, Thompson earned his master's degree in guidance counseling at the University of the District of Columbia. His coaching career began at St. Anthony's High in Washington, D.C., and he went to Georgetown in 1972.

Thompson has been known as an overprotective coach. To his critics, he replied, "I think I probably am overprotective, but I don't think that's bad . . . I'm nervous about the responsibility of 15 people who belong to somebody else."[31]

He guided his 1982–83 team to the NCAA finals, but lost when Freddy Brown made a bad pass in the last thirty seconds of the game against North Carolina. In one of the most dramatic moments in college television sports history, Thompson shocked millions of viewers by putting his arm around Brown in a consoling gesture. Most people expected outrage from him. Thompson, however, was nonplussed about his totally unexpected act. People, he said ". . . made me a saint because I put my arm around Freddy Brown . . . Shucks, man. What was I suppose to do? Chop off his head?"

On April 3, 1984, Thompson's squad, led by Patrick Ewing, won the NCAA title over Houston, 84–75. Ewing led a team that held its opponents to a 39.5 field-goal percentage—an NCAA record. Like Michael Jordan one year before him, Ewing was the 1984–85 College Player of the Year.

Thompson, Big East Coach of the Year in 1992, completed his 21st year with a 464–165 record. He completed the 1991–92 season with five Big East regular season titles and six Big East tournament championships. Also by the end of that season, 64 of 66 (97 percent) student-athletes who stayed for four years received their degrees.

Though nearly every major NCAA team took the court with predominantly black players, few of these squads had black coaches. According to the Black Coaches Association (BCA)—formed in 1987—there were only 29 black coaches at 283 Division I schools in 1988. BCA founders Rudy Washington, Wade Houston, Mike Boyd, Kenny Williamson, and Ray Martin agreed to raise awareness and push for greater black participation.

Blacks named to head NCAA-I schools prior to 1992 include: Bob Wade (Maryland), Larry Finch (Memphis State), John Chaney (Temple), Clem Haskins (Minnesota), George Raveling (USC), Walt Hazzard (UCLA), Randy Ayers (Ohio State), Frankie Allen (Virginia Tech), Wade Houston (Tennessee), Rudy Washington (Drake), and Nolan Richardson (Arkansas).

There is every indication that black players will continue to excel in college basketball. Lists of the African-American male John Wooden awardees and the African-American All-Americas since 1950 appear in the Reference section.

Notable among the black women stars were Luisa Harris of Delta State, Lynette Woodard of Kansas, Pam and Paula McGee of the University of Southern California, and Cheryl Miller, also of USC. Miller, 6-3, was acclaimed the best female player in the history of the sport.

After being named All-America four years and NCAA Player of the Year three times, she graduated in 1986 with a degree in communications. She led the U.S. to gold medals at the 1984 Olympics, the 1986 World Championships and the 1986 Goodwill Games in Moscow. Also outstanding was Clarissa Davis, who scored 24 points and grabbed 14 rebounds, leading Texas to victory against USC in the 1986 NCAA final. Through the 1960s, most women's teams played with six on a team and a regulation-sized basketball. Now the teams use five players and a slightly smaller ball. The exciting play at the 1984, 1988 and 1982 Olympic Games and at schools such as Iowa, Texas, Louisiana Tech, Old Dominion, Delta State, and St. Joseph's shows that women's basketball can indeed be very inspiring.

THE PROFESSIONALS

After World War II, professional basketball took a distinct backseat to the college game. There had been a rich black professional history, with the New York Renaissance and the Harlem Globetrotters to draw upon. By the late 1940s, the Renaissance's best days were behind them, and Abe Saperstein did not want his Globetrotters to join the new professional leagues. The Globbies, as the Globetrotters were sometimes called, had a near monopoly on the best black talent, and Saperstein wanted to keep it that way.

In 1948, for instance, the Globbies played the powerful all-white Minneapolis Lakers, led by the great George Mikan, and split a pair of games at Chicago Stadium. They won the first game 61–59 before 18,000 fans, but lost the second 75–60. There was no doubt in the mind of any professional team owner that blacks were among the best players around. When the Basketball Association of America was formed in 1946, it agreed to sign black players, so it became only a matter of time before blacks were signed by the National Basketball Association.

The thirty-nine year period between the admittance of the first three black players in the NBA in 1950 through to 1989 can be divided into three eras: Breaking In (1950–59); Wilt Chamberlain and Bill Russell Reign (1960–73); and the Kareem Abdul-Jabbar Era (1974–89).

1950 to 1960: Breaking In

The Basketball Association of America team owners were primarily interested in filling empty arenas. Doing so with blacks initially presented two problems: 1. Many BAA owners booked Globetrotter games—that outdrew BAA games—in their arenas; and 2. Saperstein wanted to continue his monopoly of the best black talent. Saperstein, however, could not hold back the tide forever.

The first three blacks signed to play in the NBA for the 1950–51 season were: Chuck Cooper, of Duquesne University, who signed with the Boston Celtics; Earl Lloyd, of West Virginia State, who went to the Washington Capitols, and Nathaniel "Sweetwater" Clifton, of Xavier University, who went to the New York Knickerbockers. The first black player to be drafted by the NBA was Harold Hunter of North Carolina College. Hunter was signed by the Baltimore Bullets, traded to the Capitols, and then cut.

In that first historic season, Cooper played in 66 games and had 562 rebounds, 174 assists, and 615 points for a 9.3 average. Clifton played in 65 games and had 491 rebounds,

162 assists, and 562 points for an 8.6 average. Lloyd played in only seven games because the team disbanded on January 9, 1951. As auspicious a start as these three players had, Globetrotter owner Saperstein was not pleased.

As Wilt Chamberlain noted in his book, "Abe [Saperstein] wasn't very happy when the NBA first started to integrate. Walter Brown, one of the founders of the NBA, was the owner of the Boston Celtics, and he was going to sign Chuck Cooper as the first black man in the league. Abe went crazy. He threatened to boycott Boston Garden."[32]

Since the Globetrotters were no longer assured of the best black players, and the team was not going to join the NBA, they decided to change their format to one that entertained spectators with comical routines and fancy ball handling, rather than playing serious basketball. They even made a movie, *The Globetrotters Story*, that debuted in 1951, and introduced the black actress, Dorothy Dandridge.

The Globbies continued as one of the most famous sports teams on earth, traveling the globe and performing before popes and kings. Stars like Marques Haynes, Reece "Goose" Tatum, Meadowlark Lemon, and Curly Neal thrilled thousands. Haynes had graduated from Langston University and was a dribbler nonpareil. In 1953, he formed a rival group, the Harlem Magicians, and also played with Lemon's Bucketeers and with the Harlem Wizards. Lemon was a superb showman, but according to Haynes, Tatum's public image belied his dislike for whites.

While Haynes readily acknowledges that "no one will ever match him [Tatum]" for having been one of the sports world's most famous personages, Tatum's funeral was a nonevent. Haynes and his wife drove to Fort Bliss, Texas, for the services, but they were ten minutes late arriving at the cemetery. Seeing no one around, Haynes asked the grave diggers what they missed. Sadly, they were told that nothing happened. "They [the funeral directors] drove up, backed the hearse up to the grave, lowered the casket and took off."[33] Haynes bought a bible for $2.98 and read the Lord's Prayer and the Twenty-third Psalm for his friend Goose Tatum.

Slow Pace: The first black players in the NBA were forwards. The first black "big man" was Ray Felix, 6-feet 10-inches, who went to the Baltimore Bullets in 1953. Felix found the pace of the game slower than necessary in the early 1950s. Coaches wanted disciplined ball handling and passing. Spectators wanted to stop the slowdowns caused when a team with a substantial lead began to stall. In the 1954–55 season, the NBA adopted a twenty-four-second rule that required teams to attempt a shot within twenty-four seconds of inbounding the ball, and limited teams to 6 fouls per period. These rules speeded up play, and the change came none too soon for William Fenton "Bill" Russell, who would combine with Bob Cousy and K.C. Jones to form the most winning professional team since World War II.

Bill Russell: Russell changed the classic theories about the way the game should be played. At the University of San Francisco he led his team to two NCAA titles, over LaSalle by a score of 77–63 in 1955 and over Iowa, 83–71, in 1956. He suffered only one loss in his college career, a 47–40 decision to UCLA in 1954. At the end of 1955, the NCAA doubled the width of the foul lane from six to twelve feet—"the Russell rule"—because Russell had been so dominating a rebounder.

No one had ever played defense so well before. More specifically, as Celtic coach Arnold "Red" Auerbach said, "Nobody had ever blocked shots in the pros before Russell came along. He upset everybody."[34] Players were afraid to drive toward the basket, and the Celtics won their first NBA title; the first of eleven NBA titles with Russell. The 6-foot 10-inch Russell, who was born in Monroe, Louisiana, also recognized his impact. "No one had ever played basketball the way I played it," noted Russell, "or as well. They had never seen anyone block shots before . . . I like to think I originated a whole new style of play."[35]

Russell's inimitable playmaker teammate, Bob Cousy, succinctly summed up his friend's worth: "He meant everything. We didn't win a championship until we got him in 1957, we lost it when he was injured in 1959, and we won it back when he was sound again in 1959."[36] Such was the relative value of one player in a sport like basketball. In addition, Auerbach stressed teamwork wherein every player had a specifically defined role to play. Auerbach also decided to utilize the faster speed of black players to his advantage by installing a "full court press" and allowing blacks to play the playground game they learned as youngsters—within limits.

Russell did have his detractors. In 1958 when he was the NBA's Most Valuable Player, the sportswriters did not name him to the All-NBA team; the insult still rankles Russell today. The overall pressure on Russell almost caused him to have a nervous breakdown in the 1963–64 season. Nevertheless, for the 1966–67 season he was named player/coach of the Celtics, the first black coach in a major sport since World War II. He later coached the Seattle Supersonics, and is currently the head coach of the Sacramento Kings.

Russell, a born leader, played through the transition period from the racial slurs that characterized the mid-1950s to the empowerment of the NBA Players Association and the era of six-figure salaries. He still remembers the game's quota system when he began. "In America," he noted then, "The practice is to put two black athletes in the basketball game at home, put three on the road, and put five in when you get behind . . ."[37] No American athlete has won as many championship titles in major sports as has Bill Russell.

Elgin Baylor: This Hall of Fame forward for the Los Angeles Lakers (previously the Minneapolis Lakers) was the first to impress crowds with an ability to seemingly defy gravity. The 6-foot 8-inch Baylor came from Washington, D.C., and its Spingarn High School. He attended the College of Idaho on a football scholarship and then transferred to Seattle University. Baylor was a 1958 first round draft choice of the Lakers.

Baylor stated that his amazing body control was "a gift from God"[38] although as a youth he had spent thousands of hours practicing on the public playgrounds of the nation's capital. As good as his on-court record was, his very presence was instrumental in the strengthening of the Players Association. In 1964, just before the All-Star Game, the players were poised to strike over the lack of an adequate pension plan. Lakers owner Bob Short sent word to Jerry West, a white player, and Baylor that they had better play—or else. Short's ultimatum to two of the game's best united the players, and the owners gave in under pressure from ABC Television to begin the game.

Baylor was named captain of the Lakers and was one of the game's most popular players. He played on one championship team, 1971–72, in his fourteen-year career. The Lakers lost to the Celtics six times in the NBA playoffs during the same period. After his retirement he became coach of the New Orleans Jazz. However, racial slurs and the lack of local support made life difficult for him and his black players. Phrases like "We're not going to make this an all-nigger team" were common, said Baylor. "Black players couldn't wait to be traded."[39]

The first black players having been big forwards, it is therefore not surprising that Ray Felix was the first black player to show up in more than one statistical category. He was fifth in scoring, fifth in field-goal percentage and fourth in rebounds. Not until the 1956–57 season did a black player, Maurice Stokes, lead the league in a category. That year, Stokes averaged 17.4 rebounds per game, almost three more per game than Bob Petitt.

Stokes began with the Rochester Royals in the 1955–56 season and finished the year second in rebounding. Unfortunately, on March 15, 1958, Stokes suffered a paralyzing stroke that ended his career. Stokes's white teammate, Dick Ricketts, remembered the stroke, which occurred on an airplane. Said Stokes to Ricketts, "Dick, every bone in my body pains me. I feel like I'm going to die."[40] After a period of recovery, a benefit game was organized by Jack Twyman, another of Stokes's white teammates.

Twyman treated his care of Stokes like a privilege, "I had to take care of Mo'. The rest of the team was leaving town. I was a hometown guy. It was my responsibility . . . taking care of Mo' has made me a better man."[41]

Hal Greer: The first of the speedy black guards in the NBA was Hal Greer of Marshall University. Players like Bob Cousy were excellent ballhandlers and passers, but they did not have Greer's blazing speed and ability to literally break open defenses. Guy Rodgers and Greer both began their NBA careers in the 1958–59 season, just one year after the St. Louis Hawks became the last all-white team to win the NBA championship.

Within two years, Rodgers was second in the assists category and Greer was second in field-goal percentage, a spectacular feat for a guard who had to shoot primarily from long range. Wilt Chamberlain was forthright in his appraisal of Rodgers: "Guy Rodgers . . . was

the best ball handler I ever saw—better than Cousy or Jerry West or Oscar Robertson or Walt Frazier or Pete Maravich or anyone."[42] Both Rodgers and Greer were prototypes of the new and faster NBA guard whose jobs were to direct a team's offense, execute steals, and play a solid defensive game.

Greer played fifteen years in the NBA, for the Syracuse Nationals and the Philadelphia 76'ers. He led his teams in average points scored three times and is one of the few players to perform in three separate decades.

Sam Jones: Jones is the second black Celtics player to be inducted into the Hall of Fame. He played at North Carolina College (now North Carolina Central University)—where he was also a member of the tennis team—in Durham. Jones later found his niche with the Celtics. His career spanned thirteen seasons, during which time he was on ten championship teams. He is best remembered for his banked shots off the backboard, and for his willingness to take the last shot in the closing minutes of a tight game.

He was never flashy, but publicly contented himself with being a part of the Celtics dynasty, and one-half of "the Jones boys"— with K.C. Jones. Celtic Coach Red Auerbach stated that Jones was one of the most selfless players in the game and that he understood the value of each player being assigned a special role (a lesson Jones no doubt learned at NCCU). Jones later coached at NCCU and at Federal City College in Washington, D.C.

An Era Closes: It is surprising to many that ten years elapsed before the last all-white NBA team, the St. Louis Hawks, signed a black player in 1959. The Hawks were also the last all-white squad to win the NBA title, in 1958. There were only eight teams in the league in 1959 and, like the Washington Redskins in football, the Hawks were the southern-most team, geographically, and in manner of operation. The Hawks were the South's team.

Still, basketball in this decade became an obsession for thousands of black youngsters who had dreams of a professional career. The fact that two of the first three black players in the NBA in 1950 were from black colleges was highly significant. That was not the case in either baseball or football. Even the percentages seemed favorable. From three players on eleven teams in 1950, the black presence grew to twenty-three players on eight teams ten years later.

The rule changes, especially the twenty-four-second clock adopted in 1954 were advantageous to traditional black playground styles of play. That same year, three blacks, Earl Lloyd, George King, and Jim Tucker, were the first to play for an NBA Championship team, the Syracuse Nationals. Blacks realized they were pioneers and that they were being judged by higher standards than those for whites. Like their baseball counterparts, black players endured instances of overt discrimination but, in the main, they felt privileged to be professional players earning salaries high above those of most wage-earning blacks and whites.

Finally, the period also marked the debut of the two most dominant players in the history of the game—Bill Russell and Wilt Chamberlain. Their personal battles and those of their respective teams provide the boundaries for the next era in the professional game.

1960 to 1973: Russell and Chamberlain Reign

Superstars in every sport need other superstars by which to measure their performances. When Bill Russell came into the league in 1956 he led the Celtics to their first NBA title. During that same year, Wilt Chamberlain began his collegiate career at the University of Kansas, scoring 52 points and grabbing 31 rebounds in his first varsity game. However, the Kansas squad lost to North Carolina in the NCAA finals, 54–53. Chamberlain left Kansas after one more season and played for the Globetrotters during the 1958–59 season.

Chamberlain later signed with the Philadelphia Warriors, chiefly because Warriors owner Eddie Gottlieb had territorial rights to him. In his first NBA game on October 24, 1959, against the New York Knickerbockers, Chamberlain scored 43 points and grabbed twenty-eight rebounds. Fourteen days later, he faced Russell for the first time and saw his first fall-away jumper blocked by his new adversary. Their rivalry had begun, and Russell had the upper hand.

Wilt Chamberlain: The NBA had decidedly better players when Chamberlain made his debut, than when Chuck Cooper began with the Celtics in 1950. Cooper's salary was under $10,000, whereas the top salary in 1959 was $25,000. Players were more accurate and better trained. The average field-goal percentage of the top ten scorers in 1950 was .432—versus .449 for the top ten in 1959. Chamberlain, however, was in an altogether different class.

Wilt, who was one of eleven children (two died), was born on August 21, 1936, in Philadelphia, Pennsylvania. He graduated from the city's famed Overbrook High School and attended the University of Kansas for two years. He was such a dominating force the *Look* magazine featured a story about him entitled "Why I Am Quitting College," an unprecedented occurrence for a black college player. Since NBA rules prohibited the signing of players before their college class graduated, Chamberlain spent the extra year with the Globetrotters.

Chamberlain was an immediate sensation in the NBA. No one, not even the great George Mikan, ever matched his offensive prowess;

he was able to score almost at will. He was named the league's MVP after his first season. Though he led the NBA in offensive statistics and never fouled out of a game during his professional career, Chamberlain was tagged with a "loser" label early on, because his teams failed to win titles. His first NBA title came in 1967, seven years after his rookie season.

As a youngster, Chamberlain led his Christian Street YMCA to a national championship and helped Overbrook to two All-City titles and three All-Public school titles. He also won shot-put titles in track and field at Overbrook and at Kansas. Part of this success was his uncommon coordination on a long frame. He was 6-feet 3-inches at twelve years of age, and was extremely dedicated to succeeding in athletics. "I'd practice afternoons and evenings and weekends, and during the summer I'd practice all day long, working on my moves and my shots and my passing and my rebounding."[43] Chamberlain eventually grew to 7-feet 1 1/16-inches and weighed 265 pounds. He was possibly the strongest professional athlete in a major sport.

While Chamberlain continued to pile up individual NBA honors, his teams failed to match the success of Bill Russell's Celtics. Though both men were superb athletes, they were different in many ways. Russell stayed with one team for his entire career; Chamberlain changed teams twice, from the Philadelphia/San Francisco Warriors to the Philadelphia 76'ers and then to the Los Angeles Lakers. Russell got along with his coach Red Auerbach and was eventually made player/coach himself; Chamberlain constantly feuded with his coaches. Russell was a leader in the NBA Players Association; Chamberlain was not. Yet Chamberlain was never afraid to speak his mind or follow his own dictates. "I never have been known for my humility."[44] Nor was he afraid to face black militants in the mid-1960s. In the early 1970s he admitted

that ". . . I do not support the militant black power 'hate whitey' types like Stokeley Carmichael and H. Rap Brown, and some of the early Black Panthers."[45] Chamberlain even publicly supported Richard Nixon for President in 1968 and attended the Republican Convention, much to the chagrin of most blacks. (He did so on the basis of a private and prolonged conversation with Nixon on a plane ride from New York City to Los Angeles).

Chamberlain also freely admitted dating white women at a time when it was frowned upon by many in the black community, and by reporters who covered his games. He said, "Back when I was getting started in the NBA, most sportswriters—like most whites—didn't like that interracial sex one bit."[46] He inadvertently incensed many black women with a passage from his book, *Wilt*, published in 1973, which sought to explain his dating philosophy: "I live in America, where there are more white women than black women available to date . . . I meet more white women than black women . . . I don't give a s—— what color a girl's skin is."[47] Though the statement itself was more of an observation than a defense of his right to date whomever he pleased, it nevertheless was cause for much discussion among blacks at a time when black militancy was high and the women's liberation movement was just getting started.

Throughout their careers, however, Russell and Chamberlain remained good friends. They even picked one another up at the airport when their respective teams arrived to play each other. These two giants left the professional game much better off than it was when they began. Russell set defensive standards and a winning percentage that remain the standard today. While Chamberlain's offensive output may perhaps never be equalled in so many different categories, both men's contributions have forever marked the sport.

Back-Court Generals: As teams moved from the era of tokenism in the 1950s to fielding the best five players on their rosters regardless of race, they were forced to acknowledge the superior speed and leadership of black guards. While theories abounded to explain the growing black point guard presence in the NBA, few argued with the results. Though some wanted to believe in the superior genetic endowment of blacks for physical expression, the more objective reasoning was that black players were simply more highly-motivated, practiced longer and harder, and made a stronger commitment to the game at an earlier age than whites.

However characterized, these exceptional players led the NBA's statistical record books for free-throw percentage, assists, field goals, and points: Hal Greer, Guy Rodgers, Sihugo Green, Lenny Wilkens, Dick Barnett, K.C. Jones, Walt Hazzard, Wally Jones, Dave Bing, Al Attles, Norm Van Lier, Clem Haskins, Art Williams, Nate Archibald, Archie Clark, Flynn Robinson, Eddie Miles, Randy Smith, Herm Gilliam, Charlie Scott, Jimmy Walker, Calvin Murphy, Jo Jo White, Walt Frazier, Earl Monroe, and Oscar Robertson, to name just some of them.

Lenny Wilkens, K.C. Jones, and Al Attles went on to coaching careers in the NBA. Walt Frazier led the New York Knicks to an NBA title in 1970 with a seventh-game performance against the Lakers that included 36 points, 7 rebounds, 19 assists, and 5 steals. Calvin Murphy, at 5-feet 9-inches, was one of the few black players under six feet. Earl Monroe performed in the quintessential black playground style. Nicknamed "the Pearl" as a professional, he was known as "the Black Jesus" on the public courts of his native Philadelphia and at Winston-Salem State College under coach Clarence "Big House" Gaines. This 6-foot 3-inch wizard was a favorite with the Baltimore Bullets and the New York Knicks fans. No guard, though,

could match the all-around skills of Oscar Robertson.

Oscar Robertson: Robertson was the modern game's first big guard at 6-feet 5-inches and 210 pounds. He could—and did— do everything well. He was born on November 24, 1938, in Charlotte, Tennessee, the son of a divorced sanitation worker. Like his black counterparts in the 1950s, he suffered his share of turmoil on and off the court. Under coach Ray Crowe, Robertson guided Indianapolis' Crispus Attucks High School team to two state titles in three years, the first black school to achieve that goal. Traditionally, Indiana's winning high school team was feted with a parade through their hometown but, Crispus Attucks' principal, Russell Lane, warned to temper their celebrations since they had defeated a white school, Shortridge, in the finals. Instead of being led through the center of town as usual, Robertson's team was taken to Northwestern Park, a remote part of town, by police to avoid racial incidents. Robertson never forgot this slight.

Robertson's motivation was no different than any other black youngster. "I practiced all the time . . . we didn't have any money and sports was the only outlet we had."[48] His views did not change much when he attended the University of Cincinnati, though he was the first college player to lead the NCAA in scoring three consecutive years. Yet he had become so disillusioned with his life that he said, "All I want is to get out of school. When I'm through, I don't want to have anything to do with this place."[49]

Robertson signed with the Cincinnati Royals in 1960 for $100,000 for three years and helped to draw more people into the arena than in the Royal's three previous seasons combined. His steady but brilliant play impressed NBA veterans immediately, but he rankled under the NBA's disguised quota system for blacks. "We [blacks] all know it. A lot of good Negro ball players should be in the league but generally only four or five spots are open on a team. Boston has five, I think. St. Louis has five . . . I don't know. It makes you wonder."[50]

Robertson's best year was the 1963–64 season when he averaged 31.4 points per game, led the league in assists with 868, and led the league in free-throw percentage with .853. The Royals had their best season ever, with 55 wins and 25 losses. Amazingly, it took four years before he was finally offered a product endorsement—for a basketball!

At the suggestion of Jack Twyman, Robertson ran for and was elected president of the NBA Players Association in 1966. He later helped hire Larry Fleischer as the Association's counsel. Under his leadership, the NBAPA established collective bargaining with the owners.

In 1971, Robertson finally won an NBA title, with the Milwaukee Bucks, where he played with Lew Alcindor (Kareem Abdul-Jabbar). He retired in 1974.

Front-Court Stars: The average fan can readily understand someone who is under 6-feet 4-inches tall being exceptionally coordinated. But the intricate moves shown by men averaging 6 feet 8 inches or taller seem somehow extraordinary. Players like George Mikan, Clyde Lovellette, and Bob Petitt—all white—were outstanding in their time. However, by the mid-1960s, the black big men brought their own distinctive style of play to the hardwood. While most of them had come from solid college experiences, they had learned to play in black environments where they impressed one another with the latest moves.

In the period between 1960 and 1973, the following forwards and centers appeared among the lists of statistical leaders: Willie Naulls, Walter Dukes, Wayne Embry, Walt Bellamy, Johnny Green, Bob Boozer, Ray Scott,

Gus Johnson, Nate Thurmond, Lucius Jackson, Zelmo Beaty, Jim Barnes, Bob Love, Bill Bridges, Leroy Ellis, Chet Walker, Wes Unseld, Paul Silas, Bob Lanier, Elmore Smith, Elvin Hayes, Willis Reed, Spencer Haywood, Curtis Rowe, Bob Dandridge, Cazzie Russell, Lou Hudson, Connie Hawkins, Joe Caldwell, and Sidney Wicks. During the fourteen-year period, 101 of the top 140 NBA rebounding leaders were black.

Through the 1984–85 season, Elvin Hayes had played in more NBA games, 1,303, than anyone else. He was also first in minutes played at 50,000, third in field goals, and fourth in blocked shots. Paul Silas was second in games played and eighth in rebounds. Among NBA career scores, Walt Bellamy was ninth, Bob Lanier was thirteenth, and Chet Walker was fifteenth.

Willis Reed: Reed was the extremely popular captain of the New York Knicks and is best remembered for his heroic play in the 1970 seven-game championship series win over the Lakers. Reed had a painful hip injury and was a doubtful starter for game seven. However, he hobbled onto the court at Madison Square Garden and promptly sunk his first two field goals to provide an emotional lift for his team. The Knicks won 113–99 for their first championship.

Reed attended college at Grambling State in Louisiana and later coached the New York Knicks and the Creighton University team. He was elected to the Hall of Fame in 1981.

Off-Court Problems: In addition to the unwritten but evident quota system for blacks through the 1960s, there were other problems that surfaced. The point shaving scandal kept Connie Hawkins from signing with an NBA team. Black players were not united enough and the NBAPA was not strong enough at the time to challenge this snub, which was based solely on unproven testimony from an indicted gambler. When Hawkins finally joined the Phoenix Suns in 1969, he led the team in scoring with a 24.6 average.

The Spencer Haywood case had also caused enmity among black players. Some black superstars even turned their backs on Haywood, an unprecedented occurrence in basketball, baseball, or football. Most did not understand at the time that Haywood had signed his ABA contract without benefit of counsel, and they erroneously connected the final resolution of his lawsuit to a merger of the ABA and NBA, which was fought by black players, because it would have reduced the competition for their talents.

The Russell-Chamberlain era was one of tremendous growth in the sport. Salaries rose, television coverage increased, and the caliber of play improved substantially; due in large measure to the excitement created by this new generation of blacks.

1973 to 1989: The Kareem Abdul-Jabbar Era

At the end of the 1960s, Wilt Chamberlain was recovering from knee surgery and the New York Knicks were about to win their first NBA title. Professional sports were providing a welcome diversion from the evening television news programs that showed the numbers of American and Vietnamese soldiers being killed in Southeast Asia. ABC Television renewed its NBA contract for another four years in spite of the league's 58 percent black roster. The rival ABA was 54 percent black in 1969.

The minimum salary for players was $15,500 with the average salary being $43,000. Statistically, blacks began the 1970s with fourteen of the top twenty scorers, five of the top ten field-goal shooters, seven of the top ten free-throw shooters, seven of the top ten assists leaders, and seven of the top ten rebounders. For all players, the average of the

top ten in field-goal percentage was an impressive .527, compared with .432 in 1951 and .449 in 1959. Unquestionably, players were not only faster, they were also better. However, for a time there was another league to contend with.

The NBA/ABA Merger: In the Fall of 1966, the American Basketball Association (ABA) began operating with eleven teams. It was clear that more large cities wanted teams than the NBA was willing to include. As a marketing ploy, the ABA introduced the 3-point field goal for shots made 25 feet or more, and they played with a red, white, and blue ball. Inevitably, a bidding war erupted between the two leagues and salaries began to rise—60 percent between 1967 and 1971—and some NBA players jumped to the ABA. The interleague competition was a boon to black players, and several, including Elgin Baylor, Wilt Chamberlain, and Nate Thurmond, began earning more than $100,000 per year by 1968.

The ABA had its best opportunity for long-term stability if, in 1969, it could sign Lew Alcindor (now Kareen Abdul-Jabbar). The ABA's commissioner was George Mikan who plainly stated, "If Lew joined our league, it would be the equivalent of the [New York] Jets beating the [Baltimore] Colts in the Super Bowl."[51] But the ABA did not get Alcindor, because he asked for a bonus atop the ABA's offer and Mikan turned him down. Mikan mistakenly thought Alcindor was just negotiating. Mikan's error turned out to be one of the most costly in American team-sport history. Alcindor later declared, "The ABA had the inside track but they had blown it."[52]

Though the NBAPA filed a class action suit in 1970 to block a proposed merger of the two leagues, the leagues eventually did merge in 1975 and the NBA was flooded with a wealth of talent.

Before the merger, however, there were some racial difficulties that plagued some

ABA teams. For instance, the Dallas franchise removed four of their ten blacks from its eleven-man roster, as a Dallas official was quoted as saying, "Whites in Dallas are simply not interested in paying to see an all-black team and the black population alone cannot support us."[53]

These problems notwithstanding, the ABA in its ten-year existence had provided professional jobs for dozens of black players and had helped increase salaries for players in both leagues.

High Salaries Change Relationships: Along with the merger proceedings of the ABA and NBA came a dissolution of the reserve system, which, as in baseball, bound a player to a team for the duration of his career. As salaries soared, so did the problems that black players had in keeping their new fortunes. In addition, alongside the box scores were stories of the profligacy of many players, most of whom were black. Said the July 17, 1978, issue of *Sports Illustrated* of Marvin "Bad News" Barnes, "After . . . Barnes signed his $2.1 million contract with St. Louis of the ABA in 1974, he spent $125,000 in six weeks. A silver Rolls-Royce, a diamond ring for each hand, a ruby necklace spelling NEWS and 13 telephones . . ."[54]

In 1975, Moses Malone became the first high school player to skip college altogether and go directly to the NBA. He had averaged 36 points per game, 26 rebounds, and 12 blocked shots in his high school senior year. He was so heavily recruited that his mother developed an ulcer. But she did remember the moment her son decided to become a professional. She said, "I didn't even think about him going pro until he came into the Safeway and told me to quit work."[55]

"Jumping" Joe Caldwell, a ten-year veteran of the ABA and NBA who once earned $210,000 per year, was broke and divorced by 1977.

Opinions about their relative economic worth varied among black players, but nearly all of them came from humble and religious beginnings. The following are sample comments from four players at the time:

Elvin Hayes: "No athlete is worth the money he is getting, including me."

Julius Erving, who remembered his poor childhood: "I have this habit. I was always so poor that if I had a dime I made sure when I went to bed that dime would be there when I got up . . . in the beginning I was taken advantage of. Players have to be careful that they don't get used and cast aside."[56]

George Gervin: "We put a lot of wear and tear on our bodies. We're sacrificing ourselves to give fans something to see. If that's not work, what is?"

Wayne Embry: "Many players are now more concerned about protecting their earning power than performing. So the quality of basketball is not what it used to be. The fans pay an inflated price for a tarnished product—all because of greed."

Embry's comment was echoed by many white sportswriters. The general feeling among white fans was that ". . . the declining intensity in play confirmed their suspicions of innate black laziness . . . [the] perception that black players were not 'putting out.' "[57] Ted Stepien, the Cleveland Cavaliers owner, said he thought attendance would rise if there were more white players. In New York City, the Knicks were sometimes referred to by some whites as the New York Niggerbockers. Some owners, though, were still prepared to pay top dollar for the best talent. In 1981, Los Angeles Lakers owner, Jerry Buss, gave Earvin "Magic" Johnson a twenty-five-year, $25-million contract, the largest total sum in team-sports history.

Due to the intense pressure to play and with players receiving such large sums, their relationships with coaches changed dramatically. Coaches simply lost much of their authority. Few of their high-priced players were hesitant in speaking up about their concerns, even as the pressure mounted to perform up to expectations. Subsequently, many players succumbed to using illegal drugs, especially cocaine. In the seventies, they had begun using marijuana. Elgin Baylor noted that: "There were guys that smoked marijuana and drank [alcohol] through the late sixties, but no one was doing cocaine."[58] That had all changed by the mid-1970s. Even Kareem Abdul-Jabbar, who came from a solid middle-class family, admitted to an early problem: "I found myself coming out of college and all of a sudden I had some money in my pocket and I was curious enough to try it [cocaine] . . . I ended up altering my personality so much that I was some type of race car driver and I ended up spinning my car out . . ."[59]

John Lucas, another product of a middle-class environment, admitted his addiction: "I became bored by what I was doing [playing basketball]. I wanted to seek some adventure. I let my teammates down, I let myself down. I lost some money. Lost my job."[60]

Michael Ray Richardson was one of the most publicized drug users. He came from a broken home, one of seven children of a twice-divorced mother in Lubbock, Texas. At one time, he was a severe stutterer. When he first joined the New York Knicks he bought a Rolls-Royce, but coach Willis Reed counselled him and persuaded him to sell it. Richardson stated that "the lifestyle that basketball has created for me, I can't handle that . . . maybe I'd be better off driving a truck."[61] He was waived from the NBA's New Jersey Nets for the 1982–83 season because of his problem. "When they put me out of the league, I started spending all my cash . . . about 60 or 70 grand easy. I've heard of guys that spent two or three million, so $60,000 is not really that much."[62]

In stories regarding drug abuse, black athletes have been mentioned in nearly every instance. The most startling case was that of the late Len Bias of the University of Maryland.

Bias, a 6-8 prodigy in the mold of Michael Jordan, died on June 19, 1986, after taking a substantial amount of cocaine. He had been signed to play as a first-round draft choice with the Boston Celtics, and the nation was stunned by his passing. Maryland's president John B. Slaughter accepted the resignation of Charles "Lefty" Driesell as coach and Dick Dull as athletic director. Bias had been dismissed from the University at the time of his death because he had failed or withdrawn from all five of his courses. More than 10,000 students and friends attended a memorial service in his honor at Cole Field House.

There were many other drug problems, as drugs had been an ever-present problem in many black communities for years. But the aforementioned case histories failed to dampen the enthusiasm of tens of thousands of black youngsters who still aspired to professional basketball careers at the expense of other, more viable options.

The Vicious Cycle Continues: As the rewards of a professional basketball career increased, so did the temptation to push through the nation's public-school systems those athletically gifted but academically unprepared players. The sport became an obsession in many black communities in the late sixties and early seventies. And why not? Basketball players were the highest paid team-sport athletes, and basketball courts were within walking distance of nearly every black American.

Many blacks graduated from high school with an elementary reading-skill level. The overwhelming majority of black professional players were from families in lower socioeconomic groups. As such, they were more inclined to spend the thousands of hours of practice necessary to make their high school and college teams. The lack of modern facilities was not a deterrent. Elvin Hayes remembered practicing with a "raggedy old wooden backboard nailed to an old light pole"[63] and playing three or four games a day.

Black colleges, the centerpieces of black culture in the South, continued to see basketball in the 1970s as a more inexpensive varsity sport than football. They derived free nationwide publicity from winning teams. Alcorn A & M, for example, would have been virtually unknown outside the black community and the South if it were not for their basketball and football squads. Thus, these institutions continued trying to field the best teams possible. Their record has been impressive.

A list of professional basketball players from both white and black colleges can be found in the Reference section.

Back-Court Stars in the Abdul-Jabbar Era: On the average, players during the last dozen years have been bigger, faster, and better trained than ever. All were born after World War II and have little recollection of the problems experienced by players of the 1950s such as Oscar Robertson and Elgin Baylor. Public-school facilities, especially in the South, improved tremendously in the 1960s, and black athletes took maximum advantage. Whereas players in the mid-1960s began playing in a distinctive black style, their counterparts in the 1970s and 1980s further widened the differences between black and white players. White players with exceptional ball-handling skills, like Pete Maravich, were prized commodities. Joe Jares of *Sports Illustrated* referred to Jerry West and John Havlicek, both whites, as "collector's items."

By the early 1980s, white guards were rare indeed. The list of black guards who appear among the leaders in NBA statistics from 1972 to 1985 includes Frank Johnson, Allen Leavell, Lafayette Lever, Kelvin Ramsey, Kenny Higgs, Rickey Green, Kevin Porter, Phil Chenier, Slick Watts, John Lucas, Henry Bibby, Phil Ford, Norm Nixon, Ray Williams, Earvin "Magic" Johnson, Maurice Cheeks, Randy Smith, Lucius Allen, Tom Henderson, Mike Gale, Lionel Hollins, Jo Jo White, Ricky Sobers, Quinn Buckner, Butch Lee, Clarence "Foots" Walker, Walter Davis, Armond Hill, Dudley Bradley, Terry Furlow, Sonny Parker, Robert Reid, Geoff Huston, Andrew Toney; World B. Free, John Moore, Darwin Cook, Isiah Thomas, Mark Aguirre, and Michael Jordan. These players had spent more hours practicing, had been more highly trained, had been more highly motivated, had been more highly paid, and were simply better than their white counterparts in any previous generation.

Some were among the most well-known faces and names in America.

Earvin "Magic" Johnson: Johnson's magnificent 12-year career ended prematurely in November 1991 when he shook the world with the announcement that he had tested positive for the AIDS virus.

"This is not like my life is over," Johnson said. "I plan on going on living for a long time. This is another challenge. It's like your back is against the wall and you just have to come out swinging. That's what I'm going to do."

Johnson, the Los Angeles Lakers 6-9 point guard, was the first well-known heterosexual to be diagnosed with the disease, and the impact was dramatic.

"Hopefully, this will end the silence regarding AIDS and its impact on the Afro-American community," said Belinda Rochelle of the AIDS Action Council. "We have been a community in denial about this epidemic when in fact over 56,000 AIDS cases are among Afro-Americans."

Johnson played in the NBA All-Star Game, winning the Most Valuable Player award and also led the Dream Team in a USA romp at the '92 Olympics. Soon afterwards, he announced he would return to the Lakers. He played in most of the team's exhibition games, but changed his mind about returning when several players expressed concern about playing against him. The concern became obvious when a game had to be stopped when Johnson had to receive treatment for a scratch on his right arm during an exhibition game.

"It has become obvious that the various controversies surrounding my return are taking away from both basketball as a sport and the larger issue of living with HIV for me and the many people affected," Johnson said. "After much thought and talking it over with Cookie, my wife, and my family, I decided I will retire—for good—from the Lakers."

Johnson, the first rookie to be named MVP in the NBA playoffs, guided the Lakers to five World Championships. He scored 17,239 career points, averaging 19.7 points per game and completed his career with 136 triple doubles.

There were definite advantages to being in a franchise in important media cities like New York, Los Angeles, Chicago, Washington, D.C., Baltimore, Philadelphia, Boston, and San Francisco. Walt Frazier, for instance, whose nickname was "Clyde" (so named because the stylish clothes he wore reminded some of bank robber Clyde Barrow), would not have been as well known as he played for Cleveland. Likewise, "Magic" Johnson graced the nation's papers and sports magazines largely because he was based in Los Angeles. The size of the city was secondary to its media importance, and for this reason the best players wanted to play where they received the most publicity.

Some players created their own persona. Lloyd Free legally changed his name to World B. Free. George Gervin, known as "The Ice Man," was a 6-foot 7-inch guard, who was eleventh on the list of all-time NBA scorers at

the end of the 1984–85 season. Only two other guards on the list, Oscar Robertson and Hal Greer, were ahead of him.

At the end of the 1979–80 season, the leaders in assists and steals—the two categories most associated with guards—were all blacks for the first time. But by the early 1980s, roughly 80 percent of the league was black, so it was no longer meaningful to speak of their statistical dominance.

Front-Court Status: The list of the game's premier big men who play the forward and center positions is not as long as that for the guards.

Kareem Abdul-Jabbar's name most certainly will be near the top of everyone's list.

Kareem Abdul-Jabbar: A sensation as a collegian at UCLA, Abdul-Jabbar became an instant NBA superstar upon joining the Milwaukee Bucks in 1969. The 7-2 center with the deadly skyhook led the Bucks to an NBA championship in 1971. He was traded to the Los Angeles Lakers in 1975 in a blockbuster deal.

He led the Lakers to five NBA titles before retiring in 1989. He remains the NBA all-time leader in several categories including: most points scored (38,387), most games played (1,560), most minutes played (57,446), most field goals made (15,837), and most field goals attempted (28,307). He won the NBA Most Valuable Player award six times and made the All-NBA first team 10 times.

There are simply fewer highly talented players over 6-feet 8-inches. Therefore, a good big man is much more valuable than a good little man. Consequently, the same names surface over and over again in those categories—points, field goals, rebounds, and blocked shots (a category first documented in 1972–73)—associated with front-court players. Players exclusive of those already named from the previous period, but who played during the Abdul-Jabbar era include: Bob McAdoo, Happy Hairston, Sam Lacey, Clifford Ray, Garfield Heard, Don Smith, Curtis Perry, Jim Chones, Sidney Wicks, Harvey Catchings, Lloyd Neal, George McGinnis, Artis Gilmore, Larry Kenon, Otto Moore, Bob Dandridge, John Drew, Billy Knight, Tree Rollins, Joe C. Meriweather, Marvin Webster, Leonard "Truck" Robinson, Robert Parish, Terry Tyler, Dan Roundfield, Caldwell Jones, Adrian Dantley, Cedric Maxwell, Kermit Washington, Jamaal Wilkes, Bill Cartwright, Buck Williams, Larry Smith, Moses Malone, Cliff Robinson, Julius Erving, David Thompson, Albert King, Bernard King, Terry Cummings, Larry Nance, Alton Lister, Herb Williams, and Darryl Dawkins.

A very good argument can be made that the foregoing players are among the world's best athletes. There is a consensus among sportswriters and fans that the incredible coordination shown on a basketball court by players such as Julius Erving, Larry Bird, Bill Walton, Kareem Abdul-Jabbar, and Bernard King is nothing short of astounding. In the sport of basketball, it is simply not enough to be tall; stamina, strength, timing, and intelligence are also needed. It is no surprise then that the all-time leaders in the majority of offensive, rebounding, and blocked-shot categories are centers and forwards. In one category, blocked shots, the entire top ten are all black. Several of these players alone are worth the price of admission. Julius Erving was perhaps the most gifted and acrobatic performer of his era. The only comparable player in past years was Elgin Baylor; the only comparable player to *follow* the man called Dr. J was Michael Jordan, "His Airness." The 6-6 Chicago Bulls guard routinely was seen walking on air. Jordan, who earned more than $36 million in endorsements in 1992, led the Bulls to back-to-back NBA titles in 1991–92. Baylor, Erving, and Jordan are among a handful of players in NBA history who literally had fans shaking their heads in disbelief at some of their exploits. Erving, for example, specialized in intricate plays such as dunks that

frequently begin with just one step from the foul line and end with different maneuvers each time.

Black players took pride in mastering assorted ways of dunking the ball. White players seldom attempted anything approaching the razzle-dazzle shown by blacks. And fewer still give labels to their favorite dunk, as did Darryl Dawkins. Dawkins, who like Moses Malone and Bill Willoughby went straight to the NBA from high school, broke several fiberglass backboards with his powerful slam dunks. He called this shattering move his Chocolate Thunder Flyin' Robinzin Cry'in Teeth Shakin' Glass Breakin' Rump Roastin' Bun Toasting' Wham Bam Glass Breaker Am Jam.

A Need to Regroup: In the early 1980s the black domination of the NBA was cause for serious concern among the owners and league officials. In spite of the natural talent displayed by black players, many continued to feel black player presence and dominance of the sport was the root cause of declining audience attendance. One team official was blunt in his sentiments: "It's race, pure and simple. No major sport comes up against it the way we do. It's just difficult to get a lot of people to watch huge, intelligent, millionaire black people on television."[64]

Correspondingly, fans had read and became tired of salary squabbles, illegal drug use, too many games, and lethargic play. As such, fan support began to decline. In 1982, ten of twenty-three NBA teams were for sale or facing liquidation. So it was that Larry Bird, the best white player in the NBA, was viewed as "the great white hope," but he was the only one. To save money, and possibly franchises, the NBAPA and the league agreed in 1983 to a shorter television schedule, revenue-sharing, and a team cap on salaries.

The league also enacted a tough new drug law that called for the expulsion of any player caught using illegal substances. Expelled players could petition for reinstatement in two years. If a player volunteered for treatment, he could receive it at league expense the first time, but had to pay for treatment a second time. There was no third chance.

The 1984–85 season, though, was a promising year. A revised television schedule and the presence of Michael Jordan, the sensational rookie from the University of North Carolina, gave the league a big lift. Jordan's college coach, Dean Smith, was effusive in his praise: "I've seen other great athletes but Michael also has the intelligence, the court savvy . . . he was a hero so many times at the end of games—it was uncanny. It really was."[65] Aside from some jealousy shown toward him at the 1985 All-Star Game, his rookie debut was cause for celebration. In the endorsement field, his basketball shoe, Air Jordan, was the largest selling ever, at $70 million. This is a tremendous increase from the paltry offers to Oscar Robertson twenty years earlier.

Indeed, total NBA revenues at the end of the 1984–85 season were $192 million, in third place behind baseball at $625 million, and football at $700 million. Like it or not, much of it was due to the exciting play of blacks.

A Look Back: The game has come a long way since 1891 when James Naismith nailed two peach baskets to a wall. Black players have weathered many difficulties since 1908, when Edwin B. Henderson began the first serious inner-city competitions between New York City and Washington, D.C. Much credit is due to those pioneering teams—Monticello, the Loendi Big Five, the Savoy Big Five, the New York Renaissance, the Philadelphia Tribune Girl's Team, the Harlem Globetrotters, Tennessee State, Winston-Salem State College, and Alcorn A & M.

Henderson himself cannot be thanked enough for his contributions. In addition, coaches and officials like Cumberland Posey,

Robert Douglas, Abe Saperstein, Holcombe Rucker, Clarence "Big House" Gaines, Johnny B. McLendon, Vivian Stringer, Dave Whitney, Bill Russell, John Thompson, Lenny Wilkins, and K.C. Jones have been outstanding.

Neither can we forget such players as Hilton Slocum, Ora Washington, "Fats" Jenkins, William "Pop" Gates, William "Dolly" King, Isadore Channels, Don Barksdale, Chuck Cooper, Wilt Chamberlain, Bill Russell, Hal Greer, Oscar Robertson, Lusia Harris, Kareem Abdul-Jabbar, Earl Monroe, Michael Jordan, Lynette Woodard, and Cheryl Miller.

When one thinks of the black athlete, thoughts inevitably settle on three sports— boxing, track and field, and basketball. Through thousands of hours of practice and dedication, black American athletes have mastered the nuances of the world's second most popular team-sport. Though alternative avenues of self-expression are now open that were closed as recently as fifteen years ago, ethnic pride in basketball excellence is now at stake. We can therefore expect more of the same in the future from the next wave of black NBA talent led by New York Knicks center Patrick Ewing and Shaquile O'Neal, the LSU phenom who signed a seven-year, $40-million deal with the Orlando Magic in 1992.

Notes

1. William "Pop" Gates, telephone interview with author, 24 April 1985.
2. *New York Age*, 9 October 1948.
3. *Ebony*, April 1956, 52.
4. Bill Libby and Spencer Haywood, *Stand Up For Something: The Spencer Haywood Story* (New York: Grosset and Dunlap, 1972), 41.
5. Joe Jares, *Basketball: The American Game*, (Chicago: Follet Publishing Company, 1971), 194.
6. Ibid.
7. Ibid.

8. Libby and Haywood, *Stand Up For Something: The Spencer Haywood Story*, 41.
9. *Sports Illustrated*, 20 November 1985, 129.
10. *Ebony*, March 1962, 109.
11. *Ebony*, May 1976, 153.
12. Ibid.
13. *Sports Illustrated*, 4 March 1985, 9.
14. *Ebony*, February 1977, 92.
15. *New York Times*, 1 January 1951.
16. *Pittsburgh Courier*, 27 January 1951.
17. *Ebony*, February 1970, 42.
18. *Sports Illustrated*, 19 May 1980, 54.
19. David Halberstam, *The Breaks of the Game* (New York: Alfred A. Knopf, 1981), 227.
20. *Miami Herald*, 16 February 1985.
21. Wilt Chamberlain and David Shaw, *Wilt: Just Like Any Other 7-Foot Black Millionaire Who Lives Next Door* (New York: Macmillan Publishing Company, 1973), 48.
23. Libby and Haywood, *Stand Up For Something: The Spencer Haywood Story*, 120.
24. Elgin Baylor, telephone interview with author, 19 August 1985.
25. "The Black Athlete, Part 3," Jack Olsen, *Sports Illustrated*, 15 July 1968, 30.
26. *Newsweek*, 15 July 1968, 56.
27. *Civil Rights Digest*, August 1972, 26.
28. Halberstam, *The Breaks of the Game*, 352.
29. *Commonwealth Magazine*, February 1983, 37.
30. *Sports Illustrated*, 19 May 1980, 60.
31. *Ebony*, February 1985, 96.
32. Chamberlain and Shaw, *Wilt: Just Like Any Other 7-Foot Black Millionaire Who Lives Next Door*, 94.
33. *Sports Illustrated*, 22 April 1985, 85.
34. Jares, *Basketball: The American Game*, 106.
35. Ibid, 67.
36. Ibid, 99.
37. Harry Edwards, *The Sociology of Sports* (Homewood, IL: The Dorsey Press, 1973), 213.
38. Elgin Baylor, telephone interview with author, 19 August 1985.
39. Ibid.
40. *Ebony*, April 1959, 59.
41. Ira Berkow, *Oscar Robertson: The Golden Year* (Englewood Cliffs, N.J.: Prentice-Hall, Inc., 1971), 48.
42. Chamberlain and Shaw, *Wilt: Just Like Any Other 7-Foot Black Millionaire Who Lives Next Door*, 113.
43. Ibid., 14.
44. Ibid., 3.
45. Ibid., 55.
46. Ibid., 111.
47. Ibid., 259.
48. Berkow, *Oscar Robertson: The Golden Year*, 122.
49. *Ebony*, March 1960, 118.
50. Berkow, *Oscar Robertson: The Golden Year*, 136.
51. Jares, *Basketball: The American Game*, 141.
52. Ibid.
53. Edwards, *The Sociology of Sport*, 214.
54. *Sports Illustrated*, 17 July 1978, 48.
55. *Commonwealth*, February 1983, 68.
56. *Sports Illustrated*, 17 July 1978, 36–41.
57. Benjamin G. Rader, *American Sports* (Englewood Cliffs, N.J.: Prentice-Hall, Inc., 1985), 299.
58. Elgin Baylor, telephone interview with author, 19 August 1985.
59. *New York Times*, 2 October 1985.
60. Ibid.
61. Ibid.
62. Ibid.
63. Elvin Hayes, *The Call Me The Big E* (Englewood Cliffs, N.J.: Prentice-Hall, Inc., 1978), 25.
64. *Esquire*, February 1985, 114.
65. "Show Time," Barry Jacobs, *Inside Sports*, November 1985, 24.

REFERENCE
SECTION

AFRICAN-AMERICAN STARS ON WHITE COLLEGE BASKETBALL TEAMS, THROUGH 1919

Samuel Ransom	1904–08	Beloit College
Wilbur Wood	1907–10	Nebraska
Fenwich Watkins	1909	Vermont
Cumberland Posey	1909, 1916	Penn State, Duquesne
Sol Butler	1910	Dubuque (Iowa)
William Kindle	1911	Springfield (Mass.)
Cleve Abbott	1913	South Dakota State
Paul Robeson	1915–18	Rutgers

SOUTHWESTERN ATHLETIC CONFERENCE CHAMPIONS (MEN, 1956–1984)

Year	School	Coach
1956	Texas Southern	Ed Adams
1957	Texas Southern	Ed Adams
1958	Texas Southern	Ed Adams
1959	Grambling	Fred Hobdy
1960	Grambling	Fred Hobdy
1961	Prairie View	Leroy Moore
1962	Prairie View	Leroy Moore
1963	Grambling	Fred Hobdy
1964	Grambling	Fred Hobdy
	Jackson State	Paul Covington
1965	Southern	Richard Mack
1966	Alcorn State	E.E. Simmons
	Grambling	Fred Hobdy
1967	Alcorn State	Bob Hopkins
	Arkansas AM&N	Coach Clemmons
1969	Alcorn State	Davey Whitney
1970	Jackson State	Paul Covington
1971	Grambling	Fred Hobdy
1972	Grambling	Fred Hobdy
1973	Alcorn State	Davey Whitney
1974	Jackson State	Paul Covington
1975	Jackson State	Paul Covington
1976	Alcorn State	Davey Whitney
1977	Texas Southern	Bob Moreland
1978	Southern	Carl Stewart
1979	Alcorn State	Davey Whitney
1980	Alcorn State	Davey Whitney
1981	Alcorn State	Davey Whitney
1982	Alcorn State	Davey Whitney
1983	Alcorn State	Davey Whitney
1984	Southern	Bob Hopkins

SIAC TOURNAMENT CHAMPIONS (1950–1984) DIVISION II

Year	School	Coach
1950	Morris Brown	H.B. Thompson
1951	Morris Brown	H.B. Thompson
1952	Florida A&M	Ed Oglesby
1953	Bethune-Cookman	Rudolph Matthews
1954	Clark	Leonidis Epps
1955	Florida A&M	Ed Oglesby
1956	Knoxville	Julian Bell
1957	Florida A&M	Ed Oglesby
1958	Knoxville	Julian Bell
1959	Florida A&M	Ed Oglesby
1960	Florida A&M	Ed Oglesby
1961	Benedict	John Brown
1962	Florida A&M	Ed Oglesby
1963	Fisk	H.B. Thompson
1964	South Carolina State	Ed Martin
1965	Clark	Leonidis Epps
1966	South Carolina State	Ed Martin
1967	Florida A&M	Ed Oglesby
1968	Bethune-Cookman	Jack McClairen
1969	Fort Valley State	Leon Lomax
1970	Savannah State	Leo Richardson
1971	Alabama State	Bernard Boozer

Reference Section

Year	School	Coach
1972	Alabama State	Bernard Boozer
1973	Albany State	Oliver Jones
1974	Fisk	Ron Lawson
1975	Alabama A&M	Clarence Blackmon
1976	Alabama A&M	Clarence Blackmon
1977	Florida A&M	Ajax Triplett
1978	Florida A&M	Ajax Triplett
1979	Tuskegee	Charles Thompson
1980	Bethune-Cookman	Jack McClairen
1981	Morehouse	Arthur McAfee
1982	Morris Brown	Billy Wade
1983	Albany State	Oliver Jones
1984	Albany State	Oliver Jones

SIAC
TOURNAMENT CHAMPIONS (1950–1984)
DIVISION III

Year	School	Coach
1979	Savannah State	Russ Ellington
1980	Savannah State	Russ Ellington
1981	Savannah State	Russ Ellington
1982	Miles	McKinley Young
1983	LeMoyne-Owen	Jerry Johnson
1984	LeMoyne-Owen	Jerry Johnson

MEAC CHAMPIONS
(1972–1984)

Year	School	Coach
1972	North Carolina A&T	Cal Irvin
1973	Maryland Eastern Shore	John Bates
1974	Morgan State	Nat Frazier
	Maryland Eastern Shore	John Bates
1975	North Carolina A&T	Warren Reynolds
1976	North Carolina A&T	Warren Reynolds
	Morgan State	Nat Frazier
1977	South Carolina State	Tim Autry
1978	North Carolina A&T	Gene Littles
1979	North Carolina A&T	Gene Littles
1980	Howard University	A.B. Williamson
1981	North Carolina A&T	Don Corbett

Year	School	Coach
1982	North Carolina A&T	Don Corbett
1983	North Carolina A&T	Don Corbett
1984	North Carolina A&T	Don Corbett

CIAA CHAMPIONS
(1950–1984)

Year	School	Coach
1950	North Carolina College	John McLendon
1951	Virginia Union	Tom Harris
1952	Virginia Union	Tom Harris
1953	Winston-Salem	Big House Gaines
1954	Virginia Union	Tom Harris
1955	Virginia Union	Tom Harris
1956	Maryland State	Nat Taylor
1957	Winston-Salem	Big House Gaines
1958	North Carolina A&T	Cal Irvin
1959	North Carolina A&T	Cal Irvin
1960	Winston-Salem	Big House Gaines
1961	Winston-Salem	Big House Gaines
1962	North Carolina A&T	Cal Irvin
1963	Winston-Salem	Big House Gaines
1964	North Carolina A&T	Cal Irvin
1965	Norfolk State	Ernie Fears
1966	Winston-Salem	Big House Gaines
1967	North Carolina A&T	Cal Irvin
1968	Norfolk State	Ernie Fears
1969	Elizabeth City	Bobby Vaughan
1970	Winston-Salem	Big House Gaines
1971	Norfolk State	Robert Smith
1972	Norfolk State	Robert Smith
1973	Fayetteville State	Thomas Reeves
1974	Norfolk State	Charles Christian
1975	Norfolk State	Charles Christian
1976	Norfolk State	Charles Christian
1977	Winston-Salem	Big House Gaines
1978	Norfolk State	Charles Christian
1979	Virginia Union	Dave Robbins
1980	Virginia Union	Dave Robbins
1981	Elizabeth City	Bobby Vaughan
1982	Hampton Institute	Hank Ford
1983	Hampton Institute	Hank Ford
1984	Norfolk State	Charles Christian

BLACK COLLEGE CONFERENCE WINNERS

	CIAA	SWAC	SIAC	EIAC	SCAC	MWAC
1916			Morehouse			
1917			Morehouse			
1918			Morehouse			
1919			Morehouse			
1920			Morehouse			
1921			Morehouse			
1922			Morehouse			
1923			Morehouse			
1924	Hampton		Morehouse			
1925	Hampton		Morehouse			
1926	Hampton		Morehouse			
1927	Hampton		Clark			
1928	Va. Seminary		Clark			
1929	Va. Seminary		M'house-Clark			
1930	Lincoln (Pa.)		Knoxville			
1931		Morgan State		Morris Brown		
1932	Morgan State		Morris Brown			
1933	Morgan State		Tuskegee			
1934	Howard		Tuskegee		Alcorn A & M	Wilberforce
1935	Howard		Alabama State		Alcorn A & M	Wilberforce
1936	Hampton		Alabama State		Alcorn A & M	Wilberforce
1937	N. Car. A & T		Morehouse		Alcorn A & M	Lincoln (Pa.)
1938	Va. State		Xavier		Alcorn A & M	W. Va. State
1939	Va. Union	Wiley	Clark		Alcorn A & M	W. Va. State
1940	*Va. Union	Bishop	Clark	Miner T.C.	Alcorn A & M	Kentucky State
1941		Bishop	Xavier	Fayetteville	Tougaloo	
1942		Langston	Fla. A & M		Tougaloo	
1943		Southern	S. Car. State		M.I. College	
1944		Langston	Tuskegee		M.I. College	
1945		Langston	Fla. A & M		S. Christian	

* The asterisk refers to a contested title. Va. Union says it won the CIAA title, but the CIAA refused to award it to them because they played against a professional team.

BLACK PLAYERS AT WHITE COLLEGES
(1920–1946)

Name	Year	College
Maynard Garner	1920–21	Hamilton
John H. Johnson	1920–21	Columbia U.
Ralph Bunche	1921–22	UCLA
Ross Owens	1923	South Dakota St.
Charles Drew	1923–25	Amherst
Ernie Page	1924–26	Western Illinois
George Gregory	1927–31	Columbia
James Barnes	1928–30	Oberlin
Sam Barnes	1928–30	Oberlin
DL:*Horace Johnson	1936–38	Dakota College
Bobby Yancey	1937	Boston U.
Ben Franklin	1937	Boston U.
Lawrence Bleach	1937	Detroit U.
William "Dolly" King	1937–39	Long Island U.
Frank "Doc" Kelker	1938–40	Western Reserve
Jim Coward	1938–41	Brooklyn College
Jackie Robinson	1939–41	UCLA
William Sidat-Singh	1939–41	Syracuse
Sonny Jameson	1941–45	CCNY
Ed Younger	1942–44	Long Island U.
Dick Wilkins	1942–44	Oregon
Clifton Mobley	1942–43	Wayne State
Jay Swift	1943–45	Yale
Arthur Wilson	1944–46	Princeton

ALL-CENTRAL INTERCOLLEGIATE ATHLETIC ASSOCIATION BASKETBALL TEAMS
(1954–1984)

Year	Name	School
1954	Jones, Samuel	North Carolina College
	Bacote, Ralph	St. Paul's College
	Harrison, Charles	North Carolina College
	Garrett, Ernest	Morgan State
	Burks, Clarence	St. Augustine's College
1955	Burks, Clarence	St. Augustine's College
	Sanders, Claude	Johnson C. Smith
	Gwinn, Stephen	Virginia Union
	Defares, Jack	Winston-Salem State
	Garrett, Ernest	Morgan State
1956	Syphax, John	Howard University
	Amos, Edwin	Hampton Institute
	Lloyd, Theophalius	Maryland State
	Defares, Jack	Winston-Salem State
	Smith, William	North Carolina A&T
	Harris, Thomas	Howard University
1957	Jones, Samuel	North Carolina Central
	Evans, Ronald	Fayetteville State
	Amos, Edwin	Hampton Institute
	Syphax, John	Howard University
	Defares, Jack	Winston-Salem State
1958	Garner, Ronald	Morgan State
	Sligh, James	North Carolina College
	Brightful, Charles	Morgan State
	John, Wilfred	Winston-Salem State
	Syphax, John	Howard University
	Howell, Joseph	North Carolina A&T
1959	Crenshaw, Joseph	Johnson C. Smith
	Trader, Nathaniel	Hampton Institute
	Bell, Carlton	North Carolina College

Year	Name	School	Year	Name	School
	Hill, Cleo	Winston-Salem State		Mitchell, Ira	Shaw University
	Howell, Joseph	North Carolina A&T		Cunningham, Tom	Winston-Salem State
1960	Spraggins, Warren	Virginia Union		Manning, Theodore	North Carolina College
	Attles, Alvin	North Carolina A&T		Ridgill, Howard	Winston-Salem State
	Simmons, Samuel	Virginia State		Stubbins, Gary	Elizabeth City State
	Johnson, Harold	Morgan State		Pitts, Richard	Norfolk State
	Hill, Cleo	Winston-Salem	1967	Monroe, Earl	Winston-Salem State
1961	Jackson, Jackie	Virginia Union		Davis, Lee	North Carolina College
	Ward, Walter	Hampton Institute		Lewis, Frederick	Elizabeth City State
	Hancock, Larry	Howard University		Reid, James	Winston-Salem State
	Hill, Cleo	Winston-Salem State		Randolph, Reginald	Johnson C. Smith
	Spraggins, Warren	Virginia Union		Horton, Ronald	Delaware State
1962	Trotman, Marvin	Elizabeth City State		Campbell, Ted	North Carolina A&T
	Foree, George	Winston-Salem State		Stubbins, Gary	Elizabeth City State
	Johnson, Harold	Morgan State		Davis, Michael	Virginia Union
	Williams, Jesse	Maryland State		Grant, James	Norfolk State
	Hester, James	Johnson C. Smith	1968	Looney, Rodney	Virginia State
1963	Neal, Fred	Johnson C. Smith		Dandridge, Robert	Norfolk State
	Stephens, Frank	Virginia Union		Smith, Oscar	Elizabeth City State
	Blount, Theodore	Winston-Salem State		Horton, Ronald	Delaware State
	Brock, Ernest	Virginia State		English, William	Winston-Salem State
	Glover, Richard	Winston-Salem State		Kirkland, Richard	Norfolk State
1964	Parker, Joseph	North Carolina College		Smiley, Eugene	Winston-Salem State
	Blount, Theodore	Winston-Salem State		Davis, Lee	North Carolina Central
	Bibby, Fred	Fayetteville State		Lewis, Frederick	Elizabeth City State
	Williams, Edward	Maryland State		Davis, Michael	Virginia Union
	McHartley, Maurice	North Carolina A&T	1969	Monroe, William	Fayetteville State
	Curry, Willie	Winston-Salem State		Bonaparte, Charles	Norfolk State
	Brock, Ernest	Virginia State		Walker, Vernon	North Carolina A&T
	Jackson, James	North Carolina A&T		Cherry, Daryl	North Carolina A&T
	Williams, Edward	Maryland State		Ford, Jake	Maryland State
	Davis, Warren	North Carolina A&T		Dandridge, Robert	Norfolk State
1965	Mulcare, Irving	North Carolina A&T		Pridgen, Joseph	North Carolina College
	Blount, Theodore	Winston-Salem State		Oliver, Israel	Elizabeth City State
	Morris, John	Norfolk State		English, William	Winston-Salem State
	Manning, Theodore	North Carolina College		Davis, Michael	Virginia Union
	Monroe, Earl	Winston-Salem State	1970	Utley, Kelly	Shaw University
	Turk, James	Morgan State		Butts, Robert	Johnson C. Smith
	Todd, Richard	Elizabeth City State		Gaie, Michael	Elizabeth City State
	Mulcare, Irving	North Carolina A&T		Ford, Jake	Maryland State
	Turner, Charles	Johnson C. Smith		McCrimmon, Ron	North Carolina Central
	Pitts, Richard	Norfolk State		Green, Michael	St. Paul's College
1966	Monroe, Earl	Winston-Salem State		Williams, Donald	Winston-Salem State
	Rue, Al	Delaware State		Oliver, Israel	Elizabeth City State
	Grant, James	Norfolk State		Morgan, James	Maryland State
	Todd, Richard	Elizabeth City State		McKinney, Johnny	Norfolk State

Year	Name	School	Year	Name	School
1971	Sneed, Michael	Fayetteville State		Carrington, Gregory	Virginia Union
	Prichett, Curtis	St. Augustine's College		Burns, Melvin	Norfolk State
	Smith, Sandy	Winston-Salem State		Cunningham, Eugene	Norfolk State
	Austin, Elmer	North Carolina A&T		Cooper, George	Johnson C. Smith
	Butts, Robert	Johnson C. Smith		Roberts, Donnie	St. Paul's College
	Harris, William	North Carolina A&T		Paulin, Thomas	Winston-Salem State
	Jones, Leroy	Norfolk State		Carr, Charles	Elizabeth City State
	Utley, Kelly	Shaw University		Hamilton, Jerry	Livingstone College
	Peele, Rudolph	Norfolk State	1976	Cozart, William	St. Paul's College
	Haskins, Raymond	Shaw University		Helton, Donald	Winston-Salem State
	Leggett, Redden	North Carolina Central		Lewis, Robert	Johnson C. Smith
	Gale, Michael	Elizabeth City State		Paulin, Thomas	Winston-Salem State
1972	Williams, Earl	Winston, Salem State		Cunningham, Eugene	Norfolk State
	Peele, Rudolph	Norfolk State		Epps, Raymond	Norfolk State
	Wilson, Ronald	Norfolk State		Bell, Jerome	Virginia State
	Sneed, Michael	Fayetteville State		Tisdol, Doward	Virginia State
	Carmichael, Len	Elizabeth City State		Roberts, Donnie	St. Paul's College
	Haskins, Raymond	Shaw University		Terry, Carlos	Winston-Salem State
	Pritchett, Curtis	St. Augustine's College	1977	Tisdol, Doward	Virginia State
	Johnson, Linwood	Virginia State		Barrows, John	Fayetteville State
	Jones, Leroy	Norfolk State		Entzminger, Herbert	Johnson C. Smith
	Smith, Sandy	Winston-Salem State		Payne, Marvin	Hampton Institute
1973	Youngblood, Willie	Hampton Institute		Blue, Thomas	Elizabeth City State
	Agee, Daniel	Shaw University		Epps, Raymond	Norfolk State
	Cogdill, Alton	Fayetteville State		Best, Tyrone	Hampton Institute
	Hunter, Ralph	Virginia Union		Lewis, Curvan	Virginia Union
	Johnson, Linwood	Virginia State		Terry, Carlos	Winston-Salem State
	Jones, Leroy	Norfolk State		Wilkerson, Jesse	Norfolk State
	Chavious, Arthur	Winston-Salem State		Powell, Sean	St. Augustine's College
	Williams, Earl	Winston-Salem State		Cozart, William	St. Paul's College
	Windley, Glen	Elizabeth City State	1978	Mayhorn, Rick	Hampton Institute
	Wilson, Ronald	Norfolk State		Threatt, Tony	Hampton Institute
	Hazley, Andrew	Virginia Union		Evans, Kenny	Norfolk State
1974	Cunningham, Eugene	Norfolk State		Entzminger, Herbert	Johnson C. Smith
	Britt, Wayne	Hampton Institute		Gaines, Reginald	Winston-Salem State
	Cooper, George	Johnson C. Smith		Proctor, Francis	Johnson C. Smith
	Hamilton, Jerry	Livingstone College		Robinson, Michael	Winston-Salem State
	Mitchell, Roosevelt	Norfolk State		Isabelle, Robert	Norfolk State
	Richardson, Andrew	Shaw University		Terry, Carlos	Winston-Salem State
	Williams, Earl	Winston-Salem State		Tolliver, Keith	Hampton Institute
	Kitt, Harold	Winston-Salem State	1979	Gaskins, Arthur	Elizabeth City State
	Johnson, Linwood	Virginia State		Evans, Kenneth	Norfolk State
	Windley, Glen	Elizabeth City State		Jefferson, Edward	Fayetteville State
1975	Blue, Thomas	Elizabeth City State		Valentine, Keith	Virginia Union
	Tisdol, Doward	Virginia State		Hart, Jon	Livingstone College
	Moye, Joseph	Shaw University		Ware, Daniel	Virginia State

Year	Name	School
	Tibbs, William	Johnson C. Smith
	Harold, David	Winston-Salem State
	Procter, Francis	Johnson C. Smith
	Gaines, Reginald	Winston-Salem State
	Payne, Marvin	Hampton Institute
	Mahorn, Rick	Hampton Institute
1980	Holmes, Larry	Virginia Union
	Robinson, Michael	Winston-Salem State
	Evans, Kenneth	Norfolk State
	Gaskins, Arthur	Elizabeth City State
	Oliver, Larcell	Johnson C. Smith
	Procter, Francis	Johnson C. Smith
	Cooper, William	St. Augustine's College
	Lily, Derwin	Virginia Union
	Jackson, Gregory	St. Paul's College
	Mahorn, Rick	Hampton Institute
	Gaines, Reginald	Winston-Salem State
	Tibbs, Terry	Norfolk State
	Bishop, John	North Carolina Central
	Warwick, Daryl	Hampton Institute
	Stith, Darrell	Virginia State
	Pope, David	Norfolk State
1981	Mims, Steve	Fayetteville State
	Norman, Julius	Virginia State
	Oliver, Larcell	Johnson C. Smith
	Lewis, Bernard	St. Paul's College
	Jackson, Gregory	St. Paul's College
	Boggan, Anthony	St. Augustine's College
	Flores, Phil	Johnson C. Smith
1982	Washington, Anthony	Hampton Institute
	Davis, Antonio	Livingstone's College
	McNeil, Bonny	Fayetteville State
	Stuckey, Sammy	Shaw University
	Greene, Therman	Winston-Salem State
	Bland, Pierce	Elizabeth City State
	Carroll, Donald	St. Augustine's College
	Oakley, Charles	Virginia Union
	Pope, David	Norfolk State
	Norman, Julius	Virginia State
	Oliver, Larcell	Johnson C. Smith
	Tibbs, William	Johnson C. Smith
1983	Pope, David	Norfolk State
	Washington, Anthony	Hampton Institute
	Hines, Gregory	Hampton Institute
	Binlon, David	North Carolina Central
	Oakley, Charles	Virginia Union

Year	Name	School
1984	McGrudder, Roosevelt	Johnson C. Smith
	Pope, David	Norfolk State
	Tally, Ralph	Norfolk State
	Russell, Troy	Winston-Salem State
	Francis, Randy	St. Augustine's College
	Lacy, David	Shaw University
	Bell, Charles	St. Paul's College
	Rogers, Anthony	St. Augustine's College
	Person, William	Fayetteville State
	Miller, Cedric	Hampton Institute
	Murphy, Charles	North Carolina Central
	Oakley, Charles	Virginia Union

ALL-SOUTHWESTERN ATHLETIC CONFERENCE BASKETBALL TEAMS (1958–1981)

Year	Name	School
1958	*First Team*	
	Taylor, Willie	Texas Southern
	Bobbitt, Robert	Texas Southern
	Hill, Roosevelt	Southern University
	Grimes, Harold	Prairie View A&M
	Swain, Ben	Texas Southern
	Second Team	
	Groce, Luther	Texas College
	Paul, Frank	Southern University
	Chatam, E.C.	Arkansas AM&N
	Hudson, Odell	Texas College
	Hayes, Ego	Southern Unviersity
1959	*First Team*	
	Beatty, Zelmo	Prairie View A&M
	Buckner, Cleveland	Jackson State
	Barr, Jerry	Grambling State
	Hooper, James	Grambling State
	Taylor, Willie	Texas Southern
	Second Team	
	Brackens, Harold	Prairie View A&M
	Willis, Howard	Grambling State
	Harper, Charles	Wiley College
	Grimes, Harold	Prairie View A&M
	Maura, Fred	Texas Southern
	Hardnett, Charles	Grambling State
1960	*First Team*	
	Tippett, Rex	Grambling State

62   *Reference Section*

Year	Name	School	Year	Name	School
	Buckner, Cleveland	Jackson State		Yarborough, Jerry	Jackson State
	Mack Allen, James	Arkansas AM&N		Comeaux, John	Grambling State
	Bond, Louis	Southern University		Richardson, Don	Arkansas AM&N
	Beatty, Zelmo	Prairie View AM&N		**Second Team**	
	Second Team			Leflore, Lyvonne	Jackson State
	Barfield, James	Jackson State		Richardson, Sam	Wiley College
	Hardnett, Charles	Grambling State		Bevins, Harold	Arkansas AM&N
	Thomas, Willie	Southern University		Hayes, Ron	Southern University
	Lackey, Cornell	Prairie View A&M		Allen, Robert	Arkansas AM&N
	Hayes, Ego	Southern University	1966	**First Team**	
1961	**First Team**			Comeaux, John	Grambling State
	Hardnett, Charles	Grambling State		Manning, Ed	Jackson State
	Reed, Willis	Grambling State		Ned, Walter	Alcorn State
	Tippett, Rex	Grambling State	1966	**Second Team**	
	Bond, Louis	Southern, University		Jones, James	Grambling State
	Mack Allen, James	Arkansas AM&N		Bingham, Charles	Jackson State
1962	**First Team**		1967	**First Team**	
	Reed, Willis	Grambling State		Allen, Robert	Arkansas AM&N
	Hardnett, Charles	Grambling State		Manning, Ed	Jackson State
	Love, Robert	Southern University		Jones, James	Grambling State
	Beatty, Zelmo	Prairie View A&M		Davis, Howard	Grambling State
	Bond, Louis	Southern, University		Wilson, Jasper	Southern University
	Mack Allen, James	Arkansas AM&N		**Second Team**	
1963	**First Team**			Norwood, Willie	Alcorn State
	Frazier, Wilbur	Grambling State		Kelly, James	Alcorn State
	Reed, Willis	Grambling State		Flowers, Robert	Alcorn State
	Love, Robert	Southern University		Long, Ron	Southern University
	West, Hershell	Grambling State		Allen, James	Texas Southern
	Mack Allen, James	Arkansas, AM&N	1968	**First Team**	
1964	**First Team**			Norwood, Willie	Alcorn State
	Love, Robert	Southern University		Flowers, Robert	Alcorn State
	Frazier, Wilbur	Grambling State		Kelly, James	Alcorn State
	Yarborough, Jerry	Jackson State		Wilson, James	Arkansas AM&N
	Mack Allen, James	Arkansas AM&N		Wilson, Jasper	Southern University
	Reed, Willis	Grambling State	1969	**First Team**	
	Second Team			Norwood, Willie	Alcorn State
	Boatwright, Homer	Southern University		Warner, Cornell	Jackson State
	Leflore, Lyvonne	Jackson State		Hilton, Fred	Grambling State
	Comeaux, John	Grambling State		Keye, Julius	Alcorn State
	Bevins, Harold	Arkansas AM&N		Hart, Herb	Texas Southern
	Hayes, Ron	Southern University	1970	**First Team**	
	Benton, James	Jackson State		Wyatt, Levi	Alcorn State
1965	**First Team**			Herdon, Lou	Jackson State
	Frazier, Wilbur	Grambling State		Hart, Herb	Texas Southern
	Love, Robert	Southern University			

Year	Name	School	Year	Name	School
	Shinall, John	Jackson State	1976	*First Team*	
	Warner, Cornell	Jackson State		Robinson, Dellie	Alcorn State
	Sing, Sam	Alcorn State		Short, Purvis	Jackson State
1971	*First Team*			Davis, Gaylord	Texas Southern
	Wyatt, Levi	Alcorn State		Saunders, Frankie	Southern University
	Brown, Marvin	Jackson State		Barrow, Ron	Southern University
	Hilton, Fred	Grambling State		Wright, Larry	Grambling State
	Aldridge, Ellis	Texas Southern	1977	*First Team*	
	Warner, Cornell	Jackson State		Sykes, Terry	Grambling State
	Second Team			Short, Purvis	Jackson State
	Bateman, Glen	Alcorn State		Jackson, Marvin	Prairie View A&M
	Kincaid, McKincey	Jakcson State		Williams, Lawrence	Texas Southern
	Mason, Floyd	Alcorn State		Bradley, Alonzo	Texas Southern
	Cannon, Emanuel	Grambling State		Green, Tom	Southern University
	Golden, Russell	Jackson State		Monroe, Alfredo	Alcorn State
1972	*First Team*		1978	*First Team*	
	James, Aaron	Grambling State		Saunders, Frank	Southern University
	Wyatt, Levi	Alcorn State		Short, Purvis	Jackson State
	McTier, Larry	Southern University		Horton, James	Alcorn State
	Ford, Charles	Texas Southern		Norris, Sylvester	Jackson State
	Aldridge, Ellis	Texas Southern		Lemelle, Martin	Grambling State
	Hart, Willie	Grambling State	1979	*First Team*	
1973	*First Team*			Murphy, Tony	Southern University
	James, Aaron	Grambling State		Garrett, Lionel	Southern Unviersity
	Keyes, Alex	Southern University		Norris, Audie	Jackson State
	Frazier, Andrew	Southern University		Davis, Collie	Alcorn State
	Short, Eugene	Jackson State		Lemelle, Martin	Grambling State
	Tatum, Andrew	Alcorn State		Smith, Larry	Alcorn State
1974	*First Team*			*Second Team*	
	Jones, Glendale	Jackson State		Walsh, Robert	Jackson State
	Short, Eugene	Jackson State		Hagan, Larry	Prairie View A&M
	Robinson, Calvin	Mississippi Valley State		Tidwell, Gary	Grambling State
				Williams, Ernest	Mississippi Valley State
	Barrow, Ron	Southern University			
	James, Aaron	Grambling State		Blue, Fred	Texas Southern
1975	*First Team*			Horton, James	Alcorn State
	Barrow, Ron	Southern University	1980	*First Team*	
	Milton, Alfred	Alcorn State		Smith, Larry	Alcorn State
	Ward, Henry	Jackson State		Norris, Audie	Jackson State
	Wright, Larry	Grambling State		Murphy, Tony	Southern University
	Robinson, Dellie	Alcorn State		Lemelle, Martin	Grambling State
	Jones, Glendale	Jackson State		Kelly, Harry	Texas Southern

Year	Name	School	Year	Name	School
	Second Team			Williams, Robert	Grambling State
	Shavers, Doc	Jackson State		Reed, Tony	Mississippi Valley State
	Reed, Tony	Mississippi Valley State		Irving, Albert	Alcorn State
	Williams, Robert	Grambling State		Loder, Kevin	Alabama State
	Baker, Eddie	Alcorn State		***Second Team***	
	Bell, E.J.	Alcorn State		Alexander, Dwight	Alcorn State
	Wyatt, Clinton	Alcorn State		Shavers, Doc	Jackson State
1981	***First Team***			Norris, Audie	Jackson State
	Jackson, Alvin	Southern University		Simpson, Ken	Grambling State
	Kelly, Harry	Texas Southern		Baker, Eddie	Alcorn State

AFRICAN-AMERICAN COLLEGE BASKETBALL PLAYER OF THE YEAR

1959–65 U.S. Basketball Writers' Association
1966–91 Associated Press

Year	Name	Position	College	Year	Name	Position	College
1959	Oscar Robertson	Guard	University of Cincinnati	1978	Alfred "Butch" Lee	Guard	Marquette
1960	Oscar Robertson	Guard	University of Cincinnati	1980	Mark Aguirre	Forward	DePaul
1964	Walt Hazzard	Guard	UCLA	1981	Ralph Sampson	Center	Virginia
1966	Cazzie Russell	Forward	Michigan	1982	Ralph Sampson	Center	Virginia
1967	Lew Alcindor	Center	UCLA	1983	Ralph Sampson	Center	Virginia
1968	Elvin Hayes	Forward	Houston	1984	Michael Jordan	Guard	North Carolina
1969	Lew Alcindor	Center	UCLA	1986	Walter Berry	Forward	St. John's University
1971	Austin Carr	Guard	Notre Dame	1987	David Robinson	Center	U.S. Naval Academy
1974	David Thompson	Forward	N.C. State	1988	Hersey Hawkins	Guard	Bradley University
1975	David Thompson	Forward	N.C. State	1990	Lionel Simmons	Forward	La Salle University
1976	Scott May	Forward	Indiana	1991	Larry Johnson	Forward	University of Nevada—Las Vegas
1977	Marques Johnson	Forward	UCLA				

BLACK CONSENSUS ALL-AMERICA BASKETBALL SELECTIONS 1953–92

1953	Walt Dukes, Seton Hall	1956	Bill Russell, USF
1955	Bill Russell, San Francisco		Si Green, Duquesne
	Si Green, Duquesne	1957	Wilt Chamberlain, Kansas

1958	Bob Boozer, Kansas State
	Elgin Baylor, Seattle
	Wilt Chamberlain, Kansas
	Guy Rodgers, Temple
1959	Bob Boozer, Kansas State
	Oscar Robertson, Cinn.
1960	Oscar Robertson, Cinn.
1961	Chet Walker, Bradley
1962	Billy McGill, Utah
	Chet Walker, Bradley
1963	Jerry Harkness, Loyola (Ill)
	Tom Thacker, Cinn.
1964	Dave Stallworth, Kansas
	Walt Hazzard, UCLA
1965	Cazzie Russell, Michigan
1966	Dave Bing, Syracuse
	Cazzie Russell, Michigan
	Jim Walker, Providence
1967	Lew Alcindor, UCLA
	Elvin Hayes, Houston
	Jim Walker, Providence
	Clem Haskins, W. Kentucky
1968	Wes Unseld, Louisville
	Elvin Hayes, Houston
	Lew Alcindor, UCLA
1969	Lew Alcindor, UCLA
	Spencer Haywood, Detroit
	Calvin Murphy, Niagara
1970	Bob Lanier, St. Bonaventure
	Calvin Murphy, Niagara
1971	Austin Carr, Notre Dame
	Sidney Wicks, UCLA
	Artis Gilmore, Jacksonville
	Dean Meminger, Marquette
	Jim McDaniels, W. Kentucky
1972	Dwight Lamar, SW Louisiana
	Ed Ratleff, Long Beach State
	Bob McAdoo, UNC
	Jim Chones, Marquette
	Henry Bibby, UCLA
1973	Ed Ratleff, Long Beach State
	Dwight Lamar, SW Louisiana
	David Thompson, NC State
	Keith Wilkes, UCLA
1974	Keith Wilkes, UCLA
	John Shumate, Notre Dame
	David Thompson, NC State
	Marvin Barnes, Providence
1975	David Thompson, NC State

	Adrian Dantley, Notre Dame
	Scott May, Indiana
	John Lucas, Maryland
1976	Scott May, Indiana
	Richard Washington, UCLA
	John Lucas, Maryland
	Adrian Dantley, Notre Dame
1977	Otis Birdsong, Houston
	Marques Johnson, UCLA
	Rickey Green, Michigan
	Phil Ford, UNC
	Bernard King, Tennessee
1978	Phil Ford, UNC
	Butch Lee, Marquette
	David Greenwood, UCLA
	Mychal Thompson, Minnesota
1979	David Greenwood, UCLA
	Earvin "Magic" Johnson, Michigan State
	Sidney Moncreif, Arkansas
1980	Mark Aguirre, DePaul
	Michael Brooks, LaSalle
	Joe Barry Carroll, Purdue
	Darrell Griffith, Louisville
1981	Mark Aguirre, DePaul
	Steve Johnson, Oregon State
	Ralph Sampson, Virginia
	Isiah Thomas, Indiana
1982	Terry Cummings, DePaul
	Quintin Dailey, San Francisco
	Eric Floyd, Georgetown
	Ralph Sampson, Virginia
	James Worthy, UNC
1983	Dale Ellis, Tennessee
	Pat Ewing, Georgetown
	Michael Jordan, UNC
	Sam Perkins, UNC
	Ralph Sampson, Virginia
	Wayman Tisdale, Oklahoma
	Keith Lee, Memphis State
1984	Wayman Tisdale, Oklahoma
	Sam Perkins, UNC
	Pat Ewing, Georgetown
	Akeem Olajuwon, Houston
	Michael Jordan, UNC
1985	Wayman Tisdale, Oklahoma
	Patrick Ewing, Georgetown
	Keith Lee, Memphis State
	Xavier McDaniel, Wichita State
	John Dawkins, Duke

1986	Len Bias, Maryland				Derrick Coleman, Syracuse
	Kenny Walker, Kentucky				Gary Payton, Oregon State
	Walter Berry, St. John's (New York)				Chris Jackson, Louisiana State
	John Dawkins, Duke				Lionel Simmons, La Salle
1987	David Robinson, Navy			1991	Kenny Anderson, Georgia Tech
	Danny Manning, Kansas				Billy Owens, Syracuse
	Reggie Williams, Georgetown				Larry Johnson, Nevada, Las Vegas
	Kenny Smith, UNC				Shaquille O'Neal, Louisiana State
1988	Gary Grant, Michigan				Jim Jackson, Ohio State
	Hersey Hawkins, Bradley			1992	Harold Minor, USC
	J.R. Reid, UNC				Jim Jackson, Ohio State
	Sean Elliott, Arizona				Shaquille O'Neal, Louisiana State
	Danny Manning, Kansas				Alonzo Mourning, Georgetown
1989	Sean Elliott, Arizona			1993	Calbert Cheaney, Indiana
	Pervis Ellison, Louisville				Chris Webber, Michigan
	Chris Jackson, Louisiana State				Anferney Hardaway, Memphis State
	Stacey King, Oklahoma				Jamal Mashburn, Kentucky
1990	Larry Johnson, Nevada, Las Vegas				Glenn Robinson, Purdue

MEN'S BASKETBALL AFRICAN-AMERICAN
JOHN WOODEN AWARD WINNERS

1977	Marques Johnson	UCLA	1986	Walter Berry	St. John's University
1978	Phil Ford	North Carolina	1987	David Robinson	U.S. Naval Academy
1980	Darrell Griffith	Louisville	1988	Danny Manning	University of Kansas
1982	Ralph Sampson	University of Virginia	1989	Sean Elliott	University of Arizona
1983	Ralph Sampson	University of Virginia	1990	Lionel Simmons	La Salle University
1984	Michael Jordan	University of North Carolina	1991	Larry Johnson	University of Nevada—Las Vegas

UNITED PRESS INTERNATIONAL DIVISION I
Men's Player of the Year Award

Year	Player	College	Year	Player	College
1956	Bill Russell	University of San Francisco	1978	Alfred Lee	Marquette University
1958	Oscar Robertson	University of Cincinnati	1980	Marke Aquirre	DePaul University
1959	Oscar Robertson	University of Cincinnati	1981	Ralph Sampson	University of Virginia
1960	Oscar Robertson	University of Cincinnati	1982	Ralph Sampson	University of Virginia
1966	Cazzie Russell	University of Michigan	1983	Ralph Sampson	University of Virginia
1967	Lew Alcindor	UCLA	1984	Michael Jordon	University of North Carolina
1968	Elvin Hayes	University of Houston	1986	Walter Berry	St. John's University
1969	Lew Alcindor	UCLA	1987	David Robinson	U.S. Naval Academy
1971	Austin Carr	University of Notre Dame	1988	Hersey Hawkins	Bradley University
1975	David Thompson	North Carolina State University	1990	Lionel Simmons	La Salle University
1976	Scott May	University of Indiana	1991	Shaquille O'Neal	Louisiana State University
1977	Marques Johnson	UCLA	1992	Jim Jackson	Ohio State University

NCAA MEN'S BASKETBALL TOURNAMENT
Most Valuable Player of the Year Award

Year	Player	College	Year	Player	College
1955	Bill Russell	University of San Francisco	1979	Earvin Johnson	Michigan State University
1957	Wilt Chamberlain	University of Kansas	1980	Darrell Griffith	University of Louisville
1958	Elgin Baylor	University of Seattle	1981	Isiah Thomas	Indiana University
1962	Paul Hogue	University of Cincinnati	1982	James Worthy	University of North Carolina
1964	Walt Hazzard	University of California, Los Angeles	1984	Patrick Ewing	Georgetown University
1966	Jerry Chambers	University of Utah	1985	Ed Pinkney	Villanova University
1967	Lew Alcindor*	University of California, Los Angeles	1986	Pervis Ellison	University of Louisville
1968	Lew Alcindor	University of California, Los Angeles	1987	Keith Smart	Indiana University
1969	Lew Alcindor	University of California, Los Angeles	1988	Danny Manning	University of Kansas
1970	Sidney Wicks	University of California, Los Angeles	1989	Glen Rice	University of Michigan
1971	Howard Porter	Villanova University	1990	Anderson Hunt	University of Nevada, Las Vegas
1974	David Thompson	North Carolina State University	1993	Donald Williams	University of North Carolina
1975	Richard Washington	University of California, Los Angeles			
1977	Alfred Lee	Marquette University		*Lew Alcindor (Kareem Abdul-Jabbar)	
1978	Jack Givens	University of Kentucky			

AFRICAN-AMERICANS ON THE NCAA FINAL FOUR ALL-DECADE TEAM

All-Time Team:

Player	College	Year
Lew Alcindor	UCLA	1967–69
Wilt Chamberlain	University of Kansas	1957
Earvin Johnson	Michigan State University	1979
Michael Jordan	University of North Carolina	1982

All-1950s

Elgin Baylor	Seattle University	1958
Wilt Chamberlain	University of Kansas	1957
K. C. Jones	University of San Francisco	1955
Oscar Robertson	University of Cincinnati	1959–60
Guy Rodgers	Temple University	1958
Bill Russell	University of San Francisco	1955–56

All-1960s

Lew Alcindor	UCLA	1967–69
Elvin Hayes	University of Houston	1967
Walt Hazzard	UCLA	1964
Cazzie Russell	University of Michigan	1965
Charles Scott	University of North Carolina	1968–69

Reference Section

Player	College	Year

All-1970s

Player	College	Year
Jack Givens	University of Kentucky	1978
Earvin Johnson	Michigan St. University	1979
Marques Johnson	UCLA	1975–76
Scott May	University of Indiana	1976
David Thompson	North Carolina State University	1974
Sidney Wicks	UCLA	1969–71
Keith Wilkes (Jamaal Wilkes)	UCLA	1972–74

All-1980s

Player	College	Year
John Dawkins	Duke University	1986
Patrick Ewing	Georgetown University	1982–84
Darrell Griffith	University of Louisville	1980
Michael Jordon	University of North Carolina	1982
Rodney McCray	University of Louisville	1980
Ed Pinckney	Villanova University	1985
Isiah Thomas	Indiana University	1981
James Worthy	University of North Carolina	1982

WOMEN'S COLLEGE BASKETBALL AFRICAN-AMERICAN ALL-AMERICAS, KODAC-WBCA, 1975–1992

1975
Lusia Harris, Delta State

1976
Lusia Harris, Delta State
Pearl Worrell, Wayland Baptist

1977
Lusia Harris, Delta State
Charlotte Lewis, Illinois State
Patricia Roberts, Tennessee

1978
Althea Gwynn, Queens
Lynette Woodard, Kansas

1979
Susan Taylor, Valdosta State
Franci Washington, Ohio State
Rosie Walker, Stephen F. Austin

1980
Pan Kelly, Louisiana Tech
Rosie Walker, Stephen F. Austin
Lynette Woodard, Kansas

1981
Pam Kelly, Louisiana Tech
Valerie Walker, Cheyney State
Lynette Woodard, Kansas

1982
Janet Harris, Georgia
Pam Kelly, Louisiana Tech
Barbara Kennedy, Clemson
Valerie Still, Kentucky
Angela Turner, Louisiana Tech
Valerie Walker, Cheyney State

1983
Priscilla Gary, Kansas State
Janice Lawrence, Louisiana Tech
Paula McGee, Southern California
Cheryl Miller, Southern California
LaTaunya Pollard, Long Beach State
Valerie Still, Kentucky
Joyce Walker, Louisiana State

1984

Tresa Brown, North Carolina
Janet Harris, Georgia
Becky Jackson, Auburn
Yolanda Laney, Cheyney State
Janice Lawrence, Louisiana Tech
Pam McGee, Southern California
Cheryl Miller, Southern California
Annette Smith, Texas
Marilyn Stephens, Temple
Joyce Walker, Louisiana State

1985

Medina Dixon, Old Dominion
Anucha Browne, Northwestern
Pam Gant, Louisiana Tech
Sheila Collins, Tennessee
Teresa Edwards, Georgia
Cheryl Miller, Southern California

1986

Katrina McClain, Georgia
Cheryl Miller, Southern California
Wanda Ford, Drake

1987

Cindy Brown, Long Beach State
Katrina McClain, Georgia
Clarissa Davis, Texas
Vickie Orr, Auburn
Teresa Weatherspoon, Louisiana Tech

1988

Michelle Edwards, Iowa
Bridgette Gordon, Tennessee
Penny Toler, Long Beach State
Vickie Orr, Auburn University

1989

Penny Toler, Long Beach State
Bridgette Gordon, Tennessee
Nora Lewis, Louisiana Tech
Clarissa Davis, Texas
Vicky Bullett, Maryland

1990

Dawn Staley, Virginia
Daedra Charles, Tennessee
Andrea Stinson, North Carolina State

1991

Daedra Charles, Tennessee
Andrea Stinson, North Carolina State
Dawn Staley, Virginia
Carolyn Jones, Auburn
Delmonica De Horney, Arkansas
Dana Chatman, LSU
Sonja Henning, Stanford

1992

Dena Head, Tennessee
Sheryl Swoopes, Texas Tech
Val Whiting, Stanford
Dawn Staley, Virginia

THOMAS BRODERICK AWARD RECIPIENTS (WOMEN'S BASKETBALL)

Year	Player	College	Year	Player	College
1977	Lusia Harris	Delta State College	1988	Katrina McClain	University of Georgia
1984	Cheryl Miller	University of Southern California	1989	Teresa Weatherspoon	Louisiana Tech University
1985	Cheryl Miller	University of Southern California	1990	Bridgette Gordon	University of Tennessee
1986	Cheryl Miller	University of Southern California	1991	Dawn Staley	University of Virginia

NAISMITH TROPHY RECIPIENTS (WOMEN'S BASKETBALL)

Year	Player	College	Year	Player	College
1984	Cheryl Miller	University of Southern California	1987	Clarissa Davis	University of Texas
1985	Cheryl Miller	University of Southern California	1991	Dawn Staley	University of Virginia
1986	Cheryl Miller	University of Southern California	1992	Dawn Staley	University of Virginia

WADE TROPHY RECIPIENTS (WOMEN'S BASKETBALL)

Year	Player	College	Year	Player	College
1981	Lynette Woodard	University of Kansas	1985	Cheryl Miller	University of Southern California
1982	Pam Kelly	Louisiana Tech University	1988	Teresa Weatherspoon	Louisiana Tech University
1983	LaTaunya Pollard	Long Beach State University	1989	Clarissa Davis	University of Texas
1984	Janice Lawrence	Louisiana Tech University	1991	Daedra Charles	University of Tennessee

WOMEN'S BASKETBALL COACHES ASSOCIATION
Coach of the Year Award

Year	Coach	College
1988	Vivian Stringer	University of Iowa

NCAA TEAM OF THE DECADE—1980s
(WOMEN'S BASKETBALL)

Player	College	Player	College
Cheryl Miller	University of Southern California	Clarissa Davis	University of Texas
Janice Lawrence	Louisiana Tech University	Bridgette Gordon	University of Tennessee
Teresa Witherspoon	Louisiana Tech University		

BLACK COLLEGE WOMEN'S NCAA
DIVISION II ALL-AMERICAS
(Basketball)

1982—Jackie White, Tuskegee
1983—Paris McWhirter, Virginia Union
      Barvenia Wooten, Virginia Union
1984—Veta Williams, Virginia Union

BLACK COLLEGE NATIONAL BASKETBALL
CHAMPIONSHIPS

	School		Coach		Final-Four Tournament Appearances	
1957	Tennessee State (men)	NAIA	John McLendon			
1958	Tennessee State (men)	NAIA	John McLendon	**NAIA Men**		**Finish**
1959	Tennessee State (men)	NAIA	John McLendon	1956	Texas Southern	2nd
1961	Grambling (men)	NAIA	Fred Hobdy	1958	Texas Southern	3rd
1962	Prairie View (men)	NAIA	Leroy Moore	1960	Tennessee State	3rd
1965	Central State (men)	NAIA	William Lucas	1963	Grambling	3rd
1967	Winston-Salem (men)	NCAA II	Big House Gaines	1966	Grambling	3rd
					Norfolk State	4th

	School		Coach
1968	Central State (men)	NAIA	William Lucas
1974	Morgan State (men)	NCAA II	Nat Frazier
1975	LeMoyne-Owen (men)	NCAA III	Jerry Johnson
1976	Coppin State (men)	NAIA	John Bates
1977	Texas Southern (men)	NAIA	Robert Moreland
1978	Cheyney State (men)	NCAA II	John Chaney
1979	S.C. State (women)	AIAW II	Willie Simon
1980	Virginia Union (men)	NCAA II	Dave Robbins
1982	University of The District of Columbia (men)	NCAA II	Will Jones
1983	Virginia Union (women)	NCAA II	Louis Hearn

Final-Four Tournament Appearances

NAIAMen		**Finish**
1969	Elizabeth City	4th
	Maryland State	2nd*
1973	Maryland Eastern Shore	2nd*
1974	Alcorn State	2nd
1975	Alcorn State	3rd
1980	Alabama State	2nd
1982	Hampton Institute	3rd

*Same School

NAIA Women

1981	Texas Southern	2nd
1984	Dillard	3rd

NCAA Men Div. II

1984	St. Augustine's	2nd

NCAA Women Div. II

1982	Tuskegee Institute	2nd
1984	Virginia Union	2nd

JOHN McLENDON'S CAREER COACHING RECORD

College	W	L	Pct.	Titles, Years
North Carolina College (now North Carolina Central University), 1941–1952	246	60	.815	CIAA, 1941, 1942, 1944, 1947, 1949, 1951; Black Champions 1950
Hampton Institute, 1953–1954	31	20	.608	
Tennessee State A&I University, 1955–1959	144	23	.862	NAIA Champions 1957, 1958, 1959; 1958 NAIA Coach of the Year
Kentucky State College, 1963–1966	51	30		
Cleveland State University, 1967–1969	27	41		
Professional				
Cleveland Pipers (semi-pro) National Industrial League, 1959–1961	72	32	.692	1961 AAU Champions 1961 Tournament Playoff Champions
Cleveland Pipers American Basketball League	27	20	.574	1961 Eastern Division Professional Champions
Denver Nuggets, 1969	9	19	.321	

WINNINGEST ACTIVE DIVISION II
MEN'S COLLEGE BASKETBALL COACHES
(By victories–Doesn't include 1992–1993 season)

Name	College	Wins	Name	College	Wins
Clarence Gaines	Winston-Salem State University	822	Oliver Jones	Albany State College (GA)	312
Jerry Johnson	LeMoyne-Owen College	626	Harvey Heartley	St. Augustine's College	296
Arthur McAfee	Morehouse College	393	Harold Deane	Virginia State University	233
Dave Robbins (Non-African American)	Virginia Union University	344	Ajac Triplett	Morris Brown College	200

WINNINGEST ACTIVE DIVISION I
MEN'S COLLEGE BASKETBALL COACHES

By Percentage

Place on Active List	Coach	Years	College	Won	Lost	PC
2nd	John Chaney	20	Temple University	458	143	.762
5th	Nolan Richardson	12	University of Arkansas	286	100	.741
6th	John Thompson	20	Georgetown University	464	165	.738
20th	Ben Jobe	21	Southern University	401	183	.687
25th	Don Corbett	21	North Carolina A&T State University	399	191	.676
43rd	James Oliver	17	Alabama State University	316	172	.648
46th	Mike Jarvis	7	George Washington University	136	75	.645
47th	Larry Finch	6	Memphis State University	125	69	.644

By Victories

Place on Active List	Coach	College	Wins
14th	John Thompson	Georgetown University	464
17th	John Chaney	Temple University	458
26th	Ben Jobe	Southern University	401
32nd	Cy McClairen	Bethune-Cookman College	380
46th	James Oliver	Alabama State University	316
48th	George Raveling	University of Southern CA	302
53rd	Nolan Richardson	University of Arkansas	286
56th	Robert Moreland	Texas Southern University	276

AFRICAN-AMERICAN BASKETBALL COACHES WHO WON AT LEAST 500 GAMES THROUGH 1992, REGARDLESS OF CLASSIFICATION OR ASSOCIATION, AT 4-YEAR COLLEGES

(* denotes coach who was still coaching the 1992–93 season)

Coach	(Alma Mater)	Colleges-Coached	Tenure	Years	Won	Lost	Pct.
Ed Adams	(Tuskegee, 1933)	North Carolina Central, Tuskegee, Texas Southern,	1935–1936 1937–1949 1950–1958	24	645	153	.808
John McClendon, Jr.	(Kansas, 1946)	North Carolina Central, Hampton Institute, Tennessee STate, Kentucky State, Cleveland State,	1941–1952 1953–1954 1955–1959 1964–1966 1967–1969	25	523	165	.760
Jerry Johnson*	(Fayetteville State, 1951)	LeMoyne-Owen,	1959–1992	34	626	287	.686
Fred Hobdy	(Grambling, 1949)	Grambling,	1957–1986	30	571	287	.666
Ed Martin	(North Carolina A&T, 1951)	South Carolina State, Tennessee State,	1956–1968 1969–1985	30	501	253	.664
Clarence "Bighouse" Gaines*	(Morgan State, 1945)	Winston-Salem State	1947–1992	46	822	430	.657
Robert Vaughn	(Virginia State, 1948)	Elizabeth City State,	1952–1986	34	501	363	.580

UPI'S NCAA COACH OF THE YEAR AWARD

Year	Coach	College
1987	John Thompson	Georgetown University
1988	John Chaney	Temple University
1992	Perry Clark	Tulane University

ASSOCIATED PRESS COACH OF THE YEAR AWARD

Year	Coach	College
1988	John Chaney	Temple University
1991	Randy Ayers	Ohio State University

U.S. BASKETBALL WRITERS ASSOCIATION COACH OF THE YEAR AWARD

Year	Coach	College
1987	John Chaney	Temple University
1988	John Chaney	Temple University
1991	Randy Ayers	Ohio State University
1992	Perry Clark	Tulane University

NATIONAL ASSOCIATION OF BASKETBALL COACHES
DIVISION I COACH OF THE YEAR AWARD

Year	Coach	College
1985	John Thompson	Georgetown University
1988	John Chaney	Temple University
1992	George Raveling	University of Southern California

AFRICAN-AMERICANS ON U.S. OLYMPIC BASKETBALL TEAMS

Men's Team

1956	K.C. Jones
	Bill Russell
	Carl Cain

1960	Walt Bellamy
	Bob Boozer
	Oscar Robertson

1964	Jim Barnes
	Joe Caldwell
	Walt Hazzard
	Luke Jackson
	George Wilson

1968	Jo Jo White
	Spencer Haywood
	Charlie Scott
	James King
	Calvin Fowles

1972	Tom Henderson
	Mike Bantom
	Dwight Jones
	Jim Brewer
	Ed Ratleff
	James Forbes

1976	Phil Ford
	Steve Sheppard
	Walter Davis
	Quinn Buckner
	Adrian Dantley
	Kenny Carr
	Scott May
	Phil Hubbard

1984	Patrick Ewing
	Michael Jordan
	Waymon Tisdale
	Alvin Robertson
	Sam Perkins
	Leon Wood
	Vern Fleming

1988	Mitchell Richmond
	Hersey Hawkins
	Willie Anderson
	Vernell Coles
	Charles D. Smith
	Charles E. Smith
	Herman "J.R." Reid
	David Robinson
	Stacey Augmon
	Danny Manning

John Thompson, Head Coach
George Raveling, Assistant

1992	Charles Barkley
	Scottie Pippen
	Michael Jordan
	Earvin "Magic" Johnson
	Clyde Drexler
	Patrick Ewing
	Karl Malone
	David Robinson

Lenny Wilkens, Assistant Coach

Women's Team

1976	Lusia Harris		Victoria Bullett
	Gail Marquis		Cynthia Brown
	Charlotte Lewis		Teresa Weatherspoon
	Patricia Roberts		Cynthia Cooper
1984	Cheryl Miller	1992	Daedra Charles
	Lynette Woodard		Medina Dixon
	Janice Lawrence		Tammie Jackson
	Pam McGee		Katrina McClain
	Teresa Edwards		Vickie Orr
	Cathy Boswell		Teresa Weatherspoon
1988	Teresa Edwards		Victoria Bullett
	Katrian McClain		Clarissa Davis
	Bridgette Gordon		Carolyn Jones

TOP AFRICAN-AMERICANS IN THE NATIONAL BASKETBALL ASSOCIATION
(Through 1992)

Scoring

	Player	Pts.	OR		Player	Pts.	OR
1.	Kareem Abdul-Jabbar	38,387	1	17.	Reggie Theus	19,015	23
2.	Wilt Chamberlain	31,419	2	18.	*Michael Jordan	19,000	24
3.	Elvin Hayes	27,313	3	19.	Chet Walker	18,831	25
4.	*Moses Malone	27,016	4	20.	Bob McAdoo	18,787	26
5.	Oscar Robertson	26,710	5	21.	Julius Erving	18,364	28
6.	Alex English	25,613	7	22.	Dave Bing	18,327	29
7.	Adrian Dantley	23,177	8	23.	World B. Free	17,955	30
8.	Elgin Baylor	23,149	9	24.	Calvin Murphy	17,949	31
9.	Hal Greer	21,586	10	25.	Lou Hudson	17,940	32
10.	Walt Bellamy	20,941	11	26.	Lenny Wilkens	17,772	33
11.	George Gervin	20,708	13	27.	*Mark Aquirre	17,542	36
12.	*Robert Parish	20,634	14	28.	Earl Monroe	17,454	37
13.	*Dominique Wilkens	19,975	15	29.	Earvin "Magic" Johnson	17,287	39
14.	Walter Davis	19,521	16	30.	*Rolando Blackmon	16,643	41
15.	*Bernard King	19,432	17	31.	*Isiah Thomas	16,575	42
16.	Bob Lanier	19,248	21				

*denotes players whose careers are still active for the 1992–93 season.

Reference Section

Rebounds

Player	Reb.	OR		Player	Reb.	OR
1. Wilt Chamberlain	23,924	1		5. *Moses Malone	15,894	5
2. Bill Russell	21,620	2		6. Nate Thurmond	14,464	6
3. Kareem Abdul-Jabbar	17,440	3		7. Walt Bellamy	14,241	7
4. Elvin Hayes	16,279	4		8. Wes Unseld	13,769	8

Most Games Played

Player	GP	OR		Player	GP	OR
1. Kareem Abdul-Jabbar	1,560	1		5. *Moses Malone	1,246	6
2. Elvin Hayes	1,303	2		6. Alex English	1,193	7
3. *Robert Parrish	1,260	4		7. Hal Greer	1,122	8
4. Paul Silas	1,254	5		8. Dennis Johnson	1,100	10

Most Field Goals Made

Player	FGM	OR		Player	FGM	OR
1. Kareem Abdul-Jabbar	15,837	1		5. Oscar Robertson	9,508	6
2. Wilt Chamberlain	12,681	2		6. *Moses Malone	9,307	7
3. Elvin Hayes	10,976	3		7. Elgin Baylor	8,693	9
4. Alex English	10,659	4		8. Hal Greer	8,504	11

Most Minutes Played

Player	Min.	OR		Player	Min.	OR
1. Kareem Abdul-Jabbar	57,446	1		5. Oscar Robertson	43,866	6
2. Elvin Hayes	50,000	2		6. Bill Russell	40,726	7
3. Wilt Chamberlain	47,859	3		7. Hal Greer	39,788	8
4. *Moses Malone	44,200	5		8. Walt Bellamy	38,940	9

Career Scoring Average

Player	Avr.	OR		Player	Avr.	OR
1. *Michael Jordon	32.3	1		5. George Gervin	26.2	7
2. Wilt Chamberlain	30.1	2		6. *Karl Malone	25.9	8
3. Elgin Baylor	27.4	3		7. Oscar Robertson	25.7	9
4. *Dominique Wilkens	26.2	6		8. Kareem Abdul-Jabbar	24.6	10

Highest Field Goal Percentage

Player	Pct.	OR		Player	Pct.	OR
1. Artis Gilmore	.599	1		5. *James Donaldson	.570	5
2. *Charles Barkley	.576	2		6. Kareem Abdul-Jabbar	.559	7
3. Steve Johnson	.572	3		7. *Buck Williams	.557	9
4. Darryl Dawkins	.572	4		8. *Otis Thorpe	.553	10

Highest Free Throw Percentage

Player	Pct.	OR		Player	Pct.	OR
1. Calvin Murphy	.892	3		3. *Ricky Pierce	.874	7
2. *Jeff Malone	.876	6		4. *Reggie Miller	.870	10

Most Free Throws Made

Player	FT	OR		Player	FT	OR
1. *Moses Malone	8,395	1		5. Wilt Chamberlain	6,057	8
2. Oscar Robertson	7,694	2		6. Elgin Baylor	5,763	9
3. Adrian Dantley	6,832	5		7. Len Wilkens	5,394	10
4. Kareem Abdul-Jabbar	6,712	6				

Most Assists

Player	Assists	OR		Player	Assists	OR
1. Earvin "Magic" Johnson	9,921	1		5. Len Wilkens	7,211	6
2. Oscar Robertson	9,887	2		6. Guy Rodgers	6,917	8
3. *Isiah Thomas	7,991	3		7. Nate Archibald	6,476	9
4. *Maurice Cheeks	7,285	5		8. John Lucas	6,454	10

Most Steals

Player	Stls.	OR		Player	Stls.	OR
1. *Maurice Cheeks	2,277	1		5. Gus Williams	1,638	5
2. *Alvin Robertson	1,791	2		6. *Michael Jordan	1,594	7
3. Earvin "Magic" Johnson	1,698	3		7. *Clyde Drexler	1,528	9
4. *Isiah Thomas	1,670	4		8. Julius Erving	1,508	10

Most Blocked Shots

Player	Blk.	OR		Player	Blk.	OR
1. Kareem Abdul-Jabbar	3,189	1		5. *Larry Nance	1,774	8
2. *Wayne Rollins	2,456	3		6. Elvin Hayes	1,771	9
3. George T. Johnson	2,082	5		7. Artis Gilmore	1,747	10
4. *Robert Parrish	2,049	6				

Most Personal Fouls

Player	F	OR		Player	F	OR
1. Kareem Abdul-Jabbar	4,657	1		5. *James Edwards	3,725	6
2. Elvin Hayes	4,193	2		6. Walt Bellamy	3,536	8
3. Hal Greer	3,855	4		7. Caldwell Jones	3,527	9
4. *Robert Parrish	3,800	5				

TOP AFRICAN-AMERICANS IN THE NATIONAL BASKETBALL ASSOCIATION AND AMERICAN BASKETBALL ASSOCIATION COMBINED

Scoring Average

Player	Avr.	OR	Player	Avr.	OR
1. *Michael Jordan	32.3	1	5. *Karl Malone	25.9	7
2. Wilt Chamberlain	30.1	2	6. Oscar Robertson	25.7	8
3. Elgin Baylor	27.4	3	7. George Gervin	25.1	9
4. *Dominique Wilkes	26.2	6			

All-Time Scoring

Player	Pts.	OR	Player	Pts.	OR
1. Kareem Abdul-Jabbar	38,387	1	6. Oscar Robertson	26,710	7
2. Wilt Chamberlain	31,419	2	7. George Gervin	26,595	8
3. Julius Erving	30,026	3	8. Alex English	25,613	10
4. *Moses Malone	29,187	4	9. Artis Gilmore	24,941	11
5. Elvin Hayes	27,313	6	10. Adrian Dantley	23,177	12

Most Field Goals

Player	FG	OR	Player	FG	OR
1. Kareem Abdul-Jabbar	15,837	1	5. Alex English	10,659	5
2. Wilt Chamberlain	12,681	2	6. George Gervin	10,368	7
3. Julius Erving	11,818	3	7. *Moses Malone	10,149	9
4. Elvin Hayes	10,976	4			

Highest Free Throw Percentage

Player	Pct.	OR	Player	Pct.	OR
1. Calvin Murphy	.892	3	3. *Ricky Pierce	.874	7
2. *Jeff Malone	.876	6			

Most Minutes Played

Player	Min.	OR	Player	Min.	OR
1. Kareem Abdul-Jabbar	57,446	1	5. Artis Gilmore	47,134	5
2. Elvin Hayes	50,000	2	6. Julius Erving	45,227	7
3. *Moses Malone	48,573	3	7. Oscar Robertson	43,866	8
4. Wilt Chamberlain	47,859	4	8. Bill Russell	40,726	10

PROFESSIONAL BASKETBALL HALL OF FAMERS

Coaches

Clarence "Bighouse" Gaines   1981

Teams

New York Renaissance   1963

Contributors

John McLendon   1978

Reference Section

KAREEM ABDUL-JABBAR

Born Lew Alcindor, April 16, 1947, in New York, N.Y.
High School—Power Memorial, New York, N.Y.
College—University of California, Los Angeles
1967, 1968, 1969 NCAA All-America
1967, 1969 United Press International College "Player of the Year"
1967, 1968, 1969 Most Outstanding Player in the NCAA Tournament
1970 NBA Rookie of the Year
NBA All-Star 1970–1974, 1976–1988
1971, 1972, 1974, 1976, 1977, 1980 NBA Most Valuable Player
1980, Chosen for the NBA 35th Anniversary Team
All-time leading scorer in the history of the NBA

Collegiate Record

Sea. — Team	G	Min.	FGA	FGM	Pct.	FTA	FTM	Pct.	Reb.	Pts.	Avg.
65–66 — UCLA	21	—	432	295	.683	179	106	.592	452	696	33.1
66–67 — UCLA	30	—	519	346	.667	274	178	.650	466	870	29.0
67–68 — UCLA	28	—	480	294	.613	237	146	.616	461	734	26.2
68–69 — UCLA	30	—	477	303	.635	188	115	.612	440	721	24.0
Varsity totals	88	—	1476	943	.639	699	439	.628	1367	2325	26.4

NBA Regular-Record Season

Season Team	G	Min.	FGM-FGA	Pct.	3-Pt.	FTM-FTA	Pct.	OFF	DEF	Tot.	Ast.	PF-OQ	ST	TO	BS	Pts.	Avg.
1969–70 Mil	82	3534	938–1810	.518	—	485–743	.653	—	—	1190	337	283-8	—	—	—	2361	28.8
1970–71 Mil	82	3288	1063–1843	.577	—	470–681	.690	—	—	1311	272	254-4	—	—	—	2596	31.7
1971–72 Mil	81	3583	1159–2019	.574	—	504–732	.598	—	—	1346	370	235-1	—	—	—	2822	34.8
1972–73 Mil	76	3254	982–1772	.554	—	328–460	.713	—	—	1224	379	207-0	—	—	—	2292	30.2
1973–74 Mil	81	3548	948–1759	.539	—	295–120	.702	287	891	1178	386	238-2	112	—	282	2191	27.0
1974–75 Mil	65	2747	812–1584	.513	—	325–426	.763	194	718	912	264	205-2	65	—	212	1949	30.0
1975–76 LA	82	3379	914–1728	.529	—	447–636	.703	272	1111	1383	413	292-6	119	—	338	2275	27.7
1976–77 LA	82	3016	888–1533	.579	—	376–536	.701	266	824	1090	319	252-4	101	—	261	2152	26.2
1977–78 LA	62	2265	662–1205	.550	—	274–350	.738	185	615	801	269	182-1	103	208	185	1600	25.8
1978–79 LA	80	3157	777–1347	.577	—	349–474	.736	207	818	1025	431	230-3	76	282	315	1903	23.9
1979–80 LA	82	3143	835–1383	.504	0–1	364–476	.765	190	696	886	371	216-2	81	297	280	2034	24.8
1980–81 LA	80	2976	836–1457	.573	0–1	423–553	.756	197	524	821	272	244-4	59	249	228	2095	26.2
1981–82 LA	76	2677	753–1301	.579	0–3	312–442	.706	172	487	659	225	224-0	53	230	207	1818	23.0
1982–83 LA	79	2554	722–1228	.588	0–2	278–371	.749	167	425	592	200	220-1	61	200	170	1722	21.8
1983–84 LA	80	2622	716–1238	.578	0–1	235–394	.723	169	418	587	211	211-1	55	221	143	1717	21.5
1984–85 LA Lakers	79	2630	723–1207	.599	0–1	289–396	.732	162	460	622	249	238-3	53	197	162	1735	22.0
1985–86 LA Lakers	79	2629	755–1338	.564	—	336–439	.765	133	345	478	280	248-2	67	130	203	1846	23.4
1986–87 LA Lakers	78	2441	560–993	.564	—	245–343	.714	152	371	523	203	245-2	49	97	186	1366	17.5
1987–88 LA Lakers	80	2308	480–903	.532	—	205–269	.762	118	360	478	135	216-1	48	92	159	1165	14.6
1988–89 LA Lakers	74	1695	313–659	.475	—	122–165	.739	103	231	334	74	196-1	38	85	95	748	10.1
Totals	1560	57446	15837–28307	.559	—	6712–9304	.721	—	—	17440	5660	4657-48	1160	3189	2527	38387	24.6

NBA Playoff Record

Sea.— Team	G	Min.	FGA	FGM	Pct.	FTA	FTM	Pct.	Reb.	Ast.	PF	Dq.	Pts.	Avg.
69–70—Milwaukee	10	435	245	139	.567	101	74	.733	168	41	25	1	352	35.2
70–71—Milwaukee	14	577	295	152	.515	101	68	.673	238	35	45	0	372	26.6
71–72—Milwaukee	11	510	318	139	.437	54	38	.704	200	56	35	0	316	28.7
72–73—Milwaukee	6	276	138	59	.428	35	19	.543	97	17	26	0	137	22.8
73–74—Milwaukee	16	758	402	224	.557	91	67	.736	253	78	41	0	515	32.2
76–77—Los Angeles	11	467	242	147	.607	120	87	.725	195	45	42	0	381	34.6
77–78—Los Angeles	3	134	73	38	.521	9	5	.556	41	11	14	1	81	27.0
78–79—Los Angeles	8	367	152	88	.579	62	52	.839	101	38	26	0	228	28.5
79–80—Los Angeles	15	618	346	198	.572	105	83	.790	181	46	51	0	479	31.9
80–81—Los Angeles	3	134	65	30	.462	28	20	.714	50	12	14	0	80	26.7
81–82—Los Angeles	14	493	221	115	.520	87	55	.632	119	51	45	0	285	20.4
82–83—Los Angeles	15	588	287	163	.568	106	80	.755	115	42	61	1	406	27.1
83–84—Los Angeles	21	767	371	206	.555	120	90	.750	173	79	71	2	502	23.9
84–85—L.A. Lakers	19	610	300	168	.560	103	80	.777	154	76	67	1	416	21.9
85–86—L.A. Lakers	14	489	282	157	.557	61	48	.787	83	49	54	0	362	25.9
86–87—L.A. Lakers	18	559	234	124	.530	122	97	.795	123	36	56	0	345	19.2
87–88—L.A. Lakers	24	718	304	141	.464	71	56	.789	131	36	81	1	338	14.1
88–89—L.A. Lakers	15	351	147	68	.463	43	31	.721	59	19	43	0	167	11.1
Totals	237	8851	4422	2356	.533	1419	1050	.740	2481	767	797	7	5762	24.3

NBA All-Star Game Record

Sea.— Team	Min.	FGA	FGM	Pct.	FTA	FTM	Pct.	Reb.	Ast.	PF	Dq.	Pts.
1970 —Milwaukee	18	8	4	.500	2	2	1.000	11	4	6	1	10
1971 —Milwaukee	30	16	8	.500	4	3	.750	14	1	2	0	19
1972 —Milwaukee	19	10	5	.500	2	2	1.000	7	2	0	0	12
1973 —Milwaukee				Selected, did not play.								
1974 —Milwaukee	23	11	7	.636	0	0	—	8	6	2	0	14
1975 —Milwaukee	19	10	3	.300	2	1	.500	10	3	2	0	7
1976 —Los Angeles	36	16	9	.563	4	4	1.000	15	3	3	0	22
1977 —Los Angeles	23	14	8	.571	6	5	.833	4	2	1	0	21
1979 —Los Angeles	28	12	5	.417	2	1	.500	8	3	4	0	11
1980 —Los Angeles	30	17	6	.353	6	5	.833	16	9	5	0	17
1981 —Los Angeles	23	9	6	.667	3	3	1.000	6	4	3	0	15
1982 —Los Angeles	22	10	1	.100	0	0	—	3	1	3	0	2
1983 —Los Angeles	32	12	9	.750	3	2	.667	6	5	1	0	20
1984 —Los Angeles	37	19	11	.579	4	3	.750	13	2	5	0	25
1985 —L.A. Lakers	23	10	5	.500	2	1	.500	6	1	5	0	11
1986 —L.A. Lakers	32	15	9	.600	4	3	.750	7	2	4	0	21
1987 —L.A. Lakers	27	9	4	.444	2	2	1.000	8	3	5	0	10
1988 —L.A. Lakers	14	9	4	.444	2	2	1.000	4	0	3	0	10
1989 —L.A. Lakers	13	6	1	.167	2	2	1.000	3	0	3	0	4
Totals	449	213	105	.493	50	41	.820	149	51	57	1	251

Reference Section

NATHANIEL ARCHIBALD (Nate—Tiny)

Born September 2, 1948, in New York, N.Y.
High School—DeWitt Clinton, Bronx, N.Y.
College—Arizona Western and University of Texas-El Paso
Inducted into the Basketball Hall of Fame, 1990
1981 NBA All-Star Game Most Valuable Player

Collegiate Record

Sea.—Team	G	Min.	FGA	FGM	Pct.	FTA	FTM	Pct.	Reb.	Pts.	Avg.
66–67—Arizona Western	27	—	—	303	—	—	190	—	—	796	29.5
67–68—Texas-El Paso	23	—	281	131	.466	140	102	.729	81	364	15.8
68–69—Texas-El Paso	25	—	374	199	.532	194	161	.830	69	559	22.4
69–70—Texas-El Paso	25	—	351	180	.513	225	176	.782	66	536	21.4
Junior college totals	27	—	—	303	—	—	190	—	—	796	29.5
Four-year-college totals	73	—	1006	510	.507	559	439	.785	216	1459	20.0

NBA Regular-Season Record

Sea.—Team	G	Min.	FGA	FGM	Pct.	FTA	FTM	Pct.	Reb.	Ast.	PF	Dq.	Pts.	Avg.
70–71—Cincinnati	82	2867	1095	486	.444	444	336	.757	242	450	218	2	1308	16.0
71–72—Cincinnati	76	3272	1511	734	.486	824	677	.822	222	701	198	3	2145	28.2
72–73—Kansas City/Omaha	80	3681	2106	1028	.488	783	663	.847	223	910	207	2	2719	34.0
73–74—K.C./Omaha	35	1272	492	222	.451	211	173	.820	85	266	76	0	617	17.6
74–75—K.C./Omaha	82	3244	1664	759	.456	748	652	.872	222	557	187	0	2170	26.5
75–76—Kansas City	78	3184	1583	717	.453	625	501	.802	213	615	169	0	1935	24.8
76–77—N.Y. Mets	34	1277	560	250	.446	251	197	.785	80	254	77	1	697	20.5
77–78—Buffalo					Selected, did not play—torn achilles tendon.									
78–79—Boston	69	1662	573	259	.452	307	242	.788	103	324	132	2	760	11.0
79–80—Boston	80	2864	794	383	.482	435	361	.830	197	671	218	2	1131	14.1
80–81—Boston	80	2820	766	382	.499	419	342	.816	176	618	201	1	1106	13.8
81–82—Boston	68	2167	652	308	.472	316	236	.747	116	541	131	1	858	12.6
82–83—Boston	66	1811	553	235	.425	296	220	.743	91	409	110	1	695	10.5
83–84—Milwaukee	46	1038	279	136	.487	101	64	.634	76	160	78	0	340	7.4
Totals	876	31159	12628	5899	.467	5760	4664	.810	2046	6476	2002	15	16481	18.8

NBA Playoff Record

Sea.—Team	G	Min.	FGA	FGM	Pct.	FTA	FTM	Pct.	Reb.	Ast.	PF	Dq.	Pts.	Avg.
74–75—K.C./Omaha	6	242	118	43	.364	43	35	.814	11	32	18	0	121	20.2
79–80—Boston	9	332	89	45	.506	42	37	.881	11	71	28	1	128	14.2
80–81—Boston	17	630	211	95	.450	94	76	.809	28	107	39	0	266	15.6
81–82—Boston	8	277	70	30	.429	28	25	.893	17	52	21	0	85	10.6
82–83—Boston	7	161	68	22	.324	29	22	.759	10	44	12	0	67	9.6
Totals	47	1642	556	235	.423	236	195	.826	77	306	118	1	667	14.2

NBA All-Star Game Record

Sea.—Team	Min.	FGA	FGM	Pct.	FTA	FTM	Pct.	Reb.	Ast.	PF	Dq.	Pts.
1973—Kansas City/Omaha	27	12	6	.500	5	5	1.000	1	5	1	0	17
1975—K.C./Omaha	36	15	10	.667	8	7	.875	2	6	2	0	27
1976—Kansas City	30	13	5	.385	3	3	1.000	5	7	0	0	13
1980—Boston	21	8	0	.000	3	2	.667	3	6	1	0	2
1981—Boston	25	7	4	.571	3	1	.333	5	9	3	0	9
1982—Boston	23	5	2	.400	2	2	1.000	2	7	3	0	6
Totals	162	60	27	.450	24	20	.833	18	40	10	0	74

ELGIN GAY BAYLOR

Born September 16, 1934, in Washington, D.C.
High Schools—Phelps Vocational (Fr.-Jr.) and Spingarn (Sr.), Washington, D.C.
Colleges—The College of Idaho, Caldwell, Idaho, and Seattle University, Seattle, Wash.
Inducted into the Basketball Hall of Fame, 1976
Chosen to the NBA 35th Anniversary All-Time Team, 1980
Chosen the Most Outstanding Player in the 1958 NCAA Tournament

Collegiate Record

Sea.—Team	G	Min.	FGA	FGM	Pct.	FTA	FTM	Pct.	Reb.	Pts.	Avg.
54–55—College of Idaho	26	—	651	332	.510	232	150	.647	492	814	31.3
55–56—Seattle			Did Not Play—Transfer Student								
56–57—Seattle	25	—	555	271	.488	251	201	.801	508	743	29.7
57–58—Seattle	29	—	697	353	.506	308	237	.769	559	943	32.5
College Totals	80	—	1903	956	.502	791	588	.743	1559	2500	31.3

NOTE: 1954–55 rebound figures are for 24 games. Baylor played for Westside Ford, an AAU team in Seattle, during 1955–56 season (averaged 34 points per game).

NBA Regular-Season Record

Sea.—Team	G	Min.	FGA	FGM	Pct.	FTA	FTM	Pct.	Reb.	Ast.	PF	Dq.	Pts.	Avg.
58–59—Minneapolis	70	2855	1482	605	.408	685	532	.777	1050	287	270	4	1742	24.9
59–60—Minneapolis	70	2873	1781	755	.424	770	564	.732	1150	243	234	2	2074	29.6
60–61—Los Angeles	73	3133	2166	931	.430	863	676	.783	1447	371	279	3	2538	34.8
61–62—Los Angeles	48	2129	1588	680	.428	631	476	.754	892	222	155	1	1836	38.3
62–63—Los Angeles	80	3370	2273	1029	.453	790	661	.837	1146	386	226	1	2719	34.0
63–64—Los Angeles	78	3164	1778	756	.425	586	471	.804	936	347	235	1	1983	25.4
64–65—Los Angeles	74	3056	1903	763	.401	610	483	.792	950	280	235	0	2009	27.1
65–66—Los Angeles	65	1975	1034	415	.401	337	249	.739	621	224	157	0	1079	16.6
66–67—Los Angeles	70	2706	1658	711	.429	541	440	.813	898	215	211	1	1862	26.6
67–68—Los Angeles	77	3029	1709	757	.443	621	488	.786	941	355	232	0	2002	26.0
68–69—Los Angeles	76	3064	1632	730	.447	567	421	.743	805	408	204	0	1881	24.8
69–70—Los Angeles	54	2213	1051	511	.486	357	276	.773	559	292	132	1	1298	24.0
70–71—Los Angeles	2	57	19	8	.421	6	4	.667	11	2	6	0	20	10.0
71–72—Los Angeles	9	239	97	42	.433	27	22	.815	57	18	20	0	106	11.8
Totals	846	33863	20171	8693	.431	7391	5763	.780	11463	3650	2596	14	23149	27.4

NBA Playoff Record

Sea.—Team	G	Min.	FGA	FGM	Pct.	FTA	FTM	Pct.	Reb.	Ast.	PF	Dq.	Pts.	Avg.
58–59—Minneapolis	13	556	303	122	.403	113	87	.770	156	43	52	0	331	25.5
59–60—Minneapolis	9	408	234	111	.474	94	79	.840	128	31	38	0	301	33.4
60–61—Los Angeles	12	540	362	170	.470	142	117	.824	183	55	44	1	457	38.1
61–62—Los Angeles	13	571	425	186	.428	168	130	.774	230	47	45	1	502	38.6
62–63—Los Angeles	13	562	362	160	.442	126	104	.825	177	58	58	0	424	32.6
63–64—Los Angeles	5	221	119	45	.378	40	31	.775	58	28	17	0	121	24.2
64–65—Los Angeles	1	5	2	0	.000	0	0	.000	0	1	0	0	0	0.0
65–66—Los Angeles	14	586	328	145	.442	105	85	.810	197	52	38	0	375	26.8
66–67—Los Angeles	3	121	76	28	.368	20	15	.750	39	9	6	0	71	23.7
67–68—Los Angeles	15	633	376	176	.468	112	76	.679	218	60	41	0	428	28.5
68–69—Los Angeles	18	640	278	107	.385	100	63	.630	166	74	56	0	277	15.4
69–70—Los Angeles	18	667	296	138	.466	81	60	.741	173	83	50	1	336	18.7
Totals	134	5510	3161	1388	.439	1101	847	.769	1725	541	445	3	3623	27.0

NBA All-Star Game Record

Sea.—Team	Min.	FGA	FGM	Pct.	FTA	FTM	Pct.	Reb.	Ast.	PF	Dq.	Pts.
1959—Minneapolis	32	20	10	.500	5	4	.800	11	1	3	0	24
1960—Minneapolis	28	18	10	.556	7	5	.714	13	3	4	0	25
1961—Los Angeles	27	11	3	.273	10	9	.900	10	4	5	0	15
1962—Los Angeles	37	23	10	.435	14	12	.857	9	4	2	0	32
1963—Los Angeles	36	15	4	.267	13	9	.692	14	7	0	0	17
1964—Los Angeles	29	15	5	.333	11	5	.455	8	5	1	0	15
1965—Los Angeles	27	13	5	.385	8	8	1.000	7	0	4	0	18
1967—Los Angeles	20	14	8	.571	4	4	1.000	5	5	2	0	20
1968—Los Angeles	27	13	8	.615	7	6	.857	6	1	5	0	22
1969—Los Angeles	32	13	5	.385	12	11	.917	9	5	2	0	21
1970—Los Angeles	26	9	2	.222	7	5	.714	7	3	3	0	9
Totals	321	164	70	.427	98	78	.796	99	38	31	0	218

NBA Coaching Record

Sea.—Club	Regular Season				Playoffs	
	W.	L.	Pct.	Pos.	W.	L.
1974–75—New Orleans	0	1	.000	– †	—	—
1976–77—New Orleans	21	35	.375	5†	—	—
1977–78—New Orleans	39	43	.476	5†	—	—
1978–79—New Orleans	26	56	.317	6†	—	—
Totals (4 seasons)	86	135	.389		—	—

†Central Division.

WALTER J. BELLAMY (Walt)

Born July 24, 1939, in New Bern, N.C.
High School—J.T. Barber, New Bern, N.C.
College—Indiana University
Inducted into the Basketball Hall of Fame, 1993
All-American, 1961
Member of the 1960 United States Olympic Team

Collegiate Record

Sea.—Team	G	Min.	FGA	FGM	Pct.	FTA	FTM	Pct.	Reb.	Pts.	Avg.
57–58—Indiana‡			Freshman team did not play intercollegiate schedule.								
58–59—Indiana	22	—	289	148	.512	141	86	.610	335	382	17.4
59–60—Indiana	24	—	396	212	.535	161	113	.702	324	537	22.4
60–61—Indiana	24	—	389	195	.501	204	132	.647	428	522	21.8
Varsity totals	70	—	1074	555	.517	506	331	.654	1087	1441	20.6

NBA Regular-Season Record

Sea.—Team	G	Min.	FGA	FGM	Pct.	FTA	FTM	Pct.	Reb.	Ast.	PF	Dq.	Pts.	Avg.
61–62—Chicago	79	3344	1875	973	.519	853	549	.644	1500	210	281	6	2495	31.6
62–63—Chicago	80	3306	1595	840	.527	821	553	.674	1309	233	283	7	2233	27.9
63–64—Baltimore	80	3394	1582	811	.513	825	537	.651	1361	126	300	7	2159	27.0
64–65—Baltimore	80	3301	1441	733	.509	752	515	.685	1166	191	260	2	1981	24.8
65–66—Baltimore-New York	80	3352	1373	695	.506	689	430	.624	1254	235	294	9	1820	22.8
66–67—New York	79	3010	1084	565	.521	580	369	.636	1064	206	275	5	1499	19.0
67–68—New York	82	2695	944	511	.541	529	350	.662	961	164	259	3	1372	16.7
68–69—New York-Detroit	88	3159	1103	563	.510	618	401	.649	1101	176	320	5	1527	17.4
69–70—Detroit-Atlanta	79	2028	671	351	.523	373	215	.576	707	143	260	5	917	11.6
70–71—Atlanta	82	2908	879	433	.493	556	336	.604	1060	230	271	4	1202	14.7
71–72—Atlanta	82	3187	1089	593	.545	581	340	.585	1049	262	255	2	1526	18.6
72–73—Atlanta	74	2802	901	455	.505	526	283	.538	964	179	244	1	1193	16.1
73–74—Atlanta	77	2440	801	389	.486	383	233	.608	740	189	232	2	1011	13.1
74–75—New Orleans	1	14	2	2	1.000	2	2	1.000	5	0	2	0	6	6.0
Totals	1043	38940	15340	7914	.516	8088	5113	.632	14241	2544	3536	58	20941	20.1

NBA Playoff Record

Sea.—Team	G	Min.	FGA	FGM	Pct.	FTA	FTM	Pct.	Reb.	Ast.	PF	Dq.	Pts.	Avg.
64–65—Baltimore	10	427	158	74	.468	92	61	.663	151	34	38	0	209	20.9
66–67—New York	4	157	54	28	.519	29	17	.586	66	12	15	0	73	18.3
67–68—New York	6	277	107	45	.421	48	30	.625	96	21	22	0	120	20.0
69–70—Atlanta	9	368	126	59	.468	46	33	.717	140	35	32	0	151	16.8
70–71—Atlanta	5	216	69	41	.594	29	22	.759	72	10	16	0	104	20.8
71–72—Atlanta	6	247	86	42	.488	43	27	.628	82	11	20	0	111	18.5
72–73—Atlanta	6	247	86	34	.395	31	14	.452	73	13	17	0	82	13.7
Totals	46	1939	686	323	.471	318	204	.642	680	136	160	0	850	18.5

Reference Section

NBA All-Star Game Record

Sea.—Team	Min.	FGA	FGM	Pct.	FTA	FTM	Pct.	Reb.	Ast.	PF	Dq.	Pts.
1962—Chicago	29	18	10	.556	8	3	.375	17	1	6	1	23
1963—Chicago	14	4	1	.250	2	0	.000	1	2	3	0	2
1964—Baltimore	23	11	4	.364	5	3	.600	7	0	3	0	11
1965—Baltimore	17	5	4	.800	4	4	1.000	5	1	3	0	12
Totals	83	38	19	.500	19	10	.526	30	4	15	1	48

DAVID BING

Born November 24, 1943, in Washington, D.C.
High School—Springarn-Washington, D.C.
College—Syracuse University
Inducted into the Basketball Hall of Fame, 1989
All-American, 1966
1976 NBA All-Star Game Most Valuable Player

Collegiate Record

Sea.—Team	G	Min.	FGA	FGM	Pct.	FTA	FTM	Pct.	Reb.	Pts.	Avg.
62–63—Syracuse	17	—	341	170	.499	131	97	.740	192	437	25.7
63–64—Syracuse	25	—	460	215	.467	172	126	.733	206	556	22.2
64–65—Syracuse	23	—	444	206	.464	162	121	.747	277	533	23.2
65–66—Syracuse	28	—	569	308	.541	222	178	.802	303	794	28.4
Varsity totals	76	—	1473	729	.495	556	425	.764	786	1883	24.8

NBA Regular-Season Record

Sea.—Team	G	Min.	FGA	FGM	Pct.	FTA	FTM	Pct.	Reb.	Ast.	PF	Dq.	Pts.	Avg.
66–67—Detroit	80	2762	1522	664	.436	370	273	.738	359	330	217	2	1601	20.0
67–68—Detroit	79	3209	1893	835	.441	668	472	.707	373	509	254	2	2142	27.1
68–69—Detroit	77	3039	1594	678	.425	623	444	.713	382	546	256	3	1800	23.4
69–70—Detroit	70	2334	1295	575	.444	580	454	.783	299	418	196	0	1604	22.9
70–71—Detroit	82	3065	1710	799	.467	772	615	.797	364	408	228	4	2213	27.0
71–72—Detroit	45	1936	891	369	.414	354	278	.785	186	317	138	3	1016	22.6
72–73—Detroit	82	3361	1545	692	.448	560	456	.814	298	637	229	1	1840	22.4
73–74—Detroit	81	3124	1336	582	.436	438	356	.813	281	555	216	1	1520	18.8
74–75—Detroit	79	3222	1333	578	.434	424	343	.809	286	610	222	3	1499	19.0
75–76—Washington	82	2945	1113	497	.447	422	332	.787	237	492	262	0	1326	16.2
76–77—Washington	64	1516	597	271	.454	176	136	.773	143	275	150	1	678	10.6
77–78—Boston	80	2256	940	422	.449	296	244	.824	212	300	247	2	1088	13.6
Totals	901	32769	15769	6962	.441	5683	4400	.775	3420	5397	2615	22	18327	20.3

NBA Playoff Record

Sea.—Team	G	Min.	FGA	FGM	Pct.	FTA	FTM	Pct.	Reb.	Ast.	PF	Dq.	Pts.	Avg.
67–68—Detroit	6	254	166	68	.410	45	33	.733	24	29	21	0	169	28.2
73–74—Detroit	7	312	131	55	.420	30	22	.733	26	42	20	0	132	18.9
74–75—Detroit	3	134	47	20	.426	13	8	.615	11	29	12	0	48	16.0
75–76—Washington	7	209	76	34	.447	35	28	.800	18	28	18	0	96	13.7
76–77—Wsahington	8	55	32	14	.438	4	4	1.000	6	5	5	0	32	4.0
Totals	**31**	**964**	**452**	**191**	**.423**	**127**	**95**	**.748**	**85**	**133**	**76**	**0**	**477**	**15.4**

NBA All-Star Game Record

Sea.—Team	Min.	FGA	FGM	Pct.	FTA	FTM	Pct.	Reb.	Ast.	PF	Dq.	Pts.
1968—Detroit	20	7	4	.571	1	1	1.000	2	4	3	0	9
1969—Detroit	13	3	1	.333	1	1	1.000	0	3	0	0	3
1971—Detroit	19	7	2	.286	0	0	—	2	2	1	0	4
1973—Detroit	19	4	0	.000	2	2	1.000	3	0	1	0	2
1974—Detroit	16	9	2	.222	1	1	1.000	6	2	1	0	5
1975—Detroit	12	2	0	.000	2	2	1.000	0	1	0	0	2
1976—Washington	26	11	7	.636	2	2	1.000	3	4	1	0	16
Totals	**125**	**43**	**16**	**.372**	**9**	**9**	**1.000**	**16**	**16**	**7**	**0**	**41**

WILTON NORMAN CHAMBERLAIN (Wilt)

Born August 21, 1936, in Philadelphia, Pa.
High School—Overbrook, Philadelphia, Pa.
College—University of Kansas, Lawrence, Kan.
Inducted into the Basketball Hall of Fame, 1978
Chosen to the NBA 35th Anniversary All-Time Team, 1980
NBA Most Valuable Player, 1960, 1966, 1967, 1968
NBA All-Star Game Most Valuable Player, 1960
NBA Rookie of the Year, 1960
Played with Harlem Globetrotters during 1958–59 season.

Collegiate Record

Year	G	Min.	FGA	FGM	Pct.	FTA	FTM	Pct.	Reb.	Pts.	Avg.
55–56			(Freshmen team did not play an intercollegiate schedule)								
56–57	27	—	588	275	.468	399	250	.627	510	800	26.6
57–58	21	—	482	228	.473	291	177	.608	367	633	30.1
Varsity Totals	**48**	**—**	**1070**	**503**	**.470**	**690**	**427**	**.619**	**877**	**1433**	**29.9**

NBA Regular-Season Record

Sea.—Team	G	Min.	FGA	FGM	Pct.	FTA	FTM	Pct.	Reb.	Ast.	PF	Dq.	Pts.	Avg.
59–60—Philadelphia	72	3338	2311	1065	.461	991	577	.582	1941	168	150	0	2707	37.6
60–61—Philadelphia	79	3773	2457	1251	.509	1054	531	.504	2149	148	130	0	3033	38.4
61–62—Philadelphia	80	3882	3159	1597	.505	1363	835	.613	2052	192	123	0	4029	50.4

Reference Section

Sea.—Team	G	Min.	FGA	FGM	Pct.	FTA	FTM	Pct.	Reb.	Ast.	PF	Dq.	Pts.	Avg.
62–63—San Francisco	80	3806	2770	1463	.528	1113	660	.593	1946	275	136	0	3586	44.8
63–64—San Francisco	80	3689	2298	1204	.524	1016	540	.531	1787	403	182	0	2948	36.9
64–65—S.F.-Phila.	73	3301	2083	1063	.510	880	408	.464	1673	250	146	0	2534	34.7
65–66—Philadelphia	79	3737	1990	1074	.540	976	501	.513	1943	414	171	0	2649	33.5
66–67—Philadelphia	81	3682	1150	785	.683	875	386	.441	1957	630	143	0	1956	24.1
67–68—Philadelphia	82	3836	1377	819	.595	932	354	.380	1952	702	160	0	1992	24.3
68–69—Los Angeles	81	3669	1099	641	.583	857	382	.446	1712	366	142	0	1664	20.5
69–70—Los Angeles	12	505	227	129	.568	157	70	.446	221	49	31	0	328	27.3
70–71—Los Angeles	82	3630	1226	668	.545	669	360	.538	1493	352	174	0	1696	20.7
71–72—Los Angeles	82	3469	764	496	.649	524	221	.422	1572	329	196	0	1213	14.8
72–73—Los Angeles	82	3542	586	426	.727	455	232	.510	1526	365	191	0	1084	13.2
Totals	1045	47859	23497	12681	.540	11862	6057	.511	23924	4643	2075	0	31419	30.1

NBA Playoff Record

Sea.—Team	G	Min.	FGA	FGM	Pct.	FTA	FTM	Pct.	Reb.	Ast.	PF	Dq.	Pts.	Avg.
59–60—Philadelphia	9	415	252	125	.496	110	49	.445	232	19	17	0	299	33.2
60–61—Philadelphia	3	144	96	45	.469	38	21	.553	69	6	10	0	111	37.0
61–62—Philadelphia	12	576	347	162	.467	151	96	.636	319	37	27	0	420	35.0
63–64—San Francisco	12	558	322	175	.543	139	66	.475	302	39	27	0	416	34.7
64–65—Philadelphia	11	536	232	123	.530	136	76	.559	299	48	29	0	322	29.3
65–66—Philadelphia	5	240	110	56	.509	68	28	.412	151	15	10	0	140	28.0
66–67—Philadelphia	15	718	228	132	.579	160	62	.388	437	135	37	0	326	21.7
67–68—Philadelphia	13	631	232	124	.534	158	60	.380	321	85	29	0	308	23.7
68–69—Los Angeles	18	832	176	96	.545	148	58	.392	444	46	56	0	250	13.9
69–70—Los Angeles	18	851	288	158	.549	202	82	.406	399	81	42	0	398	22.1
70–71—Los Angeles	12	554	187	85	.455	97	50	.515	242	53	33	0	220	18.3
71–72—Los Angeles	15	703	142	80	.563	122	60	.492	315	49	47	0	220	14.7
72–73—Los Angeles	17	801	116	64	.552	98	49	.500	383	60	48	0	177	10.4
Totals	160	7559	2728	1425	.522	1627	757	.465	3913	673	412	0	3607	22.5

NBA All-Star Game Record

Sea.—Team	Min.	FGA	FGM	Pct.	FTA	FTM	Pct.	Reb.	Ast.	PF	Dq.	Pts.
1960—Philadelphia	30	20	9	.450	7	5	.714	25	2	1	0	23
1961—Philadelphia	38	8	2	.250	15	8	.533	18	5	1	0	12
1962—Philadelphia	37	23	17	.739	16	8	.500	24	1	4	0	42
1963—San Francisco	35	11	7	.636	7	3	.429	19	0	2	0	17
1964—San Francisco	37	14	4	.286	14	11	.786	20	1	2	0	19
1965—San Francisco	31	15	9	.600	8	2	.250	16	1	4	0	20
1966—Philadelphia	25	11	8	.727	9	5	.556	9	3	2	0	21
1967—Philadelphia	39	7	6	.857	5	2	.400	22	4	1	0	14
1968—Philadelphia	25	4	3	.750	4	1	.250	7	6	2	0	7
1969—Los Angeles	27	3	2	.667	1	0	.000	12	2	2	0	4
1971—Los Angeles	18	1	1	1.000	0	0	.000	8	5	0	0	2
1972—Los Angeles	24	3	3	1.000	8	2	.250	10	3	2	0	8
1973—Los Angeles	22	2	1	.500	0	0	.000	7	3	0	0	2
Totals	388	122	72	.590	94	47	.500	197	36	23	0	191

ABA Coaching Record

Sea.—Club	W.	L.	Pct.	Pos.	W.	L.
		Regular Season			Playoffs	
1973-74—San Diego	37	47	.440	T4	2	4

JULIUS W. ERVING, II (Dr. J.)

Born February 22, 1950, in Roosevelt, N.Y.
High School—Roosevelt, Roosevelt, N.Y.
College—University of Massachusetts
Inducted into the Basketball Hall of Fame, 1993
American Basketball Association Most Valuable Player, 1974, 1976
Co-Most Valuable Player, 1975
Chosen to the NBA 35th Anniversary All-Time Team, 1980
81 NBA Most Valuable Player, 1977
NBA All-Star Game Most Valuable Player, 1985

Collegiate Record

Sea.—Team	G	Min.	FGA	FGM	Pct.	FTA	FTM	Pct.	Reb.	Pts.	Avg.
68–69—Massachusetts†	15	–	216	112	.519	81	49	.605	214	273	18.2
69–70—Massachusetts	25	969	468	238	.509	230	167	.726	522	643	25.7
70–71—Massachusetts	27	1029	609	286	.470	206	155	.752	527	727	26.9
Varsity totals	52	1998	1077	524	.487	436	322	.739	1049	1370	26.3

ABA Regular-Season Record

Sea.—Team	G	Min.	2-Point FGA	FGM	Pct.	3-Point FGA	FGM	Pct.	FTA	FTM	Pct.	Reb.	Ast.	Pts.	Avg.
71–72—Virginia	84	3513	1810	907	.501	16	3	.188	627	467	.745	1319	335	2290	27.3
72–73—Virginia	71	2993	1780	889	.499	24	5	.208	612	475	.776	867	298	2268	31.9
73–74—New York	84	3398	1742	897	.515	43	17	.395	593	454	.766	899	434	2299	27.4
74–75—New York	84	3402	1719	885	.515	87	29	.333	608	486	.799	914	462	2343	27.9
75–76—New York	84	3244	1770	915	.517	103	34	.330	662	530	.801	925	423	2462	29.3
Totals	407	16550	8821	4493	.509	273	88	.322	3102	2412	.778	4924	1952	11662	28.7

ABA Playoff Record

ABA Playoff Most Valuable Player (1974, 1976).

Sea.—Team	G	Min.	2-Point FGA	FGM	Pct.	3-Point FGA	FGM	Pct.	FTA	FTM	Pct.	Reb.	Ast.	Pts.	Avg.
71–72—Virginia	11	504	280	146	.521	4	1	.250	85	71	.835	224	72	366	33.3
72–73—Virginia	5	219	109	59	.541	3	0	.000	40	30	.750	45	16	148	29.6
73–74—New York	14	579	294	156	.531	11	5	.455	85	63	.741	135	67	390	27.9
74–75—New York	5	211	113	55	.487	8	0	.000	32	27	.844	49	28	137	27.4
75–76—New York	13	551	286	156	.545	14	4	.286	158	127	.804	164	64	451	34.7
Totals	48	2064	1082	572	.529	40	10	.250	400	318	.795	671	247	1492	31.1

Reference Section

ABA All-Star Game Record

Sea.—Team	Min.	2-Point			3-Point			FTA	FTM	Pct.	Reb.	Ast.	Pts.
		FGA	FGM	Pct.	FGA	FGM	Pct.						
1972—Virginia	25	15	9	.600	0	0	—	2	2	1.000	6	3	20
1973—Virginia	30	16	8	.500	0	0	—	8	6	.750	5	1	22
1974—New York	27	15	6	.400	0	0	—	2	2	1.000	11	8	14
1975—New York	27	11	5	.455	1	1	1.000	10	8	.800	7	7	21
1976—New York	25	12	9	.750	1	0	.000	7	5	.714	7	5	23
Totals	134	69	37	.536	2	1	.500	29	23	.793	36	24	100

NBA Regular-Season Record

Sea.—Team	G	Min.	FGA	FGM	Pct.	FTA	FTM	Pct.	Reb.	Ast.	PF	Dq.	Pts.	Avg.
76–77—Philadelphia	82	2940	1373	685	.499	515	400	.777	695	306	251	1	1770	21.6
77–78—Philadelphia	74	2429	1217	611	.502	362	306	.845	481	279	207	0	1528	20.6
78–79—Philadelphia	78	2802	1455	715	.491	501	373	.745	564	357	207	0	1803	23.1
79–80—Philadelphia	78	2812	1614	838	.519	534	420	.787	576	355	208	0	2100	26.9
80–81—Philadelphia	82	2874	1524	794	.521	536	422	.787	657	364	233	0	2014	24.6
81–82—Philadelphia	81	2789	1428	780	.546	539	411	.763	557	319	229	1	1974	24.4
82–83—Philadelphia	72	2421	1170	605	.517	435	330	.759	491	263	202	1	1542	21.4
83–84—Philadelphis	77	2683	1324	678	.512	483	364	.754	532	309	217	3	1727	22.4
84–85—Philadelphia	78	2535	1236	610	.494	442	338	.765	414	233	199	0	1561	20.0
85–86—Philadelphia	74	2474	1085	521	.480	368	289	.785	370	248	196	3	1340	18.1
86–87—Philadelphia	60	1918	850	400	.471	235	191	.813	264	191	137	0	1005	16.8
Totals	836	28677	14276	7237	.507	4950	3844	.777	5601	3224	2286	9	18364	22.0

NBA Playoff Record

Sea.—Team	G	Min.	FGA	FGM	Pct.	FTA	FTM	Pct.	Reb.	Ast.	PF	Dq.	Pts.	Avg.
76–77—Philadelphia	19	758	390	204	.523	134	110	.821	122	85	45	0	518	27.3
77–78—Philadelphia	10	358	180	88	.489	56	42	.750	97	40	30	0	218	21.8
78–79—Philadelphia	9	372	172	89	.517	67	51	.761	70	53	22	0	229	25.4
79–80—Philadelphia	18	694	338	165	.488	136	108	.794	136	79	56	0	440	24.4
80–81—Philadelphia	16	592	301	143	.475	107	81	.757	114	54	54	0	367	22.9
81–82—Philadelphia	21	780	324	168	.519	165	124	.752	156	99	55	0	461	22.0
82–83—Philadelphia	13	493	211	95	.450	68	49	.721	99	44	42	1	239	18.4
83–84—Philadelphia	5	194	76	36	.474	22	19	.864	32	25	14	0	91	18.2
84–85—Philadelphia	13	434	187	84	.449	63	54	.857	73	48	34	0	222	17.1
85–86—Philadelphia	12	433	180	81	.450	65	48	.738	70	50	32	0	212	17.7
86–87—Philadelphia	5	180	82	34	.415	25	21	.840	25	17	19	0	91	18.2
Totals	141	5288	2441	1187	.486	908	707	.779	994	594	403	1	3088	21.9

NBA All-Star Game Record

Sea.—Team	Min.	FGA	FGM	Pct.	FTA	FTM	Pct.	Reb.	Ast.	PF	Dq.	Pts.
1977—Philadelphia	30	20	12	.600	6	6	1.000	12	3	2	0	30
1978—Philadelphia	27	14	3	.214	12	10	.833	8	3	1	0	16
1979—Philadelphia	39	22	10	.455	12	9	.750	8	5	4	0	29

Sea.— Team	Min.	FGA	FGM	Pct.	FTA	FTM	Pct.	Reb.	Ast.	PF	Dq.	Pts.
1980—Philadelphia	20	12	4	.333	4	3	.750	5	2	5	0	11
1981—Philadelphia	29	15	6	.400	7	6	.857	3	2	2	0	18
1982—Philadelphia	32	16	7	.438	4	2	.500	8	2	4	0	16
1983—Philadelphia	28	19	11	.579	3	3	1.000	6	3	1	0	25
1984—Philadelphia	36	22	14	.636	8	6	.750	8	5	4	0	34
1985—Philadelphia	23	15	5	.333	2	2	1.000	4	3	3	0	12
1986—Philadelphia	19	10	4	.400	2	0	.000	4	2	2	0	8
1987—Philadelphia	33	13	9	.692	3	3	1.000	4	5	3	0	22
Totals	316	178	85	.478	63	50	.794	70	35	31	0	221

WALTER FRAZIER (Walt)

Born March 29, 1945, in Atlanta, Ga
High School—David Howard, Atlanta, Ga
College—Southern Illinois University
Inducted into the Basketball Hall of Fame, 1986
Most Valuable Player in the 1967 National Invitational Tournament
1975 NBA All-Star Game Most Valuable Player

Collegiate Record

Sea.—Team	G	Min.	FGA	FGM	Pct.	FTA	FTM	Pct.	Reb.	Pts.	Avg.
63–64—Southern Illinois	14	—	225	133	.591	85	52	.612	129	318	22.7
64–65—Southern Illinois	24	—	353	161	.456	111	88	.793	221	410	17.1
65–66—Southern Illinois					Did not play—ineligible						
66–67—Southern Illinois	26	—	397	192	.484	126	90	.714	310	474	18.2
Varsity totals	50	—	750	353	.471	237	178	.751	531	884	17.7

NBA Regular-Season Record

Sea.—Team	G	Min.	FGA	FGM	Pct.	FTA	FTM	Pct.	Reb.	Ast.	PF	Dq.	Pts.	Avg.
67–68—New York	74	1588	568	256	.451	235	154	.655	313	305	199	2	666	9.0
68–69—New York	80	2949	1052	531	.505	457	341	.746	499	635	245	2	1403	17.5
69–70—New York	77	3040	1158	600	.518	547	409	.748	465	629	203	1	1609	20.9
70–71—New York	80	3455	1317	651	.494	557	434	.779	544	536	240	1	1736	21.7
71–72—New York	77	3126	1307	669	.512	557	450	.808	513	446	185	0	1788	23.2
72–73—New York	78	3181	1389	681	.490	350	286	.817	570	461	186	0	1648	21.1
73–74—New York	80	3338	1429	674	.472	352	295	.838	536	551	212	2	1643	20.5
74–75—New York	78	3204	1391	672	.483	400	331	.828	465	474	205	2	1675	21.5
75–76—New York	59	2427	969	470	.485	226	186	.823	400	351	163	1	1126	19.1
76–77—N.Y. Knicks	76	2687	1089	532	.489	336	259	.771	293	403	194	0	1323	17.4
77–78—Cleveland	51	1664	714	336	.471	180	153	.850	209	209	124	1	825	16.2
78–79—Cleveland	12	279	122	54	.443	27	21	.778	20	32	22	0	129	10.8
79–80—Cleveland	3	27	11	4	.364	2	2	1.000	3	8	2	0	10	3.3
Totals	825	30965	12516	6130	.490	4226	3321	.786	4830	5040	2180	12	15581	18.9

NBA Playoff Record

Sea.—Team	G	Min.	FGA	FGM	Pct.	FTA	FTM	Pct.	Reb.	Ast.	PF	Dq.	Pts.	Avg.
67–68—New York	4	119	33	12	.364	18	14	.778	22	25	12	0	38	9.5
68–69—New York	10	415	177	89	.503	57	34	.596	74	91	30	0	212	21.2
69–70—New York	19	834	247	118	.478	89	68	.764	149	156	53	0	304	16.0
70–71—New York	12	501	204	108	.529	75	55	.733	70	54	45	0	271	22.6
71–72—New York	16	704	276	148	.536	125	92	.736	112	98	48	0	388	24.3
72–73—New York	17	765	292	150	.514	94	73	.777	124	106	52	1	373	21.9
73–74—New York	12	491	225	113	.502	49	44	.898	95	48	41	1	270	22.5
74–75—New York	3	124	46	29	.630	16	13	.813	20	21	4	0	71	23.7
Totals	93	3953	1500	767	.511	523	393	.751	666	599	285	2	1927	20.7

NBA All-Star Game Record

Sea.—Team	Min.	FGA	FGM	Pct.	FTA	FTM	Pct.	Reb.	Ast.	PF	Dq.	Pts.
1970—New York	24	7	3	.429	2	1	.500	3	4	2	0	7
1971—New York	26	9	3	.333	0	0	—	6	5	2	0	6
1972—New York	25	11	7	.636	2	1	.500	3	5	2	0	15
1973—New York	26	15	5	.333	0	0	—	6	2	1	0	10
1974—New York	28	12	5	.417	2	2	1.000	2	5	1	0	12
1975—New York	35	17	10	.588	11	10	.909	5	2	2	0	30
1976—New York	19	7	2	.286	4	4	1.000	2	3	0	0	8
Totals	183	78	35	.449	21	18	.857	27	26	10	0	88

WILLIAM GATES (Pop)*

College—Clark College (GA)
Inducted into the Basketball Hall of Fame, 1989

Played for—New York Renaissance
Washington, D.C. Bears
Rochester Royals, National Basketball League, 1946

*No statistics available.

HAL GREER

Born June 26, 1936, in Huntington, W. Va.
High School—Huntington, W. Va.; Douglass College-Marshall University, Huntington, W. Va.
Inducted into the Basketball Hall of Fame, 1981
NBA All-Star Game Most Valuable Player, 1968

Collegiate Record

Sea.—Team	G	Min.	FGA	FGM	Pct.	FTA	FTM	Pct.	Reb.	Pts.	Avg.
54–55	—	—	—	—	—	—	—	—	—	—	18.0
55–56	23	—	213	128	.601	145	101	.697	153	357	15.5
56–57	24	—	329	167	.508	156	119	.763	332	453	18.9
57–58	24	—	432	236	.546	114	95	.833	280	567	23.6
Varsity Totals	71	—	974	531	.545	415	315	.759	765	1377	19.4

NBA Regular-Season Record

Sea.—Team	G	Min.	FGA	FGM	Pct.	FTA	FTM	Pct.	Reb.	Ast.	PF	Dq.	Pts.	Avg.
58–59—Syracuse	68	1625	679	308	.454	176	137	.778	196	101	189	1	756	11.1
59–60—Syracuse	70	1979	815	388	.476	189	148	.783	303	188	208	4	924	13.2
60–61—Syracuse	79	2763	1381	623	.451	394	305	.774	455	302	242	0	1551	19.6
61–62—Syracuse	71	2705	1442	644	.446	404	331	.819	524	313	252	2	1619	22.8
62–63—Syracuse	80	2631	1293	600	.464	434	362	.834	457	275	286	4	1562	19.5
63–64—Philadelphia	80	3157	1611	715	.444	525	435	.829	484	374	291	6	1865	23.3
64–65—Philadelphia	70	2600	1245	539	.433	413	335	.811	355	313	254	7	1413	20.2
65–66—Philadelphia	80	3326	1580	703	.445	514	413	.804	384	384	315	6	1819	22.7
66–67—Philadelphia	80	3086	1524	699	.459	466	367	.788	422	303	302	5	1765	22.1
67–68—Philadelphia	82	3263	1626	777	.478	549	422	.769	444	372	289	6	1976	24.1
68–69—Philadelphia	82	3311	1595	732	.459	543	432	.796	435	414	294	8	1896	23.1
69–70—Philadelphia	80	3024	1551	705	.455	432	352	.815	376	405	300	8	1762	22.0
70–71—Philadelphia	81	3060	1371	591	.431	405	326	.805	364	369	289	4	1508	18.6
71–72—Philadelphia	81	2410	866	389	.449	234	181	.774	271	316	268	10	959	11.8
72–73—Philadelphia	38	848	232	91	.392	39	32	.821	106	111	76	1	214	5.6
Totals	1122	39788	18811	8504	.452	5717	4578	.801	5665	4540	3855	72	21586	19.2

NBA Playoff Record

Sea.—Team	G	Min.	FGA	FGM	Pct.	FTA	FTM	Pct.	Reb.	Ast.	PF	Dq.	Pts.	Avg.
58–59—Syracuse	9	277	93	39	.419	32	26	.813	47	20	35	2	104	11.6
59–60—Syracuse	3	84	43	22	.512	4	3	.750	14	10	5	0	47	15.7
60–61—Syracuse	8	232	106	41	.387	40	33	.825	33	19	32	1	115	14.4
61–62—Syracuse	1	5	0	0	.000	0	0	.000	0	0	1	0	0	0.0
62–63—Syracuse	5	214	87	44	.506	35	29	.829	27	21	21	1	117	23.4
63–64—Philadelphia	5	211	95	37	.389	39	33	.846	28	30	19	1	107	21.4
64–65—Philadelphia	11	505	222	101	.455	87	69	.793	81	55	45	2	271	24.6
65–66—Philadelphia	5	226	91	32	.352	23	18	.783	36	21	21	0	82	16.4
66–67—Philadelphia	15	688	375	161	.429	118	94	.797	88	79	55	1	416	27.7
67–68—Philadelphia	13	553	278	120	.432	111	95	.858	79	55	49	1	335	25.8
68–69—Philadelphia	5	204	81	26	.321	36	28	.778	30	23	23	0	80	16.0
69–70—Philadelphia	5	178	74	33	.446	13	11	.846	17	27	16	0	77	15.4
70–71—Philadelphia	7	265	112	49	.438	36	27	.750	25	33	35	4	125	17.9
Totals	92	3642	1657	705	.425	574	466	.812	505	393	357	13	1876	20.4

NBA All-Star Game Record

Sea.—Team	Min.	FGA	FGM	Pct.	FTA	FTM	Pct.	Reb.	Ast.	PF	Dq.	Pts.
1961—Syracuse	18	11	7	.636	0	0	.000	6	2	2	0	14
1962—Syracuse	24	14	3	.214	7	2	.286	10	9	3	0	8
1963—Syracuse	15	7	3	.429	0	0	.000	3	2	4	0	6
1964—Philadelphia	20	10	5	.500	4	3	.750	3	4	1	0	13
1965—Philadelphia	21	11	5	.455	4	3	.750	4	1	2	0	13
1966—Philadelphia	23	13	4	.308	1	1	1.000	5	1	4	0	9
1967—Philadelphia	31	16	5	.313	8	7	.875	4	1	5	0	17
1968—Philadelphia	17	8	8	1.000	7	5	.714	3	3	2	0	21
1969—Philadelphia	17	1	0	.000	5	4	.800	3	2	2	0	4
1970—Philadelphia	21	11	7	.636	1	1	1.000	4	3	4	0	15
Totals	207	102	47	.461	37	26	.703	45	28	29	0	120

CBA Coaching Record

Sea.—Club	Regular Season				Playoffs	
	W.	L.	Pct.	Pos.	W.	L.
1980–81—Phila. Kings	17	23	.425	3†	6	6

†Eastern Division.

CORNELIUS L. HAWKINS (Connie)

Born July 17, 1942, in Brooklyn, N.Y.
High School—Boys, Brooklyn, N.Y.
College—University of Iowa
Inducted into the Basketball Hall of Fame, 1992
American Basketball Association Most Valuable Player, 1968
High School All-American, 1960

Regular-Season Record

Sea.—Team	G	Min.	2-Point			3-Point			FTA	FTM	Pct.	Reb.	Ast.	Pts.	Avg.
			FGA	FGM	Pct.	FGA	FGM	Pct.							
67–68—Pittsburgh (A)	70	3146	1223	635	.519	9	2	.222	789	603	.764	945	320	1875	26.8
68–69—Minnesota (A)	47	1852	971	496	.511	22	3	.136	554	425	.767	534	184	1420	30.2
Reg. ABA Totals	117	4998	2194	1131	.515	31	5	.161	1343	1028	.765	1479	504	3295	26.2
69–70—Phoenix	81	3312	1447	709	.490	—	—	—	741	577	.779	846	391	1995	24.6
70–71—Phoenix	71	2662	1181	512	.434	—	—	—	560	457	.816	643	322	1481	20.9
71–72—Phoenix	76	2798	1244	571	.459	—	—	—	565	456	.807	633	296	1598	21.0
72–73—Phoenix	75	2768	920	441	.479	—	—	—	404	322	.797	641	304	1204	16.1
73–74—Phoenix	79	2761	807	404	.501	—	—	—	251	191	.761	565	407	999	12.6
74–75—Los Angeles	43	1026	324	139	.429	—	—	—	99	68	.687	198	120	346	8.0
75–76—Atlanta	74	1907	530	237	.447	—	—	—	191	136	.712	445	212	610	8.2
Reg. NBA Totals	499	17234	6453	3013	.467	—	—	—	2811	2207	.785	3971	2052	8233	16.5

Sea.—Team	G	Min.	2-Point FGA	FGM	Pct.	3-Point FGA	FGM	Pct.	FTA	FTM	Pct.	Reb.	Ast.	Pts.	Avg.
NBA Playoff Totals	12	500	210	83	.395	—	—	—	81	66	.815	137	57	232	28.2
ABA Playoff Totals	21	936	416	210	.505	8	4	.500	239	169	.707	258	91	603	19.3
NBA All-Star Totals	4	45	16	8	.500	—	—	—	10	9	.900	10	5	25	7.8
ABA All-Star Totals	1	26	6	3	.500	0	0	.000	3	1	.333	9	2	7	6.3

ELVIN E. HAYES

Born November 17, 1945 in Rayville, LA
High School—Eula D. Britton, Rayville, LA
College—University of Houston
Inducted into the Basketball Hall of Fame, 1989
All-American, 1967, 1968

Collegiate Record

Sea.—Team	G	Min.	FGA	FGM	Pct.	FTA	FTM	Pct.	Reb.	Pts.	Avg.
64–65—Houston	21	—	478	217	.454	176	93	.528	500	527	25.1
65–66—Houston	29	946	570	323	.567	257	143	.556	490	785	27.2
66–67—Houston	31	1119	750	373	.497	227	135	.595	488	881	28.4
67–68—Houston	33	1270	945	519	.549	285	176	.618	624	1214	36.8
Varsity totals	93	3335	2265	1215	.536	769	454	.590	1602	2884	31.0

NBA Regular-Season Record

Sea.—Team	G	Min.	FGA	FGM	Pct.	FTA	FTM	Pct.	Reb.	Ast.	PF	Dq.	Pts.	Avg.
68–69—San Diego	82	3695	2082	930	.447	746	467	.626	1406	113	266	2	2327	28.4
69–70—San Diego	82	3665	2020	914	.452	622	428	.688	1386	162	270	5	2256	27.5
70–71—San Diego	82	3633	2215	948	.428	676	454	.672	1362	186	225	1	2350	28.7
71–72—Houston	82	3461	1918	832	.434	615	399	.649	1197	270	233	1	2063	25.2
72–73—Baltimore	81	3347	1607	713	.444	434	291	.671	1177	127	232	3	1717	21.2
73–74—Capital	81	3602	1627	689	.423	495	357	.721	1463	163	252	1	1735	21.4
74–75—Washington	82	3465	1668	739	.443	534	409	.766	1004	206	238	0	1887	23.0
75–76—Washington	80	2975	1381	649	.470	457	287	.628	878	121	293	5	1585	19.8
76–77—Washington	82	3364	1516	760	.501	614	422	.687	1029	158	312	1	1942	23.7
77–78—Washington	81	3246	1409	636	.451	514	326	.634	1075	149	313	7	1598	19.7
78–79—Washington	82	3105	1477	720	.487	534	349	.654	994	143	308	5	1789	21.8
79–80—Washington	81	3183	1677	761	.454	478	334	.699	896	129	309	9	1859	23.0
80–81—Washington	81	2931	1296	584	.451	439	271	.617	789	98	300	6	1439	17.8
81–82—Houston	82	3032	1100	519	.472	422	280	.664	747	144	287	4	1318	16.1
82–83—Houston	81	2302	890	424	.476	287	196	.683	616	158	232	2	1046	12.9
83–84—Houston	81	994	389	158	.406	132	86	.652	260	71	123	1	402	5.0
Totals	1303	50000	24272	10976	.452	7999	5356	.670	16279	2398	4193	53	27313	21.0

Reference Section

NBA Playoff Record

Sea.—Team	G	Min.	FGA	FGM	Pct.	FTA	FTM	Pct.	Reb.	Ast.	PF	Dq.	Pts.	Avg.
68–79—San Diego	6	278	114	60	.526	53	35	.660	83	5	21	0	155	25.8
72–73—Baltimore	5	228	105	53	.505	33	23	.697	57	5	16	0	129	25.8
73–74—Capital	7	323	143	76	.531	41	29	.707	111	21	23	0	181	25.9
74–75—Washington	17	751	372	174	.468	127	86	.677	186	37	70	3	434	25.5
75–76—Washington	7	305	122	54	.443	55	32	.582	88	10	24	0	140	20.0
76–77—Washington	9	405	173	74	.428	59	41	.695	122	17	39	0	189	21.0
77–78—Washington	21	868	385	189	.491	133	79	.594	279	43	86	2	457	21.8
78–79—Washington	19	786	396	170	.429	130	87	.669	266	38	79	3	427	22.5
79–80—Washington	2	92	41	16	.390	10	8	.800	22	6	8	0	40	20.0
81–82—Houston	3	124	50	17	.340	15	8	.533	30	3	12	0	42	14.0
Totals	96	4160	1901	883	.464	656	428	.652	1244	185	378	8	2194	22.9

NBA All-Star Game Record

Sea.—Team	Min.	FGA	FGM	Pct.	FTA	FTM	Pct.	Reb.	Ast.	PF	Dq.	Pts.
1969—San Diego	21	9	4	.444	3	3	1.000	5	0	4	0	11
1970—San Diego	35	21	9	.429	12	6	.500	15	1	1	0	24
1971—San Diego	19	13	4	.308	3	2	.667	4	2	1	0	10
1972—Houston	11	6	1	.167	2	2	1.000	2	0	2	0	4
1973—Baltimore	16	13	4	.308	2	2	1.000	12	0	0	0	10
1974—Capital	35	13	5	.385	3	2	.667	15	6	4	0	12
1975—Washington	17	6	2	.333	0	0	—	5	2	1	0	4
1976—Washington	31	14	6	.429	2	0	.000	10	1	5	0	12
1977—Washington	11	6	6	1.000	10	0	.000	2	1	5	0	12
1978—Washington	11	7	1	.143	0	0	—	4	0	4	0	2
1979—Washington	28	11	5	.455	5	3	.600	13	0	5	0	13
1980—Washington	29	10	5	.500	2	2	1.000	5	4	5	0	12
Totals	264	129	52	.403	44	22	.500	92	17	37	0	126

EARVIN JOHNSON, JR. (Magic)

Born August 14, 1959, in Lansing, Michigan
High School—Everett, Lansing, Michigan
College—Michigan State University
Most Outstanding Player, 1979 NCAA-Division 1 Tournament
1980, 1982, 1987 NBA Finals Most Valuable Player
1987, 1989, 1990 NBA Most Valuable Player
1990, 1992 NBA All-Star Game Most Valuable Player
All-American, 1979

Collegiate Record

Sea.—Team	G	Min.	FGA	FGM	Pct.	FTA	FTM	Pct.	Reb.	Pts.	Avg.
77–78—Michigan State	30	—	382	175	.458	205	161	.785	237	511	17.0
78–79—Michigan State	32	1159	370	173	.468	240	202	.842	234	548	17.1
Totals	62	—	752	348	.463	445	363	.816	471	1059	17.1

NBA Regular-Season Record

Sea.—Team	G	Min.	FGA	FGM	Pct.	FTA	FTM	Pct.	Reb.	Ast.	PF	Dq.	Pts.	Avg.
79–80—Los Angeles	77	2795	949	503	.530	462	374	.810	596	563	218	1	1387	18.0
80–81—Los Angeles	37	1371	587	312	.532	225	171	.760	320	317	100	0	798	21.6
81–82—Los Angeles	78	2991	1036	556	.537	433	329	.760	751	743	223	1	1447	18.6
82–83—Los Angeles	79	2907	933	511	.548	380	304	.800	683	829	200	1	1326	16.8
83–84—Los Angeles	67	2567	780	441	.565	358	290	.810	491	875	169	1	1178	17.6
84–85—L.A. Lakers	77	2781	899	504	.561	464	391	.843	476	968	155	0	1406	18.3
85–86—L.A. Lakers	72	2578	918	483	.526	434	378	.871	426	907	133	0	1354	18.8
86–87—L.A. Lakers	80	2904	1308	683	.522	631	535	.848	504	977	168	0	1909	23.9
87–88—L.A. Lakers	72	2637	996	490	.492	489	417	.853	449	858	147	0	1408	19.6
88–89—L.A. Lakers	77	2886	1137	579	.509	563	513	.911	607	988	172	0	1730	22.5
89–90—L.A. Lakers	79	2937	1138	546	.480	637	567	.890	522	907	167	1	1765	22.3
90–91—L.A. Lakers	79	2933	976	466	.477	573	519	.906	551	989	150	0	1531	19.4
91–92—L.A. Lakers					Did not play—medical reasons.									
Totals	874	32287	11657	6074	.521	5649	4788	.848	6376	9921	2002	5	17239	19.7

NBA Playoff Record

Sea.—Team	G	Min.	FGA	FGM	Pct.	FTA	FTM	Pct.	Reb.	Ast.	PF	Dq.	Pts.	Avg.
79–80—Los Angeles	16	658	199	103	.518	106	85	.802	168	151	47	1	293	18.3
80–81—Los Angeles	3	127	49	19	.388	20	13	.650	41	21	14	1	51	17.0
81–82—Los Angeles	14	562	157	83	.529	93	77	.828	158	130	50	0	243	17.4
82–83—Los Angeles	15	643	206	100	.485	81	68	.840	128	192	49	0	268	17.0
83–84—Los Angeles	21	837	274	151	.551	100	80	.800	139	284	71	0	382	18.2
84–85—L.A. Lakers	19	687	226	116	.513	118	100	.847	134	289	48	0	333	17.5
85–86—L.A. Lakers	14	541	205	110	.537	107	82	.766	100	211	43	0	302	21.6
86–87—L.A. Lakers	18	666	271	146	.539	118	98	.831	139	219	37	0	392	21.8
87–88—L.A. Lakers	24	965	329	169	.514	155	132	.852	130	303	61	0	477	19.9
88–89—L.A. Lakers	14	518	174	85	.489	86	78	.907	83	165	30	1	258	18.4
89–90—L.A. Lakers	9	376	155	76	.490	79	70	.886	57	115	28	0	227	25.2
90–91—L.A. Lakers	19	823	268	118	.440	178	157	.882	154	240	43	0	414	21.8
Totals	186	7403	1513	1276	.508	1241	1040	.838	1431	2320	521	3	3640	19.6

NBA All-Star Game Record

Sea.—Team	Min.	FGA	FGM	Pct.	FTA	FTM	Pct.	Reb.	Ast.	PF	Dq.	Pts.
1980—Los Angeles	24	8	5	.625	2	2	1.000	2	4	3	0	12
1982—Los Angeles	23	9	5	.556	7	6	.857	4	7	5	0	16
1983—Los Angeles	33	16	7	.438	4	3	.750	5	16	2	0	17
1984—Los Angeles	37	13	6	.462	2	2	1.000	9	22	3	0	15
1985—L.A. Lakers	31	14	7	.500	8	7	.875	5	15	2	0	21
1986—L.A. Lakers	28	3	1	.333	4	4	1.000	4	15	4	0	6
1987—L.A. Lakers	34	10	4	.400	2	1	.500	7	13	2	0	9
1988—L.A. Lakers	39	15	4	.267	9	9	1.000	6	19	2	0	17
1989—L.A. Lakers				Did not play—injured.								
1990—L.A. Lakers	25	15	9	.600	0	0	—	6	4	1	0	22
1991—L.A. Lakers	28	16	7	.438	0	0	—	4	3	1	0	16
1992—L.A. Lakers	29	12	9	.750	4	4	1.000	5	9	0	0	25
Totals	331	131	64	.489	42	38	.905	57	127	25	0	176

Reference Section

K. C. JONES

Born May 25, 1932, in Taylor, Texas
High School—Commerce, San Francisco, Ca
College—University of San Francisco, San Francisco, Ca
Inducted into the Basketball Hall of Fame, 1988
Member of the 1956 United States Olympic Basketball Team
Amateur Athletic Union All-American, 1958

Collegiate Record

Sea.—Team	G	Min.	FGA	FGM	Pct.	FTA	FTM	Pct.	Reb.	Pts.	Avg.
51–52—San Francisco	24	—	128	44	.344	64	46	.719	—	134	5.6
52–53—San Francisco	23	—	159	63	.396	149	81	.544	—	207	9.0
53–54—San Francisco	1	—	12	3	.250	2	2	1.000	3	8	8.0
54–55—San Francisco	29	—	293	105	.358	144	97	.674	148	307	10.6
55–56—San Francisco	25	—	208	76	.365	142	93	.655	130	245	9.8
Totals	102	—	800	291	.364	501	319	.637	—	901	8.8

NBA Regular-Season Record

Sea.—Team	G	Min.	FGA	FGM	Pct.	FTA	FTM	Pct.	Reb.	Ast.	PF	Dq.	Pts.	Avg.
58–59—Boston	49	609	192	65	.339	68	41	.603	127	70	58	0	171	3.5
59–60—Boston	74	1274	414	169	.408	170	128	.753	199	189	109	1	466	6.3
60–61—Boston	78	1607	601	203	.338	320	186	.581	279	253	200	3	592	7.6
61–62—Boston	79	2023	707	289	.409	231	145	.628	291	339	204	2	723	9.2
62–63—Boston	79	1945	591	230	.389	177	112	.633	263	317	221	3	572	7.2
63–64—Boston	80	2424	722	283	.392	168	88	.524	372	407	253	0	654	8.2
64–65—Boston	78	2434	639	253	.396	227	143	.630	318	437	263	5	649	8.3
65–66—Boston	80	2710	619	240	.388	303	209	.690	304	503	243	4	689	8.6
66–67—Boston	78	2446	459	182	.397	189	119	.630	239	389	273	7	483	6.2
Totals	675	17472	4944	1914	.387	1853	1171	.632	2392	2904	1824	25	4999	7.4

NBA Playoff Record

Sea.—Team	G	Min.	FGA	FGM	Pct.	FTA	FTM	Pct.	Reb.	Ast.	PF	Dq.	Pts.	Avg.
58–59—Boston	8	75	20	5	.250	5	5	1.000	12	10	8	0	15	1.9
59–60—Boston	13	232	80	27	.338	22	17	.773	45	14	28	0	71	5.5
60–61—Boston	9	103	30	9	.300	14	7	.500	19	15	17	0	25	2.8
61–62—Boston	14	329	102	44	.431	53	38	.717	56	55	50	1	126	9.0
62–63—Boston	13	250	64	19	.297	30	21	.700	36	37	42	1	59	4.5
63–64—Boston	10	312	72	25	.347	25	13	.520	37	68	40	0	63	6.3
64–65—Boston	12	396	104	43	.413	45	35	.778	39	74	49	1	121	10.1
65–66—Boston	17	543	109	45	.413	57	39	.684	52	75	65	0	129	7.6
66–67—Boston	9	254	75	24	.320	18	11	.611	24	48	36	1	59	6.6
Totals	105	2494	656	241	.367	269	186	.691	320	396	335	4	668	6.4

EBL Regular-Season Record

Sea.—Team	G	Min.	FGA	FGM	Pct.	FTA	FTM	Pct.	Reb.	Ast.	PF	Dq.	Pts.	Avg.
67–68—Hartford	6	—	—	15	—	18	9	.500	24	41	—	—	39	6.5

Collegiate Coaching Record

Sea.—Team	W	L	Pct.	Finish
67–68—Brandeis	11	10	.524	
68–69—Brandeis	12	9	.571	
69–70—Brandeis	11	13	.458	
Total	34	32	.515	

ABA Coaching Record

Sea.—Team	Regular Season				Playoffs		
	W	L	Pct.	Finish	W	L	Pct.
72–73—San Diego	30	54	.357	4th/Western Division	0	4	.000
Total	30	54	.357		0	4	.000

NBA Coaching Record

Sea.—Team	Regular Season				Playoffs		
	W	L	Pct.	Finish	W	L	Pct.
73–74—Capital	47	35	.573	1st/Central Division	3	4	.429
74–75—Washington	60	22	.732	1st/Central Division	8	9	.471
75–76—Washington	48	34	.585	2nd/Central Division	3	4	.429
83–84—Boston	62	20	.756	1st/Atlantic Division	15	8	.652
84–85—Boston	63	19	.768	1st/Atlantic Division	13	8	.619
85–86—Boston	67	15	.817	1st/Atlantic Division	15	3	.833
86–87—Boston	59	23	.720	1st/Atlantic Division	13	10	.565
87–88—Boston	57	25	.695	1st/Atlantic Division	9	8	.529
90–91—Seattle	41	41	.500	5th/Pacific Division	2	3	.400
91–92—Seattle	18	18	.500		—	—	—
Total	522	252	.674	**Total**	81	57	.587

SAMUEL JONES (Sam)

Born June 24, 1933, in Wilmington, N.C.
High School—Lauringburg Institute, Lauringburg, N.C.
College—North Carolina Central University
Inducted into the Basketball Hall of Fame, 1983
Chosen the NBA 25th Anniversary All-Time Team, 1970
Inducted into the NAIA Basketball Hall of Fame, 1962

Collegiate Record

Sea.—Team	G	Min.	FGA	FGM	Pct.	FTA	FTM	Pct.	Reb.	Pts.	Avg.
51–52—North Carolina Central	22	—	263	126	.479	78	48	.615	150	300	13.6
52–53—North Carolina Central	24	—	370	169	.457	180	115	.639	248	453	18.9
53–54—North Carolina Central	27	—	432	208	.481	137	98	.715	223	514	19.0

Sea.—Team	G	Min.	FGA	FGM	Pct.	FTA	FTM	Pct.	Reb.	Pts.	Avg.
54–55—			Did not play—in military service.								
55–56—			Did not play—in military service.								
56–57—North Carolina Central	27	—	398	174	.437	202	155	.767	288	503	18.6
Totals	100	—	1463	677	.463	597	416	.697	909	1770	17.7

NBA Regular-Season Record

Sea.—Team	G	Min.	FGA	FGM	Pct.	FTA	FTM	Pct.	Reb.	Ast.	PF	Dq.	Pts.	Avg.
57–58—Boston	56	594	233	100	.429	84	60	.714	160	37	42	0	260	4.6
58–59—Boston	71	1466	703	305	.434	196	151	.770	428	101	102	0	761	10.7
59–60—Boston	74	1512	782	355	.454	220	168	.764	375	125	101	1	878	11.9
60–61—Boston	78	2028	1069	480	.449	268	211	.787	421	217	148	1	1171	15.0
61–62—Boston	78	2388	1284	596	.464	297	243	.818	458	232	149	0	1435	18.4
62–63—Boston	76	2323	1305	621	.476	324	257	.793	396	241	162	1	1499	19.7
63–64—Boston	76	2381	1359	612	.450	318	249	.783	349	202	192	1	1473	19.4
64–65—Boston	80	2885	1818	821	.452	522	428	.820	411	223	176	0	2070	25.9
65–66—Boston	67	2155	1335	626	.469	407	325	.799	347	216	170	0	1577	23.5
66–67—Boston	72	2325	1406	638	.454	371	318	.857	338	217	191	1	1594	22.1
67–68—Boston	73	2408	1348	621	.461	376	311	.827	357	216	181	0	1553	21.3
68–69—Boston	70	1820	1103	496	.450	189	148	.783	265	182	121	0	1140	16.3
Totals	871	24285	13745	6271	.456	3572	2869	.803	4305	2209	1735	5	15411	17.7

NBA Playoff Record

Sea.—Team	G	Min.	FGA	FGM	Pct.	FTA	FTM	Pct.	Reb.	Ast.	PF	Dq.	Pts.	Avg.
57–58—Boston	8	75	22	10	.455	16	11	.688	24	4	7	0	31	3.9
58–59—Boston	11	192	108	40	.370	39	33	.846	63	17	14	0	113	10.3
59–60—Boston	13	197	117	45	.385	21	17	.810	41	18	15	0	107	8.2
60–61—Boston	10	258	112	50	.446	35	31	.886	54	22	22	0	131	13.1
61–62—Boston	14	504	277	123	.444	60	42	.700	99	44	30	0	288	20.6
62–63—Boston	13	450	248	120	.484	83	69	.831	81	32	42	1	309	23.8
63–64—Boston	10	356	180	91	.506	68	50	.735	47	23	24	0	232	23.2
64–65—Boston	12	495	294	135	.459	84	73	.869	55	30	39	1	343	28.6
65–66—Boston	17	602	343	154	.449	136	114	.838	86	53	65	1	422	24.8
66–67—Boston	9	326	207	95	.459	58	50	.862	46	28	30	1	240	26.7
67–68—Boston	19	685	367	162	.441	84	66	.786	64	50	58	0	390	20.5
68 69—Boston	18	514	296	124	.419	69	55	.797	58	37	45	1	303	16.8
Totals	154	4654	2571	1149	.447	753	611	.811	718	358	391	5	2909	18.9

NBA All-Star Game Record

Sea.—Team	Min.	FGA	FGM	Pct.	FTA	FTM	Pct.	Reb.	Ast.	PF	Dq.	Pts.
1962—Boston	14	8	1	.125	1	0	.000	1	0	1	0	2
1964—Boston	27	20	8	.400	0	0	—	4	3	2	0	16
1965—Boston	24	12	2	.167	2	2	1.000	5	3	2	0	6
1966—Boston	22	11	5	.455	2	2	1.000	2	5	0	0	12
1968—Boston	15	5	2	.400	1	1	1.000	2	4	1	0	5
Totals	102	56	18	.321	6	5	.833	14	15	6	0	41

Collegiate Coaching Record

Sea. — Team	W	L	Pct.	Finish
69–70—Federal City College	5	8	.385	
70–71—Federal City College	12	9	.571	
71–72—Federal City College	11	9	.550	
72–73—Federal City College	11	13	.458	
73–74—North Carolina Central	5	16	.238	7th/Mid-Eastern Athletic Conference.
Total	**44**	**55**	**.444**	

ROBERT J. LANIER, JR. (Bob)

Born September 10, 1948, in Buffalo, N.Y.
High School—Bennett, Buffalo, N.Y.
College—St. Bonaventure University
Inducted into the Basketball Hall of Fame, 1992
All-American, 1970
1974 NBA All-Star Game Most Valuable Player

Collegiate Record

Sea.—Team	G	Min.	FGA	FGM	Pct.	FTA	FTM	Pct.	Reb.	Pts.	Avg.
66–67—St. Bonaventure†	15	—	—	—	—	—	—	—	—	450	30.0
67–68—St. Bonaventure	25	—	466	272	.584	175	112	.640	390	656	26.2
68–69—St. Bonaventure	24	—	460	270	.587	181	114	.630	374	654	27.3
69–70—St. Bonaventure	26	—	549	308	.561	194	141	.727	416	757	29.1
Varsity totals	**75**	**—**	**1475**	**850**	**.576**	**550**	**367**	**.667**	**1180**	**2067**	**27.6**

NBA Regular-Season Record

Sea.—Team	G	Min.	FGA	FGM	Pct.	FTA	FTM	Pct.	Reb.	Ast.	PF	Dq.	Pts.	Avg.
70–71—Detroit	82	2017	1108	504	.455	376	273	.726	665	146	272	4	1281	15.6
71–72—Detroit	80	3092	1690	834	.493	505	388	.768	1132	248	297	6	2056	25.7
72–73—Detroit	81	3150	1654	810	.490	397	307	.773	1205	260	278	4	1927	23.8
73–74—Detroit	81	3047	1483	748	.504	409	326	.797	1074	343	273	7	1822	22.5
74–75—Detroit	76	2987	1433	731	.510	450	361	.802	914	350	237	1	1823	24.0
75–76—Detroit	64	2363	1017	541	.532	370	284	.768	746	217	203	2	1366	21.3
76–77—Detroit	64	2446	1269	678	.534	318	260	.818	745	214	174	0	1616	25.3
77–78—Detroit	63	2311	1159	622	.537	386	298	.772	715	216	185	2	1542	24.5
78–79—Detroit	53	1835	950	489	.515	367	275	.749	494	140	181	5	1253	23.6
79–80—Detroit-Mil.	63	2131	867	466	.537	354	277	.782	552	184	200	3	1210	19.2
80–81—Milwaukee	67	1753	716	376	.525	277	208	.751	413	179	184	0	961	14.3
81–82—Milwaukee	74	1986	729	407	.558	242	182	.752	388	219	211	3	996	13.5
82–83—Milwaukee	39	978	332	163	.491	133	91	.684	200	105	125	2	417	10.7
83–84—Milwaukee	72	2007	685	392	.572	274	194	.708	455	186	228	8	978	13.6
Totals	**959**	**32103**	**15092**	**7761**	**.514**	**4858**	**3724**	**.767**	**9698**	**3007**	**3048**	**47**	**19248**	**20.1**

NBA Playoff Record

Sea.—Team	G	Min.	FGA	FGM	Pct.	FTA	FTM	Pct.	Reb.	Ast.	PF	Dq.	Pts.	Avg.
73–74—Detroit	7	303	152	77	.507	38	30	.789	107	21	28	1	184	26.3
74–75—Detroit	3	128	51	26	.510	12	9	.750	32	19	10	0	61	20.3
75–76—Detroit	9	359	172	95	.552	50	45	.900	114	30	34	1	235	26.1
76–77—Detroit	3	118	54	34	.630	19	16	.842	50	6	10	0	84	28.0
79–80—Milwaukee	7	256	101	52	.515	42	31	.738	65	31	23	0	135	19.3
80–81—Milwaukee	7	236	85	50	.588	32	23	.719	52	28	18	0	123	17.6
81–82—Milwaukee	6	212	80	41	.513	25	14	.560	45	22	21	2	96	16.0
82–83—Milwaukee	9	250	89	51	.573	35	21	.600	63	23	32	2	123	13.7
83–84—Milwaukee	16	499	171	82	.480	44	39	.886	117	55	57	1	203	12.7
Totals	67	2361	955	508	.532	297	228	.768	645	235	233	7	1244	18.6

NBA All-Star Game Record

Sea.—Team	Min.	FGA	FGM	Pct.	FTA	FTM	Pct.	Reb.	Ast.	PF	Dq.	Pts.
1972—Detroit	5	2	0	.000	3	2	.667	3	0	0	0	2
1973—Detroit	12	9	5	.556	0	0	—	6	0	1	0	10
1974—Detroit	26	15	11	.733	2	2	1.000	10	2	1	0	24
1975—Detroit	12	4	1	.250	0	0	—	7	2	3	0	2
1977—Detroit	20	8	7	.875	3	3	1.000	10	4	3	0	17
1978—Detroit	4	0	0	—	2	1	.500	2	0	0	0	1
1979—Detroit	31	10	5	.500	0	0	—	4	4	4	0	10
1982—Milwaukee	11	7	3	.429	2	2	1.000	3	0	3	0	8
Totals	121	55	32	.582	12	10	.833	45	12	15	0	74

VERNON MONROE (Earl)

Born November 21, 1944, in Philadelphia, Pa
High School—John Bartram, Philadelphia, Pa
College—Winston-Salem State University, Winston-Salem, N.C.
Inducted into the Basketball Hall of Fame, 1989
NCAA Division II All-American, 1967
Most Valuable Player Division II Tournament, 1967
Inducted into the NAIA Hall of Fame, 1975

Collegiate Record

Sea.—Team	G	Min.	FGA	FGM	Pct.	FTA	FTM	Pct.	Reb.	Pts.	Avg.
63–64—Winston-Salem State	23	—	—	71	—	—	21	—	—	163	7.1
64–65—Winston-Salem State	30	—	—	286	—	176	125	.710	211	697	23.2
65–66—Winston-Salem State	25	—	519	292	.563	187	162	.866	167	746	29.8
66–67—Winston-Salem State	32	—	839	509	.607	391	311	.795	218	1329	41.5
Totals	110	—	—	1158	—	—	619	—	—	2935	26.7

NBA Regular-Season Record

Sea.—Team	G	Min.	FGA	FGM	Pct.	FTA	FTM	Pct.	Reb.	Ast.	PF	Dq.	Pts.	Avg.
67–68—Baltimore	82	3012	1637	742	.453	649	507	.781	465	349	282	3	1991	24.3
68–69—Baltimore	80	3075	1837	809	.440	582	447	.768	280	392	261	1	2065	25.8
69–70—Baltimore	82	3051	1557	695	.446	641	532	.830	257	402	258	3	1922	23.4
70–71—Baltimore	81	2843	1501	663	.442	506	406	.802	213	354	220	3	1732	21.4
71–72—Baltimore-New York	63	1337	662	287	.434	224	175	.781	100	142	139	1	749	11.9
72–73—New York	75	2370	1016	496	.488	208	171	.822	245	288	195	1	1163	15.5
73–74—New York	41	1194	513	240	.468	113	93	.823	121	110	97	0	573	14.0
74–75—New York	78	2814	1462	668	.457	359	297	.827	327	270	200	0	1633	20.9
75–76—New York	76	2889	1354	647	.478	356	280	.787	273	304	209	1	1574	20.7
76–77—N.Y. Knicks	77	2656	1185	613	.517	366	307	.839	223	366	197	0	1533	19.9
77–78—New York	76	2369	1123	556	.495	291	242	.832	182	361	189	0	1354	17.8
78–79—New York	64	1393	699	329	.471	154	129	.838	74	189	123	0	787	12.3
79–80—New York	51	633	352	161	.457	64	56	.875	36	67	46	0	378	7.4
Totals	926	29636	14898	6906	.464	4513	3642	.807	2796	3594	2416	13	1754	18.8

NBA Playoff Record

Sea.—Team	G	Min.	FGA	FGM	Pct.	FTA	FTM	Pct.	Reb.	Ast.	PF	Dq.	Pts.	Avg.
68–69—Baltimore	4	171	114	44	.386	31	25	.806	21	16	10	0	113	28.3
69–70—Baltimore	7	299	154	74	.481	60	48	.800	23	28	23	0	196	28.0
70–71—Baltimore	18	671	356	145	.407	135	107	.793	64	74	56	0	397	22.1
71–72—New York	16	429	185	76	.411	57	45	.789	45	47	41	0	197	12.3
72–73—New York	16	504	211	111	.526	48	36	.750	51	51	39	0	258	16.1
73–74—New York	12	407	165	81	.491	55	47	.855	48	25	26	0	209	17.4
74–75—New York	3	89	45	12	.267	22	18	.818	9	6	6	0	42	14.0
77–78—New York	6	145	62	24	.387	18	11	.611	5	17	15	0	59	9.8
Totals	82	2715	1292	567	.439	426	337	.791	266	264	216	0	1471	17.9

NBA All-Star Game Record

Sea.—Team	Min.	FGA	FGM	Pct.	FTA	FTM	Pct.	Reb.	Ast.	PF	Dq.	Pts.
1969—Baltimore	27	15	6	.400	12	9	.750	4	4	4	0	21
1971—Baltimore	18	9	3	.333	0	0	—	5	2	3	0	6
1975—New York	25	8	3	.375	5	3	.600	3	2	2	0	9
1977—N.Y. Knicks	15	7	2	.286	0	0	—	0	3	1	0	4
Totals	85	39	14	.359	17	12	.706	12	11	10	0	40

Reference Section

CALVIN J. MURPHY

Born May 9, 1948, in Norwalk, Conn.
High School—Norwalk, Norwalk, Conn.
College—Niagara University
Inducted into the Basketball Hall of Fame, 1993
All-American, 1969, 1970

Collegiate Record

Sea.—Team	G	Min.	FGA	FGM	Pct.	FTA	FTM	Pct.	Reb.	Pts.	Avg.
66–67—Niagara	19	—	719	364	.506	239	201	.841	102	929	48.9
67–68—Niagara	24	—	772	337	.437	288	242	.840	118	916	38.2
68–69—Niagara	24	—	700	294	.420	230	190	.826	87	778	32.4
69–70—Niagara	29	—	692	316	.457	252	222	.881	103	854	29.4
Varsity totals	77	—	2164	947	.438	770	654	.849	308	2548	33.1

NBA Regular-Season Record

Sea.—Team	G	Min.	FGA	FGM	Pct.	FTA	FTM	Pct.	Reb.	Ast.	PF	Dq.	Pts.	Avg.
70–71—San Diego	82	2020	1029	471	.458	434	356	.820	245	329	263	4	1298	15.8
71–72—Houston	82	2538	1255	571	.455	392	349	.890	258	393	298	6	1491	18.2
72–73—Houston	77	1697	820	381	.465	269	239	.888	149	262	211	3	1001	13.0
73–74—Houston	81	2922	1285	671	.522	357	310	.868	188	603	310	8	1652	20.4
74–75—Houston	78	2513	1152	557	.484	386	341	.883	173	381	281	8	1455	18.7
75–76—Houston	82	2995	1369	675	.493	410	372	.907	209	596	294	3	1722	21.0
76–77—Houston	82	2764	1216	596	.490	307	272	.886	172	386	281	6	1464	17.9
77–78—Houston	76	2900	1737	852	.491	267	245	.918	164	259	241	4	1949	25.6
78–79—Houston	82	2941	1424	707	.496	265	246	.928	173	351	288	5	1660	20.2
79–80—Houston	76	2676	1267	624	.493	302	271	.897	150	299	269	3	1520	20.0
80–81—Houston	76	2014	1074	528	.492	215	206	.958	87	222	209	0	1266	16.7
81–82—Houston	64	1204	648	277	.427	110	100	.909	61	163	142	0	655	10.2
82–83—Houston	64	1423	754	337	.447	150	138	.920	74	158	163	3	816	12.8
Totals	1002	30607	15030	7247	.482	3864	3445	.892	2103	4402	3250	53	17949	17.9

NBA Playoff Record

Sea.—Team	G	Min.	FGA	FGM	Pct.	FTA	FTM	Pct.	Reb.	Ast.	PF	Dq.	Pts.	Avg.
74–75—Houston	8	305	156	72	.462	57	51	.895	19	45	36	2	195	24.4
76–77—Houston	12	420	213	102	.479	30	28	.933	19	75	47	1	232	19.3
78–79—Houston	2	73	31	9	.290	9	8	.889	3	6	9	0	26	13.0
79–80—Houston	7	265	108	58	.537	13	13	1.000	10	26	29	1	131	18.7
80–81—Houston	19	540	287	142	.495	60	58	.967	24	57	69	0	344	18.1
81–82—Houston	3	57	22	5	.227	8	7	.875	3	4	7	0	17	5.7
Totals	51	1660	817	388	.475	177	165	.932	78	213	197	4	945	18.5

NBA All-Star Game Record

Sea.—Team	Min.	FGA	FGM	Pct.	FTA	FTM	Pct.	Reb.	Ast.	PF	Dq.	Pts.
1979—Houston	15	5	3	.600	0	0	—	1	5	4	0	6

WILLIS REED, JR.

Born June 25, 1942, in Hico, La.
High School—West Side, Lillie, La.
College—Grambling College, Grambling, LA.
Inducted into the Basketball Hall of Fame, 1981
NBA Most Valuable Player, 1970
NBA All-Star Game Most Valuable Player, 1970
NBA Rookie of the Year, 1965

Collegiate Playing Record

Sea.—Team	G	Min.	FGA	FGM	Pct.	FTA	FTM	Pct.	Reb.	Pts.	Avg.
60–61—Grambling	35	—	239	146	.611	122	86	.705	312	378	10.8
61–62—Grambling	26	—	323	189	.585	102	80	.784	380	458	17.6
62–63—Grambling	33	—	489	282	.565	177	135	.763	563	699	21.2
63–64—Grambling	28	—	486	301	.619	199	143	.719	596	745	26.6
Totals	122	—	1537	918	.597	600	444	.740	1851	2280	18.7

NBA Regular-Season Record

Sea.—Team	G	Min.	FGA	FGM	Pct.	FTA	FTM	Pct.	Reb.	Ast.	PF	Dq.	Pts.	Avg.
64–65—New York	80	3042	1457	629	.432	407	302	.742	1175	133	339	14	1560	19.5
65–66—New York	76	2537	1009	438	.434	399	302	.757	883	91	323	13	1178	15.5
66–67—New York	78	2824	1298	635	.489	487	358	.735	1136	126	293	9	1628	20.9
67–68—New York	81	2879	1346	659	.490	509	367	.721	1073	159	343	12	1685	20.8
68–69—New York	82	3108	1351	704	.521	435	325	.747	1191	190	314	7	1733	21.1
69–70—New York	81	3089	1385	702	.507	464	351	.756	1126	161	287	2	1755	21.7
70–71—New York	73	2855	1330	614	.462	381	299	.785	1003	148	228	1	1527	20.9
71–72—New York	11	363	137	60	.438	39	27	.692	96	22	30	0	147	13.4
72–73—New York	69	1876	705	334	.474	124	92	.742	590	126	205	0	760	11.0
73–74—New York	19	500	184	84	.457	53	42	.792	141	30	49	0	210	11.1
Totals	650	23073	10202	4859	.476	3298	2465	.747	8414	1186	2411	58	12183	18.7

NBA Playoff Record

Sea.—Team	G	Min.	FGA	FGM	Pct.	FTA	FTM	Pct.	Reb.	Ast.	PF	Dq.	Pts.	Avg.
66–67—New York	4	148	80	43	.538	25	24	.960	55	7	19	1	110	27.5
67–68—New York	6	210	98	53	.541	30	22	.733	62	11	24	1	128	21.3
68–69—New York	10	429	198	101	.510	70	55	.786	141	19	40	1	257	25.7
69–70—New York	18	732	378	178	.471	95	70	.737	248	51	60	0	426	23.7
70–71—New York	12	504	196	81	.413	39	26	.667	144	27	41	0	188	15.7
72–73—New York	17	486	208	97	.466	21	18	.857	129	30	65	1	212	12.5
73–74—New York	11	132	45	17	.378	5	3	.600	22	4	26	0	37	3.4
Totals	78	2641	1203	370	.474	285	218	.765	801	149	275	4	1358	17.4

Reference Section

NBA All-Star Game Record

Sea.—Team	Min.	FGA	FGM	Pct.	FTA	FTM	Pct.	Reb.	Ast.	PF	Dq.	Pts.
1965–New York	25	11	3	.273	2	1	.500	5	1	2	0	7
1966–New York	23	11	7	.636	2	2	1.000	8	1	3	0	16
1967–New York	17	6	2	.333	0	0	.000	9	1	0	0	4
1968–New York	25	14	7	.500	3	2	.667	8	1	4	0	16
1969–New York	14	8	5	.625	0	0	.000	4	2	2	0	10
1970–New York	30	18	9	.500	3	3	1.000	11	0	6	1	21
1971–New York	27	16	5	.313	6	4	.667	13	1	3	0	14
Totals	161	84	38	.452	16	12	.750	58	7	20	1	88

NBA Coaching Record

Sea.—Club	Regular Season				Playoffs	
	W.	L.	Pct.	Pos.	W.	L.
1977–78—New York	43	39	.524	2†	2	4
1978–79—New York	6	8	.429	–†	—	—
Total	49	47	.510		2	4

Collegiate Coaching Record

Sea.—Club	Regular Season				Playoffs	
	W.	L.	Pct.	Pos.	W.	L.
1981–82—Creighton	7	20	.259	‡8		
1982–83—Creighton	8	19	.296	‡10		
1983–84—Creighton	17	14	.548	‡4		
Total	32	53	.376			

† Atlantic Division
‡ Missouri Valley Conference.

OSCAR PALMER ROBERTSON (Big O)

Born November 24, 1938, in Charlotte, Tenn. Height 6:05 Weight 220
High School—Crispus Attucks, Indianapolis, Ind.
College—University of Cincinnati, Cincinnati, O.
Inducted into the Basketball Hall of Fame, 1979
Chosen to the NBA 35th Anniversary All-Time Team, 1980
NBA Most Valuable Player, 1964
NBA All-Star Game Most Valuable Player, 1961, 1964, 1969
United Press International College Player of the Year, 1958, 1959, 1960
Member of the 1960 United States Olympic Basketball Team
NBA Rookie of the Year, 1961

Collegiate Record

Sea.—Team	G	Min.	FGA	FGM	Pct.	FTA	FTM	Pct.	Reb.	Pts.	Avg.
56–57—Cincinnati	13	—	—	151	—	178	127	.713	—	429	33.0
57–58—Cincinnati	28	1085	617	352	.571	355	280	.789	425	984	35.1
58–59—Cincinnati	30	1172	650	331	.509	398	316	.794	489	978	32.6
59–60—Cincinnati	30	1155	701	369	.526	361	273	.756	424	1011	33.7
Varsity Totals	88	3412	1968	1052	.535	1114	869	.780	1338	2973	13.8

NBA Regular-Season Record

Sea.—Team	G	Min.	FGA	FGM	Pct.	FTA	FTM	Pct.	Reb.	Ast.	PF	Dq.	Pts.	Avg.
60–61—Cincinnati	71	3012	1600	756	.473	794	653	.822	716	690	219	3	2165	30.5
61–62—Cincinnati	79	3503	1810	866	.478	872	700	.803	985	899	258	1	2432	30.8
62–63—Cincinnati	80	3521	1593	825	.518	758	614	.810	835	758	293	1	2264	28.3
63–64—Cincinnati	79	3559	1740	840	.483	938	800	.853	783	868	280	3	2480	31.4
64–65—Cincinnati	75	3421	1681	807	.480	793	665	.839	674	861	205	2	2279	30.4
65–66—Cincinnati	76	3493	1723	818	.475	881	742	.842	586	847	227	1	2378	31.3
66–67—Cincinnati	79	3468	1699	838	.493	843	736	.873	486	845	226	2	2412	30.5
67–68—Cincinnati	65	2765	1321	660	.500	660	576	.873	391	633	199	2	1896	29.2
68–69—Cincinnati	79	3461	1351	656	.486	767	643	.838	502	772	231	2	1955	24.7
69–70—Cincinnati	69	2865	1267	647	.511	561	454	.809	422	558	175	1	1748	25.3
70–71—Milwaukee	81	3194	1193	592	.496	453	385	.850	462	668	203	0	1569	19.4
71–72—Milwaukee	64	2390	887	419	.472	330	276	.836	323	491	116	0	1114	17.4
72–73—Milwaukee	73	2737	983	446	.454	281	238	.847	360	551	167	0	1130	15.5
73–74—Milwaukee	70	2477	772	338	.438	254	212	.835	279	446	132	0	888	12.7
Totals	1040	43866	19620	9508	.485	9185	7694	.838	7804	9887	2931	18	26710	25.7

NBA Playoff Record

Sea.—Team	G	Min.	FGA	FGM	Pct.	FTA	FTM	Pct.	Reb.	Ast.	PF	Dq.	Pts.	Avg.
61–62—Cincinnati	4	185	81	42	.519	39	31	.795	44	44	18	1	115	28.8
62–63—Cincinnati	12	570	264	124	.470	154	133	.864	156	108	41	0	381	31.8
63–64—Cincinnati	10	471	202	92	.455	127	109	.858	89	84	30	0	293	29.3
64–65—Cincinnati	4	195	89	38	.427	39	36	.923	19	48	14	0	112	28.0
65–66—Cincinnati	5	224	120	49	.408	68	61	.897	38	39	20	1	159	31.8
66–67—Cincinnati	4	183	64	33	.516	37	33	.892	16	45	9	0	99	24.8
70–71—Milwaukee	14	520	210	102	.486	69	52	.754	70	124	39	0	256	18.3

Reference Section

Sea.—Team	G	Min.	FGA	FGM	Pct.	FTA	FTM	Pct.	Reb.	Ast.	PF	Dq.	Pts.	Avg.
71–72—Milwaukee	11	380	140	57	.407	36	30	.833	64	83	29	0	144	13.1
72–73—Milwaukee	6	256	96	48	.500	34	31	.912	28	45	21	1	127	21.2
73–74—Milwaukee	16	689	200	90	.450	52	44	.846	54	149	46	0	224	14.0
Totals	86	3673	1466	675	.460	655	560	.855	578	769	267	3	1910	22.2

NBA All-Star Game Record

Sea.—Team	Min.	FGA	FGM	Pct.	FTA	FTM	Pct.	Reb.	Ast.	PF	Dq.	Pts.
1961—Cincinnati	34	13	8	.615	9	7	.778	9	14	5	0	23
1962—Cincinnati	37	20	9	.450	14	8	.571	7	13	3	0	26
1963—Cincinnati	37	15	9	.600	4	3	.750	3	6	5	0	21
1964—Cincinnati	42	23	10	.435	10	6	.600	14	8	4	0	26
1965—Cincinnati	40	18	8	.444	13	12	.923	6	8	5	0	28
1966—Cincinnati	25	12	6	.500	6	5	.833	10	8	0	0	17
1967—Cincinnati	34	20	9	.450	10	8	.800	2	5	4	0	26
1968—Cincinnati	22	9	7	.778	7	4	.571	1	5	2	0	18
1969—Cincinnati	32	16	8	.500	8	8	1.000	6	5	3	0	24
1970—Cincinnati	29	11	9	.818	4	3	.750	6	4	3	0	21
1971—Milwaukee	24	6	2	.333	3	1	.333	2	2	3	0	5
1972—Milwaukee	24	9	3	.333	10	5	.500	3	3	4	0	11
Totals	380	172	88	.512	98	70	.714	69	81	41	0	246

WILLIAM FENTON RUSSELL (Bill)

Born February 12, 1934, in Monroe, La.
High School—McClymonds, Oakland, Calif.
College—University of San Francisco, San Francisco, Calif.
Inducted into the Basketball Hall of Fame, 1974
Chosen to the NBA 25th Anniversary All-Time Team, 1970
Chosen to the NBA 35th Anniversary All-Time Team, 1980
NBA Most Valuable Player, 1958, 1961, 1963, 1965
NBA All-Star Game Most Valuable Player, 1963
Member of the 1956 United States Olympic Basketball Team
Chosen the Most Outstanding Player in the 1955 NCAA Tournament

Collegiate Record

Sea.—Team	G	Min.	FGA	FGM	Pct.	FTA	FTM	Pct.	Reb.	Pts.	Avg.
52–53—Univ. of San Francisco	23	—	—	—	—	—	—	—	—	461	20.0
53–54—Univ. of San Francisco	21	—	309	150	.485	212	117	.552	403	417	19.9
54–55—Univ. of San Francisco	29	—	423	229	.541	278	164	.590	594	622	21.4
55–56—Univ. of San Francisco	29	—	480	246	.513	212	105	.495	609	597	20.6
Totals	79	—	1212	625	.516	702	386	.550	1606	1636	20.7

NBA Regular-Season Record

Sea.—Team	G	Min.	FGA	FGM	Pct.	FTA	FTM	Pct.	Reb.	Ast.	PF	Dq.	Pts.	Avg.
56–57—Boston	48	1695	649	277	.427	309	152	.492	943	88	143	2	706	14.7
57–58—Boston	69	2640	1032	456	.442	443	230	.519	1564	202	181	2	1142	16.6
58–59—Boston	70	2979	997	456	.457	428	256	.598	1612	222	161	3	1168	16.7
59–60—Boston	74	3146	1189	555	.467	392	240	.612	1778	277	210	0	1350	18.2
60–61—Boston	78	3458	1250	532	.426	469	258	.550	1868	268	155	0	1322	16.9
61–62—Boston	76	3433	1258	575	.457	481	286	.594	1790	341	207	3	1436	18.9
62–63—Boston	78	3500	1182	511	.432	517	287	.555	1843	348	189	1	1309	16.8
63–64—Boston	78	3482	1077	466	.433	429	236	.550	1930	370	190	0	1168	15.0
64–65—Boston	78	3466	980	429	.438	426	244	.573	1878	410	204	1	1102	14.1
65–66—Boston	78	3386	943	391	.415	405	223	.551	1779	371	221	4	1005	12.9
66–67—Boston	81	3297	870	395	.454	467	285	.610	1700	472	258	4	1075	13.4
67–68—Boston	78	2953	858	365	.425	460	247	.537	1451	357	242	2	977	12.5
68–69—Boston	77	3291	645	279	.433	388	204	.526	1484	374	231	2	762	9.9
Totals	963	40726	12930	5687	.440	5614	3148	.561	21620	4100	2592	24	14522	15.1

NBA Playoff Record

Sea.—Team	G	Min.	FGA	FGM	Pct.	FTA	FTM	Pct.	Reb.	Ast.	PF	Dq.	Pts.	Avg.
56–57—Boston	10	409	148	54	.365	61	31	.508	244	32	41	1	139	13.9
57–58—Boston	9	355	133	48	.361	66	40	.606	221	24	24	0	136	15.1
58–59—Boston	11	496	159	65	.409	67	41	.612	305	40	28	1	171	15.5
59–60—Boston	13	572	206	94	.456	75	53	.707	336	38	38	1	241	18.5
60–61—Boston	10	462	171	73	.427	86	45	.523	299	48	24	0	191	19.1
61–62—Boston	14	672	253	116	.458	113	82	.726	370	70	49	0	314	22.4
62–63—Boston	13	617	212	96	.453	109	72	.661	326	66	36	0	264	20.3
63–64—Boston	10	451	132	47	.356	67	37	.552	272	44	33	0	131	13.1
64–65—Boston	12	561	150	79	.527	76	40	.526	302	76	43	2	198	16.5
65–66—Boston	17	814	261	124	.475	123	76	.618	428	85	60	0	324	19.1
66–67—Boston	9	390	86	31	.360	52	33	.635	198	50	32	1	95	10.6
67–68—Boston	19	869	242	99	.409	130	76	.585	434	99	73	1	274	14.4
68–69—Boston	18	829	182	77	.423	81	41	.506	369	98	65	1	195	10.8
Totals	165	7497	2335	1003	.430	1106	667	.603	4104	770	546	8	2673	16.2

NBA All-Star Game Record

Sea.—Team	Min.	FGA	FGM	Pct.	FTA	FTM	Pct.	Reb.	Ast.	PF	Dq.	Pts.
1958—Boston	26	12	5	.417	3	1	.333	11	2	5	0	11
1959—Boston	27	10	3	.300	1	1	1.000	9	1	4	0	7
1960—Boston	27	7	3	.429	2	0	.000	8	3	1	0	6
1961—Boston	28	15	9	.600	8	6	.750	11	1	2	0	24
1962—Boston	27	12	5	.417	3	2	.667	12	2	2	0	12
1963—Boston	37	14	8	.571	4	3	.750	24	5	3	0	19
1964—Boston	42	13	6	.462	2	1	.500	21	2	4	0	13
1965—Boston	33	12	7	.583	9	3	.333	13	5	6	1	17
1966—Boston	23	6	1	.167	0	0	.000	10	2	2	0	2
1967—Boston	22	2	1	.500	0	0	.000	5	5	2	0	2
1968—Boston	23	4	2	.500	0	0	.000	9	8	5	0	4
1969—Boston	28	4	1	.250	2	1	.500	6	3	1	0	3
Totals	343	111	51	.459	34	18	.529	139	39	37	1	120

Reference Section

NBA Coaching Record

Sea.—Club	Regular Season				Playoffs	
	W.	L.	Pct.	Pos.	W.	L.
1966–67—Boston	60	21	.741	2†	4	5
1967–68—Boston*	54	28	.659	2†	12	7
1968–69—Boston*	48	34	.585	4†	12	6
1973–74—Seattle	36	46	.439	3‡	—	—
1974–75—Seattle	43	39	.524	2‡	4	5
1975–76—Seattle	43	39	.524	2‡	2	4
1976–77—Seattle	40	42	.488	4‡	—	—
Total	324	249	.565		34	27

*Won NBA championship. †Eastern Division. ‡Pacific Division.

LUSIA HARRIS STEWART*

College—Delta State University
Inducted into the Basketball Hall of Fame, 1992
1977 Recipient—Thomas Broderick Award
All-American, 1975, 1976
In 1992 she became the first African-American woman inducted into the Basketball Hall of Fame.

*No data available.

NATHANIEL THURMOND (Nate)

Born July 25, 1941, in Akron, Ohio
High School—Central Hower, Akron, Ohio
College—Bowling Green State University, Bowling Green, Ohio
Inducted into the Basketball Hall of Fame, 1984
All-American, 1963

Collegiate Record

Sea.—Team	G	Min.	FGA	FGM	Pct.	FTA	FTM	Pct.	Reb.	Pts.	Avg.
59–60—Bowling Green State‡	17	—	—	—	—	—	—	—	208	225	13.2
60–61—Bowling Green State	24	—	427	170	.398	129	87	.674	449	427	17.8
61–62—Bowling Green State	25	—	358	163	.455	113	67	.593	394	393	15.7
62–63—Bowling Green State	27	—	466	206	.442	197	124	.629	452	536	19.9
Varsity totals	76	—	1251	539	.431	439	278	.633	1295	1356	17.8

NBA Regular-Season Record

Sea.—Team	G	Min.	FGA	FGM	Pct.	FTA	FTM	Pct.	Reb.	Ast.	PF	Dq.	Pts.	Avg.
63–64—San Francisco	76	1966	554	219	.395	173	95	.549	790	86	184	2	533	7.0
64–65—San Francisco	77	3173	1240	519	.419	357	235	.658	1395	157	232	3	1273	16.5
65–66—San Francisco	73	2891	1119	454	.406	428	280	.654	1312	111	223	7	1188	16.3
66–67—San Francisco	65	2755	1068	467	.437	445	280	.629	1382	166	183	3	1214	18.7
67–68—San Francisco	51	2222	929	382	.411	438	282	.644	1121	215	137	1	1046	20.5
68–69—San Francisco	71	3208	1394	571	.410	621	382	.615	1402	253	171	0	1524	21.5
69–70—San Francisco	43	1919	824	341	.414	346	261	.754	762	150	110	1	943	21.9
70–71—San Francisco	82	3351	1401	623	.445	541	395	.730	1128	257	192	1	1641	20.0
71–72—Golden State	78	3362	1454	628	.432	561	417	.743	1252	230	214	1	1673	21.4
72–73—Golden State	79	3419	1159	517	.446	439	315	.718	1349	280	240	2	1349	17.1
73–74—Golden State	62	2463	694	308	.444	287	191	.666	878	165	179	4	807	13.0
74–75—Chicago	80	2756	686	250	.364	224	132	.589	904	328	271	6	632	7.9
75–76—Chi.-Clev.	78	1393	337	142	.421	123	62	.504	415	94	160	1	346	4.4
76–77—Cleveland	49	997	246	100	.407	106	68	.642	374	83	128	2	268	5.5
Totals	964	35875	13105	5521	.421	5089	3395	.667	14464	2575	2624	34	14437	15.0

NBA Playoff Record

Sea.—Team	G	Min.	FGA	FGM	Pct.	FTA	FTM	Pct.	Reb.	Ast.	PF	Dq.	Pts.	Avg.
63–64—San Francisco	12	410	98	42	.429	53	36	.679	148	12	46	0	120	10.0
66–67—San Francisco	15	690	215	93	.433	91	52	.571	346	47	52	1	238	15.9
68–69—San Francisco	6	263	102	40	.392	34	20	.588	117	28	18	0	100	16.7
70–71—San Francisco	5	192	97	36	.371	20	16	.800	51	15	20	0	88	17.6
71–72—Golden State	5	230	122	53	.434	28	21	.750	89	26	12	0	127	25.4
72–73—Golden State	11	460	161	64	.398	40	32	.800	145	40	30	1	160	14.5
74–75—Chicago	13	254	38	14	.368	37	18	.486	87	31	36	0	46	3.5
75–76—Cleveland	13	375	79	37	.468	32	13	.406	117	28	52	2	87	6.7
76–77—Cleveland	1	1	0	0	—	0	0	—	1	0	0	0	0	0.0
Totals	81	2875	912	379	.416	335	208	.621	1101	227	266	4	966	11.9

NBA All-Star Game Record

Sea.—Team	Min.	FGA	FGM	Pct.	FTA	FTM	Pct.	Reb.	Ast.	PF	Dq.	Pts.
1965—San Francisco	10	2	0	.000	0	0	—	3	0	1	0	0
1966—San Francisco	33	16	3	.188	3	1	.333	16	1	1	0	7
1967—San Francisco	42	16	7	.438	4	2	.500	18	0	1	0	16
1968—San Francisco				Selected, did not play—injured.								
1970—San Francisco				Selected, did not play—injured.								
1973—Golden State	14	5	2	.400	0	0	—	4	1	2	0	4
1974—Golden State	5	4	2	.500	1	0	.000	3	0	0	0	4
Totals	104	43	14	.326	8	3	.375	44	2	5	0	31

Reference Section

WESTLEY UNSELD (Wes)

Born March 14, 1946, in Louisville, Kentucky
High School—Seneca-Louisville, Kentucky
College—University of Louisville
Inducted into the Basketball Hall of Fame, 1987
All American, 1968
1969 NBA Most Valuable Player
1969 NBA Rookie of the Year
1978 NBA Finals Most Valuable Player

Collegiate Record

Sea.—Team	G	Min.	FGA	FGM	Pct.	FTA	FTM	Pct.	Reb.	Pts.	Avg.
64–65—Louisville	14	—	312	214	.686	124	73	.589	331	501	35.8
65–66—Louisville	26	—	374	195	.521	202	128	.634	505	518	19.9
66–67—Louisville	28	—	374	201	.537	177	121	.684	533	523	18.7
67–68—Louisville	28	—	382	234	.613	275	177	.644	513	645	23.0
Varsity totals	82	—	1130	630	.558	654	426	.651	1551	1686	20.6

NBA Regular-Season Record

Sea.—Team	G	Min.	FGA	FGM	Pct.	FTA	FTM	Pct.	Reb.	Ast.	PF	Dq.	Pts.	Avg.
68–69—Baltimore	82	2970	897	427	.476	458	277	.605	1491	213	276	4	1131	13.8
69–70—Baltimore	82	3234	1015	526	.518	428	273	.638	1370	291	250	2	1325	16.2
70–71—Baltimore	74	2904	846	424	.501	303	199	.657	1253	293	235	2	1047	14.1
71–72—Baltimore	76	3171	822	409	.498	272	171	.629	1336	278	218	1	989	13.0
72–73—Baltimore	79	3085	854	421	.493	212	149	.703	1260	347	168	0	991	12.5
73–74—Capital	56	1727	333	146	.438	55	36	.655	517	159	121	1	328	5.9
74–75—Washington	73	2904	544	273	.502	184	126	.685	1077	297	180	1	672	9.2
75–76—Washington	78	2922	567	318	.561	195	114	.585	1036	404	203	3	750	9.6
76–77—Washington	82	2860	551	270	.490	166	100	.602	877	363	253	5	640	7.8
77–78—Washington	80	2644	491	257	.523	173	93	.538	955	326	234	2	607	7.6
78–79—Washington	77	2406	600	346	.577	235	151	.643	830	315	204	2	843	10.9
79–80—Washington	82	2973	637	327	.513	209	139	.665	1094	366	249	5	794	9.7
80–81—Washington	63	2032	429	225	.524	86	55	.640	673	170	171	1	507	8.0
Totals	984	35832	8586	4369	.509	2976	1883	.633	13769	3822	2762	29	10624	10.8

NBA Playoff Record

Sea.—Team	G	Min.	FGA	FGM	Pct.	FTA	FTM	Pct.	Reb.	Ast.	PF	Dq.	Pts.	Avg.
68–69—Baltimore	4	165	57	30	.526	19	15	.789	74	5	14	0	75	18.8
69–70—Baltimore	7	289	70	29	.414	19	15	.789	165	24	25	1	73	10.4
70–71—Baltimore	18	759	208	96	.462	81	46	.568	339	69	60	0	238	13.2
71–72—Baltimore	6	266	65	32	.492	19	10	.526	75	25	22	0	74	12.3
72–73—Baltimore	5	201	48	20	.417	19	9	.474	76	17	12	0	49	9.8
73–74—Capital	7	297	63	31	.492	15	9	.600	85	27	15	0	71	10.1
74–75—Washington	17	734	130	71	.546	61	40	.656	276	64	39	0	182	10.7
75–76—Washington	7	310	39	18	.462	24	13	.542	85	28	19	0	49	7.0
76–77—Washington	9	368	54	30	.556	12	7	.583	105	44	32	0	67	7.4
77–78—Washington	18	677	134	71	.530	46	27	.587	216	79	62	2	169	9.4

Sea.—Team	G	Min.	FGA	FGM	Pct.	FTA	FTM	Pct.	Reb.	Ast.	PF	Dq.	Pts.	Avg.
78–79—Washington	19	736	158	78	.494	64	39	.609	253	64	66	2	195	10.3
79–80—Washington	2	87	14	7	.500	6	4	.667	28	7	5	0	18	9.0
Totals	119	4889	1040	513	.493	385	234	.608	1777	453	371	5	1260	10.6

NBA All-Star Game Record

Sea.—Team	Min.	FGA	FGM	Pct.	FTA	FTM	Pct.	Reb.	Ast.	PF	Dq.	Pts.
1969—Baltimore	14	7	5	.714	3	1	.333	8	1	3	0	11
1971—Baltimore	21	9	4	.444	0	0	—	10	2	2	0	8
1972—Baltimore	16	5	1	.200	0	0	—	7	1	3	0	2
1973—Baltimore	11	4	2	.500	0	0	—	5	1	0	0	4
1975—Washington	15	3	2	.667	2	2	1.000	6	1	2	0	6
Totals	77	28	14	.500	5	3	.600	36	6	10	0	31

NBA Coaching Record

		Regular Season				Playoffs		
Sea.—Team	W	L	Pct.	Finish	W	L	Pct.
87–88—Washington	30	25	.545	T2nd/Atlantic Division	2	3	.400
88–89—Washington	40	42	.488	4th/Atlantic Division	—	—	—
89–90—Washington	31	51	.378	4th/Atlantic Division	—		
90–91—Washington	30	52	.366	4th/Atlantic Division	—	—	—
91–92—Washington	25	57	.305	6th/Atlantic Division	—	—	—
Total	156	227	.407		2	3	.400

LEONARD R. WILKENS (Lenny)

Born October 28, 1937, in Brooklyn, New York
High School—Boys, Brooklyn, N.Y.
College—Providence R.I.
Inducted into the Basketball Hall of Fame, 1988
1971 NBA All-Star Game Most Valuable Player

Collegiate Record

Sea.—Team	G	Min.	FGA	FGM	Pct.	FTA	FTM	Pct.	Reb.	Pts.	Avg.
56–57—Providence	23	—	—	—	—	—	—	—	—	488	21.2
57–58—Providence	24	—	316	137	.434	130	84	.646	190	358	14.9
58–59—Providence	27	—	390	167	.428	144	89	.618	188	423	15.7
59–60—Providence	29	—	362	157	.434	140	98	.700	205	412	14.2
Varsity totals	80	—	1068	461	.432	414	271	.655	583	1193	14.9

Reference Section

NBA Regular-Season Record

Sea.—Team	G	Min.	FGA	FGM	Pct.	FTA	FTM	Pct.	Reb.	Ast.	PF	Dq.	Pts.	Avg.
60–61—St. Louis	75	1898	783	333	.425	300	214	.713	335	212	215	5	880	11.7
61–62—St. Louis	20	870	364	140	.385	110	84	.764	131	116	63	0	364	18.2
62–63—St. Louis	75	2569	834	333	.399	319	222	.696	403	381	256	6	888	11.8
63–64—St. Louis	78	2526	808	334	.413	365	270	.740	335	359	287	7	938	12.0
64–65—St. Louis	78	2854	1048	434	.414	558	416	.746	365	431	283	7	1284	16.5
65–66—St. Louis	69	2692	954	411	.431	532	422	.793	322	429	248	4	1244	18.0
66–67—St. Louis	78	2974	1036	448	.432	583	459	.787	412	442	280	6	1355	17.4
67–68—St. Louis	82	3169	1246	546	.438	711	546	.768	438	679	255	3	1638	20.0
68–69—Seattle	82	3463	1462	644	.440	710	547	.770	511	674	294	8	1835	22.4
69–70—Seattle	75	2802	1066	448	.420	556	438	.788	378	683	212	5	1334	17.8
70–71—Seattle	71	2641	1125	471	.419	574	461	.803	319	654	201	3	1403	19.8
71–72—Seattle	80	2989	1027	479	.466	620	480	.774	338	766	209	4	1438	18.0
72–73—Cleveland	75	2973	1275	572	.449	476	394	.828	346	628	221	2	1538	20.5
73–74—Cleveland	74	2483	994	462	.465	361	289	.801	277	522	165	2	1213	16.4
74–75—Portland	65	1161	305	134	.439	198	152	.768	120	235	96	1	420	6.5
Totals	1077	38064	14327	6189	.432	6973	5394	.774	5030	7211	3285	63	17772	16.5

NBA Playoff Record

Sea.—Team	G	Min.	FGA	FGM	Pct.	FTA	FTM	Pct.	Reb.	Ast.	PF	Dq.	Pts.	Avg.
60–61—St. Louis	12	437	166	63	.380	58	44	.759	72	42	51	4	170	14.2
62–63—St. Louis	11	400	154	57	.370	49	37	.755	69	69	51	2	151	13.7
63–64–St. Louis	12	413	143	64	.448	58	44	.759	60	64	42	0	172	14.3
64–65—St. Louis	4	147	57	20	.351	29	24	.828	12	15	14	0	64	16.0
65–66—St. Louis	10	391	143	57	.399	83	57	.687	54	70	43	0	171	17.1
66–67—St. Louis	9	378	145	58	.400	90	77	.856	68	65	34	0	193	21.4
67–68—St. Louis	6	237	91	40	.440	40	30	.750	38	47	23	1	110	18.3
Totals	64	2403	899	359	.399	407	313	.769	373	372	258	7	1031	16.1

NBA All-Star Game Record

Sea.—Team	Min.	FGA	FGM	Pct.	FTA	FTM	Pct.	Reb.	Ast.	PF	Dq.	Pts.
1963—St. Louis	25	7	2	.286	1	0	.000	2	3	0	0	4
1964—St. Louis	14	5	1	.200	1	1	1.000	0	0	3	0	3
1965—St.Louis	20	6	2	.333	4	4	1.000	3	3	3	0	8
1967—St. Louis	16	6	2	.333	3	2	.667	2	6	2	0	6
1968—St. Louis	22	10	4	.400	8	6	.750	3	3	1	0	14
1969—Seattle	24	15	3	.200	5	4	.800	7	5	3	0	10
1970—Seattle	17	7	5	.714	3	2	.667	2	4	1	0	12
1971—Seattle	20	11	8	.727	5	5	1.000	1	1	1	0	21
1973—Cleveland	24	8	3	.375	2	1	.500	2	1	1	0	7
Totals	182	75	30	.400	32	25	.781	22	26	15	0	85

NBA Coaching Record

Sea.—Team	Regular Season				Playoffs		
	W	L	Pct.	Finish	W	L	Pct.
69–70—Seattle	36	46	.439	5th/Western Division	—	—	—
70–71—Seattle	38	44	.463	4th/Pacific Division	—	—	—
71–72—Seattle	47	35	.573	3rd/Pacific Division	—	—	—
74–75—Portland	38	44	.463	3rd/Pacific Division	—	—	—
75–76—Portland	37	45	.451	5th/Pacific Division	—	—	—
77–78—Seattle	42	18	.700	3rd/Pacific Division	13	9	.591
78–79—Seattle	52	30	.634	1st/Pacific Division	12	5	.706
79–80—Seattle	56	26	.683	2nd/Pacific Division	7	8	.467
80–81—Seattle	34	48	.415	6th/Pacific Division	—	—	—
81–82—Seattle	52	30	.634	2nd/Pacific Division	3	5	.375
82–83—Seattle	48	34	.585	3rd/Pacific Division	0	2	.000
83–84—Seattle	42	40	.512	3rd/Pacific Division	2	3	.400
84–85—Seattle	31	51	.378	4th/Pacific Division	—	—	—
86–87—Cleveland	31	51	.378	6th/Central Division	—	—	—
87–88—Cleveland	42	40	.512	T4th/Central Division	2	3	.400
88–89—Cleveland	57	25	.695	2nd/Central Division	2	3	.400
89–90—Cleveland	42	40	.512	T4th/Central Division	2	3	.400
90–91—Cleveland	33	49	.402	6th/Central Division	—	—	—
91–92—Cleveland	57	25	.695	2nd/Central Division	9	8	.529
Total	815	721	.531		52	49	.515

EDGE NBA MOST VALUABLE PLAYER AWARD (Maurice Podoloff Trophy)

Year	Player	Team	Year	Player	Team
1957–58	Bill Russell	Boston Celtics	1974–75	Bob McAdoo	Buffalo Braves
1959–60	Wilt Chamberlain	Philadelphia Warriors	1975–76	Kareem Abdul-Jabbar	Los Angeles Lakers
1960–61	Bill Russell	Boston Celtics	1976–77	Kareem Abdul-Jabbar	Los Angeles Lakers
1961–62	Bill Russell	Boston Celtics	1978–79	Moses Malone	Houston Rockets
1962–63	Bill Russell	Boston Celtics	1979–80	Kareem Abdul-Jabbar	Los Angeles Lakers
1963–64	Oscar Robertson	Cincinnati Royals	1980–81	Julius Erving	Philadelphia 76ers
1964–65	Bill Russell	Boston Celtics	1981–82	Moses Malone	Houston Rockets
1965–66	Wilt Chamberlain	Philadelphia 76ers	1982–83	Moses Malone	Philadelphia 76ers
1966–67	Wilt Chamberlain	Philadelphia 76ers	1986–87	Earvin Johnson	Los Angeles Lakers
1967–68	Wilt Chamberlain	Philadelphia 76ers	1987–88	Michael Jordon	Chicago Bulls
1968–69	Wes Unseld	Baltimore Bullets	1988–89	Earvin Johnson	Los Angeles Lakers
1969–70	Willis Reed	New York Knicks	1989–90	Earvin Johnson	Los Angeles Lakers
1970–71	Kareem Abdul-Jabbar	Milwaukee Bucks	1990–91	Michael Jordan	Chicago Bulls
1971–72	Kareem Abdul-Jabbar	Milwaukee Bucks	1991–92	Michael Jordan	Chicago Bulls
1973–74	Kareem Abdul-Jabbar	Milwaukee Bucks	1992–93	Charles Barkley	Phoenix Suns

AMERICAN BASKETBALL ASSOCIATION MOST VALUABLE PLAYER AWARD

Year	Player	Team	Position	Year	Player	Team	Position
1967–68	Connie Hawkins	Pittsburgh Pipers	Forward	1973–74	Julius Erving	New York Nets	Forward
1968–69	Mel Daniels	Indiana Pacers	Forward	1974–75	Julius Erving	New York Nets	Forward
1969–70	Spencer Haywood	Denver Rockets	Forward		George McGinnis	Indiana Pacers	Forward
1970–71	Mel Daniels	Indiana Pacers	Forward	1975–76	Julius Erving	New York Nets	Forward
1971–72	Artis Gilmore	Kentucky Colonels	Center				

COCA-COLA CLASSIC NBA ROOKIE OF THE YEAR AWARD (Eddie Gottlieb Trophy)

Year	Player	Team	Year	Player	Team
1953–54	Ray Felix	Baltimore Bullets	1976–77	Adrian Dantley	Buffalo Braves
1955–56	Maurice Stokes	Rochester Royals	1977–78	Walter Davis	Phoenix Suns
1957–58	Woody Sauldsberry	Philadelphia Warriors	1978–79	Phil Ford	Kansas City Kings
1958–59	Elgin Baylor	Minneapolis Lakers	1980–81	Darrell Griffith	Utah Jazz
1959–60	Wilt Chamberlain	Philadelphia Warriors	1981–82	Charles Williams	New Jersey Nets
1960–61	Oscar Robertson	Cincinnati Royals	1982–83	Terry Cummings	San Diego Clippers
1961–62	Walter Bellamy	Chicago Packers	1983–84	Ralph Sampson	Houston Rockets
1964–65	Willis Reed	New York Knickerbockers	1984–85	Michael Jordan	Chicago Bulls
1966–67	David Bing	Detroit Pistons	1985–86	Patrick Ewing	New York Knickerbockers
1967–68	Earl Monroe	Baltimore Bullets	1986–87	Chuck Pearson	Indiana Pacers
1968–69	Wes Unseld	Baltimore Bullets	1987–88	Mark Jackson	New York Knickerbockers
1969–70	Kareem Abdul-Jabbar	Milwaukee Bucks	1988–89	Mitch Richmond	Golden State Warriors
1971–72	Sidney Wicks	Portland Trailblazers	1989–90	David Robinson	San Antonio Spurs
1972–73	Robert McAdoo	Buffalo Braves	1990–91	Derrick Coleman	New Jersey Nets
1974–75	Keith Wilkes	Golden State Warriors	1991–92	Larry Johnson	Charlotte Hornets

AMERICAN BASKETBALL ASSOCIATION ROOKIE OF THE YEAR

Year	Player	Team	Position	Year	Player	Team	Position
1967–68	Mel Daniels	Minnesota Muskies	Forward	1971–72	Artis Gilmore	Kentucky Colonels	Center
1968–69	Warren Armstrong	Oakland Oaks	Guard	1972–73	Brian Taylor	New York Nets	Guard
1969–70	Spencer Haywood	Denver Rockets	Forward	1974–75	Marvin Barnes	St. Louis Spirits	Forward
1970–71	Charlie Scott	Virginia Squires	Guard (co-winner)	1975–76	David Thompson	Denver Nuggets	Guard

AMERICAN BASKETBALL ASSOCIATION ALL-STAR GAME MOST VALUABLE PLAYER AWARD

Year	Player	Team	Year	Player	Team
1970	Spencer Haywood	Denver Rockets	1974	Artis Gilmore	Kentucky Colonels
1971	Mel Daniels	Indiana Pacers	1975	Freddie Lewis	St. Louis Spirits
1973	Warren Jabali	Denver Nuggets	1976	David Thompson	Denver Nuggets

MILLER GENUINE DRAFT NBA SIXTH MAN AWARD

Year	Player	Team	Year	Player	Team
1986–87	Ricky Pierce	Milwaukee Bucks	1988–89	Eddie Johnson	Phoenix Suns
1987–88	Roy Tarpley	Dallas Mavericks	1989–90	Ricky Pierce	Milwaukee Bucks

SCHICK AWARD RECIPIENTS

Year	Player	Team	Year	Player	Team
1983–84	Earvin Johnson	Los Angeles Lakers	1988–89	Michael Jordan	Chicago Bulls
1984–85	Michael Jordan	Chicago Bulls	1989–90	David Robinson	San Antonio Spurs
1985–86	Charles Barkley	Philadelphia 76ers	1990–91	David Robinson	San Antonio Spurs
1986–87	Charles Barkley	Philadelphia 76ers	1991–92	Dennis Rodman	Detroit Pistons
1987–88	Charles Barkely	Philadelphia 76ers			

J. WALTER KENNEDY CITIZENSHIP AWARD

Year	Player	Team	Year	Player	Team
1974–75	Wes Unseld	Washington Bullets	1985–86	(tie) Michael Cooper	Los Angeles Lakers
1975–76	Slick Watts	Seattle Supersonics		Rory Sparrow	New York Knicks
1976–77	Dave Bing	Washington Bullets	1986–87	Isiah Thomas	Detroit Pistons
1977–78	Robert Lanier	Detroit Pistons	1987–88	Alexander English	Denver Nuggets
1978–79	Calvin Murphy	Houston Rockets	1988–89	Thurl Bailey	Utah Jazz
1979–80	Austin Carr	Cleveland Cavaliars	1989–90	Glenn Rivers	Atlanta Hawks
1980–81	Michael Glenn	New York Knicks	1990–91	Kevin Johnson	Phoenix Suns
1982–83	Julius Erving	Philadelphia 76ers	1991–92	Earvin Johnson	Los Angeles Lakers

Reference Section

NATIONAL BASKETBALL ASSOCIATION FINALS MOST VALUABLE PLAYER

Year	Player	Team	Year	Player	Team
1970	Willis Reed	New York Knicks	1983	Moses Malone	Philadelphia 76ers
1971	Kareem Abdul-Jabbar	Milwaukee Bucks	1985	Kareem Abdul-Jabbar	Los Angeles Lakers
1972	Wilt Chamberlain	Los Angeles Lakers	1987	Earvin Johnson	Los Angeles Lakers
1973	Willis Reed	New York Knicks	1988	James Worthy	Los Angeles Lakers
1976	JoJo White	Boston Celtics	1989	Joe Dumars	Detroit Pistons
1978	Westley Unseld	Washington Bullets	1990	Isiah Thomas	Detroit Pistons
1979	Dennis Johnson	Seattle Supersonics	1991	Michael Jordan	Chicago Bulls
1980	Earvin Johnson	Los Angeles Lakers	1992	Michael Jordan	Chicago Bulls
1981	Cedric Maxwell	Boston Celtics	1993	Michael Jordan	Chicago Bulls
1982	Earvin Johnson	Los Angeles Lakers			

NBA DEFENSIVE PLAYER OF THE YEAR AWARD

Year	Player	Team	Year	Player	Team
1982–83	Sidney Moncrief	Milwaukee Bucks	1987–88	Michael Jordan	Chicago Bulls
1983–84	Sidney Moncrief	Milwaukee Bucks	1989–90	Dennis Rodman	Detroit Pistons
1985–86	Alvin Robertson	San Antonio Spurs	1990–91	Dennis Rodman	Detroit Pistons
1986–87	Michael Cooper	Los Angeles Lakers	1991–92	David Robinson	San Antonio Spurs

IBM NBA COACH OF THE YEAR (Red Auerbach Trophy)

Year	Player	Team
1973–74	Ray Scott	Detroit Pistons
1990–91	Don Chaney	Houston Rockets

NBA EXECUTIVE OF THE YEAR

Year	Executive	Team
1991	Wayne Embry	Cleveland Cavaliers

AFRICAN-AMERICANS IN PROFESSIONAL BASKETBALL

ATLANTA HAWKS
Atlanta, Georgia 30303

St. Louis Hawks, 1955–68

Coaches
Reed, Willis (Assistant) 1985–87

All-Stars
Wilkens, Lenny 1963–68
Beatty, Zelmo 1966, 1968
Bridges, Bill 1967–68, 1970
Hudson, Lou 1969–71, 1973–74
Drew, John 1976, 1980
Johnson, Eddie 1980–81
Roundfield, Dan 1980–82
Wilkens, Dominique 1986–92

All-Time Roster of The Atlanta Hawks
Barker, Tom, University of Hawaii, 1976–77
Battle, John, Rutgers University, 1985–92

Beard, Alfred "Butch," University of Louisville, 1969–70
Behagan, Ron, University of Minnesota, 1977–78
Bellamy, Walter, Indiana University, 1969–74
Bracey, Steven, University of Tulsa, 1972–74
Bradshaw, Clyde, DePaul University, 1981–82
Bridges, William, University of Kansas, 1968–72
Brown, Rickey, Mississippi State University, 1982–85
Caldwell, Joe, Arizona State University, 1968–70
Carr, Antoine, Wichita State University, 1984–90
Chambers, Jerry, University of Utah, 1970–71
Charles, Ken, Fordham University, 1976–78
Charles, Lorenzo, North Carolina State University, 1985–86
Christian, Robert, Grambling State University, 1970–73
Collins, Don, Washington State University, 1980–81
Criss, Charles, New Mexico State University, 1977–85

Davis, John, University of Dayton, 1982–84
Drew, John, Gardner-Webb College, 1974–82
DuVal, Dennis, Syracuse University, 1975–76
Eaves, Jerry, University of Louisville, 1984–85
Edmonson, Keith, Purdue University, 1982–83
Furlow, Terry, Michigan State University, 1978–80
Gilliam, Herm, Michigan State University, 1978–80
Givens, Jack, University of Kentucky, 1978–80
Glenn, Michael, Southern Illinois University, 1981–85
Granger, Stewart, Villanova University, 1984–85
Haliburton, Jeff, Drake University, 1971–73
Halimon, Shaler, University of Utah, 1971–72
Hawkins, Connie, Iowa University, 1975–76
Hazzard, Walter (Mahdi Abdul-Rahman), University of California, LA, 1968–71
Henderson, Tom, University of Hawaii, 1974–77
Herron, Keith, Villanova University, 1978–79
Hill, Armond, Princeton University, 1976–84
Holland, Wilbur, University of New Orleans, 1975–76
Hudson, Lou, University of Minnesota, 1968–77
Jackson, Tracey, University of Notre Dame, 1985–86
Johnson, Eddie, Auburn University, 1977–85
Johnson, George, Dillard University, 1982–83
Johnson, Ollie, Temple University, 1977–78
Jones, Dwight, University of Houston, 1973–76
Lee, Alfred "Butch," Marquette University, 1978–79
Lee, Ron, University of Oregon, 1979–80
Levingston, Cliff, Wichita State University, 1984–90
Lowe, Sidney, North Carolina State University, 1984–85
Macklin, Durand "Rudy," Louisiana State University, 1981–83
Matthews, Wes, University of Wisconsin, 1980–84, 1990–91
McElroy, James, Central Michigan University, 1979–82
Meminger, Dean, Marquette University, 1974–75
Meriweather, Joe C., Southern Illinois University, 1976–77
Payne, Tom, University of Kentucky, 1971–72
Pellom, Sam, University of Buffalo, 1979–83
Rivers, Glenn "Doc," Marquette University, 1983–91
Robertson, Tony, West Virginia University, 1977–78
Robinson, Leonard, Tennessee State University, 1976–77
Rollins, Wayne "Tree," Clemson University, 1977–88
Roundfield, Dan, Central Michigan University, 1978–84
Russell, Walker D., Western Michigan University, 1984–85
Shelton, Craig, Georgetown University, 1980–82
Silas, Paul, Creighton University, 1968–69
Smith, Randy, Buffalo State University, 1982–83
Sojourner, Michael, University of Utah, 1974–77
Sparrow, Rory, Villanova University, 1981–83
Toney, Sedric, University of Dayton, 1985–86, 1990–91
Trapp, George, Long Beach State University, 1971–73

Waller, Dwight, Tennessee State University, 1968–69
Washington, Jim, Villanova University, 1971–75
Wilkins, Dominique, University of Georgia, 1982–87
Williams, Freeman, Portland State University, 1981–82
Williams, Milt, Lincoln University, 1971–72
Williams, Sylvester, University of Rhode Island, 1983–85
Willis, Kevin, Michigan State University, 1984–87
Willoughby, William, Dwight Morrow H.S. (N.J.), 1975–77
Wilson, Rick, University of Louisville, 1978–80
Wood, Al, University of North Carolina, 1981–82

ADDENDUM

Front Office Personnel

Triche, Arthur (Director of Media Relations) 1988–93
Davis, Johnny (Assistant to the President) 1989–90
Pender, Mel (Director of Community Affairs) 1989–93
May, Darrin (Assistant Director of Media Relations) 1992–93
Wimbush, Amanda (Assistant Director Community Affairs) 1992–93
Bradley, Sharon (Marketing Representative) 1992–93
Epps, Michael (Marketing Representative) 1992–93
Hensley, Don (Marketing Representative) 1992–93
Lawrence, David (Marketing Representative), 1992–93
McCoy, Teyon (Marketing Representative) 1992–93
Washington, Chuck (Marketing Representative) 1992–93

Coaches

Davis, Johnny, (Assistant), 1990–93
Hinds, Roger, (Strength and Conditioning), 1992–93
Wilkens, Lenny, (Head), 1993–94

All-Stars

Rivers, Glenn 1988
Malone, Moses 1989
Willis, Kevin 1992

All-Time Roster of The Atlanta Hawks

Augmon, Stacey, University of Nevada, Las Vegas, 1991–93
Blaylock, Darrin "Mookie," University of Oklahoma, 1992–93
Bradley, Dudley, University of North Carolina, 1988–89
Charles, Lorenzo, North Carolina State University, 1986–86
Cheeks, Maurice, West Texas State University, 1991–92
*DeZonie, Henry E. ("Hank"), Clark College (Georgia), 1950–51
Ferrell, Duane, Georgia Tech University, 1988–93
Graham, Paul, Ohio University, 1991–93
Henderson, Cedric, University of Georgia, 1986–87
Long, John, University of Detroit, 1989–90
Malone, Moses, Petersburg H.S. (Virginia), 1988–91
Marble, Roy, University of Iowa, 1989–90

Mays, Travis, University of Texas, 1991–93
McGee, Mike, University of Michigan, 1986–88
Moncrief, Sidney, University of Arkansas, 1990–91
Monroe, Rodney, North Carolina State University, 1991–92
Robinson, Rumeal, University of Michigan, 1990–92
Sanders, Jeff, Georgia Southern University, 1992–93
Smith, Ken, University of North Carolina, 1990–91
Theus, Reginald, University of Nevada, Las Vegas, 1988–89
Tolbert, Ray, Indiana University, 1988–89
Washburn, Chris, North Carolina State University, 1987–88
Webb, Anthony "Spud," North Carolina State University, 1985–91

Whatley, Ennis, University of Alabama, 1987–88
Wiley, Morlon, Long Beach State University, 1992–93
Williams, Gus, University of Southern California, 1986–87
Williams, Ray, University of Minnesota, 1985–86
Wilson, Mike, Marquette University, 1986–87
Wood, Leon, California State University Fullerton, 1987–88
Workman, Haywoode, Oral Roberts University, 1989–90

*Hank DeZonie played for the Tri-Cities Blackhawks in the National Basketball League. The team moved to Milwaukee and then to St. Louis.

BOSTON CELTICS
Boston, Massachusetts 02114

Coaches
Russell, William (Head) 1966–69
Jones, K. C. (Assistant) 1977–83
          (Head) 1983–87
Sanders, Thomas "Satch" (Assistant) 1977–78
          (Head) 1978–79

All-Stars
Russell, William 1959–69
Jones, Sam 1962, 1964–66, 1968
White, JoJo 1971–77
Archibald, Nate 1980–82
Parrish, Robert 1981–87, 1990–91
Johnson, Dennis 1985–87

All-Time Roster of The Boston Celtics
Abdul-Aziz, Zaid, Iowa State University, 1977–78
Anderson, Jerome, West Virginia University, 1975–76
Archibald, Nate, University of Texas, El Paso, 1978–83
Ard, Jim, University of Cincinnati, 1974–78
Barker, Tom, University of Hawaii, 1978–79
Barksdale, Don, University of California, LA, 1953–55
Barnes, Jim "Bad News," Texas Western University, 1968–70
Barnes, Marvin, Providence College, 1978–79
Bing, David, Syracuse University, 1977–78
Boswell, Thomas, University of South Carolina, 1975–78
Bradley, Charles, University of Wyoming, 1981–83
Bryant, Emmette, DePaul University, 1968–70
Buckner, Quinn, Indiana University, 1982–85
Carr, M. L., Guilford College, 1979–85
Chaney, Don, University of Houston, 1968–80
Clark, Carlos, University of Kansas, 1976–77
Cook, Norm, University of Houston, 1968–80

Cooper, Charles, Duquesne University, 1950–54
Downing, Steven, Indiana University, 1973–75
Duerod, Terry, University of Detroit, 1980–82
Embry, Wayne, University of Miami (Ohio), 1966–68
Glover, Clarence, Western Kentucky University, 1971–72
Green, Si Hugo, Duquesne University, 1965–66
Hankinsojn, Phil, University of Pennsylvania, 1973–75
Henderson, Gerald, Virginia Commonwealth University, 1979–85
Jackson, Tracy, University of Notre Dame, 1981–82
Johnson, Dennis, Pepperdine University, 1983–90
Johnson, Rich, Grambling College, 1968–71
Jones, John, Los Angeles State University, 1967–68
Jones, K. C., University of San Francisco, 1958–67
Jones, Sam, North Carolina Central University, 1957–69
King, Maurice, University of Kansas, 1959–60
Knight, Billy, University of Pittsburgh, 1978–79
Maxwell, Cedric, University of North Carolina, Charlotte, 1977–85
McAdoo, Robert, University of North Carolina, 1978–79
McDonald, Glenn, Long Beach State University, 1974–76
Naulls, Willie, University of California, LA, 1963–66
Parrish, Robert, Cenetary College, 1980–87
Rowe, Curtis, University of California, LA, 1976–79
Russell, William, University of San Francisco, 1956–69
Sanders, Frank, Southern University, 1978–79
Sanders, Tom, New York University, 1960–73
Sauldsberry, Woodrow, Texas Southern University, 1965–66
Scott, Charles, University of North Carolina, 1975–78
Searcy, Ed, St. John's University, 1975–76
Silas, Paul, Creighton University, 1972–76
Smith, Garfield, University of Kentucky, 1970–72
Swain, Ben, Texas Southern University, 1958–59
Tatum, Earl, Marquette University, 1978–79

Thacker, Tom, University of Cincinnati, 1967–68
Thompson, John, Providence College, 1964–66
Tillis, Darren, Cleveland State University, 1981–83
Vincent, Sam, Michigan State University, 1985–87
Washington, Kermit, American University, 1977–78
White, Joseph, University of Kansas, 1969–79
Wicks, Sidney, University of California, LA, 1976–78
Williams, Art, California Poly, 1971–74
Williams, Earl, Winston-Salem State University, 1978–79
Williams, Sylvester, University of Rhode Island, 1985–86
Williams, Willie, Florida State University, 1970–71
Wilson, Robert, Wichita State University, 1976–77

ADDENDUM

Front Office Personnel
Levy, Wayne (Coordinator of Community Relations) 1987–93
Hutcherson, Eric (Assistant Director of Public Relations) 1991–93
Carr, M. L. (Director of Community Relations) 1991–93

Coaches
1982–83

All-Stars
Barksdale, Donald 1953
Lewis, Reggie 1992

All-Time Roster of The Boston Celtics
Bagley, John, Boston College, 1989–93
Battle, Ken, University of Illinois, 1991–92
Birdsong, Otis, University of Houston, 1988–89
Brown, Dee, Jacksonville University, 1990–93
Daye, Darren, University of California, LA, 1986–88
Douglas, Sherman, Syracuse University, 1992–93
Gamble, Kevin, University of Iowa, 1988–93
Gilmore, Artis, Jacksonville University, 1987–88
Glover, Clarence, Western Kentucky University, 1987–88
Green, Rickey, University of Michigan, 1991–92
Lewis, Reggie, Northeastern University, 1987–93
Massenburg, Tony, University of Maryland, 1991–92
McDaniel, Xavier, Wichita State University, 1992–93
Minniefield, Dirk, University of Kentucky, 1987–88
Pinckney, Ed, Villanova University, 1989–93
Robinson, Ed, Centenary College, 1991–92
Shaw, Brian, University of California, Santa Barbara, 1988–92
Smith, Charles, Georgetown University, 1989–91
Smith, Derek, University of Louisville, 1990–91
Thirdkill, David, Bradley University, 1985–87
Turner, Andre, Memphis State University, 1986–87
Upshaw, Kelvin, University of Utah, 1988–90
Williams, Ray, University of Minnesota, 1984–85
Wynder, A. J., Fairfield University, 1990–91

CHARLOTTE HORNETS
Charlotte, North Carolina 28217

Board of Advisors
Albright, Dr. Robert L. 1990–93
Gantt, Harvey 1990–93

Front Office Personnel
Montgomery, Cathy (Telecommunication Administrator) 1990–93
Smith, Clayton (Director of Ticketing Operations) 1990–93
Thompson, David (Youth Program Coordinator) 1990–93

Coaches
Littles, Gene (Assistant) 1988–89
            (Head) 1989–91
Dunn, T. R. (Assistant) 1991–93

All-Stars
Johnson, Larry 1993

All-Time Roster of The Charlotte Hornets
Ansley, Michael, University of Alabama, 1991–92

Bogues, Tyrone, Wake Forest University, 1988–93
Cureton, Earl, University of Detroit, 1988–91
Curry, Del, Virginia Tech University, 1988–93
Dozier, Terry, University of South Carolina, 1989–90
Frederick, Anthony, Pepperdine University, 1991–92
Gattison, Ken, Old Dominion University, 1989–93
Gill, Kendall, University of Illinois, 1990–93
Gilliam, Armon, University of Nevada, Las Vegas, 1989–91
Grant, Greg, Trenton State College, 1991–92
Green, Rickey, University of Michigan, 1988–89
Green, Sidney, University of Nevada, Las Vegas, 1992–93
Holton, Michael, University of California, LA, 1988–90
Hammonds, Tom, Georgia Tech University, 1992–93
Hunter, Cedric, University of Kansas, 1991–92
Johnson, Larry, University of Nevada, Las Vegas, 1991–93
Keys, Randolph, University of Southern Mississippi, 1989–90
Lewis, Ralph, LaSalle University, 1988–90
Lowe, Sidney, North Carolina State University, 1988–90

Massenburg, Tony, University of Maryland, 1991–92
Mourning, Alonzo, Georgetown University, 1992–93
Newman, John, University of Richmond, 1990–93
Perry, Elliot, Memphis State University, 1991–92
Reiied, J. R., University of North Carolina, 1989–92

Reid, Robert, St. Mary's College, 1988–90
Sanders, Jeff, Georgia Southern University, 1990–91
Turner, Andre, Memphis State University, 1989–90
Williams, Michael, Baylor University, 1989–90

CHICAGO BULLS
Chicago, Illinois 60611

Board of Directors
Gardner, Edward, 1986–93

All-Stars
Rodgers, Guy 1967
Walker, Chet 1970–74
Love, Robert 1971–73
Gilmore, Artis 1978–80
Theus, Reginald 1980–83
Jordan, Michael 1985–93

All-Time Roster of The Chicago Bulls
Ard, Jim, University of Cincinnati, 1977–78
Barnes, Jim, Texas Western University, 1967–69
Baum, John, Temple University, 1969–71
Benbow, Leon, Jacksonville University, 1974–76
Blume, Ray, University of Oregon, 1981–82
Boozer, Robert, Kansas State University, 1966–69
Bowman, Nate, Wichita State University, 1966–67
Bradley, Dudley, University of North Carolina, 1982–83
Brown, Roger, University of Kansas, 1979–80
Bryant, Wallace, University of San Francisco, 1983–84
Collins, Jimmy, New Mexico State University, 1970–72
Colter, Steve, New Mexico State University, 1986–87
Dailey, Quintin, University of San Francisco, 1982–86
Dickey, Derrick, University of Cincinnati, 1977–78
Dudley, Charles, University of Washington, 1978–79
Garrett, Rowland, New Mexico State University, 1972–75
Gilmore, Artis, Jacksonville University, 1976–82
Green, Sidney, University of Nevada, Las Vegas, 1983–86
Greenwood, David, University of California, 1979–85
Halimon, Shaler, Utah State University, 1969–71
Harding, Reginald, 1967–68
Haskins, Clem, Western Kentucky University, 1967–70
Heard, Garfield, University of Oklahoma, 1972–73
Higgins, Rod, Fresno State University, 1982–86
Holland, Wilbur, University of New Orleans, 1976–79
Jackson, Tracy, University of Notre Dame, 1981–82
Johnson, Mickey, Aurora College, 1974–79

Johnson, Ollie, Temple University, 1978–79
Johnson, Steven, Oregon State University, 1983–85
Jones, Caldwell, Albany State College, 1984–86
Jones, Charles, University of Louisville, 1984–85
Jones, Dwight, University of Houston, 1979–83
Jordan, Michael, University of North Carolina, 1984–93
Kenon, Larry, Memphis State University, 1980–82
Lester, Ron, University of Iowa, 1980–84
Love, Robert, Southern University, 1968–76
Mack, Oliver, East Carolina University, 1979–81
Manning, Ed, Jackson State University, 1969–70
Matthews, Wes, University of Wisconsin, 1984–85
May, Scott, Indiana University, 1976–81
McIntosh, Ken, Michigan State University, 1971–73
Oakley, Charles, Virginia Union University, 1985–88
Paulk, Charles, Northeast Oklahoma State University, 1971–72
Pondexter, Cliff, University of Nevada, Las Vegas, 1975–78
Porter, Howard, Villanova University, 1971–74
Ray, Clifford, University of Oklahoma, 1971–74
Robinson, Flynn, University of Wyoming, 1967–69
Robinson, Jackie, University of Nevada, Las Vegas, 1981–82
Rodgers, Guy, Temple University, 1966–67
Russell, Cazzie, University of Michigan, 1977–78
Sheppard, Steve, University of Maryland, 1977–78
Smith, Sam, University of Nevada, Las Vegas, 1979–80
Smith, Willie, University of Missouri, 1976–77
Sobers, Ricky, University of Nevada, Las Vegas, 1979–80
Spriggs, Larry, Howard University, 1982–83
Starr, Keith, University of Pittsburgh, 1976–77
Theus, Reginald, University of Nevada, Las Vegas, 1978–84
Thurmond, Nate, Bowling Green State University, 1974–76
Van Lier, Norm, St. Francis College, 1971–78
Wakefield, Andre, Loyola University, Chicago, 1978–79
Walker, Chet, Bradley University, 1969–75
Washington, Jim, Villanova University, 1966–69
Weatherspoon, Nick, University of Illinois, 1977–78
Wesley, Walter, University of Cincinnati, 1969–70
Whatley, Ennis, University of Alabama, 1983–85
Wiggins, Mitchell, Florida State University, 1983–84

Wiburn, Mitchell, Central State University (Ohio), 1967–69
Wilkerson, Bob, Indiana University, 1980–81
Wilkes, James, University of California, LA, 1980–82
Wilson, George, University of Cincinnati, 1966–67
Woolridge, Orlando, University of Notre Dame, 1981–86
Worthen, Sam, Marquette University, 1980–81

ADDENDUM

Front Office Personnel
Mahoney, Ian (Manager, Corporate Sales) 1991–93
Henderson, Jacqui (Data Processor) 1991–93
McKinney, Mia (Marketing Assistant) 1991–93
Cunningham, Michele (Accountant) 1991–93
Love, Robert (Director of Community Relations) 1992–93

Coaches
Clemons, Jim (Assistant) 1989–93

All-Stars
Pippen, Scottie 1990, 1992–93

All-Time Roster of The Chicago Bulls
Armstrong, B. J., University of Iowa, 1989–93

Banks, Eugene, Duke University, 1985–87
Brewer, Ron, University of Arkansas, 1985–86
Cartwright, William, University of San Francisco, 1988–93
Cofield, Fred, Eastern Michigan University, 1986–87
Colter, Steven, New Mexico State University, 1986–87
Gervin, George, Eastern Michigan University, 1985–86
Grant, Horace, Clemson University, 1987–93
Hodges, Craig, Long Beach State University, 1988–92
Hopson, Dennis, Ohio State University, 1990–91
Jones, Anthony, University of Nevada, Las Vegas, 1988–89
King, Stacy, University of Oklahoma, 1991–93
McCray, Rodney, University of Louisville, 1992–93
Myers, Peter, University of Arkansas, Little Rock, 1986–87
Oakley, Charles, Virginia Union University, 1985–88
Pippen, Scottie, Central Arkansas University, 1987–93
Pressley, Dominique, Boston College, 1988–89
Threatt, Sedale, West Virginia Tech University, 1986–88
Turner, Elston, University of Mississippi, 1986–88
Vincent, Sam, Michigan State University, 1987–89
Waiters, Granville, Ohio State University, 1986–88
Walker, Darrell, University of Arkansas, 1992–93
White, Tony, University of Tennessee, 1987–88
Williams, Scott, University of North Carolina, 1990–93

CLEVELAND CAVALIERS
Richfield, Ohio 44286

Coaches
Johnson, Gus (Assistant) 1981–82
Littles, Eugene (Assistant) 1982–86
                    (Interim Head Coach) 1985–86

All-Stars
Johnson, John 1971–72
Beard, Alfred "Butch" 1972
Wilkens, Len 1973
Carr, Austin, 1974
Russell, Campy 1979
Mitchell, Michael 1981

All-Time Roster of The Cleveland Cavaliers
Anderson, Cliff, St. Joseph's University, 1970–71
Anderson, Ron, Fresno State University, 1984–86
Bagley, John, Boston College, 1982–87
Beard, Alfred "Butch," University of Louisville, 1971–72, 1974–75
Bennett, Melvin, University of Pittsburgh, 1981–82
Brewer, Jim, University of Minnesota, 1973–79
Brewer, Ron, University of Arkansas, 1981–83

Brokaw, Gary, University of Notre Dame, 1976–77
Calvin, Mack, University of Southern California, 1980–81
Carr, Austin, University of Notre Dame, 1971–80
Chones, Jim "Sweets," Marquette University, 1974–79
Cleamons, Jim, Ohio State University, 1972–77
Crompton, Geff, University of North Carolina, 1983–84
Davis, Charles, Wake Forest University, 1971–73
Davis, Dwight, University of Houston, 1972–75
Davis, John, University of Dayton, 1984–86
Edwards, James, University of Washington, 1981–83
Evans, Michael, Kansas State University, 1981–82
Frazier, Walter, Southern Illinois University, 1977–80
Free, World B., Guilford College, 1983–86
Furlow, Terry, Michigan State University, 1977–79
Garrett, Rowland, Florida State University, 1975–77
Garris, John, Boston College, 1983–84
Granger, Stewart, Villanova University, 1983–84
Graves, Earl "Butch," Yale University, 1985–86
Herron, Keith, Villanova University, 1981–82
Higgs, Ken, Louisiana State University, 1978–79

Hinson, Roy, Rutgers University, 1983–86
Howard, Greg, University of New Mexico, 1971–72
Howard, Maurice "Mo," University of Maryland, 1976–77
Hubbard, Phil, University of Michigan, 1982–86
Huston, Geoff, Texas Tech University, 1980–85
Johnson, John, University of Iowa, 1970–73
Johnson, Reginald, University of Tennessee, 1981–82
Jones, Edgar, University of Nevada, Reno, 1984–86
Jordan, Ed, Rutgers University, 1977–78
Kenon, Larry, Memphis State University, 1982–83
Kinch, Chad, University of North Carolina, Charlotte, 1980–81
Lacy, Sam, New Mexico State University, 1982–83
Lee, Alfred "Butch," Marquette University, 1978–80
Lee, Keith, Memphis State University, 1985–87
McLemore, McCojy, Drake University, 1970–71
Minniefield, Dirk, University of Kentucky, 1985–87
Mitchell, Michael, Auburn University, 1978–82
Moore, Lowes, West Virginia University, 1981–82
Nicks, Carl, Indiana State University, 1982–83
Packley, Luther, Xavier Ohio University, 1970–72
Roberson, Rick, University of Cincinnati, 1971–73
Robinson, Cliff, University of Southern California, 1981–84
Robinzine, Bill, DePaul University, 1980–81
Rule, Robert, Colorado State University, 1972–74
Russell, Michael "Campy," University of Michigan, 1974–80, 1984–85
Shelton, Lonnie, Oregon State University, 1983–86
Silas, James, Steven F. Austin State University, 1981–82
Smith, Bobby, University of Tulsa, 1970–80
Smith, Elmore, Kentucky State University, 1976–79
Smith, Randy, Buffalo State, 1979–81
Smith, Robert, University of Nevada, Las Vegas, 1980–81, 1984–85
Smith, William C., University of Missouri, 1979–80
Tatum, Earl, Marquette University, 1979–80
Thompson, Paul, Tulane University, 1983–85
Thurmond, Nate, Bowling Green State University, 1975–77
Tillis, Darren, Cleveland State University, 1975–77
Turpin, Melvin, University of Kentucky, 1984–87
Walker, Clarence "Foots," West Georgia State College, 1974–80
Warner, Cornell, Jackson State University, 1972–74
Warren, John, St. John's University, 1970–74
Washington, Richard, University of California, LA, 1981–83
Wesley, Walter, University of Kansas, 1970–77
West, Mark, Old Dominion University, 1985–86
Whatley, Ennis, University of Alabama, 1985–86
Whitehead, Jerome, Marquette University, 1980–81
Wilkens, Lenny, Providence College, 1972–74
Wilkerson, Bobby, Indiana University, 1981–83

Williams, Chuckie, Kansas State University, 1976–77
Williams, Kevin, St. John's University, 1984–85
Willoughby, William "Wesley," Dwight Morrow H.S. (Englewood, N.J.), 1979–80
Wilson, Michael, Marquette University, 1984–85

ADDENDUM

Front Office Personnel
Embry, Wayne (Executive Vice-President and General Manager) 1986–93
Carr, Austin (Director of Community Business Development) 1992–93

Coaches
Wilkens, Lenny (Head) 1986–93

All-Stars
Nance, Larry 1989, 1993
Daugherty, Brad 1991–93

All-Time Roster of The Cleveland Cavaliers
Battle, John, Rutgers University, 1991–93
Bennett, Winston, University of Kentucky, 1989–92
Brandon, Terrell, University of Oregon, 1991–93
Brown, Chucky, North Carolina State University, 1989–92
Chievous, Derrick, University of Missouri, 1989–91
Corbin, Tyrone, DePaul University, 1986–88
Curry, Dell, Virginia Tech University, 1987–88
Daugherty, Brad, University of North Carolina, 1986–93
Harper, Ron, University of Miami (Miami), 1986–90
Johnson, Eddie, Auburn University, 1985–86
Johnson, Kannard, Western Kentucky University, 1987–88
Johnson, Kevin, University of California, Berkeley, 1987–88
Keys, Randolph, University of Southern Mississippi, 1988–90
Lane, Jerome, University of Pittsburgh, 1992–93
McCray, Carlton "Scooter," University of Louisville, 1986–87
Morton, John, Seton Hall University, 1989–92
Nance, Larry, Clemson University, 1988–93
Newman, John, University of Richmond, 1986–87
Oliver, Jimmy, Purdue University, 1991–92
Paddio, Gerald, University of Nevada, Las Vegas, 1990–91
Rollins, Wayne, Clemson University, 1988–90
Sanders, Michael, University of California, LA, 1987–89, 1992–93
Valentine, Darnell, University of Kansas, 1988–89, 1990–91
Voce, Gary, University of Notre Dame, 1989–90
Wilkens, Gerald, University of Tennessee-Chattanooga, 1992–93
Williams, Reginald, Georgetown University, 1989–90
Woodson, Mike, Indiana University, 1990–91

Reference Section

DALLAS MAVERICKS
Dallas, Texas 75207

All-Stars
Aguirre, Mark 1984–88
Blackmon, Rolando 1985–87, 1990

All-Time Roster of The Dallas Mavericks
Aguirre, Mark, DePaul University, 1981–89
Allums, Darrell, University of California, LA, 1980–81
Blackmon, Rolando, Kansas State University, 1981–92
Boynes, Winford, University of San Francisco, 1980–81
Bryant, Wallace, University of San Francisco, 1984–86
Carr, Austin, University of Notre Dame, 1980–81
Carter, Howard, Louisiana State University, 1984–85
Cooper, Wayne, University of New Orleans, 1981–82
Davis, Monti, Tennessee State University, 1980–81
Duerod, Terry, University of Detroit, 1980–81
Ellis, Dale, University of Tennessee, 1983–86
Harper, Derek, University of Illinois, 1983–93
Huston, Geoff, Texas Tech University, 1980–81
Jeelani, Abdul (Gary Cole), University of Wisconsin-Parkside,
     1980–81
Kea, Clarence, Lamar University, 1980–82
Kinch, Chad, University of North Carolina, Charlotte, 1980–81
Mack, Oliver, East Carolina University, 1980–82
Perkins, Sam, University of North Carolina, 1984–90
Ransey, Kelvin, Ohio State University, 1982–83
Robinzine, Bill, DePaul University, 1980–81
Sluby, Tom, University of Notre Dame, 1984–85
Thompson, Corny, University of Connecticut, 1982–83
Turner, Elston, University of Mississippi, 1981–84
Vincent, Jay, Michigan State University, 1981–86
Washington, Richard, University of California, LA, 1980–81
West, Mark, Old Dominion University, 1983–84
Whitehead, Jerome, Marquette University, 1980–81

ADDENDUM
Coaches
Ray, Clifford (Special Assignment Coach) 1987–93
Heard, Garfield (Head) 1992–93
     (Assistant) 1986–92
Buckner, Quinn (Head) 1993–94

All-Stars
Donaldson, James 1988

All-Time Roster of The Dallas Mavericks
Cambridge, Dexter, University of Texas, 1992–93
Cooper, Wayne, University of New Orleans, 1988–90
Dantley, Adrian, University of Notre Dame, 1988–90
Davis, Terry, Virginia Union University, 1991–93
Donaldson, James, Washington State University, 1985–92
English, Alex, University of South Carolina, 1990–91
Garrick, Tom, University of Rhode Island, 1991–92
Hodge, Donald, Temple University, 1991–93
Howard, Brian, University of Maryland, 1992–93
Jackson, Jim, Ohio State University, 1992–93
Jones, Anthony, University of Nevada, Las Vegas, 1988–90
Keeling, Harold, Santa Clara University, 1985–86
Lever, Lafayette "Fat," Arizona State University, 1990–93
McCray, Rodney, University of Louisville, 1990–92
Moore, Tracey, University of Tulsa, 1991–93
Rooks, Sean, University of Arizona, 1992–93
Smith, Doug, University of Missouri, 1991–93
Tarpley, Roy, University of Michigan, 1986–91
Tyler, Terry, University of Detroit, 1988–89
Wade, Mark, University of Nevada, Las Vegas, 1989–90
White, Randy, Louisiana Tech University, 1989–93
Wiley, Morlon, Long Beach State University, 1988–89
Williams, Herb, Ohio State University, 1988–92
Wood, Al, University of North Carolina, 1986–87
Wright, Howard, Stamford University, 1990–91

DENVER NUGGETS
Denver, Colorado 80204

Denver Rockets, 1967–74

All-Stars (American Basketball Association Until 1975)
Haywood, Spencer 1970
Simpson, Ralph 1972–76
Jabali, Warren 1973
Calvin, Mack 1975
Thompson, David 1976–79
McGinnis, George 1979
English, Alex 1982–89
Natt, Calvin 1985

All-Time Roster of The Denver Nuggets
Anderson, Cliff, St. Joseph's College, 1969–70
Anderson, Dwight, University of Southern California, 1982–83
Barnhill, John, Tennessee State University, 1970–71
Boswell, Thomas, University of South Carolina, 1978–80
Bowens, Thomas, Grambling College, 1967–68
Bradley, Jim, Northern Illinois University, 1975–76
Brown, Roger, University of Kansas, 1975–76
Burns, David, St. Louis University, 1981–82
Calvin, Mack, University of Southern California, 1974–78
Card, Frank, South Carolina State University, 1971–73
Carter, Howard, Louisiana State University, 1983–84
Cook, Norman, University of Kansas, 1977–78
Cooper, Wayne, University of New Orleans, 1984–89
Crompton, Geoff, University of North Carolina, 1978–79
Cross, Russell, Purdue University, 1984–85
Dorsey, Jackie, University of Georgia, 1977–78
Dunn, T.R., University of Alabama, 1980–91
Edmondson, Keith, Purdue University, 1983–84
Ellis, Maurice "Bo," Marquette University, 1977–80
English, Alex, University of South Carolina, 1979–87
Evans, Michael, Kansas State University, 1982–88
Foster, Jimmy, University of Connecticut, 1975–76
Garland, Gary, DePaul University, 1979–80
Green, Michael, Louisiana Tech University, 1973–75
Haywood, Spencer, University of Detroit, 1969–70
Higgs, Ken, Louisiana State University, 1980–82
Hightower, Wayne, University of Kansas, 1967–69
Hillman, Darnell, San Jose State University, 1977–78
Hordges, Cedric, University of Kansas, 1980–82
Jabali, Warren, Wichita State University, 1972–74
Johnson, George, St. John's University, 1979–80
Jones, Steven, University of Oregon, 1973–74

Keye, Julius, Alcorn A&M University, 1969–74
Lever, Lafayette, Arizona State University, 1984–90
Long, Willie, University of New Mexico, 1972–74
McClain, Ted, Tennessee State University, 1976–77
McGill, Bill, University of Utah, 1968–69
McGinnis, George, Indiana University, 1978–80
McKinney, Bill, Northwestern University, 1980–83
Murrell, Willie, Kansas State University, 1967–68
Natt, Calvin, Northeast Louisiana University, 1984–89
Nicks, Carl, Indiana State University, 1980–81
Price, Jim, University of Louisville, 1976–78
Ray, James, Jacksonville University, 1980–83
Roberts, Anthony, Oral Roberts University, 1977–80, 1983–84
Roberts, Mary, Utah State University, 1971–74
Scott, Charles, University of North Carolina, 1978–80
Silas, Paul, Creighton University, 1976–77
Simpson, Ralph, Michigan State University, 1970–76, 1977–78
Smith, Robert, University of Nevada, Las Vegas, 1977–79
Tart, Levern, Bradley University, 1968–69
Taylor, Brian, Princeton University, 1977–78
Taylor, Roland "Fatty," La Salle College, 1974–77
Theard, Floyd, Kentucky State University, 1969–70
Thomas, Willis "Lefty," Tennessee State University, 1969–70
Thompson, David, North Carolina State University, 1975–81
Trapp, John Q., University of Nevada, Las Vegas, 1972–73
Turner, Elston, University of Mississippi, 1984–86, 1988–89
Valentine, Ron, Old Dominion University, 1980–81
Waller, Dwight, Tennessee State University, 1969–72
Warley, Ben, Tennessee State University, 1969–70
Washington, Donald, University of North Carolina, 1974–75
Webster, Marvin, Morgan State University, 1975–77
White, Willie, University of Tennessee-Chattanooga, 1984–86
Wilburn, Ken, Central State University (Ohio), 1968–69
Wilkerson, Bobby, Indiana University, 1977–80
Williams, Rob, University of Houston, 1982–84
Wise, Willie, Drake University, 1976–77
Wright, Lonnie, Colorado State University, 1967–71

ADDENDUM

Front Office Personnel
Bickerstaff, Bernie (General Manager) 1990–93
Davis, Walter (Community Ambassador) 1992–93

Coaches
Evans, Michael (Assistant) 1990–93
Littles, Eugene (Assistant) 1992–93

All-Stars (American Basketball Association Until 1975)
Lever, LaFayette 1988–90

All-Time Roster of The Denver Nuggets
Adams, Michael, Boston College, 1987–91
Anderson, Greg, University of Houston, 1990–92
Battle, Ken, University of Illinois, 1990–91
Brooks, Michael, LaSalle University, 1987–88
Brooks, Kevin, Southwestern Louisiana University, 1991–93
Carroll, Joe Barry, Purdue University, 1989–90
Cook, Anthony, University of Arizona, 1990–93
Cook, Darwin, University of Portland, 1988–89
Davis, Walter, University of North Carolina, 1988–92
Ellis, LaPhonso, University of Notre Dame, 1992–93
Gaines, Corey, Loyola Marymount University, 1990–91

Garland, Winston, Southwest Missouri State Univ., 1991–93
Greenwood, David, University of California, LA, 1988–89
Hughes, Eddie, Colorado State University, 1988–90
Jackson, Chris, Louisiana State University, 1990–93
Johnson, Avery, Southern University (Louisiana), 1990–91
Lane, Jerome, University of Pittsburgh, 1988–92
Liberty, Marcus, University of Illinois, 1990–93
Macon, Mark, Temple University, 1991–93
Martin, Maurice "Mo," St. Joseph's University, 1986–89
Mason, Anthony, Tennessee State University, 1990–91
Mills, Terry, University of Michigan, 1990–91
Moore, Andre, Loyola University of Chicago, 1987–88
Oldham, Jawann, Seattle University, 1980–81
Smith, Otis, Jacksonville University, 1986–88
Stith, Bryan, University of Virginia, 1992–93
Vincent, Jay, Michigan State University, 1987–89
Walker, Darrell, University of Arkansas, 1986–87
Williams, Reggie, Georgetown University, 1991–93
Woolridge, Orlando, University of Notre Dame, 1990–91

DETROIT PISTONS
Auburn Hills, Michigan 48326

Front Office Personnel
Robinson, Will (Administrative Assistant to the General Manager/
        Director of Community Relations), 1982–88
        (Assistant to the Director of Player Personnel)
        1988–93

Coaches
Lloyd, Earl (Assistant) 1971–73
Scott, Ray (Head) 1973–76
Chaney, Don (Assistant) 1980–83, 1992–93
        (Head), 1993–94

All-Stars
Dukes, Walter 1960, 1962
Miles, Eddie 1966
Bing, David 1968–69, 1971–75
Walker, Jimmy, 1970–72
Lanier, Robert 1972–75, 1977–79
Rowe, Curtis 1976
Thomas, Isiah 1982–93

All-Time Roster of The Detroit Pistons
Barnes, Marvin, Providence College, 1976–78
Barnhill, John, Tennessee State University, 1965–66
Behagan, Ron, University of Minnesota, 1978–79

Bellamy, Walter, Indiana University, 1968–70
Bing, David, Syracuse University, 1966–76
Black, Norman, St. Joseph's College, 1980–81
Brewer, Jim, University of Minnesota, 1978–79
Britt, Wayman, University of Michigan, 1977–78
Brown, Roger, University of Kansas, 1975–77
Buntin, Bill, University of Michigan, 1965–66
Caldwell, Joe, Arizona State University, 1964–66
Campbell, Tony, Ohio State University, 1984–87
Carr, Kenneth, North Carolina State University, 1981–82
Carr, M. L., Guilford College, 1976–79
Cash, Cornelius, Bowling Green State University, 1976–77
Clark, Archie, University of Minnesota, 1975–76
Clifton, Nat, Xavier University (Louisiana), 1957–58
Cureton, Earl, University of Detroit, 1983–86
Douglas, Leon, University of Alabama, 1976–80
Dove, Sonny, St. John's University, 1967–69
Drew, Larry, University of Missouri, 1980–81
Duerod, Terry, University of Detroit, 1979–80
Dukes, Walter, Seton Hall University, 1957–63
Dumars, Joe, McNeese State University, 1985–93
Evans, Earl, University of Nevada, Las Vegas, 1979–80
Green, Rickey, University of Michigan, 1978–79
Hagan, Glen, St. Bonaventure University, 1981–82

Harding, Reginald, 1963–65
Hardy, Alan, University of Michigan, 1981–82
Hairston, Happy, New York University, 1967–70
Hairston, Lindsay, Michigan State University, 1975–76
Hamilton, Roy, University of California, LA, 1979–80
Hawkins, Bubbles, Illinois State University, 1978–79
Herron, Keith, Villanova University, 1980–81
Hightower, Wayne, University of Kansas, 1966–67
Hollins, Lionel, Arizona State University, 1983–84
Hollis, Essie, St. Bonaventure University, 1978–79
Howard, Otis, Austin Peay State University, 1978–79
Hubbard, Phil, University of Michigan, 1979–82
Johnson, Lee, East Tennessee State University, 1980–81
Johnson, Vinnie, Baylor University, 1981–91
Jones, Edgar, University of Nevada, Reno, 1981–83
Jones, Major, Albany State College (Georgia), 1984–85
Jones, Wali, Villanova University, 1975–76
Jones, Willie, Northwestern University, 1960–65
Kelser, Gregory, Michigan State University, 1979–82
Lanier, Robert, St. Bonaventure University, 1970–80
Lee, Ron, University of Oregon, 1979–82
Levingston, Cliff, Wichita State University, 1982–84
Lloyd, Earl, West Virginia State University, 1958–60
Long, John, University of Detroit, 1978–85
Lowe, Sidney, North Carolina State University, 1984–85
Mahorn, Rick, Hampton University, 1985–87
May, Scott, Indiana University, 1982–83
McAdoo, Robert, University of North Carolina, 1979–81
McElroy, James, Central Michigan University, 1979–80
McLemore, McCoy, Drake University, 1968–70
McNeill, Larry, Marquette University, 1978–79
Mengelt, John, Auburn University, 1972–76
Miles, Eddie, Seattle University, 1963–70
Money, Eric, University of Arizona, 1974–78, 1979–80
Moore, Otto, Pan American University, 1968–71, 1974–75
Murrey, Dorie, University of Detroit, 1966–67
Norwood, Willie, Alcorn A&M University, 1971–75, 1977–78
Pierce, Rick, Rice University, 1982–83
Porter, Howard, Villanova University, 1974–78
Porter, Kevin, St. Francis College (Pennsylvania), 1975–79
Price, Jim, University of Louisville, 1977–78
Robinson, Jackie, University of Nevada, Las Vegas, 1979–80
Robinson, Wayne, Virginia Tech University, 1980–81
Romar, Lorenzo, University of Washington, 1984–85
Roundfield, Dan, Central Michigan University, 1984–85
Rowe, Curtis, University of California, LA, 1971–76
Russell, Walker, Western Michigan University, 1982–84
Scott, Ray, University of Portland, 1961–67

Sellers, Phil, Rutgers University, 1976–77
Sheppard, Steven, University of Maryland, 1978–79
Shumate, John, University of Notre Dame, 1977–80
Simpson, Ralph, Michigan State University, 1976–78
Skinner, Al, University of Massachusetts, 1977–78
Smith, Jim, Ohio State University, 1982–83
Tatum, Earl, Marquette University, 1978–79
Teagle, Terry, Baylor University, 1984–86
Thomas, Isiah, Indiana University, 1981–93
Tolbert, Ray, Indiana University, 1982–84
Trapp, George, Long Beach State University, 1973–77
Tresvant, John, Seattle University, 1965–68
Tyler, Terry, University of Detroit, 1978–85
Wakefield, Andre, Loyola University of Chicago, 1978–79
Walker, Jimmy, Providence College, 1967–72
Wilkes, James, University of California, LA, 1982–83
Williams, Earl, Winston-Salem State University, 1975–76
Wright, Larry, Grambling State University, 1980–82

ADDENDUM

Front Office Personnel
McKinney, William (Director of Player Personnel) 1992–93
Nelson, Rex K. (Director of Community Relations) 1992–93
Perrin, Walter (Director of Scouting) 1992–93

All-Stars
Rodman, Dennis 1990, 1992
Dumars, Joe 1990–92

All-Time Roster of The Detroit Pistons
Aquirre, Mark, DePaul University, 1988–93
Bedford, William, Memphis State University, 1987–92
Blanks, Lance, University of Texas, 1990–93
Dantley, Adrian, University of Notre Dame, 1986–89
Dawkins, Darryl, Maynard Evans H.S. (Florida), 1987–89
Dembo, Fennis, University of Wyoming, 1988–89
Edwards, James, University of Washington, 1987–91
Gibson, Michael, University of South Carolina-Spartanburg, 1985–86
Glass, Gerald, University of Mississippi, 1992–93
Greenwood, David, University of California, LA, 1989–90
Harris, Steven, University of Tulsa, 1988–89
Henderson, Gerald, Virginia Commonwealth University, 1989–92
Lewis, Ralph, LaSalle University, 1987–90
McAnn, Robert, Morehead State University, 1991–92
McQueen, Cozell, North Carolina State University, 1986–87
Mills, Terry, University of Michigan, 1992–93
Moore, Ron, West Virginia State University, 1987–88

Morris, Isiah, University of Arkansas, 1992–93
Polynice, Olden, University of Virginia, 1992–93
Rodman, Dennis, Southeast Oklahoma State University, 1986–93
Rollins, Wayne, Clemson University, 1990–91
Salley, John, Georgia Tech University, 1986–92

Sellers, Brad, Ohio State University, 1991–93
Walker, Darrell, University of Arkansas, 1991–92
Williams, Michael, Baylor University, 1988–89
Woolridge, Orlando, University of Notre Dame, 1991–93

GOLDEN STATE WARRIORS
Oakland, California 94621

Front Office Personnel
Attles, Alvin (Vice-President and Assistant General Manager) 1983–93
Thurmond, Nate (Director of Community Relations) 1981–92

Coaches
Attles, Alvin (Head) 1970–83

All-Stars
Sauldsberry, Woody 1959
Rodgers, Guy 1963–64, 1966
Chamberlain, Wilt 1965
Thurmond, Nate 1965–67, 1970, 1973–74
Russell, Cazzie 1972
Wilkes, Jamall 1976
Smith, Phil 1976–77
King, Bernard 1982
Short, Purvis 1986
Floyd, Eric 1987

All-Time Roster of The Golden State Warriors
Abdul-Rahman, Mahdi (Walt Hazzard), University of California, LA, 1972–73
Allen, Odis, University of Nevada, Las Vegas, 1971–72
Attles, Alvin, North Carolina A&T University, 1960–72
Beard, Alfred "Butch," University of Louisville, 1973–76
Bracey, Steven, University of Tulsa, 1974–75
Brewer, Ron, University of Arkansas, 1982–83
Bridges, William, University of Kansas, 1974–75
Brown, Rick, Mississippi State University, 1980–83
Burtt, Steven, Iona College, 1984–85
Carroll, Joe Barry, Purdue University, 1980–84, 1985–88
Chamberlain, Wilt, University of Kansas, 1959–65
Chenier, Phil, University of California, Berkeley, 1980–81
Coleman, E. C., Houston Baptist University, 1977–78
Collins, Don, Washington State University, 1983–84
Conner, Lester, Oregon State University, 1982–86
Cooper, Wayne, University of New Orleans, 1978–80
Cox, Westley, University of Louisville, 1977–79

Cross, Russell, Purdue University, 1983–84
Davis, Dwight, University of Houston, 1975–77
Dickey, Derrick, University of Cincinnati, 1973–78
Dudley, Charles, University of Washington, 1974–78
Duerod, Terry, University of Detroit, 1982–83
Ellis, Joe, University of San Francisco, 1966–74
Epps, Ray, Norfolk State University, 1978–79
Floyd, Eric, Georgetown University, 1982–87
Fontaine, Levi, Maryland State College, 1970–71
Frazier, Wilbert, Grambling State University, 1965–66
Free, World B., Guilford College, 1980–83
Gale, Michael, Elizabeth City State University, 1981–83
Green, Rickey, University of Michigan, 1977–78
Hawkins, Robert "Bubbles," Illinois State University, 1975–76
Hightower, Wayne, University of Kansas, 1962–65
Hillman, Darnell, San Jose State University, 1979–80
Johnson, Charles, University of California, Berkeley, 1972–78
Johnson, George, Dillard University, 1972–77
Johnson, Lynbert, Wichita State University, 1979–80
Johnson, Mickey, Aurora College, 1982–85
Kenon, Larry, Memphis State University, 1982–83
King, Bernard, University of Tennessee, 1980–82
Lattin, David, Texas Western University, 1967 – 68
Lear, Hal, Temple University, 1956–57
Lloyd, Lewis, Drake University, 1981–83
Lucas, John, University of Maryland, 1978–81
Marsh, Ricky, Manhattan College, 1977–78
Mayfield, William, University of Iowa, 1980–81
McLemore, McCoy, Drake University, 1964–66
McNeill, Larry, Marquette University, 1976–78
Moore, Jackie, LaSalle College, 1954–57
Naulls, Willie, University of California, LA, 1962–63
Parker, Sonny, Texas A&M University, 1976–82
Parrish, Robert, Centenary College, 1976–80
Plummer, Gary, Boston University, 1984–86
Ray, Clifford, University of Oklahoma, 1974–81
Richardson, Michael Ray, University of Montana 1982–83
Robertson, Tony, University of West Virginia, 1978–79
Rodgers, Guy, Temple University, 1958–66

Rogers, Marshall, Pan American University, 1976–77
Romar, Lorenzo, University of Michigan, 1971–74
Russell, Cazzie, University of Michigan, 1971–74
Sauldesberry, Woody, Texas Southern University, 1957–60
Short, Purvis, Jackson State University, 1978–87
Smith, Derek, University of Louisville, 1982–83
Smith, Larry, Alcorn State University, 1980–89
Smith, Phil, University of San Francisco, 1974–80
Teagle, Terry, Baylor University, 1984–86
Thibeaux, Peter, St. Mary's College, 1984–86
Thurmond, Nate, Bowling Green State University, 1963–74
Tillis, Darren, Cleveland State University, 1983–84
White, Hubie, Villanova University, 1962–63
White, JoJo, University of Kansas, 1978–80
White, Rudy, Arizona State University, 1980–81
Whitehead, Jerome, Marquette University, 1984–89
Wilkes, Jamaal, University of California, LA, 1974–77
Williams, Gus, University of Southern California, 1975–77
Williams, Nate, Utah State University, 1977–79
Williams, Ron, West Virginia University, 1968–73
Williams, Sam, Arizona State University, 1981–84

ADDENDUM

Front Office Personnel
Perry, David (Promotional Sales Manager) 1991–92
Frost, Sandria (Media Relations Coordinator) 1991–93
Eison, Rayshael (Account Executive) 1991–93
Epps, Paula (Bookkeeper) 1991–93

Coaches
Roberts, Joe (Assistant) 1976–79
Farmer, Larry (Assistant) 1990–91
Pressey, Paul (Assistant) 1992–93

All-Stars
Hardaway, Tim 1991–93

All-Time Roster of The Golden State Warriors
Alexander, Victor, Iowa State University, 1991

Askew, Vincent, Memphis State University, 1990–92
Ballard, Greg, University of Oregon, 1985–87
Battle, Ken, University of Illinois, 1991–92
Demps, Dell, University of Pacific, 1992–93
Elie, Mario, American International College, 1990–92
Frank, Tellis, Western Kentucky University, 1987–89
Garland, Winston, S.W. Missouri State University, 1987–90
Gatling, Chris, Old Dominion University, 1991–93
Grayer, Jeff, Iowa State University, 1992–93
Hardaway, Tim, University of Texas, El Paso, 1989–93
Harris, Steven, University of Tulsa, 1985–88
Higgins, Rod, Fresno State University, 1986–92
Hill, Tyrone, Xavier University (Ohio), 1990–93
Houston, Byron, Oklahoma State University, 1992–93
Jackson, Jaren, Georgetown University, 1991–92
Jenning, Keith "Mr.," East Tennessee State University, 1992–93
Johnson, Andrew "Andy," University of Portland, 1958–61
Johnson, Marques, University of California, LA, 1989–90
Johnson, Steven, Oregon State University, 1990–91
Jones, Shelton, St. John's University, 1988–89
Lister, Alton, Arizona State University, 1989–93
Massenburg, Tony, University of Maryland, 1991–92
Minnifield, Dirk, University of Kentucky, 1987–88
Moss, Perry, Northeastern University, 1986–87
Owens, Billy, Syracuse University, 1991–93
Richmond, Mitch, Kansas State University, 1988–91
Sampson, Ralph, University of Virginia, 1987–89
Smith, Clinton, Cleveland State University, 1986–87
Smith, Otis, Jacksonville University, 1987–89
Sprewell, Latrell, University of Alabama, 1992–93
Starks, John, Oklahoma State University, 1988–89
Taylor, Leonard, University of California, 1989–90
Thompson, Billy, University of Louisville, 1991–92
Upshaw, Kelvin, University of Utah, 1989–90
Wade, Mark, University of Nevada, Las Vegas, 1987–88
Washburn, Chris, North Carolina State University, 1986–88
Washington, Kermit, American University, 1987–88
White, Tony, University of Tennessee, 1987–88

HOUSTON ROCKETS
Houston, Texas 77046

San Diego Rockets, 1967–71

All-Stars
Hayes, Elvin 1969–72
Malone, Moses 1978–82
Murphy, Calvin 1979
Sampson, Ralph 1984–87

All-Time Roster of The Houston Rockets
Abdul-Aziz, Zaid, Iowa State University, 1972–75, 1977–78
Adams, Don, Northwestern University, 1970–71
Bailey, Gus, University of Texas, El Paso, 1974–76
Bailey, James, Rutgers University, 1982–84
Barker, Tom, University of Hawaii, 1978
Barnes, Harry, Northeastern University, 1968–69
Behagen, Ron, University of Minnesota, 1977
Bond, Phil, University of Louisville, 1977
Bradley, Alonzo, Texas Southern University, 1977–80
Britt, Tyrone, Johnson C. Smith University, 1967–68
Bryant, Joe, LaSalle University, 1982–83
Coleman, E. C., Houston Baptist University, 1973–74, 1978
Davis, Jim, University of Colorado, 1971
Dorsey, Jackie, University of Georgia, 1978–79
Ford, Phil, University of North Carolina, 1983–84
Garrett, Calvin, Oral Roberts University, 1980–82
Green, John, Michigan State University, 1967–68
Harris, Steve, University of Tulsa, 1985–88
Hayes, Elvin, University of Houston, 1968–76
Henderson, Tom, University of Hawaii, 1972–76
Johnson, George, Stephen F. Austin State University, 1973–74
Johnson, John, University of Iowa, 1975–77
Johnson, Lee, East Texas State University, 1980
Jones, Caldwell, Albany State College, 1982–84
Jones, Dwight, University of Houston, 1976–79
Jones, Major, Albany State College, 1979–85
Jones, Nick, University of Oregon, 1967–68
Jones, Robin, St. Louis University, 1971
Kennedy, Eugene, Texas Christian University, 1976–77
Lantz, Stu, University of Nebraska, 1968–72
Lloyd, Lewis, Drake University, 1983–87
Lucas, John, University of Maryland, 1976–78, 1984–86, 1989–90
Malone, Moses, Petersburg H.S. (Virginia), 1976–82
McCray, Rodney, University of Louisville, 1983–88
McKenzie, Stan, New York University, 1972–74
McWilliams, Eric, Long Beach State University, 1972–73
Meely, Cliff, University of Colorado, 1971–76

Meriweather, Joe C., University of Southern Illinois, 1975–76
Moffett, Larry, Long Beach State University, 1977–78
Moore, Otto, Pan American University, 1972–74
Murphy, Calvin, Niagara University, 1970–83
Perry, Curtis, S.W. Missouri State University, 1970–71
Ratleff, Ed, Long Beach State University, 1973–78
Reid, Robert, St. Mary's (Texas), 1977–87
Riley, Ron, University of Southern California, 1973–76
Sampson, Ralph, University of Virginia, 1983–87
Shuman, John, University of Notre Dame, 1979–80
Smith, Bobby, University of Tulsa, 1969–70
Spriggs, Larry, Howard University, 1982
Taylor, Jeff, Texas Tech University, 1982–83
Teagle, Terry, Baylor University, 1982–84
Trapp, John, Nevada Southern, 1968–71
Watts, Slick, Xavier University, 1978–79
Wells, Owen, University of Detroit, 1974–75
White, Rudy, Arizona State University, 1975–78, 1979–80
Wiggins, Mitchell, Florida State University, 1985–87
Williams, Art, California Poly, 1967–70
Williams, Bernie, LaSalle University, 1969–71
Willoughby, Bill, Dwight Morrow H.S. (Englewood, N.J.), 1980–82

ADDENDUM

Front Office Personnel
Rainey, Sharon (Sponsor Services Coordinator) 1991–93

Coaches
Barr, Robert (Strength Coach) 1984–93
Chaney, Don (Head) 1988–92
Murphy, Calvin (Special Assignments/Community Relations) 1989–93
Berry, Bill (Assistant) 1992–93

All-Stars
Thorpe, Otis 1992

All-Time Roster of The Houston Rockets
Berry, Walter, St. John's University, 1988–89
Blair, Curtis, University of Richmond, 1992–93
Bowie, Anthony, University of Oklahoma, 1989–90
Brown, Tony, University of Arkansas, 1988–89
Caldwell, Adrian, Lamar University, 1989–91

Carroll, Joe Barry, Purdue University, 1987–88
Chievous, Derrick, University of Missouri, 1988–90
Conner, Lester, Oregon State University, 1987–88
Dinkins, Byron, University of North Carolina-Charlotte, 1989–90
Floyd, Eric "Sleepy," Georgetown University, 1987–93
Free, World B., Guilford College, 1987–88
Harris, Steven, University of Tulsa, 1985–88
Henderson, Gerald, Virginia Commonwealth University, 1991–92
Horrey, Robert, University of Alabama, 1992–93
Johnson, Alonzo "Buck," University of Alabama, 1986–92
Johnson, Avery, Southern University, 1991–92
Johnson, Frank, Wake Forest University, 1988–89

Maxwell, Cedric, University of North Carolina, Charlotte, 1987–88
Maxwell, Vernon, University of Florida, 1990–93
Minniefield, Dirk, University of Kentucky, 1986–87
Rollins, Wayne "Tree," Clemson University, 1991–93
Short, Purvis, Jackson State University, 1987–89
Smith, Ken, University of North Carolina, 1990–93
Smith, Larry, Alcorn State University, 1989–92
Thompson, Bernard, Fresno State University, 1988–89
Thorpe, Otis, Providence College, 1988–93
Turner, Andre, Memphis State University, 1987–88
Turner, John, Phillips College (Oklahoma), 1991–92
Waiters, Granville, Ohio State University, 1985–86

INDIANA PACERS
Indianapolis, Indiana 46204

Front Office Personnel
Embry, Wayne (Vice-President/Basketball Consultant) 1985–87

Coaches
Daniels, Mel (Assistant) 1984–93

All-Stars (American Basketball Association Until 1975)
Brown, Roger 1968, 1970–71
Daniels, Mel 1969–71, 1973
McGinnis, George 1973–75
Knight, Billy 1977

All-Time Roster
Anderson, Jerome, West Virginia University, 1976–77
Armstrong, Warren, Wichita State University, 1970–71
Bantom, Michael, St. Joseph's University, 1977–82
Barnhill, John, Tennessee State University, 1969–72
Baum, John, Temple University, 1973–74
Behagan, Ron, University of Minnesota, 1977–78
Bennett, Mel, University of Pittsburgh, 1976–78
Bradley, Dudley, University of North Carolina, 1979–81
Brown, Roger, University of Dayton, 1967–75
Brown, Tony, University of Arkansas, 1984–85
Buckner, Quinn, Indiana University, 1985–86
Calhoun, Corky, University of Pennsylvania, 1978–80
Carrington, Robert, Boston College, 1977–78
Carter, Clarence "Butch," Indiana University, 1981–84
Carter, Ron, Virginia Military Institute, 1979–80
Chenier, Phil, University of California, Berkeley, 1979–80
Combs, Leroy, Oklahoma State University, 1983–84
Daniels, Mel, University of New Mexico, 1968–74
Dantley, Adrian, University of Notre Dame, 1977–78

Darden, Oliver, University of Michigan, 1967–70
Davis, John, University of Dayton, 1978–82
Duren, John, Georgetown University, 1982–83
Edelin, Kenton, University of Virginia, 1984–85
Edmonds, Bobby Joe, University of Virginia, 1984–85
Edwards, James, University of Washington, 1977–81
Elmore, Len, University of Maryland, 1974–79
English, Alexander, University of South Carolina, 1978–80
Fleming, Vern, University of Georgia, 1984–93
Freeman, Don, University of Illinois, 1972–74
Grant, Travis, Kentucky State University, 1975–76
Hackett, Rudy, Syracuse University, 1976–77
Harding, Reginald, 1967–68
Harkness, Gerald, Loyola University of Chicago, 1967–69
Hillman, Darnell, San Jose State University, 1971–77
Jackson, Ralph, University of California, LA, 1984–85
Jackson, Tracey, University of Notre Dame, 1983–84
Johnson, Clemon, Florida A&M University, 1979–83
Johnson, Gus, University of Idaho, 1972–73
Johnson, Mickey, Aurora College, 1979–80
Jones, Wilbert, Albany State College (Georgia), 1976–77
Kellogg, Clark, Ohio State University, 1982–87
Kelly, Arvesta, Lincoln University (Missouri), 1971–72
Kelser, Gregory, Michigan State University, 1984-85
Knight, Billy, University of Pittsburgh, 1974–83
Lamar, Dwight, University of Southwestern Louisiana, 1975–76
Lewis, Freddie, Arizona State University, 1967–77
Lowe, Sidney, North Carolina State University, 1983–84
Manning, Ed, Jackson State University, 1975–76
Mayes, Clyde, Furman University, 1976–77
McGinnis, George, Indiana University, 1971–82

Morgan, Guy, Wake Forest University, 1982–83
Natt, Ken, N.E. Louisiana University, 1980–81
Orr, Louis, Syracuse University, 1980–82
Pearson, Chuck, Auburn University, 1986–92
Radford, Wayne, Indiana University, 1978–79
Roundfield, Dan, Central Michigan University, 1975–78
Slaughter, Jose, University of Portland, 1982–83
Smith, Willie, University of Missouri, 1977–78
Sobers, Ricky, University of Nevada, Las Vegas, 1977–79
Stansbury, Terrence, Temple University, 1984–86
Tatum, Earl, Marquette University, 1977–78
Thacker, Tom, University of Cincinnati, 1968–71
Thomas, Jim, Indiana University, 1983–85
Waiters, Granville, Ohio State University, 1983–85
Williams, Herb, Ohio State University, 1981–89
Williamson, John, New Mexico State University, 1976–78
Wilson, Robert, Wichita State University, 1977–78
Winkler, Marvin, University of Southwestern Louisiana, 1971–72

ADDENDUM

Front Office Personnel
Brooks, Vonda (Community Relations) 1991–93
Jordan, Kathryn (Community Relations) 1991–93
McDowell, Dean (Broadcast Productions) 1991–93
Smith, Alice (Sponsorship Sales/Promotions) 1991–93

All-Stars
Miller, Reggie 1990

All-Time Roster of The Indiana Pacers
Brooks, Michael, LaSalle University, 1986–87
Davis, Dale, Clemson University, 1991–93
Dinkins, Byron, University of North Carolina, Charlotte, 1990–91
Frederick, Anthony, Pepperdine University, 1988–89
Green, Sean, Iona College, 1991–93
Green, Rickey, University of Michigan, 1989–90
Lane, Jerome, University of Pittsburgh, 1991–92
Long, John, University of Detroit, 1986–89
Martin, William, Georgetown University, 1985–86
McClain, Dwayne, Villanova University, 1985–86
McCloud, George, Florida State University, 1989–93
Miller, Reginald, University of California, LA, 1987–93
Mitchell, Sam, Mercer University, 1992–93
Natt, Calvin, Northeast Louisiana University, 1989–90
Nix, Dyron, University of Tennessee, 1989–90
Oldham, Jawann, Seattle University, 1990–91
Person, Chuck, Auburn University, 1986–92
Richardson, Clint, Seattle University, 1985–86
Richardson, Jerome "Pooh," University of California, LA, 1992–93
Russell, Walker, Western Michigan University, 1986–87
Sanders, Michael, University of California, LA, 1989–92
Sealy, Malik, St. John's University, 1992–93
Stephens, Everette, Purdue University, 1988–89
Thompson, LaSalle, University of Texas, 1988–93
Tisdale, Waymon, University of Oklahoma, 1985–89
Toney, Sedric, University of Dayton, 1988–89
Warrick, Bryan, St. Joseph's University (Pennsylvania), 1985–86
Wheeler, Clinton, William Patterson College, 1987–88
Williams, Ken, Elizabeth City State University, 1990–93
Williams, Michael, Baylor University, 1990–92

LOS ANGELES CLIPPERS
Los Angeles, California 90037

Buffalo Braves, 1970–78
San Diego Clippers, 1978–84

Front Office Personnel
Baylor, Elgin (General Manager) 1986–93

Coaches
Silas, Paul (Head) 1980–83
Chaney, Don (Head) 1985–87

All-Stars
McAdoo, Robert 1974–76
Smith, Randy 1976, 1978
Free, Lloyd 1980

Cummings, Terry 1984
Nixon, Norm 1985

All-Time Roster of The Los Angeles Clippers
Abdul-Aziz, Zaid (Don Smith), Iowa State University, 1976–77
Abdul Rahman, Mahdi (Walt Hazzard), University of California, LA, 1971–73
Archibald, Nate, University of Texas, El Paso, 1977–78 (Injured All Season)
Averitt, William "Bird," Pepperdine University, 1976–78
Barnes, Marvin, Providence College, 1977–80

Benjamin, Benoit, Creighton University, 1985–91
Bibby, Henry, University of California, LA, 1980–81
Bowman, Nate, Wichita State University, 1970–71
Bridgeman, Junior, University of Louisville, 1984–86
Brokaw, Gary, University of Notre Dame, 1977–78
Brooks, Michael, LaSalle College, 1979–82
Bryant, Emmette, DePaul University, 1970–72
Bryant, Joe, LaSalle College, 1979–82
Cage, Michael, San Diego State University, 1984–88
Carrington, Robert, Boston College, 1979–80
Catchings, Harvey, Hardin-Simmons University, 1984–85
Chambers, Jerry, University of Utah, 1971–72
Charles, Ken, Fordham University, 1973–76
Cooper, Joe, University of Colorado, 1982–83
Crawford, Fred, St. Bonaventure University, 1970–71
Criss, Charlie, New Mexico State University, 1981–82
Cummings, Terry, DePaul University, 1982–84
Dantley, Adrian, University of Notre Dame, 1976–77
Davis, Michael, Virginia Union University, 1970–72
Donaldson, James, Washington State University, 1983–86
Douglas, John, University of Kansas, 1981–83
Edwards, Franklin, Cleveland State University, 1984–86
Fox, Harold, Jacksonville University, 1972–73
Free, Lloyd, Guilford College, 1978–80
Garrett, Dick, Southern Illinois University, 1970–73
Gilliam, Herm, Purdue University, 1970–71
Glenn, Michael, Southern Illinois University, 1977–78
Gordon, Lancaster, University of Louisville, 1984–88
Harris, Bernard, Virginia Commonwealth University, 1974–75
Heard, Garfield, University of Oklahoma, 1973–76, 1980–81
Hill, Armond, Princeton University, 1981–82
Hilton, Fred, Grambling State University, 1971–73
Hodges, Craig, Long Beach State University, 1982–84
Hollins, Lionel, Arizona State University, 1982–83
Johnson, George, Dillard University, 1976–77
Johnson, Marques, University of California, LA, 1984–88
Jones, Wil, Albany State College, Georgia, 1977–78
Kelser, Gregory, Michigan State University, 1983–84
Knight, William, University of Pittsburgh, 1977–78
Loder, Kevin, Alabama State University, 1983–84
Malone, Moses, Petersburg, Virginia H.S., 1976–77
Maxwell, Cedric, University of North Carolina, Charlotte, 1985–87
Mayes, Clyde, Furman University, 1976–77
McAdoo, Robert, University of North Carolina, 1972–77
McClain, Ted, Tennessee State University, 1977–78
McDaniels, Jim, Western Kentucky University, 1977–78
McKinney, Bill, Northwestern University, 1983–84
McMillian, Jim, Columbia University, 1973–76
McNeil, Larry, Marquette University, 1977–78

Moore, Lowes, West Virginia University, 1982–83
Nixon, Norm, Duquesne University, 1983–89
Norman, Coniel, University of Arizona, 1978–79
Owens, Eddie, University of Nevada, Las Vegas, 1977–78
Price, Jim, University of Louisville, 1976–77
Price, Tony, University of Pennsylvania, 1980–81
Shumate, John, University of Notre Dame, 1975–78
Smith, Derek, University of Louisville, 1983–86
Smith, Elmore, Kentucky State University, 1971–73
Smith, Phil, University of San Francisco, 1980–82
Smith, Randy, Buffalo State University, 1971–83
Smith, Robert, University of Nevada, Las Vegas, 1982–83
Smith, Robert "Bingo," University of Tulsa, 1979–80
Taylor, Brian, Princeton University, 1978–82
Towns, Linton, James Madison University, 1983–84
Warner, Cornell, Jackson State University, 1970–73
Warrick, Bryan, St. Joseph's University, 1984–85
Washington, Jim, Villanova University, 1974–76
Washington, Kermit, American University, 1978–79
Weatherspoon, Nick, University of Illinois, 1978–80
White, Rory, University of South Alabama, 1983–86
Whitehead, Jerome, Marquette University, 1978–84
Wicks, Sidney, University of California, LA, 1978–81
Wilson, George, University of Cincinnati, 1970–71
Wiley, Michael, Long Beach State University, 1981–82
Williams, Chuck, University of Colorado, 1976–78
Williams, Freeman, Portland State University, 1978–82
Willoughby, Bill, Dwight Morgan H.S. (Englewood, N.J.), 1977–78
Wood, Al, University of North Carolina, 1981–83

ADDENDUM

Coaches
Jones, Keith (Head Trainer) 1990–93
Horne, Carl W. (Strength and Conditioning) 1991–93

All-Stars
Johnson, Marques 1986
Manning, Danny 1993

All-Time Roster of The Los Angeles Clippers
Ball, Cedric, University of North Carolina-Charlotte, 1990–91
Bannister, Ken, St. Augustine's College, 1988–91
Brown, Tony, University of Arkansas, 1991–92
Bryant, Wallace, University of San Francisco, 1985–86
Burtt, Steven, Iona College, 1987–88
Coleman, Norris, Kansas State University, 1987–88
Copeland, Lanard, Georgia State University, 1991–92
Cureton, Earl, University of Detroit, 1986–88

Dailey, Quintin, University of San Francisco, 1986–89
Drew, Larry, University of Missouri, 1986–88
Edwards, James, University of Washington, 1991–92
Edwards, Jay, Indiana University, 1989–91
Fields, Ken, University of California, LA 1986–88
Garland, Winston, Southwest Missouri State University, 1989–91
Garrick, Tom, University of Rhode Island, 1988–91
Grant, Gary, University of Michigan, 1988–93
Gregory, Claude, University of Wisconsin, 1987–88
Harper, Ron, University of Miami (Ohio), 1989–93
Harris, Steven, University of Tulsa, 1989–90
Jackson, Jaren, Georgetown University, 1992–93
Jackson, Mark, St. John's University, 1992–93
Jones, Ozell, California State University, Fullerton, 1985–86
Kimble, Bo, Loyola Marymount University, 1990–92
Manning, Danny, University of Kansas, 1988–93
Mayes, Tharon, Florida State University, 1991–92
McKinney, Carlton, Southern Methodist University, 1989–90
Norman, Ken, University of Illinois, 1987–93
Phelps, Michael, Alcorn State University, 1987–88

Polee, Dwayne, Pepperdine University, 1986–87
Polynice, Olden, University of Virginia, 1990–91
Rivers, Glen "Doc," Marquette University, 1991–92
Roberts, Stanley, Louisiana State University, 1992–93
Smith, Charles, University of Pittsburgh, 1988–92
Spencer, Elmore, University of Nevada, Las Vegas 1992–93
Thomas, Jim, Indiana University, 1985–86
Turner, Andre, Memphis State University, 1989–90
Valentine, Darnell, University of Kansas, 1985–88
Vaught, Loy, University of Michigan, 1990–93
Weatherspoon, Nick, University of Alabama, 1988–89
Wilkes, Jamaal, University of California, LA, 1985–86
Williams, John, Louisiana State University, 1992–93
Williams, Kevin, St. John's University, 1988–89
Williams, Reginald, Georgetown University, 1987–90
Woods, Randy, LaSalle University, 1992–93
Woodson, Michael, Indiana University, 1986–87
Young, Danny, Wake Forest University, 1987–88
Young, Michael, University of Houston, 1989–90

LOS ANGELES LAKERS
Inglewood, California 90306

Minneapolis Lakers, 1948–60

Front Office Personnel
Harris, Pat (Vice-President, Finance) 1981–82
Jackson, John (Assistant to the Owner) 1982–93

Coaches
Jones, K. C. (Assistant) 1971–72
Barnhill, John (Assistant) 1972–75

All-Stars
Baylor, Elgin 1959, 1961–65, 1967–70
Clark, Archie 1968
Chamberlain, Wilt 1969, 1971–73
Abdul-Jabbar, Kareem 1976–77, 1979–89
Johnson, Earvin 1980, 1982–92
Wilkes, Jamaal 1981, 1983
Nixon, Norm 1982
Worthy, James 1986–92

All-Time Roster of The Los Angeles Lakers
Abdul-Jabbar, Kareem, University of California, LA, 1975–89
Allen, Lucius, University of California, LA, 1974–77
Anderson, Cliff, St. Joseph's University, 1967–69
Barnes, Jim, Texas Western University, 1966–68

Barnett, Richard, Tennessee State University, 1962–65
Bates, Billy Ray, Kentucky State University, 1982–83
Baylor, Elgin, Seattle University, 1958–72
Boone, Ron, Idaho State University, 1978–79
Branch, Adrian, University of Maryland, 1986–87
Brewer, Jim, University of Minnesota, 1980–82
Bridges, William, University of Kansas, 1972–75
Calhoun, David, University of Pennsylvania, 1974–75
Carr, Kenneth, North Carolina State University, 1977–79
Carter, Clarence "Butch," Indiana University, 1980–81
Carter, Ron, Virginia Military Institute, 1978–79
Chamberlain, Wilt, University of North Carolina, 1968–73
Chambers, Jerry, University of Utah, 1966–67
Chones, Jim, Marquette University, 1979–81
Clark, Archie, University of Minnesota, 1966–68
Cooper, Michael, New Mexico University, 1978–90
Crawford, Fred, St. Bonaventure University, 1967–69
Dantley, Adrian, University of Notre Dame, 1977–79
Edwards, James, University of Washington, 1977–78
Ellis, Leroy, St. John's University, 1962–66
Felix, Ray, Long Island University, 1960–62
Freeman, Don, University of Illinois, 1975–76

Garrett, Calvin, Oral Roberts University, 1983–84
Garrett, Dick, Southern Illinois University, 1969–70
Grant, Travis, Kentucky State University, 1972–74
Hairston, Happy, New York University, 1969–75
Hardy, Alan, University of Michigan, 1980–81
Hawkins, Connie, University of Iowa, 1973–74
Hawkins, Tom, University of Notre Dame, 1966–69
Haywood, Spencer, University of Detroit, 1979–80
Hazzard, Walt, University of California, LA, 1964–67
Hudson, Lou, University of Minnesota, 1977–79
Johnson, Clay, University of Missouri, 1982–83
Johnson, Earvin, Michigan State University, 1979–91
Jones, Dwight, University of Houston, 1982–83
Jones, Earl, University of the District of Columbia, 1984–85
Jordan, Ed, Rutgers University, 1980–84
Lamar, Dwight, University of Southwestern Louisiana, 1976–77
Lester, Ronnie, University of Iowa, 1984–86
Lantz, Stu, University of Nebraska, 1974–76
Mack, Oliver, East Carolina University, 1979–80
McAdoo, Robert, University of North Carolina, 1981–85
McCarter, Willie, Drake University, 1969–71
McGee, Michael, University of Michigan, 1981–86
McMillian, Jim, Columbia University, 1970–73
Nixon, Norm, Duquesne University, 1977–83
Patrick, Myles, Auburn University, 1980–81
Price, Jim, University of Louisville, 1972–74
Robinson, Flynn, University of Wyoming, 1971–73
Russell, Cazzie, University of Michigan, 1974–77
Scott, Byron, Arizona State University, 1983–93
Smith, Elmore, Kentucky State University, 1973–75
Spriggs, Larry, Howard University, 1983–86
Tatum, Earl, Marquette University, 1976–78
Thompson, Bill, University of Louisville, 1986–88
Trapp, John Q., Long Beach State University, 1972–73
Tresvant, John, Seattle University, 1969–71
Warner, Cornell, Jackson State University, 1975–77
Washington, Kermit, American University, 1973–78
Wesley, Walter, University of Kansas, 1975–76
Wiley, Gene, Long Beach State University, 1962–66
Wilkes, Jamaal, University of California, LA, 1977–85
Worthy, James, University of North Carolina, 1982–93

ADDENDUM
Front Office Personnel
Cooper, Michael (Special Assistant to the General Manager) 1991–93
Lester, Ron (Scout) 1988–93

Coaches
Drew, Larry (Assistant) 1992–93

All-Stars
Green, A. C. 1990

All-Time Roster of The Los Angeles Lakers
Benjamin, Benoit, Creighton University, 1992–93
Brown, Chucky, North Carolina State University, 1991–92
Brown, Tony, University of Arkansas, 1990–91
Calip, Demetrius, University of Michigan, 1991–92
Campbell, Elden, Clemson University, 1990–93
Campbell, Tony, Ohio State University, 1987–89
Christie, Doug, Pepperdine University, 1992–93
Drew, Larry, University of Missouri, 1989–91
Green, A. C., Oregon State University, 1985–93
Henderson, Jerome, Virginia Commonwealth University, 1985–86
Lucas, Maurice, Marquette University, 1985–86
McCants, Melvin, Purdue University, 1989–90
Matthews, Wes, University of Wisconsin, 1986–88
Perkins, Sam, University of North Carolina, 1990–93
Robinson, Cliff, University of Southern California, 1991–92
Rivers, David, University of Notre Dame, 1988–89
Smith, Tony, Marquette University, 1990–93
Sparrow, Rory, Villanova University, 1991–92
Teagle, Terry, Baylor University, 1990–92
Thompson, Mychal, University of Minnesota, 1986–91
Threatt, Sedale, West Virginia Tech, 1991–93
Tolbert, Ray, Indiana University, 1987–88
Wagner, Milt, University of Louisville, 1987–88
Woolridge, Orlando, University of Notre Dame, 1988–90
Vincent, Jay, Michigan State University, 1989–90

MIAMI HEAT
Miami, Florida 33136-4102

Front Office Personnel

Green, Roger (Vice-President, Corporate Sales) 1990–93
Jones, Wali (Vice-President, Community Relations Director of Community Relations) 1991–93
George, Sybil Wilson (Director of Corporate Education) 1991–93
Green, Carmen, (Communication Coordinator) 1991–93
Laidler, Jr., Lorenzo (Sales Representative) 1991–93
Lott, Linda (Administrative Assistant) 1992–93
Evans, Celestine (Administrative Assistant) 1992–93

Coaches

Gentry, Alvin (Assistant) 1991–93

All-Time Roster of The Miami Heat

Ackles, George, University of Nevada, Las Vegas, 1992–93
Askins, Keith, University of Alabama, 1990–93
Bennett, Winston, University of Kentucky, 1991–92
Burton, Willie, University of Minnesota, 1990–93
Coles, Vernell "Bimbo," Virginia Tech University, 1990–93
Douglas, Sherman, Syracuse University, 1989–92

Edwards, Kevin, DePaul University, 1988–93
Frank, Tellis, Western Kentucky University, 1989–90
Funchess, Carlos, Northeast Louisiana University, 1992–93
Gray, Sylvester, Memphis State University, 1988–89
Long, Grant, Eastern Michigan University, 1988–93
Minor, Harold, University of Southern California, 1992–93
Mitchell, Todd, Purdue University, 1988–89
Morton, John, Seton Hall University, 1991–93
Rice, Glen, University of Michigan, 1989–93
Salley, John, Georgia Tech University, 1992–93
Shaw, Brian, University of California, Santa Barbara, 1991–93
Smith, Steve, Michigan State University, 1991–93
Sparrow, Rory, Villanova University, 1988–90
Taylor, Anthony, University of Oregon, 1988–89
Thompson, Billy, University of Louisville, 1988–89
Upshaw, Kelvin, University of Utah, 1988–89
Wagner, Milt, University of Louisville, 1990–91
Washington, Dwayne "Pearl," Syracuse University, 1988–89
Wheeler, Clinton, William Patterson College, 1988–89

MILWAUKEE BUCKS
Milwaukee, Wisconsin 53203-1312

Coaches

Jones, K. C. (Assistant) 1976–77
Calvin, Mack (Assistant) 1987–91
Carter, Clarence "Butch" (Assistant) 1991–93
Horton, Phil (Assistant Trainer) 1991–93
Lewis, Harold (Equipment Manager) 1988–93

All-Stars

Abdul-Jabbar, Kareem 1970–75
Robinson, Flynn 1970
Robertson, Oscar 1971–72
Dandridge, Robert 1973–76
Price, Jim 1975
Johnson, Marques 1979–81
Moncrief, Sidney 1982–86
Cummings, Terry 1985
Pierce, Ricky 1991
Robertson, Alvin 1991

All-Time Roster of The Milwaukee Bucks

Abdul-Jabbar, Kareem, University of California, LA, 1970–75
Archibald, Nate, University of Texas, El Paso, 1983–84

Avent, Anthony, Seton Hall University, 1992–93
Boozer, Robert, Kansas State University, 1970–71
Bradley, Dudley, University of Kansas, 1986–88
Bridgeman, Ulysses "Junior," University of Louisville, 1975–87
Brokaw, Gary, University of Notre Dame, 1974–77
Brown, Tony, University of Arkansas, 1988–90
Buckner, Quinn, Indiana University, 1976–82
Carter, Fred, Mount St. Mary's College, 1976–77
Catchings, Harvey, Hardin-Simmons University, 1979–84
Coleman, Ben, University of Maryland, 1989–90
Collins, Don, Washington State University, 1986–87
Conner, Lester, Oregon State University, 1990–92
Crawford, Fred, St. Bonaventure University, 1969–70
Criss, Charles, New Mexico State University, 1982–84
Crompton, Geoff, University of North Carolina, 1981–82
Cummings, Terry, DePaul University, 1984–89
Dandridge, Robert, Norfolk State University, 1969–77, 1981–82
Dantley, Adrian, University of Notre Dame, 1990–91
Davis, Charles, Vanderbilt University, 1984–86, 1987–88
Davis, Mark, Old Dominion University, 1988–89
Day, Todd, University of Arkansas, 1992–93
Dinwiddie, Bill, New Mexico Highlands University, 1971–72

Edwards, Theodore "Blue," East Carolina University, 1992–93
Ellis, Dale, University of Tennessee, 1990–92
Elmore, Len, University of Maryland, 1980–81
Embry, Wayne, University of Miami (Ohio), 1968–69
English, Alex, University of South Carolina, 1976–78
Evans, Michael, Kansas State University, 1980–82
Fields, Ken, University of California, LA, 1984–87
Ford, Phil, University of North Carolina, 1982–83
Garrett, Richard, Southern Illinois University, 1973–74
Garrett, Rowland, Florida State University, 1977–78
Glenn, Michael, Southern Illinois University, 1985–86
Grayer, Jeff, Iowa State University, 1988–92
Green, Rickey, University of Michigan, 1988–89
Henderson, Cedric, University of Georgia, 1986–87
Henderson, Gerald, Virginia Commonwealth University, 1989–90
Hill, Armond, Princeton University, 1982–83
Hodges, Craig, Long Beach State University, 1984–88
Howard, Otis, Austin Peay University, 1978–79
Humphries, Jay, University of Colorado, 1987–92
Johnson, George, St. John's University, 1978–79
Johnson, Marques, University of California, LA, 1977–84
Jones, Earl, University of the District of Columbia, 1985–86
Jones, Wali, Villanova University, 1971–73
Lane, Jerome, University of Pittsburgh, 1991–92
Lanier, Robert, St. Bonaventure University, 1979–84
Laurel, Rich, Hofstra University, 1977–78
Lee, Russell, Marshall University, 1972–74
Lister, Alton, Arizona State University, 1981–86
Love, Robert, Southern University, 1968–69
Lowery, Charles, University of Puget Sound, 1971–72
Lucas, John, University of Maryland, 1987–88
Malone, Moses, Petersburg High School (Virginia), 1991–93
May, Scott, Indiana University, 1981–82
Mayberry, Lee, University of Arkansas, 1992–93
Mayes, Clyde, Furman University, 1975–76
McDonald, Glenn, Long Beach State University, 1976–77
McLemore, McCoy, Drake University, 1970–72
Micheaux, Larry, University of Houston, 1984–85
Moncrief, Sidney, University of Arkansas, 1979–89
Moore, Andre, Loyola University of Chicago, 1987–88
Murdock, Eric, Providence College, 1992–93

Paulk, Charles, Northeastern Oklahoma University, 1969–70
Pellon, Sam, Buffalo State University, 1982–83
Perry, Curtis, Southwest Missouri State Univ., 1971–74
Pierce, Ricky, Rice University, 1984–91
Pressey, Paul, University of Tulsa, 1982–90
Price, Jim, University of Louisville, 1974–77
Reynolds, Jerry "Ice," Louisiana State University, 1985–88
Robertson, Alvin, University of Arkansas, 1989–93
Robertson, Oscar, University of Cincinnati, 1970–74
Robinson, Flynn, University of Wyoming, 1968–70
Rodgers, Guy, Temple University, 1968–70
Roman, Lorenzo, University of Washington, 1983–85
Rowland, Derrick, Potsdam State University, 1985–86
Rule, Robert, Colorado State University, 1974–75
Smith, Don, Iowa State University, 1968–70
Smith, Elmore, Kentucky State University, 1975–77
Smith, Greg, Western Kentucky University, 1968–72
Smith, Keith, Loyola Marymount University, 1986–87
Smith, Robert, University of Nevada, Las Vegas, 1981–82
Smith, Sam, University of Nevada, Las Vegas, 1978–79
Stephens, Everette, Purdue University, 1990–91
Thirdkill, David, Bradley, University, 1984–85
Thompson, Paul, Tulane University, 1984–85
Thompson, George, Marquette, University, 1974–75
Townes, Linton, James Madison University, 1983–84
Turner, Andre, Memphis State University, 1988–89
Van Lier, Norman, St. Francis College (PA), 1978–79
Vincent, Sam, Michigan State University, 1992–93
Walton, Lloyd, Marquette University, 1976–80
Warlick, Robert, Pepperdine University, 1968–69
Warner, Cornell, Jackson State University, 1973–75
Warrick, Bryan, St. Joseph's University, 1985–86
Washington, Richard, University of California, LA, 1979–80
Webster, Marvin, Morgan State University, 1986–87
Wesley, Walter, University of Cincinnati, 1974–75
West, Mark, Old Dominion University, 1984–85
White, Rudy, Arizona State University, 1975–78, 1979–80
Williams, Ron, West Virginia University, 1973–75
Williams, Sam, University of Iowa, 1968–70
Winkler, Marvin, University of Southwestern Louisiana, 1970–71
Winslow, Ricky, University of Houston, 1987–88

MINNESOTA TIMBERWOLVES
Minneapolis, Minnesota 55403

Front Office Personnel
McMoore, William (Community Relations Manager) 1991–93
Pierce, Kristy (Timberwolves Foundation Director) 1991–93

Coaches
Brewer, Jim (Assistant to the General Manager/ 1991–93 Assistant
 Coach)
Lowe, Sidney (Assistant) 1991–92, (Head) 1992–93

All-Time Roster of The Minnesota Timberwolves
Bailey, Thurl, North Carolina State University, 1991–93
Branch, Adrian, University of Maryland, 1989–90
Brown, Myron, Slippery Rock State University, 1991–92
Campbell, Tony, Ohio State University, 1989–92
Coffey, Richard, University of Minnesota, 1990–91
Corbin, Tyrone, DePaul University, 1989–91

Frank, Tellis, Western Kentucky University, 1991–92
Garrick, Tom, University of Rhode Island, 1991–92
Glass, Gerald, University of Mississippi, 1990–92
Johnson, Steve, Oregon State University, 1989–90
Lowe, Sidney, North Carolina State University, 1989–90
Maxey, Marlon, University of Texas, El Paso, 1992–93
Mitchell, Sam, Mercer University, 1989–92
Pearson, Charles "Chuck," Auburn University, 1992–93
Richardson, Jerome "Pooh," University of California, LA, 1989–92
Royal, Donald, University of Notre Dame, 1989–90
Sellers, Brad, Ohio State University, 1989–90
Smith, Chris, University of Connecticut, 1992–93
Spencer, Felton, University of Louisville, 1990–93
Thomas, Jim, Indiana University, 1990–91
West, Doug, Villanova University, 1989–93
Williams, Michael, Baylor University, 1992–93

NEW JERSEY NETS
East Rutherford, New Jersey 07073
New York Nets, 1968–76

Front Office Personnel
Doby, Larry (Director of Community Affairs) 1979–88
Bassett, Tim (Regional Sales Manager) 1984–85

Coaches
Silas, Paul (Assistant) 1985–86, 1992–93

All-Stars (American Basketball Association Before 1975)
Erving, Julius 1974–75
Taylor, Brian 1975
Williams, Charles "Buck" 1982–83, 1986
Richardson, Michael Ray 1985

All-Time Roster of The New Jersey Nets (American Basketball Association Before 1975)
Archibald, Nat, University of Texas, El Paso, 1976–77
Ard, Jim, University of Cincinnati, 1970–73
Austin, John, Boston College, 1967–68
Averitt, William, Pepperdine University, 1977–78
Bailey, James, Rutgers University, 1981–83, 1986–87
Bantom, Michael, St. Joseph's College, 1976–77
Bassett, Tim, University of Georgia, 1976–80
Beard, Al, Norfolk State University, 1967–68

Birdsong, Otis, University of Houston, 1981–88
Bowens, Tom, Grambling State University, 1968–69
Boynes, Winford, University of San Francisco, 1978–80
Brewer, Ron, University of Arkansas, 1984–85
Carrington, Robert, Boston College, 1977–78
Catchings, Harvey, Hardin-Simmons University, 1978–79
Chones, Jim, Marquette University, 1972–73
Christian, Robert, Grambling College, 1969–70
Cook, Darwin, University of Portland, 1980–86
Cooper, Joe, University of Colorado, 1981–82
Daniels, Mel, University of New Mexico, 1976–77
Darden, Oliver, University of Michigan, 1968–69
Davis, Mel, St. John's University, 1976–77
Dawkins, Darryl, Maynard Evans H.S. (Florida), 1982–87
DePre, Joe, St. John's University, 1969–72
Dove, Lloyd "Sonny," St. John's University, 1969–72
Elliot, Robert, University of Arizona, 1978–81
Elmore, Len, University of Maryland, 1981–83
Erving, Julius, University of Massachusetts, 1973–76
Floyd, Eric "Sleepy," Georgetown University, 1982–83
Ford, Phil, University of North Carolina, 1982–83
Frazier, Wilbert, Grambling College, 1968–69
Gale, Michael, Elizabeth City State University, 1973–75

Green, Luther, Long Island University, 1969–71
Hackett, Rudy, Syracuse University, 1976–77
Hawkins, Robert "Bubbles," Illinois State University, 1976–78
Hillman, Darnell, San Jose State University, 1977–78
Hunter, Les, Loyola University of Chicago, 1969–71
Jackson, Tony, St. John's University, 1967–69
Johnson, Ed, Tennessee State University, 1969–71
Johnson, George, Dillard University, 1977–80
Johnson, Reginald, University of Tennessee, 1982–84
Johnson, Wallace "Micky," Aurora College, 1982–83, 1985–86
Jones, Edgar, University of Nevada, Reno, 1980–81
Jones, Rich, Memphis State University, 1976–77
Jordan, Ed, Rutgers University, 1977–81
Kenon, Larry, Memphis State University, 1973–75
King, Albert, University of Maryland, 1981–87
King, Bernard, University of Tennessee, 1977–79, 1992–93
Lacey, Sam, New Mexico State University, 1981–82
Lackey, Robert, Marquette University, 1972–74
Leaks, Manny, Niagara University, 1968–72
Love, Robert, Southern University, 1976–77
Lucas, Maurice, Marquette University, 1979–81
Manning, Ed, Jackson State University, 1974–75
Mathis, John, Savannah State University, 1967–68
Jones, Mark, St. Bonaventure University, 1983–84
McAdoo, Robert, University of North Carolina, 1980–81
McClain, Ted, Tennessee State University, 1975–76
McHartley, Maurice, North Carolina A&T University, 1968–69
McNeil, Larry, Marquette University, 1976–77
Money, Eric, University of Arizona, 1978–79
Moore, Lowes, West Virginia University, 1980–81
Natt, Calvin, Northeast Louisiana University, 1979–80
Phillips, Eddie, University of Alabama, 1982–83
Porter, Kevin, St. Francis College (Pennsylvania), 1977–78
Ransey, Kelvin, Ohio State University, 1983–86
Richardson, Michael Ray, University of Montana, 1983–86
Robinson, Cliff, University of Southern California, 1979–81
Sappleton, Wayne, Loyola University of Chicago, 1984–85
Sherod, Edmund, Virginia Commonwealth University, 1981–82
Simpson, Ralph, Michigan State University, 1978–80
Skinner, Al, University of Massachusetts, 1976–79
Smith, Robert, University of Nevada, Las Vegas, 1979–80
Sojourner, Willie, Weber State College, 1973–75
Somerset, Willie, Duquesne University, 1968–69
Sparrow, Rory, Villanova University, 1980–81
Spraggins, Bruce, Virginia Union University, 1967–68
Taylor, Brian, Princeton University, 1972–76
Taylor, Ollie, University of Houston, 1970–74
Tolbert, Ray, Indiana University, 1981–82
Walker, Clarence "Foots," West Georgia College, 1980–84

Washington, Tom, Cheyney State University, 1971–73
Washington, Wilson, Old Dominion University, 1977–79
Webster, Elnardo, St. Peters' College, 1971–72
Westbrook, Dexter, Providence College, 1967–68
Williams, Charles "Buck," University of Maryland, 1981–89
Williams, Earl, Winston-Salem State University, 1976–77
Williams, Ray, University of Minnesota, 1981–82, 1985–87
Williamson, John, New Mexico State University, 1976–80
Wilson, Michael, Marquette University, 1984–85
Woodson, Michael, Indiana University, 1981–82

ADDENDUM

Front Office Personnel
Reed, Willis (Executive Vice-President/Basketball and General Manager, 1989–93

Coaches
Reed, Willis (Head) 1987–89

All-Time Roster of The New Jersey Nets
Addison, Rafael, Syracuse University, 1991–93
Anderson, Greg, University of Houston, 1990–91
Anderson, Kenny, Georgia Tech University, 1991–93
Berry, Walter, St. John's University, 1988–89
Blaylock, Daron "Mookie," University of Oklahoma, 1989–92
Bowie, Sam, University of Kentucky, 1989–93
Bradley, Dudley, University of North Carolina, 1987–88
Branch, Adrian, University of Maryland, 1987–88
Brown, Tony, University of Arkansas, 1986–88
Cattage, Robert, Auburn University, 1985–89
Cavenall, Ron, Texas Southern University, 1988–89
Cheeks, Maurice, West Texas State University, 1992–93
Coleman, Ben, University of Maryland, 1986–88
Coleman, Derrick, Syracuse University, 1990–93
Comegys, Dallas, DePaul University, 1987–88
Conner, Lester, Oregon State University, 1988–91
Gaines, Cory, Loyola Marymount University, 1988–89
George Tate, University of Connecticut, 1990–93
Gervin, Derrick, University of Texas, San Antonio, 1989–91
Higgins, Rod, Fresno State University, 1985–86
Hinson, Roy, Rutgers University, 1988–92
Hopson, Dennis, Ohio State University, 1987–90
Jackson, Jaren, Georgetown University, 1989–90
Lee, Keith, Memphis State University, 1987–89
Mason, Anthony, Tennessee State University, 1989–90
Mills, Terry, University of Michigan, 1990–92
Moore, John, University of Texas, 1987–88
Morris, Chris, Auburn University, 1988–93

Myers, Peter, University of Arkansas, Little Rock, 1989–90
Nelson, Louie, University of Washington, 1977–78
Robinson, Rumeal, University of Michigan, 1992–93
Shackleford, Charles, North Carolina State University, 1988–90
Theus, Reginald, University of Nevada, Las Vegas, 1990–91

Waller, Jamie, Virginia Union University, 1987–88
Washington, Duane, Middle Tennessee State University, 1987–88
Williams, Kevin, St. John's University, 1988–89
Wood, Leon, Loyola Marymount University, 1986–87, 1989–90
Woolridge, Orlando, University of Notre Dame, 1986–87

NEW YORK KNICKERBOCKERS
New York, New York 10121

Coaches
Reed, Willie (Head) 1977–79

All-Stars
Clifton, Nat (Sweetwater) 1957
Naulis, Willie 1958, 1960–62
Green, John 1962–63, 1965
Reed, Willis 1965–71
Barnett, Dick 1968
Frazier, Walter 1970–76
Monroe, Earl 1975, 1977
McAdoo, Robert 1977–78
Cartwright, Bill 1980
Richardson, Michael Ray 1980–82
King, Bernard 1984–85

All-Time Roster of The New York Knickerbockers
Bailey, James, Rutgers University, 1984–86
Bannister, Ken, St. Augustine's College, 1984–86
Barker, Tom, University of Hawaii, 1978–79
Barnes, Jim, Texas Western University, 1964–65
Barnett, Dick, Tennessee State University, 1965–74
Beard, Alfred "Butch," University of Louisville, 1975–79
Behagan, Ron, University of Minnesota, 1978–79
Bellamy, Walter, University of Indiana, 1965–69
Bibby, Henry, University of California, LA, 1972–75
Blackman, Rolando, Kansas State University, 1963–65
Boozer, Robert, Kansas State University, 1963–65
Bowman, Nate, Wichita State University, 1967–70
Bradley, Alex, Villanova University, 1981–82
Bryant, Emmette, DePaul University, 1964–68
Buckner, Cleveland, Jackson State University, 1961–62
Bunch, Greg, California State University, Fullerton, 1978–79
Burden, Luther "Ticky," University of Utah, 1976–78
Carter, Clarence "Butch," Indiana University, 1984–85
Carter, Reggie, St. John's University, 1980–82
Cartwright, William, University of San Francisco, 1979–87
Cavenall, Ron, Texas Southern University, 1984–85
Clemons, Jim, Ohio State University, 1977–80

Clifton, Nat, Xavier University (Louisiana), 1950–57
Copeland, Hollis, Rutgers University, 1979–82
Crawford, Fred, St. Bonaventure University, 1966–68
Dark, Jesse, Virginia Commonwealth University, 1974–75
Davis, Mel, St. John's University, 1973–77
Davis, Mike, University of Maryland, 1982–83
Demic, Larry, University of Arizona, 1979–82
Dukes, Walter, Seton Hall University, 1955–56
Eddie, Patrick, University of Mississippi, 1992–93
Elmore, Len, University of Maryland, 1983–84
Felix, Ray, Long Island University, 1954–60
Filmore, Greg, Cheyney State University, 1970–72
Fogle, Larry, Canisius College, 1975–76
Frazier, Walter, Southern Illinois University, 1967–77
Garrett, Dick, Southern Illinois University, 1973–74
Glenn, Michael, Southern Illinois University, 1978–81
Green, John, Michigan State University, 1959–65
Harkness, Gerald, Loyola University of Chicago, 1963–64
Haywood, Spencer, University of Detroit, 1975–79
Hogue, Paul, University of Cincinnati, 1962–64
Hoover, Tom, Villanova University, 1963–65
Huston, Geoff, Texas Tech University, 1979–80
Jackson, Greg, Guilford College, 1974–75
King, Bernard, University of Tennessee, 1982–87
Knight, Toby, University of Notre Dame, 1977–82
Layton, Dennis, University of Southern California, 1976–77
Lucas, Maurice, Marquette University, 1981–82
Macklin, Durand "Rudy," Louisiana State University, 1983–84
Mayfield, Kendall, Tuskegee Institute, 1975–76
McAdoo, Robert, University of North Carolina, 1976–79
McGill, Bill, University of Utah, 1963–64
McMillian, Jim, Columbia University, 1976–78
Meminger, Dean, Marquette University, 1971–74, 1976–77
Meriweather, Joe C., Southern Illinois University, 1978–80
Miles, Eddie, Seattle University, 1971–72
Monroe, Earl, Winston-Salem State University, 1971–80
Naulls, Willie, University of California, LA, 1956–63
Orr, Louis, Syracuse University, 1982–88
Paulk, Charles, N.E. Oklahoma State, 1971–72

Porter, Howard, Villanova University, 1974–75
Price, Michael, University of Illinois, 1970–72
Rackley, Luther, Xavier University, Ohio, 1971–73
Ramsey, Cal, New York University, 1959–60
Reed, Willis, Grambling University, 1964–74
Richardson, Michael Ray, University of Montana, 1978–82
Robinson, Leonard, Tennessee State University, 1982–85
Russell, Cazzie, University of Michigan, 1966–71
Russell, Michael "Campy," University of Michigan, 1980–82
Scales, DeWayne, Louisiana State University, 1980–82
Shelton, Lonnie, Oregon State University, 1976–78
Sherod, Edmund, Virginia Commonwealth University, 1982–83
Short, Eugene, Jackson State University, 1975–76
Smith, Randy, Buffalo State University, 1981–82
Sparrow, Rory, Villanova University, 1983–88
Stallworth, David, Wichita State University, 1965–67, 1969–75
Stith, Tom, St. Bonaventure University, 1962–63
Taylor, Vince, Duke University, 1982–83
Tucker, Kelvin (Trent), University of Minnesota, 1982–91
Walker, Darrell, University of Arkansas, 1983–86
Walker, Ken, University of Kentucky, 1986–91
Warren, John, St. John's University, 1969–70
Webster, Marvin, Morgan State University, 1978–84
Wilkins, Gerald, University of Tennessee at Chattanooga, 1985–92
Williams, Milt, Lincoln University, 1970–71
William, Ray, University of Minnesota, 1977–84
Wingo, Hawthorne, Friendship Junior College, 1972–76
Woodson, Michael, Indiana University, 1980–81

ADDENDUM

Front Office Personnel
Ramsey, Cal (Director of Community Relations) 1991–93
Tapscott, Ed (Director of Administration) 1992–93

Coaches
Jackson, Stu (Assistant) 1987–89
         (Head) 1989–91
Silas, Paul (Assistant) 1990–92

All-Stars
Ewing, Patrick 1986, 1988–93
Jackson, Mark 1989

All-Time Roster of The New York Knickerbockers
Anthony, Greg, University of Nevada, Las Vegas, 1991–93
Campbell, Tony, Ohio State University, 1992–93
Cheeks, Maurice "Mo," West Texas State University, 1989–91
Cofield, Fred, Eastern Michigan University, 1985–86
Davis, Hubert, University of North Carolina, 1992–93
Donalson, James, Washington State University, 1991–92
Ewing, Patrick, Georgetown University, 1985–93
Granger, Stewart, Villanova University, 1986–87
Grant, Greg, Trenton State College, 1990–91
Green, Sidney, University of Nevada, Las Vegas, 1987–89
Henderson, Gerald, Virginia Commonwealth University, 1986–88
Jackson, Mark, St. John's University, 1987–92
Kimble, Bo, Loyola Marymount University, 1992–93
Martin, William, Georgetown University, 1986–87
Mason, Anthony, Tennessee State University, 1991–93
McDaniel, Xavier, Wichita State University, 1991–92
McKinney, Carlton, Southern Methodist University, 1991–92
Mustaf, Jerrod, University of Maryland, 1990–91
Myers, Pete, University of Arkansas, Little Rock, 1988–90
Newman, John, University of Richmond, 1987–90
Oakley, Charles, Virginia Union University, 1988–93
Oldham, Jawann, Seattle University, 1986–87
Rivers, Glenn "Doc," Marquette University, 1992–93
Scurry, Carey, Long Island University, 1987–88
Singleton, McKinley, University of Alabama, Birmingham, 1986–87
Smith, Charles, University of Pittsburgh, 1992–93
Starks, John, Oklahoma State University, 1990–93
Strickland, Rod, DePaul University, 1988–90
Tolbert, Ray, Indiana University, 1987–88
Toney, Sedric, University of Dayton, 1987–88
White, Tony, University of Tennessee, 1987–88
Winchester, Kennard, Averett College, 1991–92

Reference Section

ORLANDO MAGIC
Orlando, Florida 32801

Front Office Personnel
Blue, Traci (Assistant Director of Publicity/Media Relations for Nonbasketball Events) 1992–93

All-Stars
O'Neal, Shaquille, 1993

All-Time Roster of The Orlando Magic
Anderson, Nick, University of Illinois, 1989–93
Ansley, Michael, University of Alabama, 1989–91
Bowie, Anthony, University of Oklahoma, 1991–93
Catledge, Terry, University of South Alabama, 1989–93
Conner, Lester, Oregon State University, 1992–93
Green, Litterial, University of Georgia, 1992–93

Green, Sidney, University of Michigan, 1991–92
Higgins, Sean, University of Michigan, 1991–92
O'Neal, Shaquille, Louisiana State University, 1992–93
Reynolds, Jerry, Louisiana State University, 1989–93
Roberts, Stanley, Louisiana State University, 1991–92
Royal, Donald, University of Notre Dame, 1992–93
Scott, Dennis, Georgia Tech University, 1990–93
Smith, Otis, Jacksonville University, 1989–92
Theus, Reggie, University of Nevada, Las Vegas, 1989–90
Thompson, Stephen, Syracuse University, 1991–92
Vincent, Sam, Michigan State University, 1989–92
Wiley, Morlon, Long Beach State University, 1989–92
Williams, Brian, University of Arizona, 1991–93

PHILADELPHIA 76ERS
Philadelphia, Pennsylvania 19147-0240

Syracuse Nationals, 1947–63

Front Office Personnel
Shelton, Clayton (Director of Group Sales—Tickets) 1985–88
Barnes, Marlene (Office Manager) 1985–93

All-Stars
Greer, Hal 1961–70
Jackson, Lucious 1965
Walker, Chet 1965–67
Chamberlain, Wilt 1966–68
McGinnis, George 1976–77
Erving, Julius, 1977–87
Cheeks, Maurice 1983, 1986–88
Malone, Moses 1983–86
Toney, Andrew 1983–84

All-Time Roster of The Philadelphia 76ers
Anderson, Cliff, St. Joseph's University, 1970–71
Anderson, Mitchell, Bradley University, 1982–83
Batom, Michael, St. Joseph's University, 1981–82
Barkley, Charles, Auburn University, 1984–92
Barnett, Richard, Tennessee State University, 1959–61
Bibby, Henry, University of California, LA, 1976–80
Bowman, Nate, Witchita State University, 1966–67
Boyd, Fred, Oregon State University, 1972–76
Bridges, William, University of Kansas, 1971–73
Bryant, Joe, LaSalle College, 1975–80

Carter, Fred, Mount St. Mary's College, 1971–77
Cathings, Harvey, Hardin-Simmons University, 1974–79
Chamberlain, Wilt, University of Kansas, 1964–68
Chambers, Jerry, University of Utah, 1968–69
Clark, Archie, University of Minnesota, 1968–72
Crawford, Fred, St. Bonaventure University, 1970–71
Cureton, Earl, University of Detroit, 1980–83
Davis, Monti, Tennessee State University, 1980–81
Dawkins, Darryl, Maynard Evans H.S. (Orlando, Florida), 1975–82
Durrett, Ken, LaSalle College, 1974–75
Edwards, Franklin, Cleveland State University, 1981–84
Ellis, Leroy, St. John's University, 1972–76
Erving, Julius, University of Massachusetts, 1976–87
Free, Lloyd, Guilford College, 1975–78
Furlow, Terry, Michigan State University, 1976–77
Green, John, Michigan State University, 1967–69
Green, Luther, Long Island University, 1972–73
Greer, Hal, Marshall University, 1968–69
Halimon, Shaler, Utah State University, 1968–69
Halliburton, Jeff, Drake University, 1972–73
Hinson, Roy, Rutgers University, 1986–88
Hollins, Lionel, Arizona State University, 1979–82
Hopkins, Robert, Grambling State University, 1956–60
Jackson, Lucious, Pan American University, 1964–72
Johnson, Clemon, Florida A&M University, 1982–86
Johnson, George, St. John's University, 1984–86

Johnson, Ollie, Temple University, 1980–82
Johnson, Reggie, University of Tennessee, 1982–83
Jones, Caldwell, Albany State College (Georgia), 1976–82
Jones, Charles, Albany State College (Georgia), 1983–84
Jones, Wali, Villanova University, 1965–72
Leaks, Manny, Niagara University, 1972–73
Lloyd, Earl, West Virginia State College, 1952–58
Malone, Moses, Petersburg H.S. (Virginia), 1982–86
Matthews, Wes, University of Wisconsin, 1983–84
McClain, Ted, Tennessee State University, 1977–78
McGinnis, George, Indiana University, 1975–78
Meriweather, Porter, Tennessee State University, 1962–63
Money, Eric, University of Arizona, 1978–80
Mosley, Glenn, Seton Hall University, 1977–78
Norman, Coniel, University of Arizona, 1974–76
Rackley, Luther, Xavier University (Ohio), 1973–74
Ramsey, Cal, New York University, 1960–61
Redmond, Marlon, University of San Francisco, 1978–79
Richardson, Clint, Seattle University, 1979–85
Rule, Robert, Colorado State University, 1971–73
Simpson, Ralph, Michigan State University, 1978–79
Skinner, Al, University of Massachusetts, 1978–80
Threatt, Sedale, West Virginia Tech, 1983–87
Toney, Andrew, University of Southwestern Louisiana, 1980–88
Toone, Bernard, Marquette University, 1979–80
Trapp, John Q., Nevada Southern, 1972–73
Walker, Chet, Bradley University, 1962–69
Warley, Ben, Tennessee State University, 1962–66
Washington, Jim, Villanova University, 1969–72
Washington, Wilson, Old Dominion University, 1977–78
Wesley, Walter, University of Kansas, 1974–75
White, Hubie, Villanova University, 1963–64
Williams, Sam, Arizona State University, 1983–85
Wilson, George, University of Cincinnati, 1968–70
Wood, Leon, California State University, Fullerton, 1984–86

ADDENDUM

Coaches
Carter, Fred (Assistant) 1987–93
              (Head) 1992–93
Lumpkin, Sr., Allen (Equipment Manager) 1991–93

All-Stars
Barkley, Charles 1987–92
Hawkins, Hersey 1991

All-Time Roster of The Philadelphia 76ers
Anderson, Ron, Fresno State University, 1988–93
Ansley, Michael, University of Alabama, 1991–92
Askew, William, Memphis State University, 1987–88
Carter, Clarence "Butch," Indiana University, 1985–86
Catledge, Terry, University of South Alabama, 1985–86
Cheeks, Maurice, West Texas State University, 1978–89
Coleman, Ben, University of Maryland, 1987–89
Colter, Steven, New Mexico State University, 1986–88
Dawkins, John, Duke University, 1989–93
Elie, Mario, American International University, 1990–91
Gaines, Corey, Loyola Marymount University, 1989–90
Gilliam, Armon, University of Nevada, Las Vegas, 1991–93
Grant, Greg, Trenton State College, 1991–93
Green, Kenny, Wake Forest University, 1985–87
Green, Rickey, University of Michigan, 1991–92
Harris, Tony, University of New Orleans, 1990–91
Hawkins, Hersey, Bradley University, 1988–93
Henderson, David, Duke University, 1987–88
Henderson, Gerald, Virginia Commonwealth University, 1987–89
Jones, Shelton, St. John's University, 1988–89
King, Albert, University of Maryland, 1987–88
Lang, Andrew, University of Arkansas, 1992–93
Lloyd, Lewis, Drake University, 1989–90
Mahorn, Rick, Hampton University, 1989–90
McAdoo, Robert, University of North Carolina, 1985–86
Moss, Perry, Northeastern University, 1986
Myers, Peter, University of Arkansas, Little Rock, 1988–89
Oliver, Brian, Georgia Tech University, 1990–92
Payne, Ken, University of Louisville, 1989–93
Perry, Tim, Temple University, 1992–93
Reid, Robert, St. Mary's College (Texas) 1990–91
Robinson, Cliff, University of Southern California, 1986–89
Shackleford, Charles, North Carolina State University, 1991–93
Smith, Derek, University of Louisville, 1988–90
Turner, Andre, Memphis State University, 1990–91
Vincent, Jay, Michigan State University, 1989–90
Westherspoon, Clarence, University of Southern Mississippi, 1992–93
Wiggins, Mitchell, Florida State University, 1991–92
Wingate, David, Georgetown University, 1986–89
Young, Michael, University of Houston, 1985–86

PHOENIX SUNS
Phoenix, Arizona 85004

All-Stars
Hawkins, Connie 1970–73
Silas, Paul 1972
Scott, Charlie 1973–75
Davis, Walter 1978–81, 1984, 1987
Robinson, Leonard 1981
Johnson, Dennis, 1981–82
Lucas, Maurice 1983
Nance, Larry 1985

All-Time Roster of The Phoenix Suns
Bantom, Michael, St. Joseph's University, 1973–76
Bradley, Dudley, University of North Carolina, 1981–82
Calhoun, David "Corky," University of Pennsylvania, 1972–75
Chamberlain, William, University of North Carolina, 1973–74
Chambers, Jerry, University of Utah, 1969–70
Christian, Robert, Grambling State University, 1973–74
Davis, Walter, University of North Carolina, 1977–88
Edwards, James, University of Washington, 1983–88
Foster, Rod, University of California, LA, 1983–86
Green, Lamar, Morehead State University, 1969–74
Haskins, Clem, Western Kentucky University, 1970–74
Hawkins, Connie, University of Iowa, 1969–73
Hawthorne, Nate, Southern Illinois University, 1974–76
Heard, Garfield, University of Oklahoma, 1975–80
High, Johnny, University of Nevada, Reno, 1979–83
Holton, Michael, University of California, LA, 1984–85
Humphries, Jay, University of Colorado, 1984–88
Jackson, Greg, Guilford College, 1974–75
Johnson, Dennis, Pepperdine University, 1980–83
Johnson, Gus, University of Idaho, 1972–73
Jones, Charles, University of Louisville, 1984–86
Lattin, David, University of Texas, El Paso, 1968–69
Layton, Dennis, University of Southern California, 1971–73
Lucas, Maurice, Marquette University, 1982–85
Lee, Ron, University of Oregon, 1976–79
McClain, Ted, Tennessee State University, 1978–79
McLemore, McCoy, Drake University, 1968–69
Moore, Otto, Pan American University, 1971–72
Nance, Larry, Clemson University, 1984–88
Niles, Michael, California State University, Fullerton, 1980–81
Perry, Curtis, S.W. Missouri State University, 1974–78
Pittman, Charles, University of Maryland, 1982–86
Robinson, Leonard, Tennessee State University, 1978–82
Sanders, Michael, University of California, LA, 1982–88
Scott, Alvin, Oral Roberts University, 1977–85

Scott, Charlie, University of North Carolina, 1971–75
Shumate, John, University of Notre Dame, 1975–76
Silas, Paul, Creighton University, 1969–72
Sobers, Rickey, University of Nevada, Las Vegas, 1975–77
Terrell, Ira, Southern Methodist University, 1976–77
Thirdkill, David, Bradley University, 1982–83
Thompson, Bernard, Fresno State University, 1985–88
Toney, Sedric, University of Kansas, 1972–73
Weiley, Walter, University of Kansas, 1972–73
White, Rory, University of South Arizona, 1982–84
Williams, Earl, Winston-Salem State University, 1974–75
Wilson, George, University of Cincinnati, 1968–69
Young, Michael, University of Houston, 1984–85

———————

ADDENDUM

Front Office Personnel
Hawkins, Connie (Community Relations Representative) 1992–93

Coaches
Hollins, Lionel (Assistant) 1988–93

All-Stars
Johnson, Kevin 1990–91
Barkley, Charles 1993

All-Time Roster of The Phoenix Suns
Addison, Rafael, Syracuse University, 1986–87
Bailey, James, Rutgers University, 1987–88
Barkley, Charles, Auburn University, 1992–93
Battle, Kenny, University of Illinois, 1989–91
Bedford, William, Memphis State University, 1986–87
Burtt, Steven, Iona College, 1991–92
Carroll, Joe Barry, Purdue University, 1990–91
Ceballos, Cedric, California State University, Fullerton, 1990–93
Corbin, Tyrone, DePaul University, 1987–89
Dumas, Richard, Oklahoma State University, 1992–93
Dunn, T. R., University of Alabama, 1988–89
Gattison, Ken, Old Dominion University, 1986–89
Gilliam, Armon, University of Nevada, Las Vegas, 1987–90
Grant, Greg, Trenton State College (N.J.) 1989–90
Hodges, Craig, Long Beach State University, 1987–89
Johnson, Eddie, University of Illinois, 1987–91
Johnson, Frank, Wake Forest University, 1992–93
Johnson, Kevin, University of California, Berkeley, 1988–93
Knight, Negele, University of Arkansas, 1988–92

Martin, William, Georgetown University, 1987–88
McDaniel, Xavier, Wichita State University, 1990–91
McGee, Michael, University of Michigan, 1989–90
Miller, Oliver, University of Arkansas, 1992–93
Moorison, Michael, Loyola College (Maryland), 1989–90

Mustaf, Jerrod, University of Maryland, 1991–93
Perry, Tim, Temple University, 1988–92
Pinckney, Ed, Villanova University, 1985–87
West, Mark, Old Dominion University, 1988–93

PORTLAND TRAILBLAZERS
Portland, Oregon 97232

Front Office Personnel
Scales, Wallace (Director of Community Relations/Special Events Director) 1971–87

Coaches
Wilkens, Leonard (Head) 1974–76

All-Stars
Wicks, Sidney 1972–75
Lucas, Maurice 1977–79
Hollins, Lionel 1978
Washington, Kermit 1980
Drexler, Clyde 1986, 1988–93

All-Time Roster of The Portland Trailblazers
Bailey, Carl, Tuskegee Institute, 1981–82
Bates, Billy Ray, Kentucky State University, 1979–82
Bowie, Sam, University of Kentucky, 1984–87, 1988–89
Brewer, Jim, University of Minnesota, 1979–80
Brewer, Ron, University of Arkansas, 1978–81
Calhoun, Corky, University of Pennsylvania, 1976–78
Carr, Kenneth, North Carolina State University, 1982–87
Colter, Steven, New Mexico State University, 1984–86
Cooper, Wayne, University of New Orleans, 1982–84, 1989–92
Crompton, Geoff, University of North Carolina, 1980–81
Davis, Charles, Wake Forest University, 1972–74
Davis, John, Dayton University, 1976–78
Davis, Robert, Weber State College, 1972–73
Dorsey, Jackie, University of Georgia, 1977–78
Drexler, Clyde, University of Houston, 1984–93
Dunn, T. R., University of Alabama, 1977–80
Ellis, LeRoy, St. John's University, 1970–71
English, Claude, University of Rhode Island, 1970–71
Gale, Michael, Elizabeth City State University, 1980–81
Gilliam, Herman, Purdue University, 1976–77
Gilmore, Walter, Fort Valley State College, 1970–71
Halimon, Shaler, Utah State University, 1970–71
Hamilton, Roy, University of California, LA, 1980–81
Harper, Michael, North Pack College, 1980–81

Hollins, Lionel, Arizona State University, 1975–80
Jeelani, Abdul, University of Wisconsin, Parkside, 1979–80
Johnson, Clemon, Florida A&M University, 1978–79
Johnson, John, University of Iowa, 1973–76
Johnson, Ken, Michigan State University, 1985–86
Johnson, Ollie, Temple University, 1973–74
Jones, Robin, St. Louis University, 1976–77
Jones, Steven, University of Oregon, 1975–77
Jordan, Ed, Rutgers University, 1983–84
Kersey, Jerome, Longwood College, 1984–93
Knight, Ron, Los Angeles State University, 1970–72
Layton, Dennis, University of Southern California, 1973–74
Lever, Lafayette, Arizona State University, 1982–84
Lucas, Maurice, Marquette University, 1976–80
Lumpkin, Paul, University of Miami (Ohio), 1974–75
Manning, Ed, Jackson State University, 1970–71
Martin, LaRue, Loyola University of Chicago, 1972–76
Mayes, Clyde, Furman University, 1976–77
McCarter, Andre, Drake University, 1971–72
McKenzie, Stan, New York University, 1970–73
McMillian, Jim, Columbia University, 1978–79
Murrey, Doris, University of Detroit, 1970–71
Natt, Calvin, Northeast Louisiana University, 1979–85
Neal, Lloyd, Tennessee State University, 1972–79
Norris, Audie, Jackson State University, 1982–85
Norwood, Willie, Alcorn A&M University, 1977–78
Ransey, Kelvin, Ohio State University, 1980–82
Roberson, Rick, University of Cincinnati, 1973–74
Smith, Greg, Western Kentucky University, 1972–76
Smith, Willie, University of Missouri, 1978–79
Terrell, Ira, Southern Methodist University, 1978–79
Thompson, Bernard, Fresno State University, 1984–85
Thompson, Mychal, University of Minnesota, 1978–86
Townes, Linton, James Madison University, 1982–83
Washington, Kermit, American University, 1979–82
Wicks, Sidney, University of California, LA, 1971–76
Wilkens, Lenny, Providence College, 1974–75
Valentine, Darnell, University of Kansas, 1981–86
Yelverton, Charles, Fordham University, 1971–72

ADDENDUM

Front Office Personnel
Scales, Wally (Vice-President, Special Events) 1987–93
Jones, Nick (Community Activities Coordinator) 1991–93
Cooper, Wayne (Director of Basketball and Special Services) 1992–93

All-Stars
Johnson, Steven 1988
Duckworth, Kevin 1989, 1991
Porter, Terry 1991

All-Time Roster of The Portland Trailblazers
Berry, Walter, St. John's University, 1986–87
Binion, Joe, North Carolina A&T University, 1986–87
Branch, Adrian, University of Maryland, 1988–89
Bryant, Mark, Seton Hall University, 1988–93
Davis, Walter, University of North Carolina, 1990–91
Duckworth, Kevin, Eastern Illinois University, 1986–93
Elie, Mario, American International University, 1992–93
Gamble, Kevin, University of Iowa, 1987–88

Holton, Michael, University of California, LA, 1986–88
Irvin, Byron, University of Missouri, 1989–90
Johnson, David, Syracuse University, 1992–93
Johnson, Steven, Oregon State University, 1986–89
Johnson, Nate, University of Tampa, 1989–90
Jones, Charles, University of Louisville, 1987–88
Murphy, Ronnie, Jacksonville University, 1987–88
Murray, Tracy, University of California, LA, 1992–93
Pack, Robert, University of Southern California 1991–92
Porter, Terry, University of Wisconsin-Stevens Point, 1985–93
Reid, Robert, St. Mary's College (Texas), 1989–90
Robinson, Cliff, University of Connecticut, 1989–93
Smith, Reginald, Texas Christian University, 1992–93
Strickland, Rod, DePaul University, 1992–93
Strothers, Lamont, Christopher Newport College, 1992–93
Whatley, Ennis, University of Alabama, 1991–92
Wheeler, Clinton, William Patterson College, 1988–89
Williams, Charles "Buck," University of Maryland, 1989–93
Wilson, Nikita, Louisiana State University, 1987–88
Young, Danny, Wake Forest University, 1988–92
Young, Perry, Virginia Tech University, 1986–87

SACRAMENTO KINGS
Sacramento, California 95834

Rochester Royals, 1949–57
Cincinnati Royals, 1958–72
Kansas City Kings, 1972–85

All-Stars
Stokes, Maurice 1956–58
Robertson, Oscar 1961–70
Archibald, Nate 1972–76
Ford, Phil 1979–80
Birdsong, Otis 1981

All-Time Roster of The Sacramento Kings
Adams, Michael, Boston College, 1985–86
Allen, Lucius, University of California, LA, 1977–79
Archibald, Nate, University of Texas, El Paso, 1970–76
Birdsong, Otis, University of Houston, 1977–81
Boone, Ron, Idaho State University, 1976–78
Boozer, Robert, Kansas State University, 1960–64
Buckhalter, Joe, Tennessee State University, 1961–63
Catlett, Sid, University of Notre Dame, 1971–72
Douglas, Leon, University of Alabama, 1980–83
Drew, Larry, University of Missouri, 1981–86
Durrett, Ken, LaSalle University, 1971–75

Elmore, Len, University of Maryland, 1979–80
Embry, Wayne, University of Miami (Ohio), 1957–66
Evans, Michael, Kansas State University, 1978–79
Ford, Phil, University of North Carolina, 1978–82
Gilliam, Herman, Purdue University, 1969–70
Green, John, Michigan State University, 1969–73
Green, Michael, Louisiana Tech University, 1979–80
Green, Sihugo, Duquesne University, 1956–59
Hairston, Harold "Happy," New York University, 1964–68
Hawkins, Tom, University of Notre Dame, 1962–66
Hillman, Darnell, San Jose State University, 1978–79
Jackson, Al, Wilberforce University, 1965–66
Johnson, Eddie, University of Illinois, 1981–87
Johnson, Ollie, Temple University, 1974–77
Johnson, Reggie, University of Tennessee, 1981–83
Johnson, Steve, Oregon State University, 1979–83
King, Reggie, University of Alabama, 1979–83
Knight, Billy, University of Pittsburgh, 1981–85
Lacey, Sam, New Mexico State University, 1970–82

Lewis, Freddie, Arizona State University, 1966–67
Loder, Kevin, Alabama State University, 1981–83
Love, Robert, Southern University, 1966–68
McCarter, Andre, University of California, LA, 1976–78
McKinney, Bill, Northwestern University, 1978–80
McNeill, Larry, Marquette University, 1973–76
Mengelt, John, Auburn University, 1971–73
Meriweather, Joe C., Southern Illinois University, 1980–85
Micheaux, Larry, University of Houston, 1983–84
Moore, Otto, Pan American University, 1973–74
Natt, Ken, N.E. Louisiana University, 1984–85
Nelson, Louis, University of Washington, 1977–78
Paulk, Charles, N.E. Oklahoma State University, 1970–71
Pope, David, Norfolk State University, 1984–85
Rackley, Luther, Xavier University (Ohio), 1969–70
Ratiff, Michael, Eau Claire State University, 1972–73
Redmond, Marlon, University of San Francisco, 1978–80
Ricketts, Dick, Duquesne University, 1955–58
Roberson, Rick, University of Cincinnati, 1975–76
Robertson, Oscar, University of Cincinnati, 1960–70
Robinson, Cliff, University of Southern California, 1981–82
Robinson, Flynn, University of Wyoming, 1966–68, 1970–77
Robinzine, Bill, DePaul University, 1975–80
Rodgers, Guy, Temple University, 1967–68
Sanders, Frankie, Southern University, 1980–81
Sibert, Sam, Kentucky State University, 1972–73
Smith, Don (Zaid Abdul-Aziz), Iowa State University, 1968–69
Stokes, Maurice, St. Francis College (Pennsylvania), 1955–58
Suttle, Dane, Pepperdine University, 1983–85
Taylor, Brian, Princeton University, 1976–77
Thacker, Tom, University of Cincinnati, 1963–66
Theus, Reginald, University of Nevada, Las Vegas, 1983–88
Thompson, LaSalle, University of Texas, 1982–89
Thorpe, Otis, Providence College, 1984–88
Tresvant, John, Seattle University, 1967–69
Tucker, Al, Oklahoma Baptist University, 1968–69
Van Lier, Norm, St. Francis College (Pennsylvania), 1969–72
Walker, James, Providence College, 1973–76
Walton, Lloyd, Marquette University, 1980–81
Washington, Richard, University of California, LA, 1976–79
Wesley, Walter, University of Kansas, 1966–69
White, Joseph "Jo Jo," University of Kansas, 1980–81
Whitney, Charles, North Carolina State University, 1980–82
Williams, Nate, Utah State University, 1971–75
Williams, Ray, University of Minnesota, 1982–83
Williams, Willie, Florida State University, 1970–71
Wilson, George, University of Cincinnati, 1964–67
Winfield, Lee, North Texas State University, 1975–76
Woodson, Michael, Indiana University, 1981–86

ADDENDUM

Front Office Personnel

McCullough, Michael (Vice-President, Business Development) 1992–93
Stanley, Travis (Director of Public Relations) 1992–93

Coaches

Russell, William (Head) 1987–88
Jordan, Ed (Assistant) 1992–93

All-Stars

Embry, Wayne 1961–65
Green, John 1971
Lacey, Sam 1975
Richmond, Mitch 1993

All-Time Roster of The Sacramento Kings

Behagen, Ron, University of Minnesota, 1973–75, 1979
Bonner, Anthony, St. Louis University, 1990–93
Calloway, Rick, University of Kansas, 1990–91
Carr, Antoine, Wichita State Unviersity, 1989–91
Causewell, Duane, Temple University, 1990–93
Crosby, Terry, University of Tennessee, 1979–80
Douglas, Bruce, University of Illinois, 1985–86
Douglas, Leon, University of Alabama, 1980–83
Eaves, Jerry, University of Louisville, 1986–87
Edwards, Franklin, Cleveland State University, 1986–88
Ellison, Pervis, University of Louisville, 1989–90
Frederick, Anthony, Pepperdine University, 1990–91
Gillery, Ben, Georgetown University, 1988–89
Hopson, Dennis, Ohio State University, 1991–92
Jackson, Michael, Georgetown University, 1987–90
Mays, Travis, University of Texas, 1990–91
McCray, Rodney, University of Louisville, 1988–90
Oldham, Jawann, Seattle University, 1987–89
Pinckney, Ed, Villanova University, 1987–89
Pressley, Harold, Villanova University, 1986–90
Richmond, Mitch, Kansas State University, 1991–93
Sampson, Ralph, University of Virginia, 1989–91
Simmons, Lionel, LaSalle University, 1991–93
Smith, Derek, University of Louisville, 1986–89
Smith, Ken, University of North Carolina, 1987–90
Sparrow, Rory, Villanova University, 1990–91
Stokes, Greg, University of Iowa, 1989–90
Thompson, Steve, Syracuse University, 1991–92
Tisdale, Wayman, University of Oklahoma, 1988–93
Toney, Sedric, Dayton University, 1989–90
Webb, Anthony "Spud," North Carolina State University, 1991–92
Williams, Walt, University of Maryland, 1992–93

Reference Section

SAN ANTONIO SPURS
San Antonio, Texas 78205

Dallas Chaparrals, 1967–70, 1971–73
(American Basketball Association Until 1977)

All-Stars
Powell, Cincy 1968
Freeman, Don 1971–72
Silas, James 1975–76
Gervin, George 1975–85
Kenon, Larry 1978–79
Gilmore, Artis 1983, 1986
Robertson, Alvin 1986–88

All-Time Roster of The San Antonio Spurs
Averitt, William, Pepperdine University, 1973–74
Banks, Eugene, Duke University, 1981–85
Bassett, Tim, University of Georgia, 1979–80
Bennett, Willis, Winston-Salem State University, 1968–69
Boone, Ron, Idaho State University, 1968–71
Brewer, Ron, University of Arkansas, 1983–85
Brown, Roger, University of Dayton, 1973–74
Calvin, Mack, University of Southern California, 1976–77
Chambers, Jerry, University of Utah, 1973–74
Christian, Robert, Grambling College, 1969–70
Crompton, Jeff, University of North Carolina, 1982–83
Davis, Willie, North Texas State University, 1970–71
Edmonson, Keith, Purdue University, 1983–84
Evans, Michael, Kansas State University, 1979–80
Freeman, Don, University of Illinois, 1970–72, 1974–75
Gale, Michael, Elizabeth City State University, 1975–81
Gervin, George, Eastern Michigan University, 1974–85
Gilmore, Artis, Jacksonville University, 1982–87
Green, Michael, Louisiana Tech University, 1977–79
Hallmon, Shaler, Utah State University, 1971–73
Hightower, Wayne, University of Kansas, 1970–71
Hill, Simmie, West Texas University, 1971–72
Johnson, George, St. John's University, 1980–82
Johnson, Reginald, University of Tennessee, 1980–82
Jones, Collis, University of Notre Dame, 1971–73
Jones, Edgar, University of Nevada, Reno, 1982–85
Jones, Ozell, California State University, Fullerton, 1984–86
Jones, Rich, Memphis State University, 1969–75
Jones, Steve, University of Oregon, 1971–72
Kenjon, Larry, Memphis State University, 1975–80
Kennedy, Eugene, Texas Christian University, 1971–74
Knight, Billy, University of Pittsburgh, 1984–85
Layton, Dennis, University of Southern California, 1971–78

Leaks, Manny, Niagara University, 1968–70
Lockhart, Darrell, Auburn University, 1983–84
Lucas, John, University of Maryland, 1983–84
Maloy, Michael, Davidson College, 1972–73
McGill, William, Auburn University, 1983–84
McHartley, Maurice, North Carolina A & T University, 1967–70
Miller, Robert, University of Cincinnati, 1983–84
Mitchell, Michael, Auburn University, 1982–86
Moore, Gene, St. Louis University, 1970–72
Moore, John, University of Texas, 1980–86
Mosley, Glenn, St. Bonaventure University, 1978–79
Nelson, Lou, University of Washington, 1976–77
Norris, Sylvester, Jackson State University, 1979–80
Peck, Wiley, Mississippi State University, 1979–80
Powell, Cincy, Xavier University (La.), 1967–70
Robertson, Alvin, University of Arkansas, 1984–86
Robinson, Oliver, University of Alabama, Birmingham, 1982–83
Sanders, Frank, Southern University, 1978–79
Sanders, Michael, University of California, LA, 1982–83
Scott, Willie, Alabama State University, 1969–70
Shumate, John, University of Notre Dame, 1979–81
Silas, James, Elizabeth City State University, 1972–81
Smith, Robert, University of Nevada, Las Vegas, 1982–83
Tart, Lavern, Bradley University, 1970–71
Temple, Collis, Louisiana State University, 1974–75
Thirdkill, David, Bradley University, 1984–85
Townes, Linton, James Madison University, 1984–85
Truitt, Ansley, University of California, Berkeley, 1972–73
Wiley, Gene, 1967–68
Wiley, Michael, Long Beach State University, 1980–81
Williams, Kevin, St. John's University, 1983–84
Willoughby, William, Dwight Morrow H. S. (Englewood, N.J.), 1982–83
Wise, Alan, Clemson University, 1975–76

ADDENDUM

Front Office Personnel
Gervin, George, (Community Relations Representative), 1991–93
Houston, William, (Account Executive), 1991–93

Coaches
Manning, Ed (Scout) 1988–93

Lucas, John (Head) 1992–93

All-Stars (American Basketball Association Until 1977)
Robinson, David 1990–93
Elliot, Sean 1993

All-Time Roster of The San Antonio Spurs
Anderson, Greg, University of Houston, 1987–89
Anderson, Willie, University of Georgia, 1988–93
Bardo, Steven, University of Illinois, 1991–92
Berry, Walter, St. John's University, 1986–88
Blackwell, Nate, Temple University, 1987–88
Bowie, Anthony, University of Oklahoma, 1988–89
Carr, Antoine, Wichita State University, 1991–93
Cheeks, Maurice, West Texas State University, 1989–90
Comegys, Dallas, DePaul University, 1988–89
Cook, Darwin, University of Portland, 1988–89
Corbin, Tyrone, DePaul University, 1985–87
Cummings, Terry, DePaul University, 1989–92
Daniels, Lloyd, Andrew Jackson H.S. (N.Y.), 1992–93
Davis, Charles, Vanderbilt University, 1987–88
Dawkins, John, Duke University, 1986–89
Dinkins, Bryon, University of North Carolina-Charlotte, 1990–91
Duckworth, Kevin, Eastern Illinois University, 1986–87
Elliott, Sean, University of Arizona, 1989–93
Ellis, Dale, University of Tennessee, 1992–93
Garrick, Tom, University of Rhode Island, 1991–92
Green, Sidney, University of Nevada, Las Vegas, 1990–92
Higgins, Rod, Fresno State University, 1985–86
Higgins, Sean, University of Michigan, 1990–91
Hughes, Alfredrick, Loyola University of Chicago, 1985–86
Johnson, Avery, Southern University (La.), 1990–93

Johnson, Steve, Oregon State University, 1985–86
Johnson, Vinnie, Baylor University, 1991–92
Jones, Anthony, University of Nevada, Las Vegas, 1986–87
Jones, Caldwell, Albany State College (Ga.), 1989–90
Jones, Shelton, St. John's University, 1988–89
King, Albert, University of Maryland, 1988–89
Lett, Clifford, University of Florida, 1990–91
Massenburg, Tony, University of Maryland, 1990–92
Matthews, Wes, University of Wisconsin, 1985–86
Maxwell, Vernon, University of Florida, 1988–90
Myers, Peter, University of Arkansas, Little Rock, 1987–88, 1990–91
Natt, Calvin, Northeast Louisiana University, 1988–89
Pressey, Paul, University of Tulsa, 1990–92
Reid, J.R., University of North Carolina, 1992–93
Relford, Richard, University of Michigan, 1987–88
Robinson, David, U.S. Naval Academy, 1989–93
Royal, Donald, University of Notre Dame, 1991–92
Smart, Keith, Indiana University, 1988–89
Smith, Larry, Alcorn State University, 1992–93
Strickland, Rod, DePaul University, 1989–92
Sutton, Greg, Oral Roberts University, 1991–93
Thompson, Mychal, University of Minnesota, 1986–87
Tucker, Trent, University of Minnesota, 1991–92
Vincent, Jay, Michigan State University, 1988–89
Whatley, Ennis, University of Alabama, 1985–86, 1992–93
Whitehead, Jerome, Marquette University, 1988–89
Wiley, Morlon, Long Beach State University, 1991–92
Williams, Ray, University of Minnesota, 1985–86
Williams, Reginald, Georgetown University, 1989–91
Wilson, Rick, George Mason University, 1987–88
Wingate, David, Georgetown University, 1989–91
Wood, Leon, California State University, Fullerton, 1987–88

SEATTLE SUPERSONICS
Seattle, Washington 98109

Front Office Personnel
Wilkens, Lenny (Vice-President/General Manager) 1985–86

Coaches
Wilkens, Lenny (Head) 1978–85
Bickerstaff, Bernie (Head) 1985–87

All-Stars
Hazzard, Walt 1968
Wilkens, Lenny, 1969–71
Rule, Robert 1970
Haywood, Spencer 1972–75

Brown, Fred 1976
Johnson, Dennis 1979–80
Shelton, Lonnie 1982
Williams, Gus 1982–83

All-Time Roster of The Seattle Supersonics
Abdul-Aziz, Zaid (Don Smith), Iowa State University, 1970–72, 1975–76
Abdul-Rahman, Mahdi (Walt Hazzard), University of California, LA, 1967–68, 1973–74
Allen, Lucius, University of California, LA, 1969–70
Bailey, James, Rutgers University, 1979–82

Bamton, Michael, St. Joseph's University, 1975–77
Beard, Alfred "Butch," University of Louisville, 1972–73
Blackwell, Cory, University of Wisconsin, 1984–85
Boozer, Robert, Kansas State University, 1969–70
Bradley, Charles, University of Wyoming, 1983–84
Brisker, John, University of Toledo, 1972–75
Brown, Fred, University of Iowa, 1971–84
Clark, Archie, University of Minnesota, 1974–75
Cooper, Joe, University of Colorado, 1984–85
Donaldson, James, Washington State University, 1980–87
Dorsey, Jackie, University of Georgia, 1980–81
Dudley, Charles, University of Washington, 1972–73
Fleming, Al, University of Arizona, 1977–78
Ford, Jake, Maryland State College, 1970–72
Gilliam, Herm, Purdue University, 1975–76
Gray, Leonard, Long Beach State University, 1974–77
Green, Michael, Louisiana Tech University, 1976–78
Haywood, Spencer, University of Detroit, 1970–75
Heard, Garfield, University of Oklahoma, 1970–72
Henderson, Gerald, Virginia Commonwealth University, 1984–85
Hill, Armond, Princeton University, 1980–82
Johnson, Clay, University of Missouri, 1983–84
Johnson, Dennis, Pepperdine University, 1976–80
Johnson, John, University of Iowa, 1977–82
Johnson, Vinnie, Baylor University, 1979–82
Kelser, Gregory, Michigan State University, 1981–83
King, Reggie, University of Alabama, 1983–85
Love, Robert, Southern University, 1976–77
McCray, Scooter, University of Louisville, 1983–85
McDaniel, Xavier, Wichita State University, 1985–90
McDaniels, Jim, Western Kentucky University, 1971–74
McIntoch Kennedy, Eastern Michigan University, 1972–75
Norwood, Willie, Alcorn State University, 1975–77
Robinson, Jackie, University of Nevada, Las Vegas, 1978–79
Rule, Robert, Colorado State University, 1967–72
Shelton, Lonnie, Oregon State University, 1978–83
Short, Eugene, Jackson State University, 1975–76
Shumate, John, University of Notre Dame, 1980–81
Silas, Paul, Creighton University, 1977–80
Skinner, Talvin, University of Maryland, Eastern Shore, 1974–75
Smith, Phil, University of San Francisco, 1981–83
Sobers, Ricky, University of Nevada, Las Vegas, 1984–85
Stallworth, Bud, University of Kansas, 1972–74
Thompson, David, North Carolina State University, 1982–84
Tolbert, Ray, Indiana University, 1981–83
Tresvant, John, Seattle University, 1968–70

Tucker, Al, California Batiste University, 1967–69
Watts, Don, Xavier University, 1973–78
Weatherspoon, Nick, University of Illinois, 1976–77
White, Rudy, Arizona State University, 1980–81
Wilkens, Lenny, Providence College, 1968–72
Wilkerson, Bobby, Indiana University, 1976–77
Williams, Gus, University of Southern California, 1977–83
Williams, Kevin, St. John's University, 1986–88
Williams, Milt, Lincoln University, 1973–74
Wilson, George, University of Cincinnati, 1967–68
Winfield, Lee, North Texas State University, 1969–73
Wise, Willie, Drake University, 1977–78
Wood, Al, University of North Carolina, 1983–87
Wright, Toby, Indiana University, 1972–73
Young, Danny, Wake Forest University, 1984–87

ADDENDUM

Coaches
Bickerstaff, Bernie (Head) 1985–89

All-Stars
McDaniel, Xavier 1988
Ellis, Dale 1989
Kemp, Shawn 1993

All-Time Roster of the Seattle Supersonics
Barros, Dana, Boston College, 1989–93
Benjamin, Benoit, Creighton University, 1991–93
Brown, Tony, University of Arkansas, 1991–92
Cage, Michael, San Diego State University, 1988–93
Dailey, Quintin, University of San Francisco, 1989–91
Ellis, Dale, University of Tennessee, 1986–91
Johnson, Avery, Southern University (La.), 1988–90
Johnson, Steve, Oregon State University, 1989–91
Kemp, Shawn, Concord H.S. (Elkhart, Indiana), 1989–93
Lister, Alton, Arizona State University, 1986–89
Lucas, Maurice, Marquette University, 1986–87
Mickey, Derrick, University of Alabama, 1987–93
McMillian, Nate, North Carolina State University, 1987–93
Payton, Gary, Oregon State University, 1990–93
Perkins, Sam, University of North Carolina, 1992–93
Pierce, Ricky, Rice University, 1991–93
Polynice, Olden, University of Virginia, 1987–91
Reynolds, Jerry, Louisiana State University, 1988–89
Young, Danny, Wake Forest University, 1984–88

UTAH JAZZ
Salt Lake City, Utah 84101

New Orleans Jazz, 1974–80

Coaches
Baylor, Elgin (Head) 1976–79

All-Stars
Robinson, Leonard 1978
Dantley, Adrian 1980–86
Green, Rick 1984

All-Time Roster of The Utah Jazz
Anderson, Mitchell "J.J.," Bradley University, 1982–85
Bailey, Gus, University of Texas, El Paso, 1977–78
Bailey, Thurl, North Carolina State University, 1983–92
Behagan, Ron, University of Minnesota, 1975–77
Bellamy, Walter, Indiana University, 1974–75
Bennett, Melvin, University of Pittsburgh, 1980–81
Bibby, Henry, University of California, LA, 1975–76
Boone, Ron, Idaho State University, 1979–81
Boswell, Thomas, South Carolina State University, 1979–80, 1983–84
Boyd, Fred, Oregon State University, 1975–78
Calvin, Mack, University of Southern California, 1979–80
Cattage, Robert, Auburn University, 1981–82
Coleman, E. C., Central Michigan University, 1974–77
Cooper, Wayne, University of New Orleans, 1980–81
Dantley, Adrian, University of Notre Dame, 1979–86
Dawkins, Paul, Northern Illinois University, 1979–80
Drew, John, Gardner-Webb College, 1982–85
Duren, John, Georgetown University, 1980–82
Eaves, Jerry, University of Louisville, 1982–84
Furlow, Terry, Michigan State University, 1979–80
Green, Lamar, Morehead State University, 1974
Green, Rickey, University of Michigan, 1980–88
Green, Tom, Southern University (La.), 1978–79
Griffith, Darrell, University of Louisville, 1980–91
Hardy, James, University of San Francisco, 1978–82
Haywood, Spencer, University of Detroit, 1978–79
Howard, Maurice, University of Maryland, 1977–78
James, Aaron, Grambling College, 1974–79
Johnson, Ollie, Temple University, 1974–75
King, Bernard, University of Tennessee, 1979–80
Lantz, Stu, University of Nebraska, 1974–75
Lee, Ron, University of Oregon, 1979–80
Lee, Russell, Marshall University, 1974–75
Malone, Karl, Louisiana Tech University, 1985–93
McElroy, James, Central Michigan University, 1975–79

McKinney, Bill, Northwestern University, 1980–81
Meriweather, Joe, Southern Illinois University, 1977–79
Moore, Otto, Pan American University, 1974–77
Natt, Ken, Northeast Louisiana University, 1982–83, 1984–85
Nelson, Louis, University of Washington, 1974–76
Nicks, Carl, Indiana State University, 1980–82
Roberson, Rick, University of Cincinnati, 1974–75
Robinson, Leonard, Tennessee State University, 1977–79
Robinzine, William, DePaul University, 1981–82
Smith, Robert, University of Nevada, Las Vegas, 1979–80
Stallworth, Bud, University of Kansas, 1974–77
Terrell, Ira, Southern Methodist University, 1978–79
Wakefield, Andre, Loyola University of Chicago, 1979–80
Watts, Don, Xavier University, 1977–78
Whitehead, Jerome, Marquette University, 1980
Wilkins, Jeff, Illinois State University, 1980–86
Williams, Don, University of Notre Dame, 1979–80
Williams, Freeman, Portland State University, 1982–83
Williams, Nate, Portland State University, 1975–78
Williams, Ricky, Long Beach State University, 1982–83
Wood, Howard, University of Tennessee, 1981–82
Worthen, Sam, Marquette University, 1981–82

ADDENDUM

All-Stars
Malone, Karl 1988–93

All-Time Roster of the Utah Jazz
Austin, Issac, Arizona State University, 1991–93
Benoit, David, University of Alabama, 1991–93
Brown, Michael, George Washington University, 1988–93
Brown, Tony, University of Arkansas, 1990–91
Corbin, Tyrone, DePaul University, 1991–93
Curry, Dell, Virginia Tech University, 1986–87
Dawkins, Darryl, Maynard Evans H.S. (Fla.), 1987–88
Edwards, Theodore "Blue," East Carolina University, 1989–92
Howard, Stephen, DePaul University, 1992–93
Hughes, Eddie, Colorado State University, 1987–88
Johnson, Eric, Baylor University, 1989–90
Malone, Jeff, Mississippi State University, 1990–93
Murdock, Eric, Providence College, 1991–92
Rudd, Delaney, Wake Forest University, 1989–92
Scurry, Carey, Long Island University, 1985–88
Turpin, Mel, University of Kentucky, 1987–88

WASHINGTON BULLETS
Landover, Maryland 20785

Chicago Packers, 1961–62
Chicago Zephrys, 1962–63
Baltimore Bullets, 1963–73
Capital Bullets, 1973–74

Front Office Personnel
Unseld, Westley (Vice-President/Assistant to the Chief/Administrative Office) 1983–93
Rascoe, Vivian (Administrative Officer) 1981–88
Holland, Judy (Vice-President/Community Relations) 1982–93

Coaches
Jones, K. C. (Head) 1974–76
Butler, Charles (Equipment Manager) 1978–93
Carter, Fred (Assistant) 1985–88

All-Stars
Felix, Ray 1954
Bellamy, Walter 1962–65
Johnson, Gus 1965–71
Unseld, Westley 1969–75
Monroe, Earl 1969, 1971
Clark, Archie 1972
Hayes, Elvin 1973–80
Chenier, Phil 1974–75, 1977
Bing, David 1976
Dandridge, Robert 1979
Malone, Jeff 1986
Malone, Moses 1987–88

All-Time Roster of The Washington Bullets
Adams, Michael, Boston College, 1986–87, 1991–93
Austin, John, Boston College, 1966–67
Bates, Billy Ray, Kentucky State University, 1982–83
Bailey, Gus, University of Texas, El Paso, 1979–80
Ballard, Greg, University of Oregon, 1977–85
Barksdale, Don, University of California, LA, 1951–53
Barnes, Jim "Bad News," Texas Western University, 1965–66, 1970–71
Barnhill, John, Tennessee State University, 1979–80
Behagen, Ron, University of Minnesota, 1979–80
Bellamy, Walter, Indiana University, 1961–66
Bing, David, Syracuse University, 1975–77
Boston, Lawrence, University of Maryland, 1979–80
Brown, Lewis, University of Nevada, Las Vegas, 1980–81
Carr, Austin, University of Notre Dame, 1980–81
Carter, Fred, Mount St. Mary's College, 1969–72

Chenier, Phil, University of California, Berkeley, 1971–80
Chones, Jim, Marquette University, 1981–82
Clark, Archie, University of Minnesota, 1971–74
Cox, Chubby, Villanova University, 1982–83
Dandridge, Robert, Norfolk State University, 1977–81
Davis, Charles, Vanderbilt University, 1981–85
Davis, Michael, Virginia Union University, 1969–70, 1972–73
Daye, Darren, University of California, LA, 1983–85
DuVal, Dennis, Syracuse University, 1974–75
Ellis, Leroy, St. John's University, 1966–70
Felix, Ray, Long Island University, 1953–54
Gibson, Michael, University of South Carolina, Spartanburg, 1983–84
Gray, Leonard, Long Beach State University, 1976–77
Green, John, Michigan State University, 1965–67
Green, SiHugo, Duquesne University, 1961–65
Hardnett, Charles, Grambling College, 1962–65
Haskins, Clem, Western Kentucky University, 1974–76
Hayes, Elvin, University of Houston, 1972–81
Haywood, Spencer, University of Detroit, 1981–83
Henderson, Tom, University of Hawaii, 1976–79
Hightower, Wayne, University of Kansas, 1964–66
Hogue, Paul, University of Cincinnati, 1963–64
Hunter, Leslie, Loyola (Chicago), 1964–65
Johnson, Charles, University of California, Berkeley, 1977–79
Johnson, George, Stephen F. Austin State University, 1970–71
Johnson, Gus "Honeycomb," University of Idaho, 1963–72
Johnson, Frank, Wake Forest University, 1981–88
Jones, Charles, Albany State College, 1984–93
Jones, Jimmy, Grambling College, 1974–77
King, Maurice, University of Kansas, 1962–63
Leaks, Manny, Niagara University, 1973–74
Lucas, John, University of Maryland, 1981–83
Mahorn, Rick, Hampton University, 1980–85
Malone, Jeff, Mississippi State University, 1983–90
Malone, Moses, Petersburg H.S. (Virginia), 1986–88
Manning, Ed, Jackson State University, 1967–70
Matthews, Wes, University of Wisconsin, 1980–81
McCarter, Andre, University of California, LA, 1980–81
McGill, Bill, University of Utah, 1962–64
Miles, Eddie, Seattle University, 1969–71

Monroe, Earl, Winston-Salem State University, 1967–72
Murrey, Dorie, University of Detroit, 1970–72
Nelson, Louis, University of Washington, 1973–74
Pace, Joe, Coppin State University, 1976–78
Porter, Kevin, St. Francis College (Pennsylvania), 1972–81, 1982–83
Roberts, Anthony, Oral Roberts University, 1980–81
Robinson, Cliff, University of Southern California, 1984–86
Robinson, Flynn, University of Wyoming, 1972–73
Sauldsberry, Woody, Texas Southern University, 1961–62
Scales, DeWayne, Louisiana State University, 1983–84
Scott, Ray, University of Portland, 1966–70
Sewell, Tom, Lamar University, 1984–86
Sobers, Ricky, University of Nevada, Las Vegas, 1982–84
Somerset, Willie, Duquesne University, 1965–66
Stallworth, David, Witchita State University, 1971–74
Terry, Carlos, Winston-Salem State University, 1980–83
Tresvant, John, Seattle University, 1970–73
Unseld, Westly, University of Louisville, 1968–81
Walker, Phil, Millersville State University, 1977–78
Warley, Ben, Tennessee State University, 1965–67
Warrick, Bryan, St. Joseph's College, 1982–84
Weatherspoon, Nick, University of Illinois, 1973–77
West, Roland, University of Cincinnati, 1967–68
Wesley, Walter, University of Kansas, 1973–74
Williams, Gus, University of Southern California, 1984–86
Williams, Guy, Washington State University, 1983–85
Williamson, John, New Mexico State University, 1979–80
Wilson, Michael, Marquette University, 1983–84
Wright, Larry, Grambling College, 1976–80

ADDENDUM

Front Office Personnel
Downing, Bonnie (Director of Community Relations) 1991–93
Banks, Renard (Account Manager) 1992–93
Berry, Marcus (Account Manager) 1992–93
Dawkins, Terry (Area Sales Manager) 1992–93
Finney, LeRian (Baltimore Sales) 1992–93
Humes, William (Account Manager) 1992–93
Jackson, Michael (Customer Service) 1992–93
Johnson, Sheena (Assistant to Community Relations/Advertising) 1992–93

Moss, Darryll (Account Manager) 1992–93
Owens, Kevin (Account Manager) 1992–93

Coaches
Unseld, Westly (Head) 1988–93

All-Stars
King, Bernard 1991
Adams, Michael 1992

All-Time Roster of The Washington Bullets
Bogues, Tyrone, "Muggsy," Wake Forest University, 1987–88
Burtt, Steve, Iona College, 1992–93
Catledge, Terry, University of South Alabama, 1986–89
Colter, Steven, New Mexico State University, 1987–90
Cook, Darwin, University of Portland, 1986–87
Eackles, Ledell, University of New Orleans, 1988–92
Ellison, Pervis, University of Louisville, 1990–93
Grant, Harvey, University of Oklahoma, 1988–93
Green, Kenny, Wake Forest University, 1985–86
Gregory, Claude, University of Wisconsin, 1985–86
Hammonds, Tom, Georgia Tech University, 1989–92
Horton, Ed, University of Iowa, 1989–90
Irvin, Byron, University of Missouri, 1990–91
Johnson, Alfonso "Buck," University of Alabama, 1992–93
Johnson, George L., St. John's University, 1985–86
Jones, Anthony, University of Nevada, Las Vegas, 1986–87
Jones, Charles A., University of Louisville, 1988–89
King, Albert, University of Maryland, 1991–92
King, Bernard, University of Tennessee, 1987–91
Pressley, Dominic, Boston College, 1988–89
Robinson, Larry, Centenary College, 1990–91
Roundfield, Dan, Central Michigan University, 1985–87
Sampson, Ralph, University of Virginia, 1991–92
Smith, Clinton, Cleveland State University, 1990–91
Stewart, Larry, Coppin State University, 1991–93
Turner, Andre, Memphis State University, 1991–92
Vincent, Jay, Michigan State University, 1986–87
Walker, Darrell, University of Arkansas, 1987–91
Whatley, Ennis, University of Alabama, 1985–87
Williams, Freeman, Portland State University, 1985–86
Wingate, David, Georgetown University, 1991–92
Wood, Leon, California State University, Fullerton, 1985–86
Workman, Haywood, Oral Roberts University, 1990–91

Reference Section

AFRICAN-AMERICANS WHOSE NUMBERS ARE RETIRED IN THE NATIONAL BASKETBALL ASSOCIATION

EASTERN CONFERENCE

Atlanta Hawks
Lou Hudson 23

Boston Celtics
Dennis Johnson 3
Bill Russell 6
Jo Jo White 10
Tom "Satch" Sanders 16
Sam Jones 24
K. C. Jones 25

Cleveland Cavaliers
Bobby "Bingo" Smith 7
Austin Carr 34
Nate Thurmand 42

Detroit Pistons
Dave Bing 21

Indiana Pacers
George McGinnis 30
Mel Daniels 34
Roger Brown 35

Milwaukee Bucks
Oscar Robertson 1
Junior Bridgeman 2
Sidney Moncrief 4
Bob Lanier 16

New York Knickerbockers
Walt Frazier 10
Dick Barnett 12
Earl Monroe 15
Willis Reed 19

New Jersey Nets
John Williamson 23
Julius Erving 32

Philadelphia 76ers
Julius Erving 6
Wilt Chamberlain 13
Hal Greer 15

Washington Bullets
Elvin Hayes 11
Gus Johnson 25
Wes Unseld 41

WESTERN CONFERENCE

Golden State Warriors
Alvin Attles 16
Nate Thurmond 42

Houston Rockets
Calvin Murphy 23

Phoenix Suns
Connie Hawkins 42

Portland Trailblazers
Maurice Lucas 20
Lloyd Neal 36

Sacramento Kings
Maurice Stokes 12
Oscar Robertson 14

San Antonio Spurs
James Silas 13
George Gervin 44

Seattle Supersonics
Lenny Wilkens 19
Fred Brown 32

Los Angeles Lakers
Wilt Chamberlain 13
Elgin Baylor 22
Earvin Johnson 32
Kareem Abdul-Jabbar 33

OUTSTANDING AFRICAN-AMERICANS IN COLLEGE BASKETBALL
(1919–1945)

Clark College
Atlanta, Georgia 30314

Outstanding Athletes

Henderson, Abbey, 1939–1940
DeZowie, Hank, 1939–1940
Johnson, Joe, 1939–1940
Pemberton, Dale, 1939–1940
Gates, William "Pop", 1939–1940

Columbia University
New York, New York 10027

All-American

Gregory, George[1] 1931

Outstanding Athletes

Wood, Tom[2]
Skinner, Norman[3]

[1] Gregory, George—first black American voted College All-American in basketball
[2] Wood, Tom—played for Columbia University in the mid-1940s
[3] Skinner, Norman—played for Columbia University in the mid-1940s

Howard University
Washington, D.C. 20059

Coaches of Varsity Teams

Morrison, Dr. Ed 1920–23
Burr, Jr., John H. 1923–30
Waller, Aubrey O. 1930–31
Burr, Jr., John H. 1931–46

Lincoln University
Lincoln University, Pennsylvania 19352

Coaches of Varsity Teams

Law, J. L. 1922–23
Walls, Ted 1927–28
Taylor, William S. 1929–32

Martin, Julius 1933–34
Ballard, C. 1934–38
Rivero, Manuel 1939–46

Long Island University
Brooklyn, New York 11201

Outstanding Athletes

King, William "Dolly"—played on the 1936, 1937 Long Island University basketball and baseball teams

Morgan State University
Baltimore, Maryland 21239

Outstanding Athletes

Jones, Ed "Lanky", 1930

All-American
(Black College)

Wheatley, Thomas "Rap", 1930
Murdock, Ezra "Ez", 1924–1927
Hackett, Rufus "Legs", 1924–1927
Hill, Talmadge "Marse", 1924–1927
Clark, Daniel "Pinky", 1924–1927

The 1927 undefeated Morgan State team was coached by Dr. Charles Drew.

North Carolina Central University
Durham, North Carolina 77707

Athletic Directors

Crudup, B.D. 1928–29
Waters, David, 1930–31
Townsend, Leo 1935–36
Adams, E.H. 1936–37
Burghardt, William F. 1937–40

Princeton University
Princeton, New Jersey 08544

Outstanding Athletes

Wilson, Arthur[1]

[1] Wilson, Arthur—first black basketball player in Princeton University history, 1942

San Diego State University
San Diego, California 92182

All-Southern California Intercollegiate Athletic Conference (SCIAC)
Moss, Clinton 1935

Savannah State College
Savannah, Georgia 31404

Coaches of Varsity Teams
Richardson, Richard 1928–34
Dwight, Arthur 1934–40
King, W. McKinley 1940
Bruce, Clarence 1941
Myles, John 1942

Women's Basketball
Lester, Janie 1927–39

Southern University
Baton Rouge, Louisiana 70813

Coaches of Varsity Teams
Mumford, A.W. 1937–46

Tennessee State University
Nashville, Tennessee 37203

Coaches of Varsity Teams
Kean, Henry A. 1945–46

University of California, Los Angeles
Los Angeles, California 90024

All Pacific Coast Conference (Southern Division)
Robinson, Jack 1940

University of Pennsylvania
Philadelphia, Pennsylvania 19104

Outstanding Athletes
Wideman, John E.[1]

[1] Wideman, John E.—Rhodes Scholar; Big-Five Hall of Fame

Virginia Union University
Richmond, Virginia 23220

Outstanding Athletes
Glover, Melvin, 1939–1940
Frazier, Gerald "Pickles", 1939–1940
Williams, Wendell, 1939–1940
Campbell, Wylie "Soupy", 1939–1940
Hyde, Kavanzo, 1939–1940
Storres, Alvin, 1939–1940
Atkins, Floyd, 1939–1940
Jones, Howard, 1939–1940
Hines, Norman, 1939–1940
Tensley, Vincent, 1939–1940
White, Lewis, 1939–1940

The 1940 Virginia Union team, aka "The Dream Team", beat the NCAA champion Long Island University twice.

West Virginia State College
Institute, West Virginia 25112

Coaches of Varsity Teams
Hamblin, Adolph P. 1921–33
Brown, Dallas 1933–34
Hawkins, Charles C. 1934–35
Ellis, Arthur W. 1936–37
Clement, Fred A. 1938–44
McCarthy, Horace 1944–45
Cardwell, Mark 1945–46

Xavier University
New Orleans, Louisiana 70125

Outstanding Athletes
Rhodes, Leroy, 1935–1939
Bray, Clevelan, 1935–1939

McQuitter, Williams, 1935–1939
Cole, Tilford, 1935–1939
Gant, James, 1935–1939

The 1935–1939 Xavier University team had a record of 82–2

OUTSTANDING AFRICAN-AMERICANS IN COLLEGE BASKETBALL (1946–1992) BY CONFERENCE

MISSOURI VALLEY CONFERENCE

1. Wichita State University
2. University of Tulsa
3. Indiana State University
4. Creighton University
5. Drake University

6. Southern Illinois University
7. West Texas State University
8. Southwest Missouri State University
9. Illinois State University
10. Bradley University

Wichita State University
Wichita, Kansas 67208-0018

Coach of Varsity Team

Guydon, Gus (Assistant), 1976–78
Jones, Jeff (Assistant), 1977
Sprott, Charles (Assistant), 1993

All Missouri Valley Conference

Littleton, Cleo, 1952–55
Tate, Al, 1959
Wiley, Gene, 1961–62
Stallworth, David, 1963–65
Bowman, Nate, 1964
Pete, Kelly, 1965
Armstrong, Warren, 1966–68
Carney, Greg, 1970
Benton, Terry, 1971–72
Morsden, Rich, 1974–75
Wilson, Robert, 1974–75
Elmore, Robert, 1977–79
Johnson, Lynbert "Cheese", 1977–79
Levingston, Cliff, 1980–82
Carr, Antoine,[1] 1980–83
Sherrod, Aubrey, 1983
McDaniel, Xavier,[2] 1983–85

All-American

Littleton, Cleo, 1955

Stallworth, David, 1964
Carney, Greg, 1970
Johnson, Lynbert "Cheese", 1979
Carr, Antoine, 1983[1]
Sherrod, Aubrey, 1984
McDaniel, Xavier, 1984–85[2]

Other Outstanding Athletes

Santos, Gus

[1] Carr, Antoine—1983 Missouri Valley Conference Player of the Year
[2] McDaniel, Xavier—1984 and 1985 Missouri Valley Conference Player of the Year

University of Tulsa
Tulsa, Oklahoma 74104

Coach of Varsity Team

Richardson, Nolan (Head), 1980–85
Smith, Orlando "Tubby", 1991–93

All Missouri Valley Conference

Smith, Bobby,[1] 1968–69
Lewis, Dana,[2] 1970–71
Bracey, Steven, 1972
Biles, Willie, 1973–75
Brown, David, 1981
Pressey, Paul,[3] 1981–82
Stewart, Greg, 1981–82
Ross, Ricky, 1983–84

Harris, Steven,[4] 1983–85
Moore, Tracy, 1986–88
Gordon, Marcell, 1991
Morse, Mark, 1992

All-American

Smith, Bobby, 1969
Pressey, Paul, 1982
Harris, Steven,[4] 1985

Other Outstanding Athletes

Anderson, Michael

[1] Smith, Bobby—1969 Missouri Valley Conference Player of the Year; Honorable
Mention
[2] Lewis, Dana—1970 Missouri Valley Conference Newcomer of the Year
[3] Pressey, Paul—1982 Missouri Valley Conference Player of the Year
[4] Harris, Steven—1982 Missouri Valley Conference Newcomer of the Year;
Honorable Mention

Indiana State University
Terre Haute, Indiana 47809

Coach of Varsity Team

Daniels, Mel (Assistant), 1978–82

All Missouri Valley Conference

Morgan, Harry, 1978
Nicks, Carl, 1979–80
Williams, John, 1983–84

Women's Basketball

Graves, Barbara, 1983

All-American

Nicks, Carl, 1980

Creighton University
Omaha, Nebraska 68178

Coach of Varsity Team

Reed, Willis (Head), 1980–85
Thompson, Lonnie (Assistant), 1991–93

All Missouri Valley Conference

Stovall, Daryl, 1982

Benjamin, Benoit, 1984–85
Moore, Vernon, 1984–85
Cole, Duane, 1992–93

All-American

Silas, Paul, 1962–64
Baptiste, Cyril,[1] 1971
Benjamin, Benoit,[2] 1985

Other Outstanding Athletes

Gibson, Robert[3]

[1] Baptiste, Cyril—Honorable Mention
[2] Benjamin, Benoit—Honorable Mention
[3] Gibson, Robert—competed in basketball and baseball

Drake University
Des Moines, Iowa 50311

Coach of Varsity Team

Anderson, Mark (Assistant)
Green, Mel (Assistant)
Guydon, James "Gus" (Assistant)
Proctor, Joe (Assistant)
Washington, Rudy (Head), 1990–93
Sealy, Felton (Assistant), 1990–93

All Missouri Valley Conference

Guydon, Gus, 1960–61
Foster, Jerry, 1962
Torrence, Marv, 1962
McLemore, McCoy, 1964
Foster, Billy, 1964
McCarter, Willie, 1968–69
Halliburton, Jeff,[1] 1970–71
Bell, Dennis, 1973
Harris, Ken, 1976–77
Lloyd, Lewis,[2] 1980–81
Mathis, Melvin, 1984
Lloyd, Daryl, 1985
Smith, Curt, 1993

All-American

McCarter, Willie, 1969
Lloyd, Lewis, 1980–81

Other Outstanding Athletes

Watson, Herman

[1] Halliburton, Jeff—1971 Missouri Valley Conference Player of the Year
[2] Lloyd, Lewis—1980 and 1981 Missouri Valley Conference Player of the Year

Southern Illinois University
Carbondale, Illinois 62901

Coach of Varsity Team

Weaver, Sam (Assistant), 1990–93

All Missouri Valley Conference

Abrams, Corky, 1976
Glenn, Michael,[1] 1976–77
Wilson, Gary, 1978–79
Abrams, Wayne, 1978–80
Amaya, Ashraf, 1992–93

All-American

Vaughn, Charles "Chico,"[2] 1960
Glenn, Michael, 1976

Southern Illinois University's Hall of Fame

Bryson, Seymour[3]
Vaughn, Charles "Chico"
Frazier, Walter[4]
Garrett, Dick
Glenn, Michael
Meriweather, Joe C.

[1] Glenn, Michael—1976 Missouri Valley Conference Player of the Year; Honorable Mention
[2] Vaughn, Charles "Chico"—Little All-American
[3] Bryson, Seymour—presently Dean of the College of Human Resources at Southern Illinois University
[4] Frazier, Walter—1967 National Invitational Tournament Most Valuable Player Award recipient

West Texas State University
Canyon, Texas 79016

Coach of Varsity Team

Reaux, Tom (Assistant)

All Missouri Valley Conference

Smith, Dallas, 1976

Cheeks, Maurice, 1977–78
Adolph, Terry, 1980–81
Steppes, Robert, 1983

All-American

Hill, Simmie, 1969

Illinois State University
Normal, Illinois 61761

Coach of Varsity Team

King, Billy (Assistant), 1992–93

Outstanding Athletes

Hawkins, Robert "Bubbles"
Thomas, Richard

Southwest Missouri State University
Springfield, Missouri 65804

Coach of Varsity Team

Cunning, Charles (Assistant), 1993

All Missouri Valley Conference

Reid, Darryl, 1991
Crawford, Jackie, 1992–93

Other Outstanding Athletes

Perry, Curtis
Garland, Winston, 1985–87

Bradley University
Peoria, Illinois 61625

Coach of Varsity Team

McKay, Ritchie (Assistant), 1991–93

All Missouri Valley Conference

Mason, Bobby Joe, 1958–59
Walker, Chet, 1960–62
Anderson, Mitchell, 1980–82
Winters, Voise, 1985

Hawkins, Hersey, 1986–88
Manuel, Anthony, 1989
Stuckey, Curtis, 1990–91

All-American

Walker, Chet, 1961–62
Hawkins, Hersey, 1988

Missouri Valley Conference
Player of the Year Award

Year • Player • College • Position

1968–69 • Bobby "Bingo" Smith • University of Tulsa • F
1969–70 • Jim Ard • University of Cincinnati • F/C
1970–71 • Jeff Haliburton • Drake University • F
1971–72 • Larry Finch • Memphis State University • G
1972–73 • Larry Kenon • Memphis State University • F

1973–74 • Junior Bridgeman • University of Louisville • G
1974–75 • Junior Bridgeman • University of Louisville • G
1975–76 • Mike Glenn • Southern Illinois University • G
1979–80 • Lewis Lloyd • Drake University • F
1980–81 • Lewis Lloyd • Drake University • F
1981–82 • Paul Pressey • University of Tulsa • G/F
1982–83 • Antoine Carr • Wichita State University • F
1983–84 • Xavier McDaniel • Wichita State University • F
1984–85 • Xavier McDaniel • Wichita State University • F
1986–87 • Hersey Hawkins • Bradley University • G
1987–88 • Hersey Hawkins • Bradley University • G
1988–89 • Anthony Manuel • Bradley University • G

Coach of the Year Award

1980–81 • Nolan Richardson • University of Tulsa
1982–83 • Weldon Drew • New Mexico State University
1984–85 • Nolan Richardson • University of Tulsa

SUN BELT CONFERENCE

1. University of South Alabama
2. Old Dominion University
3. Jacksonville University
4. University of North Carolina, Charlotte
5. University of New Orleans
6. Western Kentucky University

7. Louisiana Tech
8. Lamar University
9. University of Arkansas, Little Rock
10. Arkansas State University
11. University of Southwestern Louisiana
12. Virginia Commonwealth University

University of South Alabama
Mobile, Alabama 36688

All Sun Belt Conference

White, Rory,[1] 1978, 1981–82
Rains, Ed,[2] 1979–81
Andrew, Herb, 1980–81
Gerren, Michael, 1983–84
Catledge, Terry,[3] 1983–85
Hodge, Jeff, 1987–89

Other Outstanding Athletes

Women's Basketball

Jenkins, Lasandra

[1] White, Rory—1979 Sun Belt Conference Player of the Year
[2] Rains, Ed—1981 Sun Belt Conference Player of the Year
[3] Catledge, Terry—1984 Sun Belt Conference Player of the Year

Old Dominion University
Norfolk, Virginia 23508

Coach of Varsity Team

Purnell, Oliver (Head), 1989–93

Women's Basketball

Thaxton, Barbara, 1981–93

All Sun Belt Conference

West, Mark, 1983
Gattison, Ken,[1] 1985–86
Gatling, Chris, 1989–91
Carver, Anthony, 1990

All-American

Copeland, Joel, 1975

Washington, Wilson, 1977
Valentine, Ron,[2] 1980
McAdoo, Ron,[3] 1981
West, Mark,[4] 1983
Gattison, Ken,[5] 1986

Women's Basketball

Claxton, Tracey, 1984–85
Dixon, Medina, 1984–85

[1] Gattison, Ken—1986 Sun Belt Conference Player of the Year
[2] Valentine, Ron—Honorable Mention
[3] McAdoo, Ron—Honorable Mention
[4] West, Mark—Honorable Mention
[5] Gattison, Ken—Honorable Mention

Jacksonville University
Jacksonville, Florida 32211

All Sun Belt Conference

Glover, Kent, 1977
Young, Felton, 1977
Ray, James,[1] 1978–80
Hackett, Michael, 1980–82
Rouhlac, Maurice, 1982
Smith, Otis, 1983–86
Murphy, Ron, 1984, 1986–87
Brown, Dee, 1989–90
Burroughs, Tim, 1992

All-American

Gilmore, Artis, 1971

Other Outstanding Athletes

Dublin, Chip[2]
Burrows, Pembrook
Fox, Harold
Fleming, Ernest
Steward, Abe
Benbow, Leon
Williams, Henry
Taylor, Butch
Williams, Anthony "Cricket"

[1] Ray, James—1980 Sun Belt Conference Player of the Year
[2] Dublin, Chip—the first black athlete to play at Jacksonville University, 1968

University of North Carolina, Charlotte
Charlotte, North Carolina 28223

All Sun Belt Conference

Maxwell, Cedric, 1977
Massey, Lew, 1977–78
Kinch, Chad, 1978–79
Ward, Phil, 1981
Johnson, Melvin, 1983–84
Dinkins, Byron, 1988–89
Williams, Henry, 1989–91

All-American

Maxwell, Cedric, 1977

Women's Basketball

Bennett, Paula, 1981–82
Walker, Patricia, 1982

University of New Orleans
New Orleans, Louisiana 70122

All Sun Belt Conference

Cooper, Wayne,[1] 1977–78
Mills, Nate, 1977–78
Johnson, Ervin, 1991–93

All-American

Webster, Butch, 1970
Cooper, Wayne, 1978
Hodge, Sandra,[2] 1984

Other Outstanding Athletes

Holland, Wilbur
Eckles, Ledell
Simon, Melvin
Garrett, Reginald

[1] Cooper, Wayne—1978 Sun Belt Conference Player of the Year; Honorable Mention
[2] Hodge, Sandra—Honorable Mention

Western Kentucky University
Bowling Green, Kentucky 42101

Coach of Varsity Team

Haskins, Clem, 1980–86

All Ohio Valley Conference

Haskins, Clem,[1] 1965–67
McDaniels, Jim,[2] 1969–71
Bryant, Aaron, 1977
Turner, Darryl, 1978
Johnson, James, 1978
Jackson, Greg, 1979
Bryant, William, 1980

All Sun Belt Conference

Wilson, Tony, 1983
Johnson, Kannard, 1985–87
Frank, Tellis, 1987
Shelton, Roland, 1990
Jennings, Jack, 1991–92
Mee, Darnell, 1993

All-American

Haskins, Clem, 1967
McDaniels, Jim, 1971

Women's Basketball

Haskins, Clemette, 1986–87

Other Outstanding Athletes

Bell, Mark
Mee, Darnell

[1] Haskins, Clem—1981 Ohio Valley Conference Coach of the Year; 1986 Sun Belt Conference Co-Coach of the Year; 1965–67 Ohio Valley Conference Player of the Year
[2] McDaniels, Jim—1970–71 Ohio Valley Conference Player of the Year

Louisiana Tech University
Ruston, Louisiana 71272

Coach of Varsity Team

Loyd, Jerry (Head), 1990–93

All Southland Conference

Knowles, Andy, 1972
Green, Michael,[1] 1972–73
Wells, Lanky, 1975–77
Alexander, Randy, 1978
King, Victor, 1978–79
Ivory, Joe, 1980
Simmons, David, 1981
Malone, Karl, 1983–85
Simmons, Willie, 1985
White, Randy, 1988–89

All-American

Green, Michael, 1973
Malone, Karl, 1985

Women's Basketball

Kelly, Pam,[2] 1980–82
Turner, Angela,[3] 1982
Lawrence, Janis,[4] 1983–84
Weatherspoon, Teresa, 1987–88

Other Outstanding Athletes

Brown, P.J., 1989–92

[1] Green, Michael—All Gulf States Conference, 1971
[2] Kelly, Pam—1982 Wade Trophy recipient; 1982 Broderick Award recipient
[3] Turner, Angela—1981 Most Valuable Player at the AIAW National Tournament
[4] Lawrence, Janis—member of the 1984 United States Olympic Women's Basketball Team; 1984 Wade Trophy recipient; Most Valuable Player at the 1984 NCAA Final Four Tournament

Lamar University
Beaumont, Texas 77710

All Southland Conference

Dow, Earl, 1968–69
Adams, Luke, 1970–71
Nickson, Alfred, 1974
Jones, Henry, 1976
Davis, B.B., 1978–79, 1981
Oliver, Michael, 1979–81
Kea, Clarence, 1980
Sewel, Thomas, 1983–84
Robinson, Lamont, 1984

All-American

Dow, Earl, 1969

Lamar University's Hall of Fame

Dow, Earl

University of Arkansas, Little Rock
Little Rock, Arkansas 72204

All Sun Belt Conference

Martin, Tony, 1992–93
Chime, Tony, 1993

Other Outstanding Athletes

Scott, James
Williams, Vaughn
Myers, Peter

Arkansas State University
State University, Arkansas 72467

All Sun Belt Conference

Shepherd, Fred, 1992

Other Outstanding AThletes

Scaife, Donald

University of Southwestern Louisiana
Lafayette, Louisiana 70501

Coach of Varsity Team

Donaldson, Dennis (Assistant), 1984

All Southland Conference

Lamar, Dwight, 1972–73
Ebron, Roy, 1972–73
Toney, Andrew, 1978–80
Figaro, Kevin, 1981

All-American

Winkler, Marvin, 1970
Lamar, Dwight, 1972–73
Toney, Andrew, 1980

All Sun Belt Conference

Stokes, Marcus, 1992
Hill, Todd, 1993

Other Outstanding Athletes

Ivory, Elvin
Warner, Graylin
Allen, Alonzo

Virginia Commonwealth University
Richmond, Virginia 23284

All Sun Belt Conference

Knight, Monty, 1980, 1982
Sherrod, Edmund, 1980–81
Stancell, Ken, 1981–82
Duncan, Calvin, 1983–85
Brown, Fred, 1983
Lamb, Rolando, 1985
Jones, Nicky, 1986
Brown, Michael, 1986
Warren, Kendrick, 1991

Other Outstanding Athletes

Dark, Jesse
Harris, Bernard

Sun Belt Conference Player of the Year

Year • Player • College • Position
1977 • Cedric Maxwell • University of North Carolina, Charlotte • F
1978 • Wayne Cooper • University of New Orleans • C
1979 • Rory White • University of South Alabama • F
1980 • James Ray • Jacksonville University • F
1981 • Ed Rains • University of South Alabama • F
1982 • Oliver Robinson • University of Alabama, Birmingham • G
1983 • Charles Bradley • University of South Florida • F
1983 • Calvin Duncan • Virginia Commonwealth University • G
1984 • Terry Catledge • University of South Alabama • F
1985 • Terry Catledge • University of South Alabama • F
1986 • Kenny Gattison • Old Dominion University • F
1987 • Tellis Frank • Western Kentucky University • F
1988 • Byron Dinkins • University of North Carolina, Charlotte • G
1989 • Jeff Hodge • University of South Alabama • G
1990 • Chris Gatling • Old Dominion University • C
1991 • Chris Gatling • Old Dominion University • C
1992 • Ron Ellis • Louisiana Tech University • F

Sun Belt Conference Coach of the Year

1986 • Clem Haskins • Western Kentucky University

BIG WEST CONFERENCE
(Pacific Coast Athletic Association until 1988)

1. University of Nevada, Las Vegas
2. University of California, Irvine
3. California State University, Long Beach
4. New Mexico State University
5. California State University, Fullerton
6. San Jose State University
7. University of California, Santa Barbara
8. University of Pacific
9. Utah State University

University of Nevada, Las Vegas
Las Vegas, Nevada 89154

Coach of Varsity Team

Bennett, Melvin (Assistant), 1988–89

All West Coast Athletic Conference

Washington, Booker, 1971–73
Baker, Jimmie, 1973–74
Sobers, Ricky, 1975
Owens, Eddie, 1975

All Pacific Coast Athletic Association

Green, Sidney,[1] 1983
Adams, Richie,[2] 1984–85
Jones, Anthony,[3] 1986
Banks, Fred, 1986–87
Gilliam, Armon, 1987

All Big West Conference

Basnight, Jarvis, 1988
Paddio, Gerald, 1988
Augmon, Stacey, 1989, 1991
Butler, David, 1989–90
Anthony, Greg, 1989–91
Johnson, Larry, 1990–91
Hunt, Anderson, 1991
Ackles, George, 1991
Gray, Evric, 1992
Spencer, Elmore, 1992
Rider, J.R., 1992–93

All-American

Gilliam, Armon, 1987
Johnson, Larry, 1990–91
Augmon, Stacey, 1991
Rider, J.R., 1993

Other Outstanding Athletes

Theus, Reginald
Williams, Flintie Ray
Smith, Robert
James, Frank
Basknight, Jarvis
Paddio, Gerald
Graham, Gary

[1] Green, Sidney—1983 Pacific Coast Athletic Association Player of the Year
[2] Adams, Richie—1984 and 1985 Pacific Coast Athletic Association Player of the Year
[3] Jones, Anthony—1986 Pacific Coast AThletic Association Co-Player of the Year

University of California, Irvine
Irvine, California 92717

Coach of Varsity Team

Baker, Rod (Head), 1991–93

All Pacific Coast Athletic Association

Magee, Kevin, 1981–82
McDonald, Ben, 1983–84

Other Outstanding Athletes

Women's Basketball
Hamilton, Katherine[1]
Lewis, Dorothy[2]

[1] Hamilton, Katherine—played on the 1979–83 University of California, Irvine, team (All-Time Leading Scorer—1,768 Points)
[2] Lewis, Dorothy—played on the 1981–85 University of California, Irvine, team

California State University, Long Beach
Long Beach, California 90840

Coach of Varsity Team
Palmer, Ron, 1984–87

Women's Basketball
McDonald, Glen (Head), 1990–93

All Pacific Coast Athletic Association

Trapp, George,[1] 1970–71
Ratleff, Ed,[2] 1971–73
Pondexter, Roscoe, 1973
Gray, Leonard,[3] 1974
Johnson, Richard, 1975
Ruffen, Clarence, 1976
McMillian, Lloyd,[4] 1977
Wise, Francois, 1978–80
Williams, Rickey, 1979
Wiley, Michael, 1980
Hodges, Craig, 1982

All Big West Conference

Wiley, Morlon, 1988
Harris, Lucious, 1990

All-American

Trapp, George, 1971
Ratleff, Ed, 1972–73
Gray, Leonard, 1974
Pondexter, Clifton, 1974
McMillian, Lloyd, 1977

Women's Basketball
Brown, Cindy, 1986–87
Toler, Penny, 1988–89

[1] Trapp, George—1970 and 1971 Pacific Coast Athletic Association Player of the Year

[2] Ratleff, Ed—1972 and 1973 Pacific Coast Athletic Association Player of the Year
[3] Gray, Leonard—1974 Pacific Coast Athletic Association Player of the Year
[4] McMillian, Lloyd—1977 Pacific Coast Athletic Association Player of the Year

New Mexico State University
Las Cruces, New Mexico 88003

Coach of Varsity Team
Drew, Weldon (Head), 1984–85

All Pacific Coast Athletic Association

Grant, Roland, 1974
Jones, Albert "Slab", 1978–80
Patterson, Ernest, 1983
Colter, Steven, 1984

All Big West Conference

Brown, Randy, 1990–91
Jordon, Reggie, 1991

All-American

Criss, Charles, 1969
Collins, Jimmy, 1970
Lacey, Sam, 1970
Williamson, John, 1972

Other Outstanding Athletes

Crawford, Sam, 1991–93
Benjamin, William, 1989–92

California State University, Fullerton
Fullerton, California 92634

Coach of Varsity Team
McQuarm, George, (Head), 1981–83

All Pacific Coast Athletic Association

Bunch, Gregory, 1976–78
Roberts, Calvin, 1979–80
Wood, Leon, 1982–84
Neal, Tony, 1985
Henderson, Kevin, 1985

All Big West Conference

Morton, Richard, 1987–88
Ceballos, Cedric, 1989–90
Small, Joe, 1991–92

All-American

Wood, Leon,[1] 1983–84

[1] Wood, Leon—member of the 1984 United States Olympic Basketball Team

San Jose State University
San Jose, California 95192-0062

Coach of Varsity Team

Berry, William (Head), 1980–89

All Pacific Coast Athletic Association

Williams, Sid, 1981
McNealy, Chris, 1982–83

All Big West Conference

Owens, Reginald, 1985
Berry, Ricky, 1986–88

All-American

Williams, Sid, 1981
McNealy, Chris, 1983

University of California, Santa Barbara
Santa Barbara, California 93106

All Big West Conference

Shaw, Brian, 1987–88
DeHart, Carrick, 1989–90
McArthur, Eric, 1989–90

All-American

Shaw, Brian, 1988

Other Outstanding Athletes

Kelly, Ray, 1990–93
Davis, Lucious, 1990–92

Utah State University
Logan, Utah 84322

All Big West Conference

Youngblood, Kendall, 1990–91

Big West Conference Player of the Year Award

Year • Player • College • Position

1970 • George Trapp • Long Beach State University • F
1971 • George Trapp • Long Beach State University • F
1972 • Ed Ratleff • Long Beach State University • G/F
1973 • Ed Ratleff • Long Beach State University • G/F
1974 • Leonard Gray • Long Beach State University • F
1976 • Greg Bunch (tie) • California State University, Fullerton • F
1977 • Lloyd McMillian • Long Beach State University • F
1981 • Kevin Magee • University of California, Irvine • F
1982 • Kevin Magee • University of California, Irvine • F
1983 • Sidney Green • University of Nevada, Las Vegas • F
1984 • Richie Adams • University of Nevada, Las Vegas • C
1985 • Richie Adams • University of Nevada, Las Vegas • C
1986 • Anthony Jones (tie) • University of Nevada, Las Vegas • G/F
1987 • Armon Gilliam • University of Nevada, Las Vegas • F
1988 • Brian Shaw • University of California, Santa Barbara • G
1989 • Stacey Augmon • University of Nevada, Las Vegas • G/F
1990 • Larry Johnson • University of Nevada, Las Vegas • F
1991 • Larry Johnson • University of Nevada, Las Vegas • F

Members of the Big West Conference 20-Year All-Star Team

Chosen in 1989 by past and present conference media coaches, and league officials

First Team

Name • College • Career

Ed Ratleff • Long Beach State University • 1971–73
Kevin Magee • University of California, Irvine • 1981–82
Leon Wood • California State University, Fullerton • 1982–84
Armon Gilliam • University of Nevada, Las Vegas • 1985–87

Second Team

Name • College • Career

Sidney Green • University of Nevada, Las Vegas • 1983
Ricky Berry • San Jose State University • 1986–88

George Trapp • Long Beach State University • 1970–71
Brian Shaw • University of California, Santa Barbara • 1987–88

Most Valuable Player
Ed Ratleff • Long Beach State University

WESTERN ATHLETIC CONFERENCE

1. University of Wyoming
2. University of Utah
3. University of Texas at El Paso
4. San Diego State University
5. Colorado State University

6. University of New Mexico
7. Fresno State University
8. University of Hawaii
9. Air Force Academy

University of Wyoming
Laramie, Wyoming 82071

Coaches of Varsity Teams

Anderson, Tevester (Assistant)

All Western Athletic Conference

Robinson, Flynn, 1963–65
Clark, Leon, 1964–66
Hall, Harry, 1967–69
Ashley, Carl, 1968–70
Roberson, Willie, 1971
Bradley, Charles, 1978, 1980–81
Martin, Tony, 1984
Dembo, Fennis, 1986–88
Slater, Reginald, 1990–92
Alexander, Maurice, 1991

All-American

Robinson, Flynn, 1965
Dembo, Fennis[1], 1987–88

Other Outstanding Athletes

Women's Basketball
Curry, Donna, 1989–92

[1] Dembo, Fennis—Honorable Mention

University of Utah
Salt Lake City, Utah 84112

All Sky-line Conference

McGill, William, 1960–62

All Western Athletic Conference

Chambers, Jerry, 1966
Jackson, Merv, 1967–68
Sojourner, Michael, 1974
Burden, Luther, 1974–75
Matheney, Buster, 1978

All High Country Conference

Women's Basketball
Lee, Leshia, 1985

All-American

McGill, William, 1961–62
Chambers, Jerry, 1966
Jackson, Merv, 1968
Sojourner, Michael, 1974
Burden, Luther, 1975

Other Outstanding Athletes

Wilson, Byron, 1990–93
Davis, Antoine, 1989–92

University of Texas, El Paso
El Paso, Texas 79968

Coach of Varsity Team

Shed, Nevil (Assistant), 1980–81
Forbes, James (Assistant), 1981–83

Women's Basketball

Thornton, Wayne (Head), 1978–83
Stoney, Be (Assistant), 1981–88

All Border Conference

Hill, Bobby Joe, 1962
Richardson, Nolan, 1962

All Western Athletic Conference

Archibald, Nate, 1970
Bailey, Gus, 1974
Forbes, James, 1974
Burns, Anthony, 1979–80
Amie, Roshern, 1981
White, Terry, 1982
Reynolds, Fred, 1982–84
Walker, Byron, 1983
Goodwin, Luster, 1984
Jackson, Jeep, 1987
Hardaway, Tim, 1988–89
Sandle, Chris, 1988
Davis, Antoine, 1989
Maxey, Marlon, 1990, 1992

All-American

Barnes, Jim, 1964
Hill, Tyrone Bobby Joe, 1966

Other Outstanding Athletes

Brown, Charles[1]
Artis, Orsten[2]
Worsley, Willie[3]
Florney, Harry[4]
Lattin, David[5]
Cager, Willie[6]
Melvin, Johnny, 1990–93
Rivera, Eddie, 1991–93
Davis, Ralph, 1991–93

[1] Brown, Charles—first black athlete to receive a basketball scholarship at University of Texas, El Paso, 1956

[2] Artis, Orsten—started on the 1966 NCAA National Championship
[3] Worsley, Willie—started on the 1966 NCAA National Championship teams
[4] Florney, Harry—started on the 1966 NCAA National Championship teams
[5] Lattin, David—started on the 1966 NCAA National Championship teams
[6] Cager, Willie—member of the 1966 NCAA National Championship teams

San Diego State University
San Diego, California 92182

Coach of Varsity Team

Gaines, David "Smokey" (Head), 1980–87
Evans, Jesse (Assistant), 1982–91
Fuller, Tony (Head), 1993–

Women's Basketball

Riggins, Earnest (Head), 1983–90

All California Collegiate Athletic Association CCAA

Pinkins, Tony, 1955–57

All Pacific Coast Athletic Association

McMurray, Chris, 1972

All Western Athletic Conference

Cage, Michael,[1] 1983–84

Women's Basketball

Perry, Chana, 1988–89

All-American

Cage, Michael, 1983–84

Women's Basketball

Hutchinson, Tina,[2] 1985
Perry, Chana, 1989

[1] Cage, Michael—1983 Western Athletic Conference Co-Player of the Year; 1983 United Press International West Coast Player of the Year
[2] Hutchinson, Tina—Honorable Mention

Colorado State University
Fort Collins, Colorado 80523

All Skyline Conference

All Western Athletic Conference

Shegogg, Cliff, 1970

Fisher, Rick, 1971
Childress, Michael, 1971
Price, George, 1972
Cash, Lorenzo, 1976
Cunningham, Alan, 1977–78
Hughes, Eddie, 1979–80

All-American

Green, William, 1963

Other Outstanding Athletes

Rule, Bob
Wright, Lonnie

University of New Mexico
Albuquerque, New Mexico 87131

All Skyline Conference

All Western Athletic Conference

Harge, Ira, 1963–64
Daniels, Mel, 1965–67
Monroe, Ben, 1967
Howard, Greg, 1968–69
Long, Willie, 1970–71
Minniefield, Darryl, 1973
Hardin, Bernard, 1974
Cooper, Michael, 1977–78
Johnson, Marvin, 1977–78
Belin, Larry, 1979
Page, Ken, 1980–81
Smith, Phil, 1984
Thomas, Charles, 1987–89
Banks, Willie, 1992
Jaxon, Khari, 1992–93

All-American

Daniels, Mel, 1967

Fresno State University
Fresno, California 93740

All Big West Conference

Williams, Art, 1978–79

Higgins, Rod, 1980–82
Thompson, Bernard, 1983–84
Arnold, Mitchell, 1984–85
Cole, Jervis, 1989
Bernard, Todd, 1992

All-American

Other Outstanding Athletes

Women's Basketball
Beckley, Tammie, 1990–93

University of Hawaii
Honolulu, Hawaii 96822

All Western Athletic Conference

U.S. Air Force Academy
Colorado Springs, Colorado 80840

Coach of Varsity Team

Minton, Reginald (Head), 1985–93

Western Athletic Conference Player of the Year

Year • Player • College • Position

1983 • Michael Cage Co-winner • San Diego State University • F
1984 • Michael Cage • San Diego State University • F
1986 • Anthony Watson • San Diego State University • G
1987 • Fennis Dembo • University of Wyoming • G/F
1989 • Tim Hardaway • University of Texas, El Paso • G
1992 • Reginald Slater • University of Wyoming • G

Western Athletic Conference Coach of the Year

Year • Player • College

1985 • David "Smokey" Gaines • San Diego State University

MID-AMERICAN CONFERENCE

1. Ohio University
2. University of Toledo
3. Miami University
4. Eastern Michigan University
5. Kent State University
6. Northern Illinois University

7. Western Michigan University
8. Bowling Green State University
9. Central Michigan University
10. Ball State University
11. University of Akron

Ohio University
Athens, Ohio 45701-2979

Coach of Varsity Team

Brown, Bill (Assistant)
Backus, Michael (Assistant), 1978–80

All Mid-American Conference

Adams, Bunk, 1960–61
Jackson, Jerry, 1964
Hill, Don, 1964–65
Fowlkes, Ken, 1966
McKee, Gerald, 1969
Corde, Tom, 1972
Green, George, 1973
Brown, Bill, 1974
Luckett, Walter,[1] 1974–75
Devereaux, John,[2] 1983–84
Graham, Paul, 1988–89
Geter, Lewis, 1991–92

All-American

Adams, Bunk,[3] 1960–61
Luckett, Walter, 1975

[1] Luckett, Walter—1974 Mid-American Conference Player of the Year
[2] Devereaux, John—1984 Mid-American Conference Player of the Year
[3] Adams, Bunk—selected as an alternate member on the 1964 United States
 Olympic Basketball Team; Honorable Mention

University of Toledo
Toledo, Ohio 43606

Coach of Varsity Team

Joplin, Stan (Assistant)

All Mid-American Conference

Jones, Larry, 1962
Aston, Robert, 1966
Cole, Larry, 1975–76
Knuckles, Harvey, 1981

Miami University
Oxford, Ohio 45056

Coach of Varsity Team

Wright, Joby (Head), 1990–93

All Mid-American Conference

Barnette, Don, 1956–57
Embry, Wayne, 1958
Winguard, Ed, 1959
Benson, LeVern, 1962
Foster, Fred,[1] 1967–68
Dunlap, Darrell, 1972
Hampton, Rich, 1973
Lumpkin, Phil, 1973–74
Aldridge, Archie, 1978
Harper, Ron,[2] 1984–86

Miami University's Hall of Fame

Embry, Wayne
Bronston, Robert
Lumpkin, Phil

[1] Foster, Fred—1968 Mid-American Conference Player of the Year
[2] Harper, Ron—1985 and 1986 Mid-American Conference Player of the Year

Eastern Michigan University
Ypsilanti, Michigan 48197

Athletic Directors

Smith, Dr. Albert E., 1975–76
Smith, Gene, 1985–93

Coach of Varsity Team

Scott, Ray (Head), 1976–79
Boyce, James (Head), 1979–93

All Mid-American Conference

Cofield, Fred, 1984–85
Long, Grant, 1987–88
Neely, Lorenzo, 1991
Kennedy, Marcus, 1991

All-American

Gervin, George,[1] 1972

Eastern Michigan University's Hall of Fame

Campbell, Garion H.
Beatty, Charles Eugene
Pureifory, David
Sabbath, Clarence
Bibbs, James
Kirksey, Daniel Webster

[1] Gervin, George—Little All-American

Kent State University
Kent, Ohio 44242

Coach of Varsity Team

Boyd, Michael (Interim Head), 1/9/78–6/78

All Mid-American Conference

Wallace, Oliver, 1958–60
Yance, Ruben, 1971–72
McGhee, Burrell, 1977–79
Grooms, Trent, 1980
Adams, Reginald, 1988–89

Other Outstanding Athletes

Walton, Harold, 1990–92

Northern Illinois University
Dekalb, Illinois 60115

Athletic Director

Davis, McKinley "Deacon" (Executive Director for Intercollegiate Athletics), 1968–82

Coach of Varsity Team

Luck, Emory (Head), 1973–77

All Mid-American Conference

Hicks, Matt,[1] 1976–77
Dawkins, Paul,[2] 1978–79

All-American

Bradley, Jim, 1972–73
Hicks, Matt,[3] 1977
Dawkins, Paul,[4] 1979

Other Outstanding Athletes

Booker, Abe

Northern Illinois University's Hall of Fame

Bradley, Jim

[1] Hicks, Matt—1977 Mid-American Conference Player of the Year
[2] Dawkins, Paul—1979 Mid-American Conference Player of the Year
[3] Hicks, Matt—Honorable Mention
[4] Dawkins, Paul—Honorable Mention

Western Michigan University
Kalamazoo, Michigan 49008

Athletic Directors

Brinn, Chauncey (Interim AD), 1/79–6/79

Coach of Varsity Team

Roberts, Joe (Assistant), 1970–71
Walker, Rich (Assistant), 1975–78
Quarles, Larry (Assistant), 1979
Byrdsong, Rick (Assistant), 1980
Wesley, Walter (Assistant), 1981–84

All Mid-American Conference

Newsome, Manny, 1962–64

Ford, Gene, 1968–69
Washington, Chuck, 1971
Jenkins, Earl, 1971
Pettis, Earnest, 1972
Cunningham, Ken, 1980
Russell, Walker D., 1981–82
James, Booker, 1987

Women's Basketball
Charity, Pat, 1981

All-American

Newsome, Manny, 1964
Ford, Gene, 1969

Western Michigan University's Hall of Fame

Coleman, Sr., Horace
Dunlap, Sam
Mallard, Louis "Bo"
Newsome, Manny
Salter, Ed

Bowling Green State University
Bowling Green, Ohio 43403

All-Mid-American Conference

Thurmond, Nate, 1961–63
Cash, Cornelius, 1973–75
Newbern, Marcus, 1982
Venable, Clinton, 1990

All-American

Thurmond, Nate, 1963

Central Michigan University
Mt. Pleasant, Michigan 48859

All Mid-American Conference

Roundfield, Dan, 1974–75
Leavy, Ervin, 1987

Ball State University
Muncie, Indiana 47306

All Mid-American Conference

Wesley, Derrick, 1988
McCurdy, Paris, 1989–90
Kidd, Curtis, 1989
Cross, Emanuel, 1991

University of Akron
Akron, Ohio 44325-5205

Coach of Varsity Team

Crawford, Coleman (Head), 1990–93

Mid-American Conference Player of the Year

Year • Player • College • Position
1974 • Walter Luckett • Ohio University • G/F
1975 • Dan Roundfield • Central Michigan University • F
1977 • Matt Hicks • Northern Illinois University • G
1978 • Archie Aldridge • Miami University (Ohio) • G
1979 • Paul Dawkins • Northern Illinois University • F
1981 • Harvey Knuckles • Toledo University • G/F
1982 • Melvin McLaughin • Central Michigan University • G
1983 • Ray McCallum • Ball State University • G
1984 • John Devereaux • Ohio University • F
1985 • Ron Harper • Miami University (Ohio) • G
1986 • Ron Harper • Miami University (Ohio) • G
1987 • Booker James • Western Michigan University • G
1988 • Grant Long • Eastern Michigan University • F
1989 • Paul Graham • Ohio University • G
1991 • Marcus Kennedy • Eastern Michigan University • F
1992 • Lewis Geter • Ohio University • F

SOUTHEASTERN CONFERENCE

1. University of Georgia
2. University of Kentucky
3. Mississippi State University
4. Vanderbilt University
5. University of Mississippi
6. Auburn University

7. University of Alabama
8. University of Tennessee
9. University of Florida
10. Louisiana State University
11. University of Arkansas
12. University of South Carolina

University of Georgia
Athens, Georgia 30613

Coach of Varsity Team

Anderson, Tevester (Assistant), 1987–93

Women's Basketball

Green-Williams, Carla (Assistant), 1991–93

All Southeastern Conference

Hogue, Ronnie, 1972
Bassett, Tim, 1973
Dorsey, Jackie, 1975–76
Daniels, Walter, 1976–79
Mercer, Lavon, 1979–80
Wilkins, Dominique,[1] 1981–82
Fleming, Vern,[2] 1983–84
Henderson, Cedric, 1985
Ward, Joe, 1986
Anderson, Willie, 1987–88
Green, Litterial, 1991–92

Women's Basketball

Edwards, Teresa, 1985–86
McClain, Katrina, 1986–87
Jenkins, Tammye, 1988–90

All-American

Wilkins, Dominique, 1982
Fleming, Vern, 1984

Women's Basketball

Locke, Bernadette, 1980
Harris, Janet, 1983–85
Edwards, Teresa, 1984–86
McClain, Katrina, 1986–87

[1] Wilkins, Dominique—1981 United Press International Southeastern Conference Player of the Year; 1981 Associated Press Southeastern

Conference Player of the Year; 1981 Most Valuable Player at the Southeastern Conference Tournament
[2] Fleming, Vern—1983 Most Valuable Player at the Southeastern Conference Tournament; member of the 1984 United States Olympic Basketball Team

University of Kentucky
Lexington, Kentucky 40506-0019

Coach of Varsity Team

Hamilton, Leonard (Assistant), 1974–86
Locke-Mattox, Bernadette (Assistant), 1990–93

All Southeastern Conference

Payne, Tom, 1971
Givens, Jack, 1976–78
Bowie, Sam, 1980
Minniefield, Dirk,[1] 1981–83
Hord, Derrick, 1982
Turpin, Melvin, 1982–84
Walker, Ken,[2] 1984–86
Bennett, Winston, 1988
Miller, Derrick, 1990
Hanson, Reginald, 1991
Mashburn, Jamal, 1992–93

Women's Basketball

Still, Valerie, 1982–83

All-American

Givens, Jack, 1977–78
Bowie, Sam,[3] 1980–84
Mashburn, Jamal, 1992–93

Women's Basketball

Still, Valerie, 1982–83

Other Outstanding Athletes

Woods, Sean
Rhodes, Roderick

[1] Minniefield, Dirk—1982 Southeastern Conference Tournament Most Valuable Player Award recipient
[2] Walker, Ken—1986 Southeastern Conference Player of the Year
[3] Bowie, Sam—member of the 1980 United States Olympic Basketball Team

Mississippi State University
Mississippi State, Mississippi 39762

Coach of Varsity Team

Jeffries, Edgar (Assistant), 1977–79
Peck, Wiley (Assistant), 1980–81
Brown, Michael (Assistant), 1981–82
Kirby, Robert (Assistant), 1988–93

Southeastern Conference

Jenkins, Jerry, 1975
White, Ray, 1976, 1978–79
Brown, Ricky, 1977–78
Peck, Wiley, 1979
Malone, Jeff,[1] 1981–83

All-American

Brown, Rickey, 1980
Malone, Jeff, 1983

Other Outstanding Athletes

Evans, Chuck

[1] Malone, Jeff—1983 United Press International Southeastern Conference Player of the Year

Vanderbilt University
Nashville, Tennessee 37240

Coach of Varsity Team

Culley, David (Assistant), 1979–81
McClendon, Leroy (Assistant), 1984

Women's Basketball

Lawrence, Teresa (Assistant), 1981–88

All Southeastern Conference

Wallace, Perry,[1] 1970
Davis, Charles, 1978–79, 1981
Springer, Tom, 1979
Jones, Willie, 1982

Women's Basketball

Brumfield, Harriet, 1982–83

Other Outstanding Athletes

Sneed, John

[1] Wallace, Perry—first black American to compete in basketball in the Southeastern Conference and at Vanderbilt University, 1968; 1980 Southeastern Conference Sportsmanship Award recipient

University of Mississippi
University, Mississippi 38677

Coach of Varsity Team

Evans, Rob (Head), 1992–93
Alexander, Denny (Assistant), 1990–93

Women's Basketball

Gillom, Peggie (Assistant), 1990–93

All Southeastern Conference

Ball, Coolidge, 1972–73
Turner, Elston, 1980–81
Clark, Carlos, 1982–83
Laird, Eric, 1984
Glass, Gerald, 1989–90
Harvell, Joe, 1992–93

Auburn University
Auburn University, Alabama 36849

Coach of Varsity Team

Anderson, Tevester (Assistant)

Women's Basketball

Orr, Vickie (Assistant), 1992–93
Thomas, Charlene (Assistant), 1992–93

All Southeastern Conference

Johnson, Eddie, 1974–76

Mitchell, Michael, 1977–78
Barkley, Charles,[1] 1983–84
Pearson, Charles,[2] 1984–86
Ford, Frank, 1987
Moore, Jeff, 1987
Morris, Chris, 1987–88
Battle, Ronnie, 1990–91

Women's Basketball

Jackson, Becky, 1981–84
Monroe, Lori, 1983
Orr, Vickie, 1986–89
Jones, Carolyn, 1989–91

All-American

Mitchell, Michael, 1978
Barkley, Charles, 1984
Person, Charles, 1985–86

Women's Basketball

Orr, Vickie, 1987–89
Jones, Carolyn, 1990–91

[1] Barkley, Charles—1984 Southeastern Conference Tournament Most Valuable Player Award recipient; 1984 United Press International Southeastern Conference Player of the Year Award recipient; 1984 Associated Press Southeastern Conference Player of the Year Award recipient
[2] Pearson, Charles—member of the 1984 United States Olympic Basketball team

University of Alabama
University, Alabama 35486

Coach of Varsity Team

Gray, Kevin (Assistant), 1984–88
Green, James (Assistant), 1992–93

Women's Basketball

Kelso, Dottie (Assistant), 1991–93

All Southeastern Conference

Hudson, Wendell,[1] 1972–73
Cleveland, Charles, 1973–75
Douglas, Leon, 1974–76
Murray, Anthony, 1976–78
Dunn, T.R., 1977
King, Reginald,[2] 1977–79
Phillips, Eddie, 1980–82
Whatley, Ennis, 1982–83

Hurt, Bobby Lee, 1983–85
Richardson, Eric, 1984
Johnson, Buck, 1984–85
McKey, Derrick, 1986–87
Ansley, Michael, 1988–89
Cheatum, Melvin, 1990–91
Horry, Robert, 1992
Robinson, James, 1992–93

All-American

Hudson, Wendell, 1973
Douglas, Leon, 1975–76
Dunn, T.R., 1977
King, Reginald, 1978–79
Whatley, Ennis,[3] 1984
Johnson, Buck,[4] 1985–86
McKey, Derrick,[5] 1987

[1] Hudson, Wendell—1973 United Press International Southeastern Conference Player of the Year; 1973 Associated Press Southeastern Conference Player of the Year
[2] King, Reginald—1978 and 1979 United Press International Southeastern Conference Player of the Year; 1978 and 1979 Associated Press Southeastern Conference Play of the Year
[3] Whatley, Ennis—Honorable Mention
[4] Johnson, Buck—Honorable Mention
[5] McKey, Derrick—Honorable Mention

University of Tennessee
Knoxville, Tennessee 37901-9926

Coach of Varsity Team

Men's Basketball

Houston, Wade (Head), 1989–93
Martin, Ray (Assistant), 1989–93

All Southeastern Conference

Robinson, Larry, 1973
King, Bernard,[1] 1975–77
Jackson, Michael, 1976–77
Darden, John, 1977–78
Johnson, Reginald, 1978–80
Carter, Gary, 1981
Wood, Howard, 1981
Ellis, Dale,[2] 1981–83
White, Tony, 1986–87
Nix, Dyron, 1988–89
Houston, Allan, 1990–93

Women's Basketball
Gordon, Bridgette, 1988–89
Charles, Daedra, 1990–91
Head, Dena, 1991–92

All-American
King, Bernard, 1975–77
Johnson, Reginald, 1979–80
Ellis, Dale, 1982–83
White, Tony, 1987
Houston, Allen, 1993

Women's Basketball
Roberts, Patricia, 1977
Gordon, Bridgette, 1977
Charles, Daedra, 1990–91
Head, Dena, 1992

[1] King, Bernard—1975 and 1976 United Press International Southeastern Conference Player of the Year; 1976 and 1977 (co-winner in 1977) Associated Press Southeastern Conference Player of the Year
[2] Ellis, Dale—1982 United Press International and Associated Press Southeastern Conference Player of the Year; 1983 Associated Press Southeastern Conference Player of the Year

University of Florida
Gainesville, Florida 32604

Athletic Directors
Tribble, Keith (Assistant Athletic Director), 1981–88

Coaches of Varsity Teams
Brown, James (Assistant), 1975–81
McCraney, Ken (Assistant), 1982–Present
McCullum, Robert (Assistant), 1990–93

Women's Basketball
Murphy, Donna (Assistant)
Ola Bolton, Mae (Assistant), 1990–93
Williams, Joi (Assistant), 1990–93

All Southeastern Conference
Glasper, Richard, 1978
Hanna, Reginald, 1980
Williams, Ron, 1981–84
McDowell, Eugene, 1983–85
Moten, Andrew, 1985–87
Maxwell, Vernon, 1986–87

Davis, Dwayne, 1989–90
Chatman, Livingstone, 1989
Poole, Stacey, 1992

Women's Basketball
Jackson, Tammy

Louisiana State University
Baton Rouge, Louisiana 70893

Coach of Varsity Team
Abernathy, Ron (Assistant), 1976–84
Jones, Johnny (Assistant), 1985–93

Women's Basketball
Chatman, Dana "Pokey," (Assistant), 1992–93

All Southeastern Conference
Temple, Collis,[1] 1974
Higgs, Ken, 1976–78
Macklin, Durand, 1978, 1980–81
Green, Al, 1979
Scales, DeWayne,[2] 1979–80
Green, Lionel, 1979
Martin, Ethan, 1980–81
Carter, Howard, 1982–83
Mitchell, Leonard, 1982–83
Taylor, Derrick, 1984
Reynolds, Jerry, 1984–85
Williams, John, 1986
Wilson, Nikita, 1987
Jackson, Chris, 1989–90
O'Neal, Shaquille, 1990–92
Roberts, Stanley, 1990
Singleton, Vernell, 1991–92

Women's Basketball
Walker, Joyce,[3] 1982–84
Doucet, Madaline, 1984
Chatman, Dana "Pokey," 1989–91

All-American
Macklin, Durand, 1981
Jackson, Chris, 1989–90
O'Neal, Shaquille, 1991–92

Women's Basketball

Walker, Joyce, 1982–84

Chatman, Dana, 1991

Other Outstanding Athletes

Irvin, Fess

Wilson, Anthony

Woodside, Bernard

Williamson, Maurice

Brandon, Jamie

Caesar, Clarence

[1] Temple, Collis—first black American to compete in basketball at Louisiana State University
[2] Scales, DeWayne—1980 Southeastern Conference Tournament Most Valuable Player Award recipient
[3] Walker, Joyce—alternate member of the 1984 United States Olympic Basketball team

University of Arkansas
Fayetteville, Arkansas 72701

Athletic Director

Richardson, Nolan (Assistant), 1991–93

Coach of Varsity Team

Richardson, Nolan (Head), 1986–93

Anderson, Michael (Assistant), 1987–93

Richardson, III, Nolan (Assistant), 1990–93

All-Southwest Conference

Brewer, Ron, 1977–78

Delph, Marvin, 1977–78

Moncrief, Sidney, 1977–79

Walker, Darrell, 198

Robertson, Alvin, 1984

Huery, Ron, 1988

Day, Todd, 1990–91

Mayberry, Lee, 1990–91

Miller, Oliver, 1991

All-American

Brewer, Ron, 1977–78

Moncrief, Sidney, 1978–79

Walker, Darrell, 1983

Robertson, Alvin, 1984

Day, Todd, 1991–92

Women's Basketball

DeHorney, Delmonica, 1989–90

Other Outstanding Athletes

Morris, Isiah

Reed, U.S.

Williamson, Corlis, 1992–93, All-Southeastern Conference

University of South Carolina
Columbia, South Carolina 29208

Athletic Directors

White, Harold (Academic Counselor, formerly Assistant Football Coach), 1972–1988

Dickerson, Ron (Assistant Athletic Director, Non Revenue Sports), 1981–82

Coaches of Varsity Teams

Jobe, Ben (Assistant), 1973–78

All-American

Boswell, Thomas, 1975

English, Alexander, 1976

Frederick, Zam, 1981

Women's Basketball

Foster, Sheila, 1982

Other Outstanding Athletes

Hodges, Cedrick

Dozier, Perry

Dozier, Terry

Associated Press Southeastern Conference Player of the Year Award

Year • Player • College • Position

1973 • Wendell Hudson (tie) • University of Alabama • G

1976 • Bernard King • University of Tennessee • F

1977 • Bernard King (tie) • University of Tennessee • F

1978 • Reggie King • University of Alabama • F

1979 • Reggie King • University of Alabama • F

1981 • Dominique Wilkens • University of Georgia • F

1982 • Dale Ellis • University of Tennessee • G/F

1983 • Dale Ellis • University of Tennessee • G/F

1984 • Charles Barkley • Auburn University • F

1985 • Kenny Walker • University of Kentucky • F
1986 • Kenny Walker • University of Kentucky • F
1987 • Derrick McKey • University of Alabama • F
1989 • Chris Jackson • Louisiana State University • G
1990 • Chris Jackson • Louisiana State University • G
1991 • Shaquille O'Neal • Louisiana State University • C
1992 • Shaquille O'Neal • Louisiana State University • C

United Press International Southeastern Conference Player of the Year Award

Year • Player • College • Position

1973 • Wendell Hudson • University of Alabama • G
1975 • Bernard King • University of Tennessee • F
1976 • Bernard King • University of Tennessee • F
1978 • Reggie King • University of Alabama • F
1979 • Reggie King • University of Alabama • F
1981 • Dominique Wilkins • University of Georgia • F
1982 • Dale Ellis • University of Tennessee • G/F
1983 • Jeff Malone • Mississippi State University • G
1984 • Charles Barkley • Auburn University • F
1985 • Kenny Walker • University of Kentucky • F
1986 • Kenny Walker • University of Kentucky • F
1987 • Derrick McKay • University of Alabama • F
     • Tony White • University of Tennessee • G
1989 • Chris Jackson • Louisiana State University • G
1990 • Chris Jackson • Louisiana State University • G
1991 • Shaquille O'Neal • Louisiana State University • C
1992 • Shaquille O'Neal • Louisiana State University • C

Coaches Southeastern Conference Player of the Year Award

Year • Player • College • Position

1987 • Derrick McKey • University of Alabama • F
1989 • Chris Jackson • Louisiana State University • G
1990 • Chris Jackson • Louisiana State University • G
1991 • Shaquille O'Neal • Louisiana State University • C
1992 • Shaquille O'Neal • Louisiana State University • C

Members of the 25-Year All Southeastern Basketball Team selected in 1986 by the Lakeland Ledger

First Team

Name • University • Career

Bernard King • University of Tennessee • 1975–77

Second Team

Name • University • Career

John Mengelt • Auburn University • 1969–71
Reggie King • University of Alabama • 1976–79
Dominque Wilkens • University of Georgia • 1980–82

Members of the Southeastern Conference Team of the 1980's

Dominque Wilkins • University of Georgia • 1980–1982
Dale Ellis • University of Tennessee • 1980–1983
Charles Barkley • Auburn University • 1982–1984
Chuck Pearson • Auburn University • 1983–1986
Kenney Walker • University of Kentucky • 1983–1986

TRANS-AMERICAN CONFERENCE

1. Northwestern State University
2. Houston Baptist University
3. Centenary College

4. North Texas State University
5. Mercer University
6. Stetson University

Northwestern State University of Louisiana Natchitoches, Louisiana 71497

Coaches of Varsity Teams

Russell, Melvin (Assistant), 1984–88

Houston Baptist University Houston, Texas 77074

All Trans-America Athletic Conference

England, Matt, 1985

All-American

England, Matt,[1] 1984

Other Outstanding Athletes

Coleman, E.C.

[1] England, Matt—Honorable Mention

Centenary College
Shreveport, Louisiana 71134-0188

All Trans-America Athletic Conference

Lett, George, 1978–79
Rhone, Cherokee, 1980–81
Jackson, Willie,[1] 1981–84
Thomas, Albert, 1985–86
Robinson, Larry, 1990
Taylor, Nate, 1992–93

All-American

Parish, Robert, 1974–76

[1] Jackson, Willie—leading scorer in Centenary College history

North Texas State University
Denton, Texas 76203

All Missouri Valley Conference

Savage, John, 1962–64
Russell, Rubin, 1966–67
Hamilton, Joe, 1969–70
Iverson, Robert, 1974–75

All Southland Conference

Lyons, Kenneth, 1983
Jones, Albert
Winfield, Leroy

Mercer University
Macon, Georgia 31207

All Trans-America Athletic Conference

Mitchell, Sam, 1984–85
Thompson, Shaun, 1992

Stetson University
Deland, Florida 32720

All Trans-America Athletic Conference

Brisker, Mark, 1991–92

EAST COAST CONFERENCE

1. American University

2. Hofstra University

American University
Washington, D.C. 20016

Coaches of Varsity Teams

Tapscott, Ed (Head), 1982–90

All East Conference

Thomas, Wilbur,[1] 1975

Brown, Calvin, 1975–77
Bowers, Russell, 1978–81
Nickens, Mark,[2] 1981–83
Sloane, Ed, 1983

All-American

Jones, Wil,[3] 1960
Washington, Kermit,[4] 1974

Other Outstanding Athletes

Lloyd, John

Hoey, Robin

Jones, Juan

Women's Basketball

Frazier, Jackie

[1] Thomas, Wilbur—1975 East Coast Conference Player of the Year
[2] Nickens, Mark—1982 East Coast Conference Co-Player of the Year
[3] Jones, Wil—College Division All-American
[4] Washington, Kermit—chosen to the 1970–80 Eastern College Athletic Conference All-Decade Team

Hofstra University
Hempstead, Long Island 11550

Coaches of Varsity Teams

Tomlin, Bernard (Assistant)

All East Coast Conference

Tomlin, Bernard, 1975

Irving, John, 1975–77

Laurel, Rich,[1] 1976–77

Harvey, Lionel, 1981

WEST COAST CONFERENCE

1. University of San Francisco   2. Pepperdine University

University of San Francisco
San Francisco, California 94117

All West Coast Athletic Conference

Russell, William, 1954–56

Jones, K.C., 1955–56

Brown, Gene, 1958

Johnson, Ollie, 1963–65

Ellis, Joseph, 1964–65

Smith, Phil, 1972–74

Redmond, Marion, 1975–76

Boynes, Winford, 1976–78

Hardy, James, 1976–77

Cartwright, William, 1976–79

Cox, Chubby, 1977–78

Dailey, Quintin, 1980–82

Bryant, Wallace, 1981–82

All-American

Russell, William,[1] 1955–56

Cartwright, William, 1977–79

Dailey, Quintin, 1982

[1] Russell, William—member of the 1956 United States Olympic Basketball team; 1956 United Press International College "Player of the Year" award recipient

Pepperdine University
Malibu, California 90265

All West Coast Athletic Conference

Dugan, Larry, 1954–55

Taylor, Mack, 1957

Forbes, Sterling, 1958–60

Blue, Robert, 1959

Sims, Robert, 1960

Warlick, Robert, 1962–63

Betts, Roland, 1964–65

Holmes, Tandy, 1966

Grant, Hal, 1967

Averitt, William, 1972–73

Johnson, Dennis, 1976

Matson, Ollie, Jr., 1976–79

Williams, Flintie Ray, 1977

Brown, Ricardo, 1979–80

Fuller, Tony, 1980

Sadler, William, 1981

Bond, Roylin, 1981–82

Phillips, Orlando, 1982–83

Suttle, Dane, 1982–83

Anger, Victor, 1984

Polee, Dwayne,[1] 1985

Christie, Doug, 1991–92

Dugan, Larry, 1955

Forbes, Sterling, 1960

Warlick, Robert, 1962
Averitt, William, 1973
Bond, Roylin, 1982

Pepperdine University's Hall of Fame

Dugan, Larry
Forbes, Sterling

Sims, Robert
Warlick, Robert
Averitt, William
Matson, Ollie, Jr.
Johnson, Dennis

[1] Polee, Dwayne—1985 West Coast Athletic Conference Player of the Year

MID-WESTERN CITY CONFERENCE

1. Detroit Mercy University
2. University of Evansville
3. Loyola University of Chicago
4. Oklahoma City University

Detroit Mercy University
Detroit, Michigan 48221

Coaches of Varsity Teams

Boyce, James (Assistant), 1973–75
Gaines, David (Assistant), 1973–77
Gaines, David "Smokey" (Head), 1977–79
McCarter, Willie (Assistant), 1978–79
McCarter, Willie (Head), 1979–82
Byrdsong, Rickey (Head), 1988–93

Women's Basketball

Sims, Lydia (Assistant), 1978–81
Jones, DeWayne (Head), 1983–90

All Mid-Western City Conference

Davis, Jerry, 1981–82
McNatt, Clarence, 1983
Simms, Roy, 1983
Ross, Bryan, 1984
Gray, Keith, 1984
Kelly, Dwayne, 1991–93

Women's Basketball

Pack, Cassandra, 1984
Pierce, Regina, 1984

All-American

Murray, Dorle, 1966
Haywood, Spencer, 1969
Long, John, 1978
Tyler, Terry, 1978
Duerod, Terry, 1979

Ross, Bryan,[1] 1984
Gray, Keith,[2] 1984

Women's Basketball

Johnson, Lydia, 1980
Williams, Cheryl, 1981
Pack, Cassandra, 1984

Detroit Mercy University Hall of Fame

Murray, Dorrie

Other Outstanding Athletes

Women's Basketball

Daniels, Coretta
Blackburn, Lisa
Perry, Cynthia

[1] Ross, Bryan—Honorable Mention
[2] Gray, Keith—Honorable Mention

University of Evansville
Evansville, Indiana 47702-0329

All Indiana Collegiate Conference

Smallwood, Ed,[1] 1958–60
Humes, Larry,[2] 1965–66

All Mid-Western City Conference

Johnson, Richard, 1982

All-American

Smallwood, Ed, 1958–60

Humes, Larry, 1965–66
Johnson, Richard,[3] 1982

Other Outstanding Athletes

Scott, Tyrone

[1] Smallwood, Ed—1958 and 1960 Indiana Collegiate Conference Player of the Year
[2] Humes, Larry—1966 Indiana Collegiate Conference Player of the Year
[3] Johnson, Richard—Honorable Mention

Loyola University of Chicago
Chicago, Illinois 60626

Coaches of Varsity Teams

Wakefield, Andre (Assistant), 1981–90

All Mid-Western Collegiate Conference

Clemons, Darius,[1] 1980–82
Sappleton, Wayne,[2] 1981–82
Hughes, Alfrederick,[3] 1983–85
Battle, Andre, 1983–85
Golston, Carl, 1984–85
Moore, Andre, 1985

All-American

Harkness, Gerald, 1963
Sappleton, Wayne, 1982
Hughes, Alfrederick, 1985

Loyola University's Hall of Fame

Bluitt, Benjamin
Coleman, James
Harkness, Gerald
Hunter, Leslie
Martin, La Rue
Rouse, M. Victor
Tillman, Jim
White, Jr., Arthur M.
Billups, Ernest
White, Henry G.

[1] Clemons, Darius—1981 Mid-Western Collegiate Conference Co-Player of the Year
[2] Sappleton, Wayne—1982 United Press International Mid-Western Collegiate Conference Player of the Year
[3] Hughes, Alfrederick—1983–85 Associated Press Mid-Western Collegiate Conference Player of the Year; 1983 United Press International Mid-Western Collegiate Conference Co-Player of the Year; 1985 United Press International Mid-Western Collegiate Conference Player of the Year

Oklahoma City University
Oklahoma City, Oklahoma 73106

All Mid-Western City Conference

Hill, Ernest 1980
Jackson, Rubin,[1] 1980–82
Henry, Carl, 1981
Campbell, James, 1982
Johnson, Gary, 1982

All-American

Wells, Jerry Lee, 1966
Travis, Rich, 1968–69
Edwards, Ozzie, 1973

[1] Jackson, Rubin—1981 Mid-Western City Conference Co-Player of the Year

BIG EAST CONFERENCE

1. Georgetown University
2. Providence College
3. University of Pittsburgh
4. University of Connecticut
5. Seton Hall University

6. Boston College
7. St. John's University
8. Villanova University
9. Syracuse University
10. University of Miami (Florida)

Georgetown University
Washington, D.C. 20057

Coaches of Varsity Teams

Thompson, John,[1] (Head), 1972–93
Riley, Michael, (Assistant), 1982–93
Wilson, Gary (Volunteer Assistant), 1981–88

All Big East Conference

Duren, John,[2] 1980
Shelton, Craig,[3] 1980
Floyd, Eric,[4] 1981–82
Ewing, Pat,[5] 1982–85
Wingate, David, 1985
Martin, Bill, 1985
Jackson, Michael, 1985
Williams, Reginald, 1986–87
McDonald, Perry, 1987
Smith, Charles, 1988–89
Mourning, Alonzo, 1989–92
Tillmon, Mark, 1990
Harrington, Othello, 1993

All-American

Floyd, Eric, 1982
Ewing, Pat, 1983–85
Williams, Reginald, 1986–87
Mourning, Alonzo, 1990, 1992

Other Outstanding Athletes

Holloway, Alonzo
Smith, Jonathan
Wilson, Merlin
Brooks, Gregory
Dutch, Al
Yeoman, Felix
Jackson, Derrick
Brown, Fred[6]
Smith, Gene
Graham, Michael
Riley, Michael
Spriggs, Ed
Hancock, Michael
Dalton, Ralph
Lynn, William
Long, Larry

Hopkins, Ed
Duren, Lonnie
Scates, Tom
Bryant, Dwayne
Churchwell, Robert
Brown, Joey
Thompson, Ronnie
Spencer, Duane

[1] Thompson, John—first black American to coach a Division 1 NCAA basketball championship, 1984; 1980 Big East Coach of the Year; 1982 United States Basketball Writers Association Coach of the Year; 1985 National Association of Basketball Coaches' "Coach of the Year" Award recipient
[2] Duren, John—1980 Big East Conference Player of the Year
[3] Shelton, Craig—Most Valuable Player, 1980 Big East Tournament
[4] Floyd, Eric—Most Valuable Player, 1982 Big East Tournament
[5] Ewing, Pat—1984 and 1985 Big East Conference Co-Player of the Year; Most Valuable Player, 1984 Big East Tournament; 1982–85 Big East Conference Defensive Player of the Year; member of the 1984 United States Olympic Basketball Team; Most Valuable Player, 1984 NCAA Final Four Tournament
[6] Brown, Fred—1981 Big East Conference Rookie of the Year

Providence College
Providence, Rhode Island 02918

All Big East Conference

Thorpe, Otis, 1984
Wright, Steve, 1988
Murdock, Eric, 1989, 1991
Screen, Carlton, 1990

All-American

Wilkins, Leonard R., 1959–60
Thompson, Jr., John R., 1963–64
Walker, James, 1967
Barnes, Marvin,[1] 1973–74
Thorpe, Otis, 1984

Providence College's Hall of Fame

Wilkens, Leonard R.
Thompson, Jr., John R.

Other Outstanding Athletes

Westbrook, Dexter
Campbell, Bruce
King, Nehru
Tucker, Ricky
Knight, Raymond
Brooks, Delray

Wright, Steve
Smith, Michael
Simpkins, Dickey
Forbes, Trent
Bragg, Marques
Phelps, Robert

[1] Barnes, Marvin—a member of the 1970–80 Eastern Collegiate Athletic
Conference All-Decade Team

University of Pittsburgh
Pittsburgh, Pennsylvania 15213

Coaches of Varsity Teams

Warford, Reginald, (Assistant), 1979

Women's Basketball

Bruce, Kirk, 1986–93

All Eastern Athletic Association

Harris, Larry, 1977–78
Knight, Terry, 1979
Ellis, Sammie, 1979–80
Clancy, Sam, 1979–81
Everson, Carlton, 1981
Vaughn, Clyde, 1982

All Big East Conference

Vaughn, Clyde, 1984
Smith, Charles,[1] 1985–89
Lane, Jerome, 1987–88
Mathews, Jason, 1989–91
Shorter, Brian, 1989–91
McCullough, Jerry, 1993

All-American

Knight, William, 1974–75
Vaughn, Clyde, 1984

Other Outstanding Athletes

Jinks, Ben
Bryant, Ernest
Shelfield, Cal
Edwards, Cleveland
Mobley, Eric
Martin, Bobby

Shareef, Ahmad

[1] Smith, Charles—1985 Big East Conference Rookie of the Year

University of Connecticut
Storrs, Connecticut 06268

All Big East Conference

Thompson, Corny, 1981–82
Kelly, Earl,[1] 1985–86
Robinson, Cliff, 1988–89
Smith, Chris, 1990–92
Burrell, Scott, 1991–92
George, Tate, 1990
Marshall, Donyell, 1993

Other Outstanding Athletes

Foster, Jimmy
Hanson, Anthony C.[2]
Thomas, John[3]
McKay, Michael[4]
Hobbs, Karl[5]
Griscombe, Vernon[6]
Gamble, Phil

[1] Kelly, Earl—1983 Big East Conference Rookie of the Year; 1983 Widmer's
Eastern College Freshman of the Year
[2] Hanson, Anthony C.—played on the 1974–77 teams, University of
Connecticut Career Scoring Leader
[3] Thomas, John—played on the 1974–76 teams
[4] McKay, Michael—played on the 1979–82 teams
[5] Hobbs, Karl—played on the 1981–84 teams
[6] Griscombe, Vernon—played on the 1981–84 teams

Seton Hall University
South Orange, New Jersey 07079

Coaches of Varsity Teams

Brown, Michael (Assistant), 1982–84, 1989–93

All Eastern College Athletic Conference

Mosley, Glenn, 1976–77
Tynes, Greg, 1977–78

All Big East Conference

McCloud, Andre 1985
Major, James, 1987
Bryant, Mark, 1988

Morton, John, 1989
Avent, Anthony, 1991
Dehere, Terry, 1991–93
Walker, Jerry, 1992–93

Women's Basketball
Bradley, Gloria, 1984

All-American

Dukes, Walter,[1] 1953
Mosley, Glenn,[2] 1977
McCloud, Andre[3] 1985
Dehere, Terry, 1993

Seton Hall University's Hall of Fame

House, Kenneth
Dukes, Walter

Other Outstanding Athletes

Gaines, Richard W.[4]
Collins, Sir John
McNeil, Howard, 1978–82
Greene, Gerald, 1985–89
Walker, Daryll, 1985–89
Taylor, Oliver, 1990–91
Wright, Luther, 1991–93

Women's Basketball
Fairbanks, Leslie
Gorham, Ozelina

[1] Dukes, Walter—1953 Haggerty Award recipient (given to the best player in the New York, New Jersey, Connecticut Tri-State area by the Metropolitan Basketball Writers Association)
[2] Mosley, Glenn—Honorable Mention
[3] McCloud, Andre—Honorable Mention
[4] Gaines, Richard W.—competed in basketball 1954–57

Boston College
Chestnut Hill, Massachusetts 02167

All Big East Conference

Bagley, John,[1] 1981–82
Garris, John, 1983
Adams, Michael, 1983–85
McCready, Roger, 1986
Barros, Dana, 1987–89

Other Outstanding Athletes

Carrington, Robert
Cobb, Ernest[2]
McCready, Roger
Weldon, Melvin
Barros, Dana[3]

All-American

Austin, John, 1966

[1] Bagley, John—1981 Big East Conference Player of the
[2] Cobb, Ernest—recipient of the 1979 Eagle Award (given to school's best student athlete)
[3] Barros, Dana—1986 Big East Rookie of the Year

St. John's University
Jamaica, New York 11439

Coaches of Varsity Teams

Rutledge, Ron (Assistant), 1983–93

All Big East Conference

Carter, Reginald, 1980
Russell, David,[1] 1982
Berry, Walter,[2] 1985–86
Jackson, Mark,[3] 1986–87
Jones, Shelton, 1988
Williams, Jayson, 1989
Harvey, Greg "Boo," 1990
Sealy, Malik, 1990–92
Buchanan, Jason, 1991
Cain, David, 1993
Scott, Shawnelle, 1993

All-American

Jackson, Tony, 1960–61
Berry, Walter, 1986
Jackson, Mark, 1987

Other Outstanding Athletes

Dove, Lloyd "Sonny"
Ellis, Leroy
Johnson, George
Searcy, Ed
Smith, Bill "Beaver"
Goodwin, Bill

Abraham, Ralph
Williams, Kevin
Moses, Michael
Stewart, Ron
McKoy, Wayne
Utley, Mel
Williams, Glen
Dupre, Joe
Middleton, Lamont, 1991–93
Brown, Derek
Green, Lee
Foster, Mitchell
Brown, Maurice
Singleton, Billy, 1988–91
Sproling, Chuck, 1989–92

[1] Russell, David—1980 Big East Rookie of the Year
[2] Berry Walter—1986 Big East Conference Player of the Year; 1986 John Wooden Award recipient (given to the Player of the Year in college basketball); 1986 Associated press Player of the Year; 1986 United Press International Player of the Year; 1986 United States Basketball Writers Association Player of the Year
[3] Jackson, Mark—1987 co-recipient of the Haggerty Award (given to the best player in New York, New Jersey, Connecticut Tri-State area by the Metropolitan Basketball Association)

Villanova University
Villanova, Pennsylvania 19085

Coaches of Varsity Teams

Raveling, George (Assistant), 1967–68
Littlepage, Craig (Assistant), 1973–75

All East

White, Hubie,[1] 1961–62
Jones, Wall,[2] 1962–64
Washington, Jim,[3] 1964–65
Jones, John, 1968
Porter, Howard,[4] 1969–71

All Eastern Athletic League

Herron, Keith, 1977–78
Bradley, Alexander, 1979–80
Sparrow, Rory, 1980

All Big East Conference

Granger, Stewart, 1981–83
Pinckney, Ed,[5] 1983–85
McClain, Dwayne, 1984–85

Pressley, Harold, 1984–86
West, Doug, 1988–89
Miller, Lance, 1991–92

All-American

Raveling, George, 1960
White, Hubie, 1962
Jones, Wali, 1964
Porter, Howard,[6] 1969–71
Pinckney, Ed,[7] 1983

[1] White, Hubie—1960–62 All Big-Five; 1962 Robert Geasey Memorial Trophy recipient (Big-Five Most Valuable Player)
[2] Jones, Wall—1962–64 All Big-Five 1963 and 1964 Robert Geasey Memorial Trophy recipient (Big-Five Most Valuable Player)
[3] Washington, Jim—1965 Robert Geasey Memorial Trophy recipient (Big-Five Most Valuable Player); 1963 and 1965 All big-Five
[4] Porter, Howard—1969 and 1970 Robert Geasey Memorial Trophy recipient; co-winner each year (Big-Five Most Valuable Player); member of the 1970–80 Eastern College Athletic Conference All-Decade Team; 1971 Most Valuable Player in the NCAA Final Four Tournament
[5] Pinckney, Ed—1985 Most Valuable Player in the NCAA Final Four Tournament

Syracuse University
Syracuse, New York 13210

All Big East Conference

Bouie, Roosevelt, 1980
Orr, Louis, 1980
Santifer, Eric, 1983
Waldren, Eugene, 1984
Addison, Rafael, 1984–86
Washington, Dwayne "Pearl,"[1] 1984–86
Douglas, Sherman, 1987–89
Coleman, Derrick, 1987–90
Thompson, Stephen, 1989–90
Owens, Billy, 1990–91
Moten, Lawrence, 1992–93

All-American

Bing, David, 1966
Duval, Dennis, 1972
Hackett, Rudy, 1975
Bouie, Roosevelt,[2] 1980
Orr, Louis,[3] 1980
Santifer, Eric,[4] 1983
Washington, Dwayne, 1985–86
Douglas, Sherman, 1989
Coleman, Derrick, 1990
Owens, Billy, 1991

Other Outstanding Athletes

Moss, Ed
Bruin, Tony "Red"[5]
Hawkins, Andre[6]
Alexis, Wendell
Triche, Howard
McRae, Conrad
Autry, Adrian

[1] Washington, Dwayne "Pearl"—1984 Big East Conference Rookie of the Year
[2] Bouie, Roosevelt—Honorable Mention
[3] Orr, Louis—Honorable Mention
[4] Santifer, Eric—Honorable Mention
[5] Bruin, Tony "Red"—1981 Big East Conference All-Tournament Team
[6] Hawkins, Andre—1984 Big East Conference All-Tournament Team

University of Miami (Florida)
Miami, Florida 33124

Bryant, Clint (Assistant), 1985–89
Hamilton, Leonard (Head), 1990–93
Fitzpatrick, Thad (Assistant), 1990–93

Women's Basketball

Rivers, Cherry (Assistant), 1984–89
Smiley, Toni (Assistant), 1989–93

Big East Conference Player of the Year Award

Year • Player • College • Position

1979–80 • John Duren • Georgetown University • G
1980–81 • John Bagley • Boston College • G
1983–84 • Patrick Ewing (co-winner) • Georgetown
  University • C
1984–85 • Patrick Ewing (co-winner) • Georgetown
  University • C
1986–87 • Reggie Williams • Georgetown University • F
1987–88 • Charles Smith • University of Pittsburgh • C
1988–89 • Charles Smith • Georgetown University • G
1989–90 • Derrick Coleman • Syracuse University • F
1990–91 • Billy Owens • Syracuse University • F
1991–92 • Alonzo Mourning • Georgetown University • C
1992–93 • Terry Dehere • Seton Hall University • G

Big East Conference Defensive Player of the Year Award

Year • Player • College • Position

1981–82 • Patrick Ewing • Georgetown University • C

1982–83 • Patrick Ewing • Georgetown University • C
1983–84 • Patrick Ewing • Georgetown University • C
1984–85 • Patrick Ewing • Georgetown University • C
1986–87 • Mark Jackson • St. John's University • G
1987–88 • Gary Massey • Villanova University • G
1988–89 • Alonzo Mourning • Georgetown University • C
1989–90 • Alonzo Mourning • Georgetown University • C
1991–92 • Alonzo Mourning • Georgetown University • C
1992–93 • Jerry Walker • Seton Hall University • F

Big East Conference Rookie of the Year Award

Year • Player • College • Position

1979–80 • David Russell • St. John's University • F
1980–81 • Fred Brown • Georgetown University • G
1981–82 • Patrick Ewing • Georgetown University • C
1982–83 • Earl Kelly • University of Connecticut • G
1983–84 • Dwayne Washington • Syracuse University • G
1984–85 • Charles Smith • University of Pittsburgh • F
1985–86 • Dana Barros • Boston College • G
1986–87 • Derrick Coleman • Syracuse University • F
1988–89 • Brian Shorter • University of Pittsburgh • F
1991–92 • Lawrence Moten • Syracuse University • G/F
1992–93 • Othello Harrington • Georgetown University • C

Big East Conference Coach of the Year Award

Year • Coach • College

1979–80 • John Thompson • Georgetown University
1986–87 • John Thompson • Georgetown University

DAVE GAVITT TROPHY RECIPIENT
Big East Conference Tournament Most Valuable Player Award

Year • Player • College • Position

1980 • Craig Shelton • Georgetown University • F
1982 • Eric Floyd • Georgetown University • G
1984 • Patrick Ewing • Georgetown University • C
1985 • Patrick Ewing • Georgetown University • C
1986 • Dwayne Washington • Syracuse University • G
1987 • Reggie Williams • Georgetown University • G/F
1988 • Sherman Douglas • Syracuse University • G
1989 • Charles Smith • Georgetown University • G
1990 • Chris Smith • University of Connecticut • G
1991 • Oliver Taylor • Seton Hall University • G
1993 • Terry Dehere • Seton Hall University • G

BIG EIGHT CONFERENCE

1. Oklahoma State University
2. University of Nebraska
3. University of Colorado
4. Iowa State University

5. University of Oklahoma
6. Kansas State University
7. University of Kansas
8. University of Missouri

Oklahoma State University
Stillwater, Oklahoma 74078

Coaches of Varsity Teams

Hamilton, Leonard (Head),[1] 1986–89
Smith, Steven (Assistant), 1973–77
Turner, Ken (Assistant), 1979–82
Stoglin, Andy (Assistant), 1984–85
Drew, Weldin (Assistant), 1985
Moulder, Fred, 1965
King, James, 1965
Odom, Ed, 1980
Clark, Matt, 1981–83
Hudson, James, 1982
Combs, Leroy, 1983
Dumas, Richard, 1989
Houston, Byron, 1990–92

All-American

Houston, Byron, 1991

Other Outstanding Athletes

Starks, John

Women's Basketball

Nixon, Bridget

[1] Hamilton, Leonard—the first black head coach in basketball in Big-Eight Conference history

University of Nebraska
Lincoln, Nebraska 68588-0123

Coaches of Varsity Teams

Porter, Lonnie (Assistant)
Carter, Tim (Assistant)
Farley, Doug (Assistant)

Women's Basketball

Washington, Mavis (Assistant)

All Big-Eight Conference

Turner, Hershell, 1960
Lantz, Stuart, 1967–68
Stewart, Marvin, 1971
Fort, Jerry, 1974–76
Banks, Brian, 1978

All Big-Eight Conference

Smith, Andre, 1980–81

University of Colorado
Boulder, Colorado 80309

Coaches of Varsity Teams

Gentry, Alvin (Assistant)
Whittenburg, Derek (Assistant), 1990–93

All Big-Eight Conference

Gilmore, Wilky, 1962
Davis, Jim, 1963–64
Meely, Cliff, 1969–71
Lewis, Emmett, 1979
Hunter, Anthony "JoJo," 1981
Humphries, Jay, 1984
Vandiver, Shaun, 1990–91

All-American

Meely, Cliff, 1971

Iowa State University
Ames, Iowa 50011

All Big-Eight Conference

Crawford, John, 1958
Whitney, Henry, 1961
Smith, Don, 1966–68
Cain, William, 1969–70
Ivy, Hercle "Poison," 1975
Parker, Andrew, 1978–79
Stevens, Barry, 1984–85
Grayer, Jeff, 1986–88
Alexander, Victor, 1989, 1991

All American

Smith, Don, 1967

University of Oklahoma
Norman, Oklahoma 73019

All Big-Eight Conference

Heard, Garfield, 1970
Barnett, Chuck, 1982
Tisdale, Waymon,[1] 1983–85
Kennedy, Darryl, 1986–87
McAllister, Tim, 1986–87
Grant, Harvey, 1988
Blaylock, Darrin "Mookie," 1989
King, Stacey, 1989
Henry, Skeeter, 1990

All American

Tisdale, Waymon, 1983–85
King, Stacey, 1989
Blaylock, Darrin "Mookie," 1989
Grant, Harvey
Johnson, David

[1] Tisdale, Waymon—1983 and 1984 Big-Eight Conference Player of the Year; member of the 1984 United States Olympic Basketball Team

Kansas State University
Manhattan, Kansas 66506

All Big-Eight Conference

Boozer, Robert, 1957–1959
Murrell, Willie, 1963–64
Honeycutt, Steven, 1969
Venable, Jerry, 1970
Hall, David, 1972
Williams, Charles "Chuckie," 1975–76
Evans, Michael, 1976–78
Redding, Curtis, 1977
Blackmon, Rolando, 1979–81
Coleman, Norris, 1986–87
Richmond, Mitch, 1988

Women's Basketball

Gary, Priscilla, 1982–83
Boner, Angela, 1983–84
Dixon, Trina, 1984

All American

Boozer, Robert,[1] 1958–59
Blackman, Rolando,[2] 1981
Richmond, Mitchell, 1988

Women's Basketball

Gary, Priscilla, 1983

[1] Boozer, Robert—member of the 1960 United States Olympic Basketball Team
[2] Blackman, Rolando—member of the 1980 United States Olympic Basketball team; 1980 Big-Eight Conference Player of the Year

University of Kansas
Lawrence, Kansas 66045

Coaches of Varsity Teams

White, Joseph (Assistant), 1981–83
Manning, Ed (Assistant), 1983–89

Women's Basketball

Washington, Marian (Head), 1972–93
Woodard, Lynette (Assistant), 1984–85

All Big-Eight Conference

King, Maurice,[1] 1956
Chamberlain, Wilt,[2] 1957–58
Bridges, William, 1959–61

Hightower, Wayne, 1960–61
Unseld, George, 1964
Wesley, Walter, 1965–66
White, Joseph "Jo Jo," 1967–69
Stallworth, Bud, 1971–72
Suttle, Rick, 1975
Cook, Norman, 1976
Douglas, John, 1977
Valentine, Darnell, 1978–81
Henry, Carl, 1984
Kellogg, Ron, 1986
Manning, Danny, 1986–88
Jordan, Adonis, 1992–93

Women's Basketball
Adams, Vickie, 1984–85

All-American

Chamberlain, Wilt, 1957–58
Bridges, William, 1961
Wesley, Walter, 1966
White, Joseph "Jo Jo,"[3] 1968–69
Stallworth, Bud, 1972
Valentine, Darnell,[4] 1980–81
Manning, Danny, 1986–87

Women's Basketball
Woodard, Lynette,[5] 1978–81

Other Outstanding Athletes

Thompson, Calvin
Marshall, Archie
Hancock, Darrin
Woodberry, Steven
Davis, Ben

University of Kansas Hall of Fame

Chamberlain, Wilt
Bridges, William
Westley, Walter
Stallworth, Bud
White, Joseph "Jo Jo"
Woodard, Lynette

[1] King, Maurice—All Big-Seven Conference
[2] Chamberlain, Wilt—All Big-Seven Conference
[3] White, Joseph "Jo Jo"—member of the 1968 United States Olympic
   Basketball Team
[4] Valentine, Darnell—member of the 1980 United States Olympic Basketball
   Team

[5] Woodard, Lynette—member of the 1984 United States Olympic Women's
   Basketball Team

University of Missouri
Columbia, Missouri 65205

All Big-Eight Conference

Smith, Willie, 1975–76
Drew, Larry, 1980
Berry, Curtis, 1980
Frazier, Ricky, 1981–82
Chievious, Derrick, 1986–87
Irvin, Byron, 1989
Peeler, Anthony, 1990, 1992
Smith, Doug, 1991

All-American

Smith, Willie, 1976
Frazier, Ricky, 1982
Chievious, Derrick,[1] 1987
Smith, Doug, 1990
Peeler, Anthony, 1991

[1] Chievious, Derrick—Honorable Mention

Big-Eight Conference Player of the Year
AP—Associated Press
UPI—United Press International

Year • Player • College • Position

1976 • Willie Smith • University of Missouri • G
1977 • Mike Evans (AP) • Kansas State University • G
1978 • Mike Evans • Kansas State University • G
1980 • Rolando Blackman • Kansas State University • G
1981 • Andre Smith • University of Nebraska • G
1982 • Ricky Frazier • University of Missouri • G
1983 • Wayman Tisdale (AP) • University of Oklahoma • F
1984 • Wayman Tisdale • University of Oklahoma • F
1985 • Wayman Tisdale • University of Oklahoma • F
1986 • Danny Manning • University of Kansas • F
1987 • Danny Manning • University of Kansas • F
1988 • Danny Manning • University of Kansas • F
1989 • Stacey King • University of Oklahoma • F
1990 • Doug Smith • University of Missouri • F
1991 • Doug Smith • University of Missouri • F
      • Byron Houston (UPI) • Oklahoma State University • F
1992 • Anthony Peeler • University of Missouri • G

SOUTHERN CONFERENCE

1. Furman University
2. Marshall University
3. Appalachian State University

4. Davidson College
5. University of Tennessee-Chattanooga
6. East Tennessee State University

Furman University
Greenville, South Carolina 29409

All Southern Conference

Mayes, Clyde,[1] 1973–75
Leonard, Foster, 1973–75
Moore, Jonathan,[2] 1977–80
Daniel, Mel, 1980–81

All-American

Moore, Jonathan,[3] 1980

[1] Mayes, Clyde—1974, 1975 Malcolm U. Pitt Award recipient (given to the Most Valuable Player in the Southern Conference); 1975 Southern Conference Athlete of the Year
[2] Moore, Jonathan—1979 and 1980 Malcolm U. Pitt Award recipient (given to the Most Valuable Player in the Southern Conference)
[3] Moore, Jonathan—Honorable Mention

Marshall University
Huntington, West Virginia 25715-1360

Coaches of Varsity Teams

Freeman, Dwight (Head), 1991–93

All Mid-American Conference

Greer, Hal,[1] 1958

All Southern Conference

Evans, Laverne,[2] 1984
Henderson, Skip, 1986–88
Taft, John, 1989–90
Phillips, Tyrone, 1992

All-American

Lee, Russell,[3] 1972
Evans, Laverne,[4] 1984

Other Outstanding Athletes

Carter, Phil

Stone, George
Gibson, Carlos

[1] Greer, Hal—First American athlete to compete in a Collegiate Sport at Marshall University
[2] Evans, Laverne—Most Valuable Player at the 1984 Southern Conference Tournament
[3] Lee, Russell—Honorable Mention
[4] Evans, Laverne—Honorable Mention

Appalachian State University
Boone, North Carolina 28608

Coaches of Varsity Teams

Littles, Eugene (Assistant)
Searcy, Tony (Assistant)

Women's Basketball

Horton, Angelita (Assistant)
Moody, Gail (Assistant)

All Southern Conference

Searcy, Tony, 1978
Hubbard, Mel, 1979
Robinson, Darryl, 1979
Payton, Charles,[1] 1981–82

Women's Basketball

Whiteside, Valorie, 1985

[1] Payton, Charles—1981 Malcolm U. Pitt Award recipient (given to the Player of the Year in the Southern Conference)

Davidson College
Davidson, North Carolina 28036

Coaches of Varsity Teams

Brown, James (Assistant), 1975–76
Wilson, Ray (Assistant), 1976–77

All Southern Conference

Maloy, Michael,[1] 1968–70
Wilson, Kenny, 1983–84

All-American

Maloy, Michael, 1970

Other Outstanding Athletes

Strong, Lester

[1] Maloy, Michael—1969 and 1970 Malcolm U. Pitt Award recipient (given to the Player of the Year in the Southern Conference)

University of Tennessee-Chattanooga
Chattanooga, Tennessee 37403

All Southern Conference

White, Willie, 1984
Wilkens, Gerald, 1985

Green, Benny, 1988–89
Nelson, Keith, 1991–92
Sutton, Kelly, 1992
Threats, LeVert, 1992

East Tennessee State University
Johnson City, Tennessee 37614

All Southern Conference

Dennis, Greg, 1988–90
Jennings, Keith, 1989–91
English, Rodney, 1992
Talford, Calvin, 1992

NORTH ATLANTIC CONFERENCE

1. Boston University
2. University of Hartford
3. Northeastern University

4. University of Delaware
5. University of Vermont
6. University of Maine

Boston University
Boston, Massachusetts 02215

Coaches of Varsity Teams

Jarvis, Michael (Head), 1985–90
Hobbs, Karl (Assistant), 1989–93

All North Atlantic Conference

Irving, Drederick, 1985–88
Jones, Larry, 1987–88

All New England

Cross, Randy, 1963–65

All Yankee Conference

Boyd, Ken, 1972–74

All Eastern College Athletic Conference (North Atlantic)

Plummer, Gary, 1984
Teague, Shawn, 1984–85
Irving, Dedrick, 1986–87

Boston University's Hall of Fame

Cross, Randy
Boyd, Ken

Other Outstanding Athletes

Brown, Arturo
Brown, James
Chesley, Walter

University of Hartford
West Hartford, Connecticut 06117

All North Atlantic Conference

Middleton, Lamont, 1988–90
Baker, Vin, 1990–93

Northeastern University
Boston, Massachusetts 02115

All Eastern College Athletic Conference (North Atlantic)

Harris, Peter, 1980–81

Moss, Perry,[1] 1982
Halsel, Mark,[2] 1982–84
Lewis, Reginald,[3] 1984–87
Lafleur, Andre, 1986–87

All North Atlantic Conference

Anderson, Marcellus, 1990–91

[1] Moss, Perry—1982 Eastern College Athletic Conference North Atlantic Player
 of the Year
[2] Halsel, Mark—1984 Eastern College Athletic Conference North Atlantic Player
 of the Year
[3] Lewis, Reginald—1984 Eastern College Athletic Conference North Atlantic
 Rookie of the Year; 1985 Eastern College Athletic Conference North Atlantic
 Player of the Year; 1986 Eastern College Athletic Conference Player of the Year

University of Delaware
Newark, Delaware 19716

All East Coast Conference

Luck, Ken, 1981–82

Women's Basketball
Price, Linny, 1984

All North Atlantic Conference

Coles, Alex, 1991–92

All-American

Luck, Ken,[1] 1982

Other Outstanding Athletes

Women's Basketball

Phipps, Cynthia

[1] Luck, Ken—Honorable Mention *(Sporting News)*

University of Vermont
Burlington, Vermont 05405

All Yankee Conference

Lord, Clyde O., 1957–59
Isles, Jr. Charles H., 1960
Becton, Benjamin, 1961

All North Atlantic Conference

Roberson, Kevin, 1990–92

University of Maine
Orono, Maine 04469

Coaches of Varsity Teams

Keeling, Rudy (Head), 1988–93

All North Atlantic Conference

Harris, Rufus, 1979–80

Division II Colleges

1. California State University, Los Angeles
2. California Polytechnic State University
3. Chicago State University
4. Texas A&I University
5. University of Puget Sound

6. Philadelphia College of Textiles and Sciences
7. University of Tennessee, Martin
8. City College of New York
9. Wesleyan University
10. Seattle University

California State University, Los Angeles
Los Angeles, California 90032

Coaches of Varsity Teams

Maxey, Ken (Head), 1981–83
Newman, James (Head), 1984–85

All California Collegiate Athletic Association

Barber, John, 1953–54
Jackson, Frank, 1958
Hill, Leo, 1959–61
Wilson, C.D., 1964–65
Davis, Joe, 1966–67
Thomas, Charles, 1967–68

Smith, Cary, 1967–68
Knight, Ron, 1968–69
Pate, Edgar, 1978–79
Hester, Michael, 1979–80
Jordan, Mark, 1980
Bellamy, Nate, 1981
Catchings, Ed, 1982
Brown, Anthony, 1984–85
Yeal, Sam, 1985

Women's Basketball

Rhodes, Johanna, 1982
Finley, Veronda, 1985

All Pacific Coast Athletic Association

Knight, Ron, 1970
Thomas, Morris, 1970
Adolph, Mose, 1970–72
Murray, Rodney, 1971
Jackson, Michael, 1972
Lewis, Raymond, 1973
Lipsey, Tom, 1974
Mallory, William, 1974

All-American

Hill, Leo[1]—Honorable Mention, 1959–60
Smith, Cary[2]—College Division, 1968
Lewis, Raymond[3]—Division I Honorable Mention, 1973
Lipsey, Tommie,[4] 1976
Brown, Darrell,[5] 1977
Veal, Sam,[6] 1985

California State University's Hall of Fame

Hill, Leo

[1] Hill, Leo—Little All-American
[2] Smith, Cary—Little All-American
[3] Lewis, Raymond—Little All-American
[4] Lipsey, Tommie—*Basketball Weekly*
[5] Brown, Darrell—Division II All-American
[6] Veal, Sam—National Association of Basketball Coaches All-American

California Polytechnic State University
San Luis Obispo, California 93407

Other Outstanding Athletes

Keys, Andre
Lucas, Kevin

Chicago State University
Chicago, Illinois 60628

Coaches of Varsity Teams

Buckhalter, Joe, 1975–77
Woods, Ed, 1977–78
McCray, Kevin, 1981–90
Pryor, Rick, 1990–93

Women's Basketball

Sailes, Gary, 1979–80

All Chicagoland Collegiate Athletic Conference

Tillman, Curtis,[1] 1981
Leonard, Percy,[2] 1981

All Chicagoland Athletic Conference

Women's Basketball

Gilkey, Anita, 1984

All-American

Cyrus, Ken, NAIA, 1978
Eversley, Michael, NAIA, 1979
Dancey, Ken, NAIA, 1980
Arnold, Sherron, NAIA, 1982–83
Perry, Charles, NAIA, 1984

[1] Tillman, Curtis—1981 Chicagoland Collegiate Athletic Conference Most Valuable Player
[2] Leonard, Percy—1981 Chicagoland Collegiate Athletic Conference Most Valuable Player

Texas A & I University
Kingsville, Texas 78363

Coaches of Varsity Teams

Thomas, Roy, 1980–83

All Lone Star Conference

Neal, Algie, 1972
Simmons, Hoegie, 1973
Johnson, James, 1976–78
Staten, Eric, 1978
Kinzer, Robert, 1978
Turner, Ed, 1979–81
Daniel, Michael, 1981–82

Farmer, Joe, 1982
Bailey, James, 1982
McCain, Michael, 1983

NAIA All-American
Turner, Ed, 1979–81

All Lone Star Conference

Women's Basketball
Goodwin, Kay, 1982
Campbell, Sheryl,[1] 1982

Other Outstanding Athletes
Smith, Charles

Women's Basketball
Denley, Altanette
Bonner, Rhonda
Glass, Owen

[1] Campbell, Sheryl-American Women's Sports Federation All-American, 1987

University of Puget Sound
Tacoma, Washington 98416

All-American NAIA
Lowery, Charles, 1971

Philadelphia College of Textiles and Sciences
Philadelphia, Pennsylvania 19144

All-American
Poole, Carlton, 1970
Sammons, Emery, 1976–77
Owens, Randy, 1979

Women's Basketball
Morris, Vincene, 1984

University of Tennessee at Martin
Martin, Tennessee 38238-5028

All Gulf South Conference
Carter, Larry, 1976–77
Boddie, Joe, 1978
Brooks, Larry, 1982
Smith, Darrell, 1982
Rudolph, Gus, 1983
Cherry, Sam, 1984

University of Tennessee at Martin's Hall of Fame
Hamilton, Leonard—the first black athlete recruited to the University of Tennessee at Martin

City College of New York
New York, New York 10031

Coaches of Varsity Teams
Layne, Floyd (Head), 1974–1989

All-American
Jameson, Spenser—Honorable Mention, 1949
Warner, Ed,[1] 1950

City College of New York's Hall of Fame
Warner, Ed—played on the 1949 and 1950 City College of New York team that won the National Invitational Tournament and National Collegiate Athletic Association titles in 1950
Layne, Floyd—played on the 1949 and 1950 City College of New York Jameson, Spencer—played on the 1949 City College of New York team
Loyd, Otis, Jr.—City College of New York's All-Time leading scorer, 1970–1973.

[1] Warner, Ed—the first African-American to be named the Most Valuable Player at the National Invitational Tournament, 1950

Seattle University
Seattle, Washington 98122

All West Coast Athletic Conference
Richardson, Clint, 1976–79

All-American

Baylor, Elgin—1958 NCAA University Division Tournament Most
  Valuable Player

GULF STAR CONFERENCE

1. Stephen F. Austin State University

Stephen F. Austin State University
Nacogdoches, Texas 75962

Oliver, Surry, 1967
Johnson, George, 1968–69
Silas, James, 1970–71
Harris, Pete, 1972–73
Evans, Vernon, 1976
Harrison, Hiram, 1982
Harrison, Winston, 1982
Hagan, Chris, 1983

All-American

Oliver, Surry, 1967
Johnson, George, 1968
Silas, James, 1970–71
Harris, Pete, 1972–73

Women's Basketball

Walker, Rosie,[1] 1979–80

[1] Walker, Rosie—member of the 1980 United States Olympic Women's
  Basketball Team

CENTRAL INTERCOLLEGIATE ATHLETIC ASSOCIATION

1. Virginia State University
2. Norfolk State University
3. Virginia Union University
4. Fayetteville State University
5. Hampton University
6. Livingstone College
7. Johnson C. Smith University
8. Elizabeth City State University
9. Winston-Salem State University
10. Shaw University
11. St. Augustine's College
12. St. Paul's College
13. North Carolina Central University
14. Bowie State University

Virginia State University
Petersburg, Virginia 23803

Coaches of Varsity Teams

Jefferson, Harry, 1946–48
Matthews, Shelton, 1949–54, 1957–63
Deane, Harold A., 1971–77, 1979
Laisure, Floyd, 1981–89
Deane, Harold, 1990–93

Women's Basketball

Bey, Leon, 1980–88
Cummings, Bertha, 1989–93

All-Central Intercollegiate Athletic Association

Simmons, Samuel, 1960
Stephens, Frank, 1963
Brock, Ernest, 1968
Looney, Rodney, 1972–74
Johnson, Linwood, 1975–77
Tisdol, Doward, 1976
Bell, Jerome, 1976
Ware, Daniel, 1979
Stith, Darryl, 1981
Norman, Julius, 1981–82
Harris, Leonard, 1988
Walker, Lamont, 1989–90

Women's Basketball

Baxter, Sheila, 1977
Cummings, Bertha, 1977–80
McKinney, Pat, 1978
Jackson, Johnna, 1983–84
Burgess, Tonya, 1985
Brown, Kammy, 1986, 1988, 1990

All Tournament Team

Bennett, Cleveland, 1947
Hurley, Walter, 1947
Banks, Leroy,[1] 1947
Oliver, Percy, 1957
Deane, Harold, 1961
Stephens, Frank, 1963
Johnson, Linwood,[2] 1974
Bell, Jerome, 1976
Tisdol, Doward, 1976–77
Stith, Darrell, 1981
Norman, Julius,[3] 1981

All-American

Brown, Kammy, 1990

[1] Banks, Leroy—1947 CIAA Tournament Most Valuable Player
[2] Johnson, Linwood—1974 CIAA Tournament Most Valuable Player
[3] Norman, Julius—1981 CIAA Tournament Most Valuable Player

Norfolk State University
Norfolk, Virginia 23504

Coaches of Varsity Teams

Porter, Leroy
Turpin, John, 1953–62
Fears, Ernest, 1962–69
Smith, Robert, 1969–73
Christian, Charles, 1974–78
Mitchell, Lucias, 1979–81
Christian, Charles, 1982–90
Bernard, Michael, 1991–93

Women's Basketball

Sweat, James E., 1989–93

All Central Intercollegiate Athletic Association

Morris, John, 1965
Pitts, Richard, 1966

Grant, James, 1966–67
Kirkland, Richard, 1968
Dandridge, Robert, 1968–69
Bonaparte, Charles, 1969
McKinney, John, 1970
Peele, Rudolph, 1971–72
Jones, Leroy, 1971–73
Wilson, Ronald, 1972–73
Mitchell, Roosevelt, 1974
Cunningham, Eugene, 1974–76
Burns, Melvin, 1975
Epps, Raymond, 1976–77
Wilkerson, Jesse, 1977
Isabelle, Robert, 1978
Evans, Ken, 1978
Tibbs, Terry, 1981
Pope, David, 1981–84
Tally, Ralph, 1984–87
Mitchell, Barry, 1987
Johnson, Lee, 1988
Coles, Jerome, 1989–91
McLean, Richard, 1990
Whitfield, Marcus, 1992

Women's Basketball

Greene, Vivian, 1977–78
Stewart, Jewel, 1978
Davis, Beverly, 1981
Wallace, Sharon, 1981
Knight, Norma, 1982–83
Theus, Ann, 1984
Johnson, Valetta, 1986
Tapps, Sharron, 1988
Saunders, Tracy, 1990
Tanks, Jennine, 1991–92
Thompson, Samantha, 1991
Rice, Lisa, 1992
Spells, Hycynthia, 1992

All Tournament Team

Pitts, Richard, 1964–66
Grant, James,[1] 1965–68
Thompson, Essex, 1966
Kirkland, Richard,[2] 1968
Bonaparte, Charles, 1968–69
Dandridge, Robert,[3] 1968–69
Smith, Gerald, 1971
Peele, Rudolph, 1971–72

James, Morrall,[4] 1971
Jones, Leroy, 1971–73
Lassiter, Randolph, 1972
Wilson, Ronald, 1973
Mitchell, Roosevelt, 1973–74
Parks, James, 1974
Cunningham, Eugene,[5] 1974–76
Epps, Raymond, 1975–76
Burns, Melvin, 1975–76
Isabelle, Robert,[6] 1978–79
Evans, Kenneth, 1978–79
Simon, Lewis, 1979
Tibbs, Terry, 1980
Haynes, Ken, 1983
Allen, Tim, 1983
Pope, David, 1983–84
Talley, Ralph,[7] 1984–87

All-American

Talley, Ralph, 1987

Women's Basketball

Saunders, Tracey, 1991

Norfolk State Alumni in the National Basketball Association

Dandridge, Robert, Milwaukee Bucks, (F), 1969–71;
   Washington Bullets, (F), 1977–81 ·
Epps, Ray, Golden State Warriors, (G), 1978–79
Pope, David, Utah Jazz, (F), 1984; Kansas City Kings, (F), 1985

[1] Grant, James—1965 CIAA Tournament Most Valuable Player
[2] Kirkland, Richard—1968 CIAA Tournament Most Valuable Player
[3] Dandridge, Robert—1969 CIAA Tournament Most Valuable Player
[4] James, Morrall—1971 CIAA Tournament Most Valuable Player
[5] Cunningham, Eugene—1975 and 1976 CIAA Tournament Most Valuable Player
[6] Isabelle, Robert—1978 CIAA Tournament Most Valuable Player
[7] Talley, Ralph—1984 CIAA Tournament Most Valuable Player; 1986 NCAA
   Division II Player of the Year

Virginia Union University
Richmond, Virginia 23220

Coaches of Varsity Teams

Hucles, Henry
Harris, Thomas, 1950–73
Moore, Robert, 1974–79
Robbins, David (Non-African-American), 1980–93

Women's Basketball

Harris, Thomas
Cannady, Nathan, 1974–82
Hearn, Louis, 1983–89
Golatt, Moses, 1989–93

All Central Intercollegiate Athletic Association

Gwin, Stephen, 1955
Spraggins, Warren, 1960–61
Jackson, Jackie, 1961
Davis, Michael, 1968–69
Hunter, Ralph, 1973
Hazley, Andrew, 1973
Carrington, Gregory, 1975
Valentine, Keith, 1979
Holmes, Larry, 1980
Lily, Derwin, 1980
Oakley, Charles, 1982–85
Waller, Jamie, 1985–87
Williams, Greg, 1987
Dallas, Tony, 1988
Davis, Terry, 1988–89
English, A.J., 1988–90
Walker, Jonathan, 1990
Hurd, Walter, 1991–92
Jones, Reginald, 1991
Johnson, Derrick, 1992

Women's Basketball

Turner, Corrine, 1978
Reynolds, Sharon, 1980
Owens, Sheila, 1981
McWhirter, Paris, 1982–84
Wooten, Barvenia, 1982
Nicholson, Maria, 1984
Walker, Sylvia, 1985
Drayton, Michelle, 1990–91

All Tournament Team

Bressant, Howard, 1946
Dilworth, James,[1] 1946
Ross, Donald,[2] 1947–49
Clements, Ozelius, 1951
Johnson, William, 1951
King, William, 1952
Wilson, William, 1952
Jones, Howard, 1954–55
Spraggins, Warren, 1959

Simmons, Edward,[3] 1959
Davis, Michael, 1967–69
Niles, Arthur, 1968
Cannady, Nathan, 1972
Hazley, Andrew, 1972
Hunter, Ralph, 1972–74
Benson, Charles, 1977
Lewis, Curvan, 1977
Holmes, Larry,[4] 1979
Echols, Lamont, 1979
Lilly, Derwin, 1979–80
Valentine, Keith,[5] 1979–80
Oakley, Charles,[6] 1985
Waller, Jamie, 1986–87

All-American (Black Colleges or NCAA Division II)

Oakley, Charles, 1985
Waller, Jamie, 1986–87
English, A.J., 1990

Virginia Union Alumni in the National Basketball Association

Oakley, Charles, Chicago Bulls, (F), 1985–87; N.Y. Knicks, 1987–93

English, A.J., Washington Bullets (G), 1992–93

[1] Dilworth, James—1946 CIAA Tournament Most Valuable Player
[2] Ross, Donald—1949 CIAA Tournament Most Valuable Player
[3] Simmons, Edward—1959 CIAA Tournament Most Valuable Player
[4] Holmes, Larry—1979 CIAA Tournament Most Valuable Player
[5] Valentine, Keith—1980 CIAA Tournament Most Valuable Player
[6] Oakley, Charles—1985 NCAA Division II Player of the Year

Fayetteville State University
Fayetteville, North Carolina 28301

Coaches of Varsity Teams

Gaines, William A. "Gus," 1946–57
Bryant, William, 1957–62
Robinson, Frank, 1962–69
Reeves, Thomas, 1969–75
Hawkins, Otis, 1975–76
Robinson, Joe, 1976–79
Ford, Jake, 1979–86
Jones, Jeff, 1986–90
Capel, Jeff, 1991–93

Women's Basketball
Taylor, Leoretta, 1944–77

Hatcher, Cleophus, 1977–78
Smith, Maceo, 1978–79
Henderson, Robert, 1979–80
Edwards, Yvonne, 1980–82
Lamb, Mary, 1982–91
Tucker, Eric, 1992–93

All Central Intercollegiate Athletic Association

Evans, Ronald, 1957
Bibby, Fred, 1964
Monroe, William, 1969
Sneed, Michael, 1971–72
Barrows, John, 1977
Jefferson, Edward, 1979
Mims, Steve, 1981
McNeil, Bonny, 1982
Person, William, 1984
James, Edward, 1985
Adams, Travis, 1986
Armstrong, Darrell, 1991
Broughton, Vernon, 1992
Calloway, Emmanuel, 1992
Spells, Travis, 1992

Women's Basketball

Cameron, Gail, 1977
Barnes, Sandra, 1978
Newsome, Angela, 1978–79
Owens, Katrine, 1978–79
Morris, Dianthia, 1979, 1981–82
Smith, Concentha, 1983
White, Dimple, 1985–86
Steward, Shelia, 1988, 1990

All Tournament Team

Evans, Ronald, 1957
Morgan, John, 1957
Sneed, Michael, 1972
McNeil, Earl, 1972
Cogdell, Alton, 1973
Tyus, James, 1973
McNeil, Bonny, 1982

Hampton University
Hampton, Virginia 23668

Coaches of Varsity Teams

McClendon, John, 1952–54
Whaley, Ben, 1954–57
Enty, Frank, 1957–61
Smith, Willie, 1961–62
Enty, Frank, 1962–63
Royster, Lee, 1963–64
Moorehead, Ike, 1964–71
Shackleford, Louis, 1971–73
Frazier, Solomon, 1973–75
Ford, Hank, 1975–86
Avery, Malcolm, 1986–93

Women's Basketball

Gatling, Alberta, 1975–80
Sinclair, Marilyn, 1980–81
Sweat, James, 1981–86
Laster, Jr., Tiny, 1986–93

All-Central Intercollegiate Athletic Association

Amos, Edwin, 1956–57
Trader, Nathaniel, 1959
Ward, Walter, 1961
Youngblood, Willie, 1973
Britt, Wayne, 1974
Best, Tyrone, 1977
Payne, Marvin, 1977–79
Threatt, Tony, 1978
Tolliver, Keith, 1978
Mahorn, Rick,[1] 1978–80
Warwick, Darryl, 1981
Washington, Anthony, 1982–83
Hines, Gregory, 1983
Miller, Cedric, 1984–85
Stevens, John, 1986
Clark, Stacey, 1989–90
Brown, Kenny, 1991
Childs, Marvin, 1991

Women's Basketball

Hundley, Joan, 1977
Thompson, Cynthia, 1977
Hannah, Sonja, 1978
Goodman, Toni, 1979
Jordan, Gwen, 1980–81

Hillman, Shelia, 1984–85
Cooper, Anita, 1985
Dolberry, Jackie, 1986, 1988
Frazier, Venise, 1988
McWilliams, Jackie, 1991
Blue, Thelka, 1992

All-Tournament Team

Trader, Nathaniel, 1960
Threatt, Tony, 1978
Tolliver, Keith, 1978
Mahorn, Rick, 1978–80
Warwick, Darryl, 1979
Hines, Gregory,[2] 1980–83
Moore, Gerald, 1982
Miller, Cedric, 1982
Washington, Tony,[3] 1982–83

All-American (Black College)

Best, Tyrome, 1977
Tolliver, Keith, NAIA 1978
Mahorn, Ricky, NAIA 1978–80
Warrick, Darryl, NAIA 1981–82
Washington, Tony, NAIA 1982–82
Hines, Gregory, NAIA 1982–83

All American

Chaney, Darlene, 1985
Cooper, Anita, 1985
Dolberry, Jackie, 1987–89

Hampton University Alumni in the National Basketball Association

Mahorn, Rick, Washington Bullets, (F), 1980–85; Detroit Pistons, (F), 1985–87; N.J. Nets (F) 1992–93

[1] Mahorn, Rick—1979 Central Intercollegiate Athletic Association Player of the Year
[2] Hines, Gregory—1982 Central Intercollegiate Athletic Most Valuable Player
[3] Washington, Tony—1983 Central Intercollegiate Athletic Associate Tournament Most Valuable Player

Livingstone College
Salisbury, North Carolina 28144

Coaches of Varsity Teams

Mitchell, Edward L., 1949–58

Warner, L.A., 1959–64
Brown, Walter L., 1965–70
Wiggins, Morris, 1970–74
Porter, Willie, 1974–76
Thomas, Fred, 1976–79
Robinson, Joe E., 1979–83
Fitch, Jerry, 1983–84
Corley, David, 1984–85
Lewter, Stan, 1990–93

Women's Basketball

Davis, Jeanne, 1947–48
Mitchell, Florence N., 1949–64
Martin, Rose, 1964–65
Williams, Anne L., 1965–69
Wrightsell, Emma M., 1969–74
Lawson, Patricia, 1974–79
Corley, David, 1979–83
Green, Peggy, 1983
Howell, Cassandra, 1991–93

All-Central Intelligence Athletic Association

Hamilton,Jerry, 1974–75
Davis, Antonio, 1982
Adams, Anthony, 1986

Women's Basketball

Downing, Beverly, 1977–78
Jenkins, Debra, 1982–84
Anderson, Jackie, 1986, 1988
Coefield, Georgia, 1992

Johnson C. Smith University
Charlotte, North Carolina 28216

Coaches of Varsity Teams

Bynum, George, 1946
McKenney, T.E., 1948
Irvin, Calvin, 1950–52
Brayboy, Jack, 1953–54
McGirt, Edward C., 1960–62
McCullough, William, 1963–68
Fitch, Jerome, 1975–78
Moore, Robert, 1979–86
Joyner, Steven, 1986–93

Women's Basketball

Evans-Liebert, Hythia, 1986–93

All Central Intercollegiate Athletic Association

Sanders, Claude, 1955
Crenshaw, Joseph, 1959
Hester, James, 1962
Neal, Fred, 1963
Turner, Charles, 1965
Randolph, Reginald, 1967
Butts, Robert, 1970–71
Cooper, George, 1974–75
Lewis, Robert, 1976
Entzminger, Herbert, 1977–78
Proctor, Francis, 1978–80
Tibbs, William, 1979–82
Oliver, Larcell, 1980–82
Flores, Phil, 1981
McGrudder, Roosevelt, 1984
Johnson, Dante, 1985–87
Brown, Vincent, 1986–87
Jones, Chris, 1988
Hurd, Walter, 1989
Sherrill, Mark, 1990–92
Parker, Columbus, 1991–92

Women's Basketball

Alexander, Marsha, 1982
Johns, Odelia, 1983
Howell, Cassandra, 1984–85
Hamilton, Angela, 1986, 1988
Beard, Sharrion, 1986, 1988
Brewington, Kim, 1990
McKoy, Mary, 1991
Baraka, Shani, 1992

All Tournament Team

Saunders, Claude, 1952
Hargett, James, 1952
Hester, James, 1961
Neal, Fred, 1961–63
McMorris, Stoney, 1964
Schley, Stephen, 1964
Wilson, Jackie, 1965–67
Sanders, James, 1973–74
Cooper, George, 1973–75
Joplin, Willie, 1974
Wallace, Derek, 1975
Lewis, Robert, 1976
Entzminger, Herbaert, 1978
Flores, Phil, 1982

Oliver, Larcell, 1982
Smith, Phil, 1982

Elizabeth City State University
Elizabeth City, North Carolina 27909

Coaches of Varsity Teams
Mackey, Dr. Claudie, 1987–93

Women's Basketball
Crump, Wanda, 1992–93

All Central Intercollegiate Athletic Association
Trotman, Marvin, 1962
Todd, Richard, 1965–66
Stubbins, Gary, 1966–67
Lewis, Frederick, 1967–68
Smith, Oscar, 1968
Oliver, Israel, 1969–70
Gale, Michael, 1970–71
Carmichael, Len, 1972
Windley, Glen, 1973–74
Carr, Charles, 1975
Blue, Thomas, 1975–77
Gaskins, Arthur, 1979–80
Bland, Pierre, 1982
Brown, Benjamin, 1985
McDaniels, Tim, 1986–87
Griffin, Ernest, 1989
Higgs, Nathan, 1992

Women's Basketball
Jackson, Tara, 1990
Rowe, Demetrius, 1991
Taylor, Patricia, 1992

All Tournament Team
Smith, Oscar, 1968
Oliver, Israel, 1969
Moorer, Hubert, 1969–70
Gale, Michael, 1969–71
Carmichael, Len, 1972
Carr, Charles, 1975
Blue, Thomas, 1975
Gaskins, Thomas, 1975
Bland, Pierre, 1981

Alumni in the National Basketball Association
Gale, Michael, San Antonio Spurs, (G), 1976–80; Portland Trailblazers, (G), 1980–81

Winston-Salem State University
Winston-Salem, North Carolina 27110

Coaches of Varsity Teams
Gaines, Clarence, 1947–93

Women's Basketball
Conley, Stenson, 1981–93

All Central Intercollegiate Athletic Association
Defares, Jack, 1955–56
John, Wilfred, 1958
Hill, Cleo, 1959–61
Foree, George, 1962
Glover, Richard, 1963
Blount, Theodore, 1963–65
Curry, Willie, 1964
Monroe, Earl, 1965–67
Cunningham, Tom, 1966
Ridgill, Howard, 1966
Reid, James, 1967
Smiley, Eugene, 1968
English, William, 1968–69
Williams, Donald, 1970
Smith, Sandy, 1971–72
Williams, Earl, 1972–74
Chavious, Arthur, 1973
Kitt, Harold, 1974
Paulin, Thomas, 1975
Helton, Donald, 1976
Terry, Carlos, 1976–78
Gaines, Reginald, 1978–80
Robinson, Michael, 1978–80
Harold, David, 1979
Greene, Therman, 1982
Russell, Troy, 1984
Gorham, Linwood, 1985
Hooper, Alex, 1986–87
Cromartie, Gary, 1987
Spell, Charles, 1987–88
Barber, Toby, 1990
Hardin, Jonathan, 1990–91

Women's Basketball

Winfield, Brenda, 1977–80
Jenkins, Laurience, 1979
Lee, Linda, 1979
Dabbs, Phyllis, 1980
Huntley, Carolyn, 1985–86
Henderson, Angela, 1988
Courtney, Angela, 1991–92

All Tournament Team

Defares, Jack, 1955–57
John, Wilfred,[2] 1955–57
Hill, Cleo,[3] 1959–61
Foree, George,[4] 1960–62
Riley, Charles, 1961
Glover, Richard, 1963
Blunt, Theodore,[5] 1962–63
Monroe, Earl,[6] 1965–67
Reid, James, 1967
English, William, 1967–69
Kimbrough, Vaughn, 1969
McManus, Allen,[7] 1970
Garner, Robert, 1973
Williams, Earl, 1973–74
Paulin, Thomas, 1975
Helton, Donald, 1975–76
Terry, Carlos,[8] 1975–78
Brown, Michael, 1976
Gibson, George, 1977
Dillard, Marco, 1977
Robinson, Michael, 1978
Gaines, Reginald, 1978–79
Whitfield, Cliff, 1983
Womack, Dan, 1983

All-American

Monroe, Earl, 1967
Gaines, Reginald, 1980

Winston Salem State Alumni in the National Basketball Association

Monroe, Earl, Baltimore Bullets, (G), 1967–72; New York Knickerbockers, (G), 1972–70
Reid, Jim, Philadelphia 76ers, (F), 1967–68
Williams, Earl, Phoenix Suns, (F), 1974–75; New Jersey Nets, (F), 1976–77
Terry, Carlos, Washington Bullets, (F), 1980–83

[1] Gaines, Clarence—has more career wins than any other active collegiate coach
[2] John, Wilfred—1957 CIAA Tournament Most Valuable Player
[3] Hill, Cleo—CIAA Tournament Most Valuable Player, 1960, 1961
[4] Foree, George—1962 CIAA Tournament Most Valuable Player
[5] Blount, Theodore—1963 CIAA Tournament Most Valuable Player
[6] Monroe, Earl—1966 CIAA Tournament Most Valuable Player
[7] McManus, Allen—1970 CIAA Tournament Most Valuable Player
[8] Terry, Carlos—1977 CIAA Tournament Most Valuable Player

Shaw University
Raleigh, North Carolina 27611

Coaches of Varsity Teams

Ford, Jake, 1992–93

Women's Basketball

Sanders, Bobby L., 1986–93

All Central Intercollegiate Athletic Association

Mitchell, Ira, 1966
Utley, Kelly, 1970–71
Haskins, Raymond, 1971–72
Agee, Daniel, 1973
Richardson, Andrew, 1974
Moye, Joseph, 1975
Stuckey, Sammy, 1982
Lacy, David, 1984–85
Joseph, Anthony, 1987
King, Anthony, 1988–89
Owens, Sheldon, 1990–92
McCoy, Terrence, 1992

Women's Basketball

Craig, Denise, 1977
Gerideau, Robin, 1980
Ambrose, Kim, 1982–84
Kemp, Mary, 1984
Staples, Carlissa, 1986
Howell, Debra, 1988
Jefferson, Edith, 1990–91

All Tournament Team

Keitt, Frank, 1958
Utley, Kelly, 1971
Haskins, Raymond, 1971–72
Murchinson, Terrance, 1973
Richardson, Andrew, 1976
Hicks, Larry, 1977

St. Augustine's College
Raleigh, North Carolina 27611

Coaches of Varsity Teams

Heartley, Harvey, 1974–93

Women's Basketball

Downing, Dr. Beverly, 1983–93

All Central Intercollegiate Athletic Association

Pritchett, Curtis, 1971–72
Powell, Sean, 1977
Cooper, William, 1980
Boggan, Anthony, 1981
Carroll, Donald, 1982
Franks, Randy, 1984
Rogers, Anthony, 1984
Coates, Al, 1985
Mounts, Randall, 1987
Johnson, Darryl, 1988
McDaniel, Lashun, 1989
Mattison, Gary, 1990

Women's Basketball

Grant, Ruby, 1978–80
McCarter, Audrey, 1978
Wilfe, Ida, 1978
Williams, Janice, 1980
Combo, Jackie, 1981
White, Lisa, 1981
Douglas, Sabrina, 1984
Wells, Pam, 1986
Anderson, Lisa, 1990
Hunter, Rhonda, 1990
Seward, Shelia, 1990
Hackney, Delbra, 1991
Brown, Carolyn, 1992
Miller, Natasha, 1992

All Tournament Team

Burks, Clarence, 1953
Stirrup, Al, 1960
Rand, Calvin, 1976
Powell, Sean, 1977
Rhodes, Larry, 1977
Preston, Calvin, 1980
Taylor, Gary, 1980

Cooper, William, 1980
Bogan, Anthony, 1980–81
Cook, Marvin, 1982
Carroll, Donald, 1982–83
Rogers, Anthony, 1982–83
Davis, Mark, 1983
Bannister, Ken, 1984
Franks, Randy, 1984

St. Augustine's Alumni in the
National Basketball Association

Bannister, Ken, New York Knickerbockers, (F), 1984–86

St. Paul's College
Lawrenceville, Virginia 23868

Coaches of Varsity Teams

Bradley, Harry, 1989–93

Women's Basketball

Freeman, Julianna, 1991–93

All Central Intercollegiate Athletic Association

Bacote, Ralph, 1954
Green, Michael, 1970
Roberts, Donnie, 1975–76
Cozart, William, 1976–77
Jackson, Gregory, 1980–81
Lewis, Bernard, 1981
Bell, Charles, 1984

Women's Basketball

Cox, Karen, 1980
Lashley, Juliana, 1981
Jones, Renee, 1985–86
Trusty, Daphne, 1990–92

North Carolina Central University
Durham, North Carolina 27707

Coaches of Varsity Teams

McLendon, John B., 1940–52
Brown, Floyd H., 1952–70
Edmonds, Harry J., 1970–73
Jones, Samuel, 1973–74

Holt, Sterlin M., 1974–78
Silva, Francis A., 1978–79
Clements, Jesse, 1979–84
Edmonds, Harry, 1984–87
Bernard, Michael, 1987–91
Jackson, Gregory, 1991–93

Women's Basketball
McCormick, Mickie, 1975–78
Wade, Calvin, 1978–79
Silva, Francis A., 1979–80
Gatling, Alberta W., 1980–82
Edwards, Yvonne M., 1982
Pinnix, Jacqueline, 1987–93

All Central Intercollegiate Athletic Association
Harrison, Charles, 1954
Jones, Samuel, 1954–57
Sligh, James, 1958
Bell, Carlton, 1959
Parker, Joseph, 1964
Manning, Theodore, 1965–66
Davis, Lee, 1967–68
Pridgen, Joseph, 1969
McCrimmon, Ronald, 1970
Leggett, Redden, 1971
Binion, David, 1983
Jennette, Willie, 1986
Howell, Wayne, 1988
Leak, Derrick, 1988–90
Clark, Miles, 1989
Sifford, Antoine, 1990

Women's Basketball
Floyd, Metrial, 1981
Judkins, Carmen, 1983
McLaurin, Mona, 1983
Pinnix, Jacqueline, 1984
Fulmore, Yon, 1985–86

Sawyer, Pame, 1990
Stewart, Monica, 1991

All Mid-Eastern Athletic Conference
Reddish, Allen, 1972
Little, Robert, 1975
Harrell, John, 1976
Monroe, Floyd, 1977
McClellan, Robert, 1977

All-American

Women's Basketball
Fulmore, Yon, 1986

North Carolina Central Alumni in the National Basketball Association
Jones, Sam, Boston Celtics, 1957–69

[1] Harvey, Earl—1985 Central Intercollegiate Athletic Association Offensive Player of the Year

Bowie State University
Bowie, Maryland 20715

Coaches of Varsity Teams
Hart, Tyrone, 1984–93

Women's Basketball
Davis, Edward, 1992–93

All Central Intercollegiate Athletic Association
Sinclair, Michael, 1987–89

Women's Basketball
Rolle, Annette, 1981
Goodwyn, Jackie, 1984
Belk, Demetress, 1990

MID-EASTERN ATHLETIC CONFERENCE

1. Morgan State University
2. Delaware State College
3. South Carolina State College
4. University of Maryland, Eastern Shore
5. Florida A&M University

6. North Carolina A&T State University
7. Howard University
8. Coppin State University
9. Bethune-Cookman College

Morgan State University
Baltimore, Maryland 21239

Coaches of Varsity Teams

Wilson, Howard A. "Brutus," 1957–66
Frazier, Nathaniel, 1967–76
Johnson, Aaron, 1976–78
Goydon, Gus, 1978–80
Dean, Tom, 1984–85
McMillian, Ray, 1984–85
Frazier, Nathaniel, 1985–90
Taylor, Nat, 1990
Holmes, Michael, 1990–93

Women's Basketball

Fields, LaRue, 1978–85
Powell, Andy, 1985–93

All Central Intercollegiate Athletic Association

Garrett, Ernest, 1954–55
Garner, Ronald, 1958
Brightful, Charles, 1958
Johnson, Harold, 1960–62
Turk, James, 1965

All Mid-Eastern Athletic Conference

Davis, Chester, 1972–73
Webster, Marvin,[1] 1972–75
Newton, William, 1975–76
Evans, Eric,[2] 1976–78
Jennings, Maurice, 1977
Young, Anthony, 1977–79
Hopkins, Garcia, 1979
Witherspoon, Byron, 1979
Roberts, Yarborough, 1980
Reid, Anthony, 1989
McCoy, James, 1990
Smith, Glenn, 1991

All-American (Black College)

Webster, Marvin, 1973–74
O'Neal, Alvin, 1974

Morgan State University's
Athletic Hall of Fame

Jones, Ed "Lanky"
Sheffey, Powell B.
Hackett, Rufus "Legs"
Jones, William "Babe"
Murdock, Ezra "Ez"
Payne, William "Mack"
Spencer, Howard "Jack"
Garrett, Ernest
Cornish, Howard Lee
Covert, Bettilee "Jenks"
Whitted, Carl "Jet"
James, Albert "Sonny"
Clarke, Wilbur "Ace"

[1] Webster, Marvin—1973–74 Mid-Eastern Athletic Conference Player of the Year
[2] Evans, Eric—1977 Mid-Eastern Conference Player of the Year

Delaware State College
Dover, Delaware 19901

Coaches of Varsity Teams

George, Bennie J., 1949–71
Mitchell, Ira, 1971–75
Emery, Marshall, 1976–79
Triplett, Ajac, 1979–83
Davidson, Joe Dean, 1983–85
Emery, Marshall, 1985–88
Jones, Jeff, 1988–93

Women's Basketball

George, Bennie J., 1953–56
Franklin, Lucille, 1956–68
Wyche, Mary, 1968–69

McQuire, june, 1969–71
Johnson, Sal, 1971–76
Russell, Carrie, 1976–80
Jones, Byarie, 1980–81
Freeman, Marriana, 1981–83
McDowell, Stanley, 1983–85
Lamb-Bowman, Mary, 1985–93

All Mid-Eastern Athletic Conference

Sheppard, Sam, 1972, 1974–75
Roundtree, James, 1973–75
Simmons, Fred, 1975
Rogers, James, 1976
Shealy, Charles, 1979–80
Maybin, Charles, 1979
Hill, William, 1979, 1980–82
Hunter, Robert, 1980
Gumbs, Jeff, 1981
Wallace, Edward, 1983
Sapp, Danny, 1983
Campbell, Bernard, 1984–85
Snowden, Dominic, 1984–85
Ball, Terrence, 1986
Davis, Tom, 1989–91
Davis, Emanuel, 1991
Boger, Tyrone, 1992

Women's Basketball

Leonard, Sabrina, 1984
Albury, Carlene, 1985–86
Hunter, Shervon, 1992

All-American (Black College)

Campbell, Bernard, 1985

Women's Basketball

McCormick, Eve, 1978

South Carolina State College
Orangeburg, South Carolina 29117

Coaches of Varsity Teams

Martin, Edward A., 1955–67
Jobe, Ben, 1968–71
Autry, Tim, 1972–79
Jones, John, 1980–82
Caldwell, Percy "Chico," 1983–87
Alexander, Cy, 1987–93

Women's Basketball

Simon, Willie J., 1974–85
Foster, Lyman, 1988–93

All Southern Intercollegiate Athletic Conference

Wright, Ted, 1956, 1958–59
Morgan, William, 1961
Jackson, Ernest, 1961–62, 1964
Moody, Lindberg, 1961–62
Myles, Ron, 1962–64
Williams, Robert, 1964
Shields, Tyrone, 1965
Hillary, William, 1966
Lewis, Robert, 1966
Keye, Julius, 1966
Lewis, Robert, 1968

All Mid-Eastern Athletic Conference

Thornton, John, 1972
Boswell, Thomas, 1972–73
Williams, Michael, 1974
Barron, Alex, 1974–75
Nickens, Harry, 1975–78
Green, Carl, 1976
Brown, Willie, 1977
Snipes, Arthur, 1978–79
Lane, Marty, 1980
Wilson, Gregory, 1980–81
Robinson, Joe, 1981–82
Haynes, Marvin, 1983
Giles, Franklin, 1983–84
Miller, Ralph, 1984
Parson, Sylvester, 1985
Williams, Dennis, 1985
Joyner, MacArthur, 1986–87
Mack, Rodney, 1988–89
Bowman, Bernard, 1988
Jeter, Eric, 1989
Williams, Travis, 1990–91
Robinson, Jackie, 1992

Women's Basketball

Wiggins, Wanda, 1992
Barber, Tabitha, 1992

University of Maryland, Eastern Shore
Princess Anne, Maryland 21853

Coaches of Varsity Teams

Kiah, Waldo, 1945
Waters, Slim, 1946–48
McCain, Vernon "Skip," 1948–54
Taylor, Robert, 1955–65
Davis, Howard, 1965–66
Robinson, Joe, 1966–71
Bates, John, 1971–74
Jones, Dan, 1974–77
Hall, Kirkland, 1977–84
Evans, Howie, 1984–86
Williams, Steven, 1986–90
Hopkins, Robert, 1990–92
Wilkerson, Robert, 1992

All Central Intercollegiate Athletic Association

Williams, Sonny, 1956
Lloyd, Sonny, 1962
Santio, Al, 1962
Williams, Edward, 1963–65
Ford, Jake, 1968–70
Fontaine, Levi, 1969–70
Morgan, James, 1970–72
Bryant, Jackie, 1971–72

All Mid-Eastern Athletic Conference

Bryant, Jackie, 1972
Collins, Rubin, 1973–74
Skinner, Talvin, 1973–74
Pace, Joe, 1974
Gordon, William, 1974
Simmons, Kenneth "Chick," 1977–79
Hay, Steve, 1980
Bonney, Donnell, 1984–85
Robinson, Derek, 1986–87
Liverpool, Noel, 1987
Blye, Marvin, 1987

Women's Basketball

Dallas, Cherryl, 1983
Felder, Monica,[2] 1984–85
Fowler, Angie, 1992
Cookfield, Sondra, 1992

All-American (Black College)

Williams, Ed, 1965
Ford, Jake, 1970
Pace, Joe, 1974
Collins, Rubin,[7] 1974
Simmons, Ken, 1979

Florida A&M University
Tallahassee, Florida 32207

Coaches of Varsity Teams

King, W. McKinley, 1930–33
Wright, Ted, 1933–37
Gaither, Alonzo "Jake," 1937–42
Nelson, Buck, 1942–50
Oglesby, Edward "Rock," 1950–73
Triplett, Ajax, 1973–79
Giles, James, 1979–83
Fields, Tony, 1983–84
Booker, Willie, 1984–93

Women's Basketball

Farmer, Claudette, 1990–93

All Southern Intercollegiate Athletic Conference

Bostic, Charles, 1951
Pittman, Herman, 1951
Fears, Ernie, 1951
Washington, Earl, 1952
Hearns, Sam, 1952
Donald, Harold, 1953
Clayton, Mack, 1954
Beachum, Herb, 1954
Young, Roy, 1954–57
Cuyler, John, 1955
Stanley, James, 1955–60
Morgan, Leo, 1956–57
Gibson, Leroy, 1956–59
Collier, Leon, 1957–58
Forchion, James, 1960
Johnson, Melvin, 1960
Bellamy, Wate, 1960–62
Barnes, William, 1962
Kennedy, Walter, 1962
Allen, Ted, 1964

Collier, Willie, 1964–65
Walls, James, 1967
Lawson, Alfred, 1967–68

All Mid-Eastern Athletic Conference

Taylor, Walter, 1981
Spence, Darrell, 1981–82
Toomer, Michael, 1982–84
Broner, Larry, 1983
Henry, Reginald, 1988
King, Leonard, 1989
Giles, Terry, 1989–90
Glover, Kevin, 1990
Turner, Delon, 1991–92
Finney, Reginald, 1992

Florida A&M Alumni in the National Basketball Association

Johnson, Clemon, Portland Trailblazers, (F), 1978–79;
Indiana Pacers, (F), 1979–82;
Philadelphia 76ers, (F), 1982–85;
Seattle Supersonics, 1986–88

North Carolina A&T State University
Greensboro, North Carolina 27411

Coaches of Varsity Teams

Irvin, Cal, 1954–72
Reynolds, Warren, 1972–77
Littles, Eugene, 1977–79
Corbett, Don,[1] 1979–93

Women's Basketball
Spruill, Joyce, 1975–86
Abney, Tim, 1986–93

All Mid-Eastern Athletic Conference

Austin, Elmer,[2] 1972
Harris, William, 1972–73
Outlaw, James, 1972, 1974
Spruill, Allen, 1975
Johnson, Ron, 1976
Sparrow, James,[3] 1976, 1978–79
Brawner, Joseph,[4] 1979–80
Anderson, James, 1981

Binion, Joe,[5] 1982–84
Brown, Jr., James, 1984–85
Boyd, Eric, 1984–85
Williams, Claude, 1986–87
Cale, George, 1986–87
Williams, Claude, 1985–88
Griffis, Thomas, 1988
Taggart, Glenn, 1989, 1991
Becton, Carlton, 1989
Elliott, Dana, 1991–92
Williams, Jamaine, 1992

Women's Basketball
Williams, Robbin, 1992

All-American (Black College)

Cotton, Joseph, 1958
Attles, Al, 1960
Harris, William, 1972–73
Sparrow, James, 1976
Binion, Joseph, 1983–84
Boyd, Eric, 1985
Brown, Jr., James, 1985

North Carolina A&T Alumni in the National Basketball Association

Attles, Alvin, San Francisco Warriors, (G), 1960–71

[1] Corbett, Don—1981–82; 1984–85 Mid-Eastern Athletic Conference Coach of the Year
[2] Austin, Elmer—1972 Mid-Eastern Conference Player of the Year
[3] Sparrow, James—1976 Mid-Eastern Athletic Conference Player of the Year
[4] Brawner, Joseph—1979 Mid-Eastern Athletic Conference Player of the Year
[5] Binion, Joe—1982–83 Mid-Eastern Athletic Conference Player of the Year

Howard University
Washington, D.C. 20059

Coaches of Varsity Teams

Burr, Jr., John H., 1946–49
Jackson, Edward, 1949–51
Hart, Tom, 1951–58
Emery, Marshall, 1971–75
Williamson, A.B., 1975–90
Beard, Alfred "Butch", 1990–93

Women's Basketball
Tyler, Sanya, 1980–93

All Central Intercollegiate Athletic Association

Harris, Thomas, 1956
Syphax, John, 1956–58
Hancock, Larry, 1961

All Central Intercollegiate Athletic Association Tournament Team

Jett, George, 1948
Harris, Thomas, 1956
Taylor, Edward, 1966–67
Shingler, Aaron, 1967
Williams, Frank, 1967

All Mid-Eastern Athletic Conference

Lewis, Robert, 1973
Hollins, Warren, 1973
Young, Arnold, 1973
Carroll, Achilles, 1974
Cotton, Vadnay, 1975–76
Glover, Gerald,[1] 1977–78
Dent, Dorian, 1978–79
Ratiff, James,[2] 1980–82
Spriggs, Larry,[3] 1980–81
Wright, Rodney, 1980, 1982
Perry, Bernard, 1983
Scott, Kevin, 1984
Wynn, David, 1984
Hill, Fred, 1985–86
McIlwaine, Robert, 1985–86
Spencer, Howard, 1987
Stuart, William, 1987
Spencer, John, 1988
Hamilton, George, 1988
Powell, Tyrone, 1990
McNeil, Julius, 1992

Women's Basketball

Lee, Annette, 1992

All-American (Black College)

Glover, Gerald, 1978
Ratiff, James, 1980
Spriggs, Larry, 1981

Other Outstanding Athletes

Council, Angelo
Hamilton, George

Wilson, Louis
Speight, Nate
Gaskins, Gerald
Terry, Chauncey
Pressley, Michael

Howard University's Alumni in the National Basketball Association

Spriggs, Larry, Houston Rockets, (F), 1982;
Chicago Bulls, (F), 1982–83;
Los Angeles Lakers, (F), 1983–86

[1] Glover, Gerald—1978 Mid-Eastern Athletic Conference Player of the Year
[2] Ratiff, James—1980 Mid-Eastern Athletic Conference Player of the Year
[3] Spriggs, Larry—1981 Mid-Eastern Athletic Conference Player of the Year; 1979–81 Most Valuable Player at the Mid-Eastern Athletic Conference Tournament

Coppin State College
Baltimore, Maryland 21216

Coaches of Varsity Teams

Byron, Dr. Cyril O., 1958–65
Jones, Joseph A.,[1] 1965–69
Hardnett, Charles, 1969–74
Bates, John,[2] 1974–86
Mitchell, Ron, 1986–9

Women's Basketball

Alexander, Celestine, 1974–75
Bishop, Barbara, 1975–76
Koger, Anne, 1976–78
Travis, Ruth, 1978–80
Harrison, Tori, 1992–93

All Mid-Eastern Athletic Conference

Edwards, Sidney, 1962
Briscoe, Thomas, 1963
Hayman, Warren, 1963
Bennett, James, 1964
Lee, Earl, 1986–87
Miller, Steven, 1987
Booth, Phil, 1988, 1990
Isaac, Reginald, 1989–91
Stewart, Larry, 1989–91
Yarbray, Larry, 1990
McCollum, Larry, 1991
Saunders, Tarig, 1992

Women's Basketball
McCallum, FAye, 1992
Scott, La Shawn, 1992

All Potomac Intercollegiate Conference
Martin, Hayzon, 1966
Green, Walter, 1966–68
Parker, Clyde, 1967
McNeil, Clayton, 1967
Hall, Larry, 1967
Carter, Colbert, 1968
Carter, Anthony, 1976–77
Heard, Warren, 1977

NAIA All-American
Hayman, Warren, 1963
Briscoe, Thomas, 1963
Parker, Clyde, 1967
Hall, Larry, 1967
Green, Walter, 1967–68
Carter, Colbert, 1968
Pace, Joe, 1976–77
Heard, Warren, 1977
Carter, Anthony, 1977

Coppin State Alumni in the National Basketball Association
Pace, Joe, Washington Bullets (C), 1976–78
Stewart, Larry, Washington Bullets, 1991–93

[1] Jones, Dr. Joseph A.—coached the first Coppin team that won an intercollegiate championship
[2] Bates, John—won the NAIA National Basketball Championship in 1976

Bethune-Cookman College
Daytona Beach, Florida 32015

Coaches of Varsity Teams
McClairen, Jack "Cy", 1961–93

Women's Basketball
Wyatt, Alvin, 1978–93

All Mid-Eastern Athletic Conference
Hill, Donald, 1985–86
Reed, Clifford, 1991
Cunningham, Reginald, 1992

Women's Basketball
Jones, Amanda, 1992

Mid-Eastern Athletic Conference Basketball Awards

Year • Player • College

1971–72 • Elmer Alston • North Carolina A&T State University
1972–73 • Marvin Webster • Morgan State University
1973–74 • Marvin Webster • Morgan State University
1974–75 • Marvin Webster • Morgan State University
1975–76 • James Sparrow • North Carolina A&T State University
1976–77 • Eric Evans • Morgan State University
1977–78 • Gerald Glover • Howard University
1978–79 • Joe Brawner • North Carolina A&T State University
1979–80 • James Ratiff • Howard University
1980–81 • Larry Spriggs • Howard University
1981–82 • Joe Binion • North Carolina A&T State University
1982–83 • Joe Binion • North Carolina A&T State University
1983–84 • Joe Binion • North Carolina A&T State University
1984–85 • Eric Boyd • North Carolina A&T State University
1985–86 • Don Hill • Bethune-Cookman College
1986–87 • George Cale • North Carolina A&T State University
1987–88 • Claude Williams • North Carolina A&T State University
1988–89 • Tom Davis • Delaware State College
1989–90 • Larry Stewart • Coppin State College
1990–91 • Larry Stewart • Coppin State College
1991–92 • Delon Turner • Florida A&M University

Coach of the Year:
Year • Coach • College

1971–72 • John Bates • University of Maryland, Eastern Shore (co-winner) • Nathaniel Frazier • Morgan State 1972–73 • John Bates • University of Maryland, Eastern Shore
1973–74 • John Bates • University of Maryland, Eastern Shore
1974–75 • Warren Reynolds • North Carolina A&T State 1975–76 • Nathaniel Frazier • Morgan State University
1976–77 • Tim Autry • South Carolina State University
1977–78 • Marshall Emery • Delaware State College
1978–79 • Eugene Littles • North Carolina State University
1979–80 • A. B. Williamson • Howard University
1980–81 • Don Corbett • North Carolina A&T State University
1981–82 • Don Corbett • North Carolina A&T State University
1982–83 • A. B. Williamson • Howard University
1983–84 • Don Corbett • North Carolina A&T State University
1984–85 • Don Corbett • North Carolina A&T State University

Reference Section

1985–86 • Don Corbett • North Carolina A&T State University
1986–87 • A. B. Williamson • Howard University
1987–88 • Don Corbett • North Carolina A&T State University
1988–89 • Cy McClairen • Bethune-Cookman College

1989–90 • Ron Mitchell • Coppin State College
1990–91 • Ron Mitchell • Coppin State College
1991–92 • Alfred "Butch" Beard • Howard University

SOUTHWESTERN ATHLETIC CONFERENCE

1. Alcorn State University
2. Grambling State University
3. Prairie View A&M University
4. Southern University

5. Jackson State University
6. Texas Southern University
7. Mississippi Valley State University
8. Alabama State University

Alcorn State University
Lorman, Mississippi 39096

Coaches of Varsity Teams

Whitney, Sr., David, 1968–89
Walker, Lonnie, 1989–93

Women's Basketball

Walker, Shirley, 1978–93

All Southwestern Athletic Conference

Ned, Walter, 1966
Kelly, James, 1967–68
Norwood, Willie, 1967–69
Flowers, Robert, 1968
Keye, Julius, 1969
Wyatt, Levi, 1970, 1972
Sing, Sam, 1970
Bateman, Glen, 1971
Tatum, Andrew, 1973
Milton, Alfred, 1975
Robinson, Dellie, 1975–76
Monroe, Alfredo, 1977
Horton, James, 1978–79
Davis, Collie, 1979
Smith, Larry, 1979–80
Baker, Eddie, 1980
Wyatt, Clinton, 1980
Bell, E.J., 1980
Alexander, Dwight, 1981
Archie, Eddie, 1981
Irving, Albert, 1981–82
Collier, Thomas, 1983–84

Phelphs, Michael, 1983–84
Brandon, Aaron, 1985
Whitney, Jr., David, 1986
Palmer, David, 1986
Malone, Michael, 1989
Ward, Reginald, 1991

Women's Basketball

Hooker, Teresa, 1986–87
Powell, Lisa, 1989–90
Varnado, Tracey, 1989
Powell, Robbie, 1989
Lewis, Sherlanda, 1990–91
Barksdale, Tammi, 1991

All-American (Black College)

McGill, John, 1976

Alcorn State Alumni in the
National Basketball Association

Smith, Larry, Golden State Warriors, (F), 1980–88

Grambling State University
Grambling, Louisiana 71245

Coaches of Varsity Teams

Hobdy, Frederick, 1956–86
Hopkins, Robert, 1986–89
James, Aaron, 1989–93

Women's Basketball

Bibbs, Patricia, 1984–93

All Southwestern Athletic Conference

Barry, Jerry, 1959
Hooper, James, 1959
Willis, Howard, 1959
Hardnett, Charles, 1959, 1962
Tippett, Rex, 1960–61
Reed, Willis, 1961, 1964
West, Hershell, 1963
Frazier, Wilbur, 1963–65
Comeaux, John, 1964–66
Jones, James, 1966–67
Davis, Howard, 1967
Hilton, Fred, 1969, 1971
Cannon, Emanuel, 1971
James, Aaron, 1972, 1974
Hart, Willie, 1972
Wright, Larry, 1975–76
Sykes, Terry, 1977
Lemelle, Martin, 1978–80
Tidwell, Gary, 1979
Williams, Robert, 1980–81
Simpson, Ken, 1981–82
Johnson, Napoleon, 1983–84
Lapoole, Willie, 1985
Wesley, Terrell, 1989
Glover, Andrew, 1991

Women's Basketball

Dillard, Elsie, 1989–90
Hollis, Tarcha, 1990–91
Paul, Karman, 1991
Locklin, Arlene, 1992

All-American (Black College)

Hardnett, Charles, 1961–62
Reed, Willis, 1964
Comeaux, John, 1966
Wright, Larry, 1976

Grambling State Alumni in the National Basketball Association

Hopkins, Robert, Syracuse Nationals, (F), 1957–60
Reed, Willis, New York Knickerbockers, (C), 1964–74
Jones, James, Washington Bullets, (G), 1974–77
Hilton, Fred, Buffalo Braves, (G), 1971–73
Christian, Robert, Atlanta Hawks, (F), 1970–73; Phoenix Suns, (F), 1973–74
James, Aaron, New Orleans Jazz, (F), 1974–79

Wright, Larry, Washington Bullets, (G), 1976–80; Detroit Pistons, (G), 1980–81

Prairie View A&M University
Prairie View, Texas 77445

Coaches of Varsity Teams

Loore, Leroy, 1961–62
Duplantier, Jim, 1981–87
Plummer, Elwood, 1990–93

Women's Basketball

Atkins, Robert, 1985–93

All Southwestern Athletic Conference

Justice, Irving, 1953
Ludd, Clarence, 1954–56
Grimes, Harold, 1958
Beatty, Zelmo, 1959–60, 1962
Brackens, Harold, 1959
Lackey, Cornell, 1960
Jackson, Marvin, 1977
Hagan, Larry, 1979
Stevenson, Steven, 1989–90
Irvin, Michael, 1989

Women's Basketball

Burnice, Frederica, 1990

All-American (Black College)

Beatty, Zelmo, NAIA 1960–62

Other Outstanding Athletes

Himes, Douglas
McQueen, Dewey
Lackey, Cornell
Manning, Guy
Gamble, James
Grimes, Harold
Stubblefield, Clarence
Redmond, Thomas

Prairie View A&M Alumni in the National Basketball Association

Beatty, Zelmo, St. Louis Hawks, (C), 1962–68; Atlanta Hawks, (C), 1968–69

Southern University
Baton Rouge, Louisiana 70813

Coaches of Varsity Teams

Stewart, Carl E., 1972–82
Stoglin, Andrew, 1982–85
Hopkins, Robert, 1985–86
Jobe, Ben, 1986–93

Women's Basketball

Turner, James, 1987–93

All Southwestern Athletic Conference

Wyatt, Lawrence, 1952
Norwood, Sylvester, 1952
Johnson, James, 1952
Singleton, James, 1953
Cunningham, Clarence, 1953
Gray, Robert, 1953–56
Wise, Ellis, 1954
Hill, Roosevelt, 1957–58
Paul, Frank, 1958
Hayes, Ego, 1958
Thomas, Willis, 1960
Bond, Louis, 1960–62
Love, Robert, 1963–65
Boatwright, Homer, 1964
Hayes, Ron, 1964–65
Long, Ron, 1967
Wilson, Jasper, 1967–68
McTier, Larry, 1972
Frazier, Andrew, 1973
Keyes, Alexander, 1973
Barrow, Ron, 1974–76
Saunders, Frank, 1976–78
Green, Tom, 1977
Murphy, Tony, 1979–80
Garrett, Lionel, 1979
Jackson, Alvin, 1981
Broadway, Bryan, 1984
Lee, James, 1984
Gabriel, Byron, 1986
Battles, Daryl, 1989
Youngblood, Robert, 1989–91
Faulkner, Joe, 1990
Phills, Robert, 1991

Women's Basketball

Stovall, Claudene, 1989

Other Outstanding Athletes

Johnson, Avery

Southern University Alumni in the National Basketball Association

Love, Robert, Cincinnati Royals, (F), 1966–68; Milwaukee Bucks, (F), 1968–69; Chicago Bulls, (F), 1969–76; New Jersey Nets, (F), 1976–77
Green, Tom, Utah Jazz, (G), 1978–79
Saunders, Frank, Boston Celtics, (F), 1976–78; San Antonio Spurs, (F), 1978–79; Kansas City Kings, (F), 1981

Jackson State University
Jackson, Mississippi 39217

Coaches of Varsity Teams

Ellis, T.B., 1949–51
Wilson, Harrison B., 1951–67
Covington, Paul, 1967–86
Prince, John, 1986–89
Stoglin, Andy, 1989–93

Women's Basketball

Tucker, Peggy, 1948–52
Magee, Sadie, 1975–89
Pennington, Andrew, 1989–93

All Southwestern Athletic Conference

Buckner, Cleveland, 1959–60
Barfield, James, 1960
Benton, James, 1964
Yarborough, Jerry, 1964–65
LeFlore, Lyvonne, 1964–65
Bingham, Charles, 1966
Manning, Ed, 1966–67
Warner, Cornell, 1969–71
Herdon, Lou, 1970
Shinall, John, 1970
Brown, Marvin, 1971
Kincaide, McKinley, 1971
Short, Eugene, 1973–74
Jones, Glendale, 1974–75
Ward, Henry, 1975
Short, Purvis, 1976–78
Norris, Sylvester, 1978
Walsh, Robert, 1979
Norris, Audie, 1979–82

Shavers, Doc, 1980–81
Williams, Henry, 1983
Walker, Jackie, 1984
Fonville, Lester, 1987
Hart, Jeff, 1985–87
Kidd, Tyrone, 1984
Abram, Demetrius, 1989
Strothers, Eric, 1991
Hunter, Lindsay, 1991–93

Jackson State University's Athletic Hall of Fame
Ingram, Joel
Wood, Melvin
Buckner, Cleveland
Manning, Edward
Short, Eugene
Short, Purvis
Ward, Henry
Norris, Audie

Women's Basketball
Paige, Gloria
Hardy, Bertha
Bender, Evelyn
Robinson, Vanetta
Thomas, Lisa
Freeman, Gloria

Jackson State University Alumni in the National Basketball Association
Buckner, Cleveland, New York Knickerbockers, (F), 1961–62
Manning, Ed, Baltimore Bullets, (F), 1967–69; Chicago Bulls, (F), 1969–70; Portland Trailblazers, (F), 1970–71
Short, Purvis, Golden State Warriors, (F), 1978–89
Short, Eugene, New York Knickerbockers, (F), 1975–76; Seattle Supersonics, (F), 1976–77
Norris, Audie, Portland Trailblazers, (F, C), 1982
Norris, Sylvester, San Antonio Spurs, (F), 1979–80

Texas Southern University
Houston, Texas 77004

Coaches of Varsity Teams
Ewell, C.T.,[2] 1935–36
Patterson, Pat,[3] 1937–40
Redding, E.V., 1946–47

Lattimore, Oliver, 1948–49
Adams, Edward H., 1950–59
Morehead, I. Thomas, 1960–64
Whitney, David, 1964–69
Gordon, Lavalius, 1969–73
McCowan, Kenneth, 1973–75
Moreland, Robert E., 1975–93

All Southwestern Athletic Conference
Bolen, Ruben, 1955
Crawford, Clifford, 1955
Sauldsberry, Woody, 1955
Swain, Ben, 1955–58
Dunbar, Earl, 1956
Maura, Fred, 1956–57, 1959
Bobbitt, Robert, 1957–58
Taylor, Willie, 1957–59
Allen, James, 1967
Hart, Herbert, 1970
Aldridge, Ellis, 1971–72
Ford, Charles, 1972
Davis, Gaylord, 1976
Williams, Lawrence, 1977
Bradley, Alonzo, 1977
Blue, Fred, 1979
Kelly, Harry, 1980–83
Mitchell, Lattrell, 1983
Hilliard, Ed, 1984
Applewhite, Andre, 1984–85
Brooks, Lester, 1984–86
Gatlin, Robert, 1987
West, Fred, 1989–90
Price, Charles, 1989–90
Younger, Ray, 1991

Women's Basketball
Mosley, Tracey, 1989
Wilson, Michelle, 1989
Long, Doretha, 1989
Dixon, Sonja, 1990
Yates, Valerie, 1991

All-American
Swain, Bennie, 1958
Bradley, Alonzo, 1977

Texas Southern Alumni in the
National Basketball Association

Sauldesberry, Woodrow, Philadelphia Eagles, (F), 1957–60;
   Chicago Packers, (F), 1961–62; St. Louis Hawks, (F), 1962–
   63; Boston Celtics, (F), 1965–66
Swain, Ben, Boston Celtics, (F, C), 1958–59
Bradley, Alonzo, Houston Rockets, (F), 1977–80

Mississippi Valley State University
Itta Bena, Mississippi 38941

Coaches of Varsity Teams

Stribling, Lafayette, 1983–93

Women's Basketball

Harris, Jesse L., 1974–93

All Southwestern Athletic Conference

Robinson, Calvin, 1974
Williams, Ernest, 1979
Reed, Tony, 1980–81
Ellis, Henry, 1982–83
Phillips, Robert, 1984
Sanders, Robert, 1984–85
Coleman, Roderick, 1989
Johnson, Jammie, 1989
Pollard, Tim, 1989
Ford, Alphonso, 1990–91

Women's Basketball

Hoskins, Patricia, 1989
Brown, Stephanie, 1989
Shields, Kathy, 1989
McGary, Donna, 1989–91

Alabama State University
Montgomery, Alabama 36101

Coaches of Varsity Teams

Oliver, James, 1978–93

Women's Basketball

Mitchell, Ron, 1986–93

All Southwestern Athletic Conference

Mayo, Darrin, 1989–90
Brooks, Terry, 1989
Smith, Gerald, 1989
Rogers, Steve, 1990–91

Women's Basketball

Hall, Neacole, 1989
Archie, Michelle, 1989
MeMullen, Lisa, 1990–91

Southwestern Athletic Conference
Basketball Awards

Player of the Year:
Year • Player • College

1988–89 • Terry Brooks • Alabama State University
1989–90 • Joe Faulkner • Southern University
1990–91 • Steve Rogers • Alabama State University

Men's Coach of the Year:
Year • Coach • College

1988–89 • Ben Jobe • Southern University
1989–90 • Ben Jobe • Southern University
1990–91 • Andy Stoglin • Jackson State University

Women's Coach of the Year:
Year • Coach • College

1981–82 • Jessie Harris • Mississippi Valley State University
1982–83 • Sadie Magee • Jackson State University
1983–84 • Shirley Walker • Alcorn State University
1984–85 • Shirley Walker • Alcorn State University
1985–86 • Shirley Walker • Alcorn State University
1986–87 • Patricia Bibbs • Grambling State University
1987–88 • Jessie Harris • Mississippi Valley State University
1988–89 • Patricia Bibbs • Grambling State University
1989–90 • Patricia Bibbs • Grambling State University
1990–91 • Shirley Walker • Alcorn State University

Southwestern Athletic Conference Hall of Fame

Inductees (May 1992)
College • Player • Titles/Sport

Alabama State University • Charles J. Dunn, Basketball

BIG TEN CONFERENCE

1. Purdue University
2. University of Wisconsin
3. Northwestern University
4. Indiana University
5. Ohio State University
6. Iowa University

7. University of Illinois at Urbana-Champaign
8. University of Minnesota
9. Michigan State University
10. University of Michigan
11. Pennsylvania State University

Purdue University
West Lafayette, Indiana 47097

All Big Ten Conference

Merriweather, Willie, 1959
Gilliam, Herman, 1969
Kendrick, Frank, 1974
Jordan, Walter, 1977–78
Carroll, Joe Barry, 1979–80
Edmonson, Keith, 1982
Cross, Russell, 1983
Mitchell, Todd, 1986–87
Lewis, Troy, 1986
Mitchell, Todd, 1988
Oliver, Jimmy, 1991
Austin, Woody, 1992
Robinson, Glen, 1993

All-Amereican

Robinson, Glen, 1993

Women's Basketball

Holmes, Joy, 1992

Other Outstanding Athletes

McCants, Melvin

University of Wisconsin
Madison, Wisconsin 53711

Coaches of Varsity Teams

Cofield, William L. (Head), 1976–80
Weaver, Larry (Assistant), 1974–76
Reed, Larry (Assistant), 1976–80
McCallum, Ray (Assistant), 1984–93
Jackson, Stu (Head), 1992–93

Women's Basketball

Qualls, Edwina (Head), 1976–86
Richey-Walton, Kathy 1979–82

All Big-Ten Conference

Franklin, Joe, 1968
Gaines, Arnold, 1978
Matthews, Westley, 1979
Gregory, Claude, 1981
Blackwell, Cory, 1983–84
Finley, Michael, 1993

Women's Basketball

Huff, Janet, 1984
Pruitt, Chris, 1984
Threatt, Robin, 1992

Northwestern University
Evanston, Illinois 60201

All Big-Ten Conference

McKinney, William, 1977

Women's Basketball

Browne, Anucha, 1983–85
Savage, Michele, 1990–92

All-American

Women's Basketball

Browne, Anucha, 1985

Indiana University
Bloomington, Indiana 47405

Coaches of Varsity Teams

Wright, Joby (Assistant), 1985–90

All Big-Ten Conference

Garrett, William,[1] 1951
Bellamy, Walter, 1960–61
McGinnis, George, 1971
Wright, Joby, 1972
Downing, Steven,[2] 1973
Buckner, Quinn, 1974–75
May, Scott,[3] 1975–76
Woodson, Michael,[4] 1979
Thomas, Isiah, 1980–81
Tolbert, Ray,[5] 1981
Garrett, Dean, 1988
Edwards, Jay, 1989
Cheaney, Calbert, 1991–93
Henderson, Alan, 1993

All-American

Garrett, William, 1951
Bellamy, Walter,[6] 1960–61
McGinnis, George, 1971
May, Scott, 1975–76
Thomas, Isiah,[7] 1981
Turner, Landon,[8] 1982
Cheaney, Calbert, 1992–93

Indiana University's Hall of Fame

Bellamy, Walter

Other Outstanding Athletes

Wilkerson, Robert
Carter, Butch
Thomas, Jim
Thomas, Daryl
Smart, Keith
Garrett, Dean

[1] Garrett, William—the first black American to play basketball in the Big-Ten Conference
[2] Downing, Steven—1973 *Chicago Tribune* Trophy recipient (given to the Most Valuable Player in the big-Ten Conference)
[3] May, Scott—1975 and 1976 *Chicago Tribune* Trophy recipient (given to the Most Valuable Player in the big-Ten Conference); 1976 United Press International and Associated Press Player of the Year; member of the 1976 United States Olympic Basketball Team
[4] Woodson, Michael—1980 *Chicago Tribune* Trophy recipient (given to the Most Valuable Player in the Big-Ten Conference)
[5] Tolbert, Ray—1981 *Chicago Tribune* Trophy recipient (given to the Most Valuable Player in the Big-Ten Conference)
[6] Bellamy, Walter—member of the 1960 United States Olympic Basketball Team
[7] Thomas, Isiah—1981 Most Valuable Player in the Final Four Tournament; member of the 1980 United States Olympic Basketball Team
[8] Turner, Landon—(honorary)

Ohio State University
Columbus, Ohio 43210-1166

Coaches of Varsity Teams

Cleamons, Jim (Assistant), 1980–86
Ayers, Randy (Head), 1989–93

All Big-Ten Conference

Cleamons, Jim, 1971
Ransey, Kelvin, 1978–80
Williams, Herb, 1980
Kellogg, Clark, 1982
Campbell, Tony, 1983–84
Stokes, Ron, 1985
Taylor, Troy, 1985
Sellers, Brad,[1] 1986
Hopson, Dennis, 1986–87
Jackson, Jim, 1991j–92

Women's Basketball

Hall, Tracey, 1986–88
Roberts, Averill, 1992
Keyton, Nikki, 1992

All-American

Jackson, Jim, 1991–92

Women's Basketball

Hall, Tracy, 1987–88

Ohio State University's Hall of Fame

Cleamons, Jim

[1] Sellers, Brad—1986 Most Valuable Player in the National Invitational Tournament

Iowa University
Iowa City, Iowa 52242

Coaches of Varsity Teams

Raveling, George (Head), 1983–86

Women's Basketball

Stringer, Vivian (Head), 1983–93
Freeman, Mariana (Assistant), 1992–93

All Big-Ten Conference

Cain, Carl, 1956
Williams, Sam,[1] 1967–68
Johnson, John, 1970
Brown, Fred, 1971
Lester, Ron, 1978–79
Stokes, Greg, 1985
Marble, Roy, 1987
Horton, Ed, 1989
Earl, Acie, 1992–93

Women's Basketball

Edwards, Michelle, 1986–88
Foster, Toni, 1991–93

All-American

Cain, Carl, 1956
Brown, Fred, 1971
Lester, Ron, 1979–80

Women's Basketball

Edwards, Michelle, 1986–87
Foster, Toni, 1991–93

Other Outstanding Athletes

Payne, Michael
Horton, Ed

[1] Williams, Sam—1968 *Chicago Tribune* Trophy recipient (given to the Most Valuable Player in the Big-Ten

University of Illinois at Urbana-Champaign
Champaign, Illinois 61820

Coaches of Varsity Teams

Yates, Tony (Assistant), 1974–83
Collins, James (Assistant), 1983–93

All Big-Ten Conference

Freeman, Don, 1966
Weatherspoon, Nick, 1973
Johnson, Eddie, 1981
Harper, Derek, 1983
Winters, Efrem, 1984–85
Douglas, Bruce, 1984–85
Welch, Anthony, 1985
Norman, Ken, 1986–87

Anderson, Nick, 1989
Gill, Kendall, 1990
Thomas, Deon, 1993

Women's Basketball

Gantt, Kendra, 1982

All-American

Freeman, Don, 1966
Harper, Derek, 1983

Other Outstanding Athletes

Vaughn, Govoner[1]
Jackson, Mannie[2]
Montgomery, George
Matthews, Audie

[1] Vaughn, Govoner—one of the first black Americans to start for a University of Illinois basketball team
[2] Jackson, Mannie—one of the first black Americans to start for a University of Illinois basketball team

University of Minnesota
Minneapolis, Minnesota 55455

Coaches of Varsity Teams

Williams, James (Assistant, Interim Head Coach), 1985–86
Haskins, Clem (Head), 1986–Present

All Big-Ten Conference

Hudson, Lou, 1965
Turner, Clyde, 1972
Behagan, Ron, 1973
Brewer, Jim,[1] 1973
Thompson, Mychal,[2] 1976–78
Mitchell, Darryl, 1982
Davis, Tom, 1985
Burton Willie, 1990

All-American

Hudson, Lou, 1965
Brewer, Jim, 1973
Behagan, Ron, 1973
Thompson, Mychal, 1978

Other Outstanding Athletes

Clark, Archie

Lockhart, Osborne
Williams, Ray
Tucker, Trent
Hall, Mark
Wilson, Mark

[1] Brewer, Jim—1972 *Chicago Tribune* Trophy recipient (given to the Most Valuable Player in the Big Ten Conference)
[2] Thompson, Mychal—1978 *Chicago Tribune* Trophy recipient (given to the Most Valuable Player in the Big Ten Conference)

Michigan State University
East Lansing, Michigan 48824

Coaches of Varsity Teams

Williams, Herb (Assistant), 1984
Perry, Derek (Assistant), 1985

All Big-Ten Conference

McCoy, Julius, 1956
Green, John,[1] 1958–59
Walker, Horace, 1960
Washington, Stanley, 1966
Lafayette, Lee, 1969
Simpson, Ralph, 1970
Robinson, Michael, 1972–74
Hairston, Lindsay, 1974–75
Furlow, Terry, 1975–76
Johnson, Earvin,[2] 1978–79
Kelser, Gregory, 1979
Vincent, Jay, 1980–81
Smith, Kevin, 1982
Vincent, Sam, 1985
Johnson, Darryl, 1987
Smith, Steve, 1990–91

All-American

Green, John, 1959
Simpson, Ralph, 1970
Robinson, Michael, 1974
Johnson, Earvin, 1979

[1] Green, John—1959 *Chicago Tribune* Trophy recipient (given to the Most Valuable Player in the Big-Ten Conference)
[2] Johnson, Earvin—1979 *Chicago Tribune* Trophy recipient (given to the Most Valuable Player in the Big-Ten Conference)

University of Michigan
Ann Arbor, Michigan 48109

Coaches of Varsity Teams

Watson, Perry (Assistant), 1992–93

All Big-Ten Conference

Burton, Memie C., 1959
Buntin, William, 1963–65
Russell, Cazzie,[1] 1964–66
Wilmore, Henry, 1971–72
Russell, Campy,[2] 1974
Green, Rick, 1976–77
Hubbard, Phil, 1977
McGee, Michael, 1978–81
Turner, Eric, 1983
Tarpley, Roy,[3] 1985–86
Grant, Gary, 1985–88
Joubert, Antoine, 1986
Rice, Glen, 1988–89
Robinson, Rumeal, 1990
Webber, Chris, 1992–93
Rose, Jalen, 1993

All-American

Buntin, William, 1964–65
Russell, Cazzie, 1965–66
Wilmore, Henry, 1971–72
Russell, Campy, 1974
Green, Rick, 1977
Tarpley, Roy, 1985
Grant, Gary, 1988
Webber, Chris, 1993

Other Outstanding Athletes

Howard, Juwan
King, Jimmy
Jackson, Ray
Higgins, Sean
Calip, Demetrius
Talley, Michael
Riley, Eric

[1] Russell, Cazzie—1965 and 1966 *Chicago Tribune* Trophy recipient (given to the Most Valuable Player in the Big-Ten Conference)
[2] Russell, Campy—1974 *Chicago Tribune* Trophy recipient (given to the Most Valuable Player in the Big-Ten Conference)
[3] Tarpley, Roy—1985 *Chicago Tribune* Trophy recipient (given to the Most Valuable Player in the Big-Ten Conference)

Pennsylvania State University
University Park, Pennsylvania 16802

All-American

Arnette, Jesse, 1954–55

Chicago Tribune Trophy Recipients (Big Ten Most Valuable Player Award)

Year • Player • College • Position

1965 • Cazzie Russell • University of Michigan • G
1966 • Cazzie Russell • University of Michigan • G
1968 • Sam Williams • Iowa University • F
1971 • Jim Cleamons • Ohio State University • G
1972 • Jim Brewer • University of Minnesota • C
1973 • Steve Downing • Indiana University • C
1974 • Campy Russell • University of Michigan • F
1975 • Scott May • Indiana University • F
1976 • Scott May • Indiana University • F
1978 • Mychal Thompson • University of Minnesota • C
1979 • Earvin Johnson • Michigan State University • G
1980 • Mike Woodson • Indiana University • F
1981 • Ray Tolbert • Indiana University • C
1985 • Roy Tarpley • University of Michigan • C

1988 • Gary Grant • University of Michigan • G
1989 • Glen Rice • University of Michigan • F
1990 • Steve Smith • Michigan State University • G
1991 • Jim Jackson • Ohio State University • G/F
1992 • Jim Jackson • Ohio State University • G/F
1993 • Calbert Cheaney • Indiana University •G/F

Big Ten Most Valuable Player (Chosen by Media Panel and Coaches)

Year • Player • College • Position

1985 • Roy Tarpley • University of Michigan • C
1987 • Dennis Hopson • Ohio State University • G
1988 • Gary Grant • University of Michigan • G
1989 • Jay Edwards • Indiana University • G
    • Glen Rice • University of Michigan • F
1991 • Jim Jackson • Ohio State University • G/F
1992 • Jim Jackson • Ohio State University • G/F

Big Ten Coach of the Year

Year • Name • College

1991 • Randy Ayers • Ohio State University
1992 • Randy Ayers • Ohio State University

ATLANTIC COAST CONFERENCE

1. University of North Carolina, Chapel Hill
2. University of Virginia
3. Wake Forest University
4. University of Maryland, College Park
5. Georgia Institute of Technology

6. Duke University
7. Clemson University
8. North Carolina State University
9. Florida State University

University of North Carolina
Chapel Hill, North Carolina 27514

Coaches of Varsity Teams

Women's Basketball

Stroman, Debbie (Assistant), 1983

All Atlantic Coast Conference

Scott, Charles,[1] 1968–70
McAdoo, Robert,[2] 1972
Davis, Walter, 1976–77
Ford, Phil,[3] 1976–78

Wood, Al, 1979–81
Worthy, James,[4] 1981–82
Perkins, Sam,[5] 1982–84
Jordan, Michael,[6] 1983–84
Smith, Ken, 1985–87
Daugherty, Brad, 1985–86
Reid, Herman "J.R.", 1987–88
Madden, Kevin, 1989
Davis, Hubert, 1992
Lynch, George, 1993

Women's Basketball

Brown, Teresa, 1982–83

All-American

Scott, Charles, 1969–70
Chamberlain, William, 1972
McAdoo, Robert, 1972
Ford, Phil, 1976–78
Wood, Al,[7] 1980–81
Worthy, James, 1982
Perkins, Sam 1982–83
Jordan, Michael, 1983–84
Smith, Ken,[8] 1985–86
Daugherty, Brad,[9] 1985
Reid, J.R., 1988–89

Women's Basketball

Brown, Teresa, 1984–85

Other Outstanding Athletes

Bradley, Dudley[10]

[1] Scott, Charles—1969 Everett Case Award recipient (given to the Most Valuable Player at the Atlantic Coast Conference Tournament)
[2] McAdoo, Robert—1972 Everett Case Award recipient (given to the Most Valuable Player at the Atlantic Coast Conference Tournament)
[3] Ford, Phil—1978 Atlantic Coast Conference Player of the Year; 1977 and 1978 Atlantic Coast Conference Athlete of the Year; member of the 1976 United States Olympic Basketball Team
[4] Worthy, James—1982 Everett Case Award recipient (most valuable player of the Atlantic Coast Conference Tournament)
[5] Perkins, Sam—1981 Atlantic Coast Conference Rookie of the Year; 1981 Everett Case Award recipient (Most Valuable Player of the Atlantic Coast Conference Tournament); member of the 1984 United States Olympic Basketball Team
[6] Jordan, Michael—1984 Atlantic Coast Conference Player of the Year; 1982 Atlantic Coast Conference Rookie of the Year; 1984 Atlantic Coast Conference Athlete of the Year; member of the 1984 United States Olympic Basketball Team
[7] Wood, Al—member of the 1980 United States Olympic Basketball Team
[8] Smith, Ken—Honorable Mention
[9] Daugherty, Brad—Honorable Mention
[10] Bradley, Dudley—1979 Everett Case Award recipient (Atlantic Coast Conference Tournament Most Valuable Player)

University of Virginia
Charlottesville, Virginia 22903

All Atlantic Coast Conference

Sampson, Ralph,[1] 1981–83
Wilson, Othell,[2] 1982–84
Polynice, Olden, 1986
Kennedy, Mel, 1988
Stith, Bryant, 1990–92

Women's Basketball

Staley, Dawn, 1989–92

All-American

Sampson, Ralph, 1981–83

Women's Basketball

Staley, Dawn, 1990–92

Other Outstanding Athletes

Drummond, Al[3]
Stroman, Debra[4]
Stokes, Ricky[5]
Edelin, Kenton

[1] Sampson, Ralph—1981–83 Atlantic Coast Conference Player of the Year; 1981–83 United Press International Player of the Year; 1981–83 Associated Press Player of the Year; 1981–83 United States Basketball Writers Association Player of the Year; 1982–83 John Wooden Award recipient
[2] Wilson, Othell—Honorable Mention
[3] Drummond, Al—first black American to receive a scholarship to play basketball at the University of Virginia, 1970
[4] Stroman, Debra—first black woman to receive a scholarship to play basketball at the University of Virginia, 1978
[5] Stokes, Ricky—received the 1984 Frances Pomeroy Naismaith Hall of Fame Award (given to the most outstanding senior male basketball player under six feet tall)

Wake Forest University
Winston-Salem, North Carolina 27109

Coaches of Varsity Teams

Stokes, Ricky (Assistant), 1991–93

All Atlantic Coast Conference

Davis, Charles,[1] 1969–71
Byers, Tony, 1973–74
Brown, Skip, 1975–77
Griffin, Rod,[2] 1976–78
Johnson, Frank, 1978–79, 1981
Teachey, Anthony, 1984
Green, Ken, 1984–85
Bogues, Tyrone "Muggsy," 1986–87
Rogers, Rodney, 1991–93
Childress, Randolph, 1993

All-American

Davis, Charles, 1971
Griffin, Rod, 1977–78
Johnson, Frank, 1981
Rogers, Rodney, 1993

Women's Basketball

Jackson, Keeva

Wake Forest University's Hall of Fame

Davis, Charles[3]

Other Outstanding Athletes

Rudd, Delaney
Castle, Stacey
Tucker, Anthony

[1] Davis, Charles—1971 Atlantic Coast Conference Player of the Year
[2] Griffin, Rod—1977 Atlantic Coast Conference Player of the Year
[3] Davis, Charles—first black American elected to the Wake Forest University Sports Hall of Fame

University of Maryland
College Park, Maryland 20740

Coaches of Varsity Teams

Dillard, Sherman (Assistant), 1980–85
Wade, Robert (Head), 1986–89
McCready, Roger (Assistant), 1989–91

All Atlantic Coast Conference

Elmore, Len, 1972–74
Lucas, John, 1974–76
Brown, Owen, 1975
Howard, Maurice, 1975
Gibson, Larry, 1979
Williams, Charles "Buck," 1980–81
King, Albert,[1] 1980–81
Coleman, Ben, 1983
Branch, Adrian, 1983–85
Bias, Len,[2] 1985–86
Lewis, Derrick, 1988
Massenburg, Tony, 1990
Williams, Walt, 1992

All-American

Elmore, Len, 1974
Lucas, John, 1974–76
Gibson, Larry, 1980
King, Albert, 1980–81
Williams, Charles "Buck," 1980–81
Branch, Adrian, 1984–85
Bias, Len, 1985–86
Williams, Walt, 1992

Other Outstanding Athletes

Brown, Darryl
Patton, Chris
Sheppard, Steve[3]
Graham, Ernest
Boston, Lawrence
Jones, Tom
Lewis, Derrick
Gatlin, Keith
Baxter, Jeff

[1] King, Albert—1980 Atlantic Coast Conference Player of the Year; 1980 Everett Case Award recipient (given to the Most Valuable Player at the Atlantic Coast Conference Tournament)
[2] Bias, Len—1985 Atlantic Coast Conference Player of the Year; 1986 Atlantic Coast Conference Player of the Year; 1984 Everett Case Award recipient (given to the Most Valuable Player at the Atlantic Coast Conference Tournament)
[3] Sheppard, Steve—member of the 1976 United States Olympic Basketball Team

Georgia Institute of Technology
Atlanta, Georgia 30332

Coaches of Varsity Teams

Jobe, Ben (Assistant), 1981–82
Clark, Perry (Assistant), 1983–90
Dillard, Sherman (Assistant), 1990–93

All Metro Conference

Brown, Tico, 1977
Drummer, Sam, 1978
Horton, Lenny, 1977–78

All Atlantic Coast Conference

Salley, John, 1985–86
Dalrymple, Bruce,[1] 1985–86
Ferrell, Duane, 1987–88
Hammonds, Tom, 1988–89
Oliver, Brian, 1990
Anderson, Kenny, 1990–91
Scott, Dennis, 1990
Mackey, Malcolm, 1991
Best, Travis, 1993
Forest, James, 1993

All-American

Salley, John, 1986
Hammonds, Tom, 1989
Scott, Dennis, 1990
Anderson, Kenny, 1990–91

Duke University
Durham, North Carolina 27706

Coaches of Varsity Teams

Amaker, Tommy (Assistant), 1990–93

All Atlantic Coast Conference

Banks, Eugene,[1] 1978–81
Taylor, Vince, 1982
Dawkins, John,[2] 1983–85
Amaker, Tom, 1987
Henderson, Phil, 1990
Hill, Grant, 1992–93
Hill, Thomas, 1992

All-American

Banks, Eugene, 1981
Dawkins, John, 1985–86
Hill, Grant, 1993

Other Outstanding Athletes

Hodge, Willie
Moses, George
Harrell, John
Henderson, David
King, Bill
Lang, Antonio

Women's Basketball

Matthews, Kim

[1] Banks, Eugene—1978 Atlantic Coast Conference Rookie of the Year;
Honorable Mention
[2] Dawkins, John—alternate member of the 1984 United States Olympic
Basketball Team

Clemson University
Clemson, South Carolina 29631

Coaches of Varsity Teams

Bryant, Client (Assistant), 1977–84
Harris, Eugene (Assistant), 1984–93
Washington, Rudy (Assistant), 1984–88

All Atlantic Coast Conference

Wise, Alan, 1975

Rollins, Wayne, 1975–77
Rome, Stan, 1977
Williams, Billy, 1980
Nance, Larry, 1981
Hamilton, Vincent, 1982
Grant, Horace, 1986–87
Campbell, Elden, 1990
Davis, Dale, 1991

All-American

Rollins, Wayne, 1977

North Carolina State University
Raleigh, North Carolina 27650

Coaches of Varsity Teams

Martin, Ray (Assistant), 1983–89

All Atlantic Coast Conference

Heartly, Al,[1] 1971
Thompson, David,[2] 1973–75
Carr, Kenneth, 1976–77
Austin, Clyde, 1978
Whitney, Charles, 1978–80
Lowe, Sidney,[3] 1981–83
Whittenberg, Derek, 1982
Bailey, Thurl, 1983
Charles, Lorenzo, 1984–85
Washburn, Chris, 1986
Shackleford, Charles, 1987, 1988
Monroe, Rodney, 1989–91

All-American

Thompson, David, 1973–75
Carr, Kenneth, 1976
Whitney, Charles "Hawkeye,"[4] 1980
Charles, Lorenzo,[5] 1985

Women's Basketball

Stinson, Andrea, 1989–90
Mapp, Rhonda, 1991

Other Outstanding Athletes

McMillan, Nate
Myers, Ernest

[1] Heartly, Al—the first black American to play basketball at North Carolina State University
[2] Thompson, David—1973, 1974, and 1975 Atlantic Coast Conference Player of the Year; 1973 and 1975 Atlantic Coast Conference AThlete of the Year; 1974 and 1975 Associated Press Player of the Year; 1975 United Press International Player of the Year; 1975 U.S. Basketball Writers Association Player of the Year; Most Valuable Player in the 1974 NCAA Final Four Tournament
[3] Lowe, Sidney—1983 Everett Case Award recipient (given to the Most Valuable Player at the Atlantic Coast Conference Tournament)
[4] Whitney, Charles "Hawkeye"—Honorable Mention
[5] Charles, Lorenzo—Honorable Mention

Florida State University
Tallahassee, Florida 32316

Coaches of Varsity Teams

Williamson, Ken (Assistant), 1989–93

All-Atlantic Coast Conference

Cassell, Sam, 1992–93
Edwards, Doug, 1992–93

All-American

King, Ron, 1973

Atlantic Coast Conference Player of the Year Award

Year • Player • College • Position

1971 • Charles Davis • Wake Forest University • F
1973 • David Thompson • North Carolina State University • G/F
1974 • David Thompson • North Carolina State University • G/F
1975 • David Thompson • North Carolina State University G/F
1977 • Rod Griffin • Wake Forest University • F
1978 • Phil Ford • University of North Carolina • G
1980 • Albert King • University of Maryland • F
1981 • Ralph Sampson • University of Virginia • C
1982 • Ralph Sampson • University of Virginia • C
1983 • Ralph Sampson • University of Virginia • C
1984 • Michael Jordan • University of North Carolina • G
1985 • Len Bias • University of Maryland • F
1986 • Len Bias • University of Maryland • F
1987 • Horace Grant • Clemson University • F
1990 • Dennis Scott • Georgia Tech University • G/F
1991 • Rodney Monroe • North Carolina State University • G
1993 • Rodney Rodgers • Wake Forest University • F

Atlantic Coast Conference Tournament Most Valuable Player Award

Year • Player • College • Position

1969 • Charles Scott • University of North Carolina • G
1972 • Robert McAdoo • University of North Carolina • F/C
1975 • Phil Ford • University of North Carolina • G
1979 • Dudley Bradley • University of North Carolina • G/F
1980 • Albert King • University of Maryland • F
1981 • Sam Perkins • University of North Carolina • C
1982 • James Worthy • University of North Carolina • F
1983 • Sidney Lowe • North Carolina State University • G
1984 • Len Bias • University of Maryland • F
1986 • Johnny Dawkins • Duke University • G
1989 • J.R. Reid • University of North Carolina • F/C
1990 • Brian Oliver • Georgia Tech University • G

PAC-TEN CONFERENCE

1. Stanford University
2. University of Washington
3. University of Southern California
4. University of California, Los Angeles
5. University of Arizona
6. Arizona State University
7. University of California, Berkeley
8. University of Oregon
9. Oregon State University
10. Washington State University

Stanford University
Stanford, California 94305

Coaches of Varsity Teams

Hunter, Robert (Assistant), 1982–84

All Pacific-eight or Pacific-Ten Conference

Harris, Art, 1966
Belton, Kimberly, 1980
Jones, Keith, 1983
Wright, Howard, 1988–89

Women's Basketball
Henning, Sonya, 1991
Whiting, Val, 1991–93

All-American
Henning, Sonya, 1991
Whiting, Val, 1992–93

Other Outstanding Athletes
Tucker, Ed[8]
Griffin, Don
Perry, Wolfe

Women's Basketball
Wilkes, Lucy
Smith, Louise[9]
Gore, Debbie

University of Washington
Seattle, Washington 98105

Coaches of Varsity Teams
Johnson, Robert (Assistant), 1975

All Coast
Edwards, James, 1977

All Pacific-Eight or Pacific-Ten Conference
Edwards, James, 1977
Fortier, Paul, 1986
Recasner, Eldridge, 1988–90

All American
Edwards, James, 1976

Other Outstanding Athletes
Romar, Lorenzo[10]

University of Southern California
Los Angeles, California 90089-0602

Coaches of Varsity Teams
Raveling, George (Head), 1986–93

Young, Draff (Assistant)
Washington, Rudy (Assistant)
Stewart, Stan (Assistant)

Women's Basketball
Williams, Fred (Assistant)

All Pacific-Eight or Pacific-Ten Conference
Hewitt, William, 1967–68
Calvin, Mack, 1969
Riley, Ron, 1972
Williams, Gus, 1975
Robinson, Cliff, 1978–79
Williams, Maurice, 1981–82
Anderson, Dwight, 1982
Hill, Jacques, 1983
Minor, Harold, 1990–92
Coleman, Ron, 1991
Cooper, Duane, 1992

Women's Basketball
Nelson, Cherie, 1989
Leslie, Lisa, 1991–93

All-American
Williams, Gus, 1975
Minor, Harold, 1991–92

Women's Basketball
McGee, Paula, 1982–83
Miller, Cheryl,[1] 1983–86
Lamb, Monica, 1987

[1] Miller, Cheryl—1984 James Naismith Memorial Trophy recipient; member of the 1984 United States Olympic Basketball Team; 1985 and 1986 James Naismith Memorial Trophy recipient; 1984, 1985, and 1986 Broderick Award recipient; 1985 Wade Trophy recipient

University of California, Los Angeles
Los Angeles, California 90024

Coaches of Varsity Teams
Farmer, Larry (Head), 1981–84
Hazzard, Walt (Head), 1984–88
Romar, Lorenzo (Assistant), 1988–93
McCarter, Andre (Assistant)

All-Pacific Coast Conference (Southern division)

Barksdale, Donald,[1] 1947
Minor, David, 1947–48
Moore, John, 1955
Naulls, Willie, 1955

All Pacific Coast and All Pacific-Ten Conference

Naulls, Willie, 1956
Taft, Morris, 1956
Torrence, Walter, 1959
Hazzard, Walter, 1963–64
Lynn, Michael, 1966
Allen, Lucius, 1967
Alcindor, Lewis,[2] 1967–69
Warren, Michael, 1968
Rowe, Curtis, 1969–71
Wicks, Sidney, 1970–71
Wilkes, Keith, 1973–74
Washington, Richard, 1976
Johnson, Marques,[3] 1976–77
Greenwood, David,[4] 1977–79
Hamilton, Roy, 1978–79
Sanders, Michael, 1981–82
Foster, Rod, 1981–83
Fields, Ken,[5] 1982–84
Jackson, Ralph, 1984
Miguel, Nigel, 1985
Miller, Reginald,[6] 1985–87
Richardson, Jerome, 1987, 1988–89
Wilson, Trevor, 1990
Murray, Tracy, 1991–92
O'Bannon, Ed, 1993

Women's Basketball
Stephens, Rehema, 1990–91
Williams, Natalie, 1991–92

All-American

Naulls, Willie, 1956
Hazzard, Walter,[7] 1964
Alcindor, Lewis, 1967–69
Allen, Lucius, 1968
Rowe, Curtis, 1970
Wicks, Sidney,[8] 1970–71
Bibby, Henry, 1972
Wilkes, Keith, 1973–74
Washington, Richard, 1976

Johnson, Marques, 1977
Greenwood, David, 1978–79
Fields, Ken, 1984
Miller, Reginald, 1986–87

All Western Collegiate Athletic Association

Thompson, Necie, 1980–83
Jones, Char, 1982–83
Joyner, Jackie, 1984

Other Outstanding Athletes

Bunche, Dr. Ralph
Madkins, Gerald
Butler, Mitchell
Tarver, Shon
Martin, Darrick

[1] Barksdale, Donald—first black American to be chosen for an Olympic team for basketball; member of the 1948 United States Olympic Basketball Team
[2] Alcindor, Lewis—aka Kareem Abdul-Jabbar; 1967 and 1969 United Press International Player of the Year; 1967 and 1969 Associated Press Player of the Year; 1967 and 1969 United States Basketball Writers Association Player of the Year
[3] Johnson, Marques—1977 Pacific-Eight Conference Player of the Year; 1977 United Press International Player of the Year; 1977 Associated Press Player of the Year; 1977 United States Basketball Writers Association Player of the Year; 1977 National Association of Basketball Coaches Player of the Year
[4] Greenwood, David—1978 Pacific-Eight Conference Player of the Year; 1979 Pacific-Ten Conference Player of the Year
[5] Fields, Ken—1983 Pacific-Ten Conference Player of the Year
[6] Miller, Reginald—1986 Pacific-Ten Conference Player of the Year
[7] Hazzard, Walter—1964 United States Basketball Writers Association Player of the Year
[8] Wicks, Sidney—1971 United States Basketball Writers Association Player of the Year

University of Arizona
Tucson, Arizona 85721

Coaches of Varsity Teams

Snowden, Fred[1] (Head), 1972–82
Byrdsong, Rick (Assistant), 1983–88

All Border Conference

Johnson, Leo, 1950–51

All Western Athletic Conference

Norman, Coniel, 1973–74
Fleming, Al, 1974–76
Money, Eric, 1973–74
Elliott, Robert, 1975–77
Harris, Helman, 1977

All Pacific-Eight or Pacific-Ten Conference

Elliott, Sean, 1987–89
Cook, Anthony, 1988–89
Williams, Brian, 1991
Mills, Chris, 1992–93
Rooks, Sean, 1992

Women's Basketball

Clark, Margo, 1992–93

All-American

Elliott, Robert, 1976–77
Elliott, Sean, 1988–89

[1] Snowden, Fred—first black head basketball coach at the University of Arizona; first black basketball coach at a major university

Arizona State University
Tempe, Arizona 85287

All Western Athletic Conference

Caldwell, Joe, 1963–64
Lewis, Fred, 1966
Hollins, Lionel, 1974–75
White, Rudy, 1975

All Pacific-Ten Conference

Williams, Sam, 1981
Lister, Alton, 1981
Lever, Lafayette, 1981–82
Scott, Byron, 1983
Edwards, Trent, 1989
Austin, Issac, 1991

All-American

Williams, Sam,[1] 1981
Lister, Alton,[2] 1981
Scott, Byron, 1983

[1] Williams, Sam—Honorable Mention
[2] Lister, Alton—Honorable Mention

University of California, Berkeley
Berkeley, California 97420

Coaches of Varsity Teams

Berry, William (Assistant), 1972–73

Bankhead, Robert (Assistant), 1976–77
Williams, Ronald (Assistant), 1983–85
Hodges, Morris (Assistant), 1984–85
Bozeman, Todd (Head), 1992–93

All Pacific-Ten or Pacific-Eight Conference

Schultz, Earl, 1960
Johnson, Charles, 1969
Chenier, Phil, 1971
Truitt, Ansley, 1972
Johnson, Kevin, 1986–87
Taylor, Leonard, 1989
Hendrick, Brian, 1990–93
Kidd, Jason, 1993

Women's Basketball

Cook, Cynthia, 1983
Garrett, Mazetta, 1984

Other Outstanding Athletes

Pressley, Robert

Women's Basketball

Martin, Kasha

University of Oregon
Eugene, Oregon 97403

Coaches of Varsity Teams

Billingslea, Ron (Assistant), 1973–78
Kent, Ernest (Assistant), 1978–80
Jackson, Stuart (Assistant), 1983–84
Adams, Debbie (Assistant), 1983–84
Rice, King (Assistant), 1992–93

All Pacific Coast, All Pacific-Eight, or All Pacific-Ten Conference

Franklin, Charles, 1957
Lee, Ron,[1] 1973–76
Ballard, Greg, 1977
Brandon, Terrell, 1990–91

All-American

Lee, Ron, 1975
Ballard, Greg, 1977

Other Outstanding Athletes

Patterson, Charles[2]
Jones, Steven

[1] Lee, Ron—1976 Pacific-Eight Conference Player of the Year
[2] Patterson, Charles—the first black American to compete in basketball in the Pacific Coast Conference

Oregon State University
Corvallis, Oregon 97331

All Pacific Coast or Pacific-Ten Conference

White, Charles, 1966
Boyd, Fred, 1972
Shelton, Lonnie, 1975
Smith, Rocky, 1977
Lee, Ricky, 1978
Johnson, Steven,[1] 1979–80
Blume, Ray, 1980–81
Radford, Mark, 1981
Conner, Lester,[2] 1982
Green, A.C.,[3] 1983–84
Payton, Gary, 1988–90

Women's Basketball
Shannon, Judy, 1991–92

All-American

White, Charles, 1966
Boyd, Fred, 1972
Blume, Ray, 1980
Johnson, Steven, 1980–81
Conner, Lester, 1982
Payton, Gary, 1990

[1] Johnson, Steven—1981 Pacific-Ten Conference Player of the Year
[2] Conner, Lester—1982 Pacific-Ten Conference Player of the Year
[3] Green, A.C.—1984 Pacific-Ten Conference Player of the Year

Washington State University
Pullman, Washington 99164-1610

Coaches of Varsity Teams

Raveling, George (Head), 1973–83
Sampson, Kelvin (Head), 1988–93

Women's Basketball
Rhodes, Harold (Head), 1983–93

All Pacific-Eight or All Pacific-Ten Conference

Rhodes, Harold, 1977
Donaldson, James, 1978
Collins, Don,[1] 1978–80
Rison, Bryan, 1980
Harriel, Steven, 1983
Lewis, Terrence, 1992

All-American

Collins, Don, 1980

Other Outstanding Athletes

Miller, Sam
Jeffries, Edgar
Davis, Ron
Hill, Angelo
House, Stuart

[1] Collins, Don—1980 Pacific-Ten Conference Player of the Year; Honorable Mention

Pacific-Ten Conference Player of the Year Award

Year • Player • College • Position

1976 • Ron Lee • University of Oregon • G
1977 • Marques Johnson • University of California, Los Angeles • F
1978 • David Greenwood • University of California, Los Angeles • F/C
1979 • David Greenwood • University of California, Los Angeles • F/C
1980 • Don Collins • Washington State University • G/F
1981 • Steven Johnson • Oregon State University • C
1982 • Lester Conner • Oregon State University • G
1983 • Kenny Fields • University of California, Los Angeles • F
1984 • A.C. Green • Oregon State University • F
1988 • Sean Elliott • University of Arizona • G/F
1989 • Sean Elliott • University of Arizona • G/F
1990 • Gary Payton • Oregon State University • G
1991 • Terell Brandon • University of Oregon • G
1992 • Harold Minor • University of Southern California • G

Pacific-Ten Conference Tournament Most Valuable Player Award

Year • Player • College • Position

1987 • Reggie Miller • University of California, Los Angeles • G
1988 • Sean Elliott • University of Arizona • G/F
1989 • Sean Elliott • University of Arizona • G/F

Pacific-Ten Conference Coach of The Year Award

Year • Coach • College

1976 • George Raveling (Co-Winner) • Washington State University
1983 • George Raveling • Washington State University
1987 • Walt Hazzard • University of California, Los Angeles
1991 • Kelvin Sampson • Washington State University
1992 • George Raveling • University of Southern California

IVY LEAGUE CONFERENCE

1. Harvard University
2. Princeton University
3. Dartmouth College
4. Cornell University

5. Columbia University
6. Yale University
7. University of Pennsylvania
8. Brown University

Harvard University
Cambridge, Massachusetts 02138

Coaches of Varsity Teams

Sanders, Tom (Head), 1973–77
Roby, Peter P. (Head), 1985–91

All Ivy League

Lewis, Floyd, 1971
James, Ralph, 1990
Mitchell, Ron, 1991–92

Other Outstanding Athletes

Brown, James[1]

[1] Brown, James—played on the 1970–71 Harvard University teams

Princeton University
Princeton, New Jersey 08544

All Ivy League

Taylor, Brian,[1] 1971–72
Hill, Armond, 1975–76
Melville, Randy, 1981
Robinson, Craig,[2] 1982–83
Leftwich, Jr., George, 1992

All-American

Taylor, Brian, 1972

[1] Taylor, Brian—member of the Ivy League Silver Anniversary All-Star Team; Ivy League Silver Anniversary Player of the Era
[2] Robinson, Craig—1982 Ivy League Player of the Year (Co-Winner); 1983 Ivy League Player of the Year

Dartmouth College
Hanover, New Hampshire 03755

Coaches of Varsity Teams

Jackson, Marcus (Head), 1974–75
Minton, Reginald (Head), 1983–84

All Ivy League

Brown, James, 1973
Edmonds, Sterling, 1978
Lawrence, Larry,[1] 1979

All-American

Lawrence, Larry, 1979
Raynor, Bill[2]
Cubas, Larry[3]

[1] Lawrence, Larry—1981 Ivy League Player of the Year
[2] Raynor, Bill—1972 Ivy League Rookie of the Year
[3] Cubas, Larry—1975 Ivy League Rookie of the Year

Cornell University
Ithaca, New York 14851

Coaches of Varsity Teams

Bluitt, Ben[1] (Head), 1974–81

Women's Basketball

Anderson, Rhonda (Assistant), 1983–84
Jordan, Kim (Head), 1988–93

All Ivy League

Morris, Gregory, 1967
Brown, Maynard, 1975
Vaughn, Bernard, 1977

Cornell University's Hall of Fame

Esdaile, Walter
Davis, Michael

[1] Bluitt, Ben—first black head coach on Cornell University's history

Columbia University—Barnard College
New York, New York 10027

Coaches of Varsity Teams

Women's Basketball

Samuel, Pat (Head, Barnard College), 1977–79

All Ivy League

McMillan, Jim,[1] 1968–70
Dotson, Heyward, 1969–70
Evans, Robert, 1973
Free, Ricky, 1977–78
Byrd, Alton,[2] 1977–79
Burnett, Darren, 1982–83
Jenkins, Buck, 1991–93

All-American

McMillian, Jim, 1968–70
Dotson, Heyward, 1968–70
Byrd, Alton,[3] 1978–79
Free, Ricky,[4] 1979
Burnett, Darren,[5] 1982–83

Other Outstanding Athletes

Steward, Russell

[1] McMillian, Jim—member of the Ivy League Silver Anniversary All-Star Team (First Team); Ivy League Silver Anniversary Player of the Era; member of the Ivy League Silver Anniversary All-Star Team (Second Team)
[2] Byrd, Alton—member of the Ivy League Silver Anniversary All-Star Team (Second Team)
[3] Byrd, Alton—Honorable Mention
[4] Free, Ricky—Honorable Mention
[5] Burnett, Darren—Honorable Mention

Yale University
New Haven, Connecticut 06250

All Ivy League

Graves, Earl (Butch), 1981–83
McCready, Travis, 1992

All-American

Graves, Earl "Butch,"[1] 1982–83

Other Outstanding Athletes

Swift, Jay
Robinson, Ed

[1] Graves, Earl "Butch"—Honorable Mention

University of Pennsylvania
Philadelphia, Pennsylvania 19104

Coaches of Varsity Teams

Littlepage, Craig (Head), 1982–85

All Ivy League

Calhoun, David "Corky,"[1] 1970–72
Hankinson, Phil,[2] 1972–73
Haigler, Ron,[3] 1973–75
McDonald, Keven,[4] 1976–78
Price, Anthony "Tony,"[5] 1979
Salters, James, 1980
Hall, Ken, 1981
Little, Paul,[6] 1982–83
Brown, Michael, 1983
Racine, Karl, 1984
Bromwell, Perry, 1987
Frazier, Jr., Walter, 1989

All-American
Calhoun, David, 1972

Other Outstanding Athletes
Littlepage, Craig[7]
Willis, Robert
Allen, Jerome

[1] Calhoun, David "Corky"—member of the Ivy League Silver Anniversary All-Star Team (First Team); Ivy League Silver Anniversary Player of the Era; 1972 Robert Geasey Memorial Trophy recipient (Big-Five Most Valuable Player); Big-Five Hall of Fame; member of the 1970–80 Eastern College Athletic Conference All-Decade Team
[2] Hankinson, Phil—Big-Five Hall of Fame
[3] Haigler, Ron—1975 Ivy League Player of the Year; member of the Ivy League Silver Anniversary All-Star Team (First Team); Ivy League Silver Anniversary Player of the Era; Big-Five Hall of Fame
[4] McDonald, Keven—1978 Ivy League Player of the Year; member of the Ivy League Silver Anniversary All-Star Team (Second Team)
[5] Price, Anthony "Tony"—1979 Ivy League Player of the Year; member of the Ivy League Silver Anniversary All-Star Team (Second Team)
[6] Little, Paul—1982 Ivy League Co-Player of the Year
[7] Littlepage, Craig—Captain, 1973

Brown University
Providence, Rhode Island 02912

Coaches of Varsity Teams
Dobbs, Frank (Head), 1991–93

All Ivy League
Morris, Eddie, 1974
Brown, Phil, 1974–75
Saunders, Brian, 1976–77
Moss, Peter,[1] 1979–80
Savage, Chuck, 1992–93

Other Outstanding Athletes
Clarke, Vaughn
Armstead, Wayne

[1] Moss, Peter—1980 Ivy League Player of the Year

Ivy League Player of the Year

Year • Player • College • Position

1975 • Ron Haigler • University of Pennsylvania • G
1976 • Armond Hill • Princeton University • G
1978 • Keven McDonald • University of Pennsylvania • F
1979 • Anthony Price • University of Pennsylvania • F
1980 • Peter Moss • Brown University • G/F
1981 • Larry Lawrence • Dartmouth College • F
      • Craig Robinson • Princeton University • F
1987 • Perry Bromwell • University of Pennsylvania • G

SOUTHWEST CONFERENCE

1. Texas Christian University
2. Rice University
3. Baylor University
4. Texas Tech University

5. Texas A&M University
6. Southern Methodist University
7. University of Texas, Austin
8. University of Houston, University Park

Texas Christian University
Fort Worth, Texas 76129

All Southwest Conference
Kennedy, Eugene, 1971
Degrate, Simpson, 1972
Browder, Darrell, 1983
Lott, Carl, 1986

Other Outstanding Athletes
Cash, James[1]

[1] Cash, James—first black athlete to play basketball in the Southwest Conference, 1968

Rice University
Houston, Texas 77251

Coaches of Varsity Teams
Wilson, Willis (Head), 1992–93
Pierce, Ricky, 1980–82

All-American
Pierce, Ricky, 1982

Baylor University
Waco, Texas 76706

Coaches of Varsity Teams

Thomas, Roy (Assistant), 1976–80
Gentry, Alvin (Assistant), 1980–81
Proctor, Joe (Assistant), 1981–90

All Southwest Conference

Bowman, Tommy, 1968–69
Chatmon, William, 1970–71
Johnson, Vinnie, 1978–79
Teagle, Terry, 1980–82
Middleton, Darryl, 1987–88
Sublett, Willie, 1992

Women's Basketball
Stinnett, Maggie, 1989, 1991

All-American

Johnson, Vinnie, 1978

Women's Basketball
Polk, Debbie, 1981

Texas Tech University
Lubbock, Texas 79409

All Southwest Conference

Knolle, Gene, 1970–71
Lowery, Greg, 1972
Richardson, Ron, 1973
Bullock, Rick, 1974–76
Johnson, William, 1975
Russell, Michael, 1977–78
Flemons, Will, 1992, 93

Women's Basketball
Swoopes, Sherryl, 1992–93

All-American

Women's Basketball
Swoopes, Sherryl, 1992–93

Texas A&M University
College Station, Texas 77843-1228

All Southwest Conference

Davis, Barry, 1975
Parker, Sonny, 1975–76
Wright, Rynn, 1980
Edwards, David, 1992–93

Southern Methodist University
Dallas, Texas 75275

Coaches of Varsity Teams
Shumate, John (Head), 1988–93

All Southwest Conference

Triplett, Ruben, 1972
Hervey, Sam, 1973
Terrell, Ira, 1973–74, 1976
Wright, Carl, 1984
McKinney, Carlton, 1987

University of Texas at Austin
Austin, Texas 78713–7389

Coaches of Varsity Teams

Women's Basketball
Page, Rod (Head), 1973–76

All Southwest Conference
Robinson, Larry, 1972–74
Baxter, Ron, 1978–80
Moore, John, 1979
Thompson, LaSalle, 1981–82
Mays, Travis, 1988, 1990
Wright, Joey, 1991
Cambridge, Dexter, 1992
Rencher, Terrence, 1992–93

Women's Basketball
Mackey, Terri, 1983
Whaley, Esoleta, 1983
Smith, Annette,[2] 1983–84
Harris, Fran, 1984
Davis, Clarissa, 1986–87
Henderson, Cinietra, 1991

All-American

Women's Basketball

Mackey, Terri, 1982–83
Smith, Annette, 1983–84
Harris, Fran, 1984
Davis, Clarissa, 1986–87, 1989

University of Houston, University Park, Houston, Texas 77004

Coaches of Varsity Teams

Women's Basketball

Kenlaw, Jessie (Head), 1990–93

All Southwest Conference

Birdsong, Otis, 1976–77
Williams, Rob, 1980–82
Drexler, Clyde, 1983
Young, Michael, 1983–84
Franklin, Alvin, 1984–85
Winslow, Rick, 1987
Anderson, Greg, 1986–87
Upchurch, Craig, 1991–92

Women's Basketball

Watkins, Sonya, 1986

All-American

Hayes, Elvin, 1966–68
Taylor, Ollie, 1970
Chaney, Don, 1970
Davis, Dwight, 1972
Birdsong, Otis, 1977
Williams, Rob, 1982

Other Outstanding Athletes

Dunbar, Louis
Rose, Cecile
Micheaux, Larry

Southwest Conference Tournament Most Valuable Player of the Year

Year • Player • College • Position

1976 • Rick Bullock • Texas Tech University • F
1977 • Ron Brewer • University of Arkansas • G
1978 • Michael Shultz • University of Houston • F
1979 • Sidney Moncrief • University of Arkansas • G/F
1980 • David Britton • Texas A&M University • G
1981 • Rob Williams • University of Houston • G
1982 • Alvin Robertson • University of Arkansas • G
1983 • Michael Young • University of Houston • G/F
1986 • Tony Benford • Texas Tech University • G
1987 • Winston Crite • Texas A&M University • F
1988 • Michael Williams • Baylor University • G
1989 • Lenzie Howell • University of Arkansas • F
1990 • Todd Day • University of Arkansas • G
1991 • Oliver Miller • University of Arkansas • C
1992 • Dexter Cambridge • University of Texas • F

Southwest Conference Player of the Year

Year • Player • College • Position

1983 • Annette Smith • University of Texas • G
1984 • Annette Smith • University of Texas • G
1985 • Fran Harris • University of Texas • G
1986 • Sonya Watkins • University of Houston • F
1989 • Clarissa Davis • University of Texas • G
1990 • Delmonica DeHorney • University of Arkansas • G/F
1991 • Delmonica DeHorney • University of Arkansas • G/F
1993 • Sherryl Swoopes • Texas Tech. University • G

Southwest Conference Athlete of the Year (Male and Female)

Year • Player • College • Sport

1989 • Clarissa Davis • University of Texas • Women's Basketball
1990 • Delmonica DeHorney • University of Arkansas • Women's Basketball

ATLANTIC-TEN CONFERENCE

1. West Virginia University
2. St. Bonaventure University
3. Temple University
4. Duquesne University
5. Rutgers University

6. University of Massachusetts
7. University of Rhode Island
8. St. Joseph's University
9. George Washington University

West Virginia University
Morgantown, West Virginia 26507

Coaches of Varsity Teams

Robinson, Jackie Joe (Assistant)
Nance, Stanford (Assistant), 1989–93

All Southern Conference

Williams, Ron,[1] 1966–68

All Atlantic-Ten Conference

Robertson, Anthony, 1977
Robinson, Maurice, 1977–78
Moore, Lowes, 1978–80
Todd, Russell, 1981–83
Jones, Greg,[3] 1981–83
Rowe, Lester, 1984–85
Prue, Darryl, 1988
Shaw, Tyrone, 1988
Brooks, Chris, 1989, 1991
Boyd, Mike, 1992

All-American

Williams, Ron, 1968
Jones, Greg,[3] 1983

West Virginia University's Hall of Fame

Williams, Ron

Other Outstanding Athletes

Robinson, Will
Prue, Darryl

[1] Williams, Ron—1968 Southern Conference Athlete of the Year; 1968 Southern
   Conference Player of the Year
[2] Jones, Greg—1982 Atlantic-Ten Conference Player of the Year; 1983 Atlantic-
   Ten Conference Co-Player of the Year; Honorable Mention

St. Bonaventure University
St. Bonaventure, N.Y. 14778

All Atlantic-Ten Conference

Belcher, Earl,[1] 1980–81
Jones, Mark, 1982–83
Brower, Jason, 1992

All-American

Stith, Tom, 1961
Lanier, Robert, 1969–70
Sanders, Greg, 1978
Belcher, Earl, 1981

Other Outstanding Athletes

Crawford, Fred[2]
Gantt, Matt
Stith, Tom
Hagan, Glenn[3]
Harrod, Delmar
Lanier, Jr., Robert

[1] Belcher, Earl—Honorable Mention
[2] Crawford, Fred—sixth all-time leading scorer in Saint Bonaventure
   University's history
[3] Hagan, Glenn—all-time assist leader in Saint Bonaventure University's history

Temple University
Philadelphia, Pennsylvania 19122

Coaches of Varsity Teams

Chaney, John,[1] (Head), 1983–93

Women's Basketball

Curtis, Charlene (Head), 1991–93

All Atlantic-Ten Conference

Stansbury, Terence,[2] 1983–84
Hall, Granger,[3] 1984–85
Rayne, Charles, 1985
Blackwell, Nate,[4] 1986–87
Evans, Howard, 1988
Macon, Mark, 1989–91
Causwell, Duane, 1989
Kilgore, Mik, 1991–92
McKie, Aaron, 1993

All-American

Lear, Hal, 1956
Rodgers, Guy,[5] 1957–58
Hall, Granger, 1982, 1984–85
Stansbury, Terence, 1984
Rayne, Charles,[6] 1985
Macon, Mark, 1991

Other Outstanding Athletes

Women's Basketball

Perry, Sonya

Temple University's Hall of Fame

Lear, Hal[7]
Rodgers, Guy
Williams, Jim[8]
Baum, John[9]
Brookins, Clarence
Johnson, Ollie[10]

[1] Chaney, John—1985 Atlantic-Ten Conference Coach of the Year
[2] Stansbury, Terence—1983 Robert Geasey Memorial Trophy recipient (Big-Five Most Valuable Player); 1984 Atlantic-Ten Conference Player of the Year
[3] Hall, Granger—1985 Atlantic-Ten Conference Player of the Year; Honorable Mention
[4] Blackwell, Nate—1987 Atlantic-Ten Conference Player of the Year
[5] Rodgers, Guy—1956–58 Robert Geasey Memorial Trophy recipient (Big-Five Most Valuable Player); Big-Five Hall of Fame
[6] Rayne, Charles—Honorable Mention
[7] Lear, Hal—Big-Five Hall of Fame
[8] Williams, Jim—Big-Five Hall of Fame
[9] Baum, John—Big-Five Hall of Fame
[10] Johnson, Ollie—Big-Five Hall of Fame

Duquesne University
Pittsburgh, Pennsylvania 15282

Coaches of Varsity Teams

Harris, Larry, 1990–93

All Atlantic-Ten Conference

Nixon, Norm, 1977
Arnold, Doug, 1980
Flenory, B.B., 1980
Moore, John, 1981
Dixon, Ron, 1981
Atkins, Bruce,[1] 1981–82
Sellers, Emmett, 1984
Alston, Derrick, 1992

All-American

Cooper, Charles, 1950
Ricketts, Richard, 1955
Green, Sihugo, 1955–56

Duquesne University's Hall of Fame

Cooper, Charles
Ricketts, Richard
Green, Sihugo
Somerset, Willie
Nixon, Norm
Ricketts, Dave

Other Outstanding Athletes

Johnson, Fletcher[2]
Gilbert, Mark
Hargrove, James
Whitehead, Efrem

[1] Atkins, Bruce—1979 Atlantic-Ten Conference Rookie of the Year
[2] Johnson, Fletcher—sixth man on the 1952–54 basketball team

Rutgers University
New Brunswick, New Jersey 08903

Coaches of Varsity Teams

Littlepage, Craig (Head), 1985–88
Jordan, Ed (Assistant), 1991–93
Baker, Joseph (Assistant), 1976–79

Perry, Art (Assistant), 1973–76, 1978–88
Nance, Stanford (Assistant), 1978–79
Sellers, Phil (Assistant), 1980–88

All Atlantic-Ten Conference

Jordan, Ed, 1977
Bailey, James,[1] 1977–79
Troy, Kelvin, 1980–81
Hinson, Roy, 1982–83
Battle, John, 1984–85
Savage, Tom, 1989
Hughes, Keith, 1990–91
Duncan, Earl, 1990–91
Worthy, Steve, 1992

All-American

Sellers, Phil, 1975–76
Dabney, Michael,[2] 1976
Copeland, Hollis,[3] 1977
Jordan, Ed,[4] 1977
Bailey, James, 1978
Hinson, Roy,[5] 1983
Battle, John,[6] 1984–85

Women's Basketball
Lawrence, Lorrie,[11] 1982

Other Outstanding Athletes

Armstead, Eugene
Roundtree, Vinnie
Cason, Les
Anderson, Abdul
Black, Kevin
Tillman, Clarence

[1] Bailey, James—1978 and 1979 Atlantic-Ten Conference Player of the Year;
member of the Eastern College Athletic Conference 1970–80 All Decade
Basketball Team
[2] Dabney, Michael—Honorable Mention
[3] Copeland, Hollis—Honorable Mention
[4] Jordan, Ed—Honorable Mention
[5] Hinson, Roy—Honorable Mention
[6] Battle, John—Honorable Mention

University of Massachusetts
Amherst, Massachusetts 01003

Coaches of Varsity Teams

Wilson, Ray (Assistant)

Smith, Carl (Assistant), 1991–93

All Atlantic-Ten Conference

Pyatt, Michael, 1978
Green, Edwin, 1984
Neysmith, Horace, 1985
Sutton, Lorenzo, 1986–88
McCoy, Jim, 1989–92
Herndon, William, 1990
Williams, Harper, 1991–93
Barbee, Tony, 1993
Roe, Louis, 1993

All-American

Erving, Julius,[1] 1970–71
Skinner, Al,[2] 1974

Other Outstanding Athletes

Eldridge, Alexander
Claiborne, Derrick
Russell, Donald
Green, Edwin
Young, Ron
Smith, Carl
Brown, Anton
Bright, Donta
Williams, Michael
Dingle, Dana

[1] Erving, Julius—member of the 1970–80 Eastern College Athletic Conference
All Decade Basketball Team
[2] Skinner, Al—Honorable Mention

University of Rhode Island
Kingston, Rhode Island 02881

Coaches of Varsity Teams

English, Claude (Head), 1981–88
Skinner, Al (Head), 1988–93
   (Assistant), 1984–88

All Yankee Conference

Lee, Charles, 1962
Carey, Henry, 1966
Stephenson, Art, 1967–68
Johnson, Larry, 1967–68
English, Claude, 1969–70

Adger, Nate, 1971
Tolliver, Dwight, 1971
Hickson, Phil, 1972
Williams, Sylvester "Sly," 1978–79

All Atlantic-Ten Conference

Wright, Jimmy, 1981
Owens, Horace "Pappy," 1981–83
Upshaw, Mark, 1982
Owens, Carlton, 1987–88
Leslie, Eric, 1989–90
Green, Kenny, 1990

Women's Basketball
Washington, Michelle, 1984

All-American

Owens, Horace "Pappy,"[1] 1973
Williams, Sylvester "Sly," 1978–79

Other Outstanding Athletes

Women's Basketball
Games, Monica

University of Rhode Island's Hall of Fame

Adams, James

[1] Owens, Horace "Pappy"—Honorable Mention

St. Joseph's University
Philadelphia, Pennsylvania 19131

All East Coast Conference

Black, Norman, 1976–79
Williams, Marcellus "Boo," 1978–81
Griffin, Luke, 1980
Warrick, Bryan, 1981–82
Clark, Jeffrey A.,[1] 1982
Costner, Anthony, 1982

All Atlantic-Ten Conference

Costner, Anthony, 1983–84
Martin, Maurice,[2] 1984–85
Blake, Rodney, 1987
Blunt, Bernard, 1991–92

All-American

Anderson, Clifford T.,[3] 1967
Bantom, Michael,[4] 1973

Other Outstanding Athletes

McFarlan, Alonzo
Benson, Edward L.
Grundy, Alfred L.
Mitchell, Dr., Eric I.

[1] Clark, Jeffrey A.—1982 All Big-Five; 1982 Robert Geasey Memorial Trophy winner (Big-Five Most Valuable Player)
[2] Martin, Maurice—1986 Atlantic-Ten Conference Player of the Year
[3] Anderson, Clifford, T.—1965–67 All Big-Five; 1967 Robert Geasey Memorial Trophy winner (Big-Five Most Valuable Player)
[4] Bantom, Michael—member of the 1972 United States Olympic Basketball Team; 1972–73 All Big-Five

George Washington University
Washington, D.C. 20052

Coaches of Varsity Teams

Jarvis, Michael (Head), 1990–93
Meyers, Ed (Assistant), 1990–93

All Atlantic-Ten Conference

Brown, Michael, 1982–85
Holland, Sonni, 1991–93

Other Outstanding Athletes

Webster, Darryl
Pearsall, Alvin, 1991)93

Atlantic-Ten Conference Player of the Year Award (Conference was called Eastern Athletic Association before 1982–83 season)

Year • Player • College • Position

1977–78 • James Bailey • Rutgers University • C
1978–79 • James Bailey • Rutgers University • C
1979–80 • Earl Belcher • St. Bonaventure University • F
1980–81 • Earl Belcher • St. Bonaventure University • F
1981–82 • Greg Jones • West Virginia University • G
1982–83 • Greg Jones • West Virginia University • G
         • Roy Hinson • Rutgers University • C
1983–84 • Terence Stansbury • Temple University • G
1984–85 • Granger Hall • Temple University • F

1985–86 • Maurice Martin • St. Joseph's University • G
1986–87 • Nate Blackwell • Temple University • G
1987–88 • Tim Perry • Temple University • F
1988–89 • Mark Macon • Temple University • G
1989–90 • Kenny Green • University of Rhode Island • F
1990–91 • Keith Hughes • Rutgers University • F
1991–92 • Harper Williams • University of Massachusetts • C/F

Atlantic-Ten Conference Coach of the Year

Year • Coach • College

1980–81 • Claude English (Co-Winner) • University of Rhode
Island
1983–84 • John Chaney • Temple University
1984–85 • John Chaney • Temple University
1986–87 • John Chaney (Co-Winner) • Temple University
1987–88 • John Chaney • Temple University
1991–92 • Al Skinner • University of Rhode Island

INDEPENDENTS

1. Case Western Reserve University

2. University of Notre Dame

University of Notre Dame
Notre Dame, Indiana 46556

Coaches of Varsity Teams

Brokaw, Gary (Assistant), 1981–86

All-American

Hawkins, Tom, 1958–59
Carr, Austin,[1] 1970–71
Jones, Collis, 1971
Shumate, John, 1973–74
Dantley, Adrian,[2] 1975–76
Woolridge, Orlando,[3] 1982
Rivers, David,[4] 1985–86

Other Outstanding Athletes

Catlett, Sid
Brokaw, Gary
Clay, Dwight
Martin, Ray
Ellis, LaPhonso
Bennett, Elmer
Williams, Monte
Russell, Malik
Royal, Donald

[1] Carr, Austin—1971 United Press International Player of the Year; 1971 Associated Press Player of the Year
[2] Dantley, Adrian—1976 United States Basketball Writers Association Player of the Year; member of the 1976 United States Olympic Basketball Team
[3] Woolridge, Orlando—Honorable Mention
[4] Rivers, David—Honorable Mention

SOUTHERN INTERCOLLEGIATE
ATHLETIC CONFERENCE*

1. Savannah State College
2. Fort Valley State College
3. Morris Brown College
4. Alabama A&M University

5. Clark College
6. Morehouse College
7. Fisk University

* The SIAC office did not provide information for the update of this edition.

Savannah State College
Savannah, Georgia 31404

Coaches of Varsity Teams

Myles, John,[1] 1946–47
Wright, Theodore,[2] 1947–62
Frazier, Albert, 1962–64
Richardson, Leo, 1964–71
Backus, Michael, 1971–76
Ellington, Russell, 1976–93

Women's Basketball

Webb, Ella, 1946–51
Fisher, Ella W., 1951–57
Westley, Jimmy, 1974–78
Trudell, Saralyn, 1978–84

All Southeastern Athletic Conference

Jackson, Alfred, 1950–52
Brock, Otis, 1954–56
Lewis, Robert, 1954–56
Wright, Noel, 1954–56
Mathis, Johnny, 1963–64
Westley, Jimmy, 1967
Crump, Carl, 1967–68
Nichols, Alan, 1968
White, Vincent,[3] 1968–69

All Southeastern Intercollegiate Athletic Conference

Jordan, Michael, 1971
White, Vincent, 1971
Ogden, Turner, 1975
Kenlaw, Sam, 1975
Grant, Sherman, 1977
Hubbard, Harold,[4] 1979–80
Riley, Ted[5]
Stocks, Michael, 1982

All Southeastern Athletic Conference

Women's Basketball

Girvin, Ida[6]
Gross, Eunice
Keith, Gwendolyn[7]
Moore, Rosa Lee
Bryant, Clara

Johnson, Luella
Bonner, Susie

[1] Myles, John—he was a Student Player and Head Coach
[2] Wright, Theodore—1960 Southeastern Athletic Conference Coach of the Year
[3] White, Vincent—1969 Most Valuable Player of the South Eastern Athletic Conference Tournament; 1970 Most Valuable Player of the Southern Intercollegiate Athletic Conference Tournament
[4] Hubbard, Harold—1979 Southern Intercollegiate Athletic Conference Most Valuable Player
[5] Riley, Ted—1980 Southern Intercollegiate Athletic Conference Tournament Most Valuable Player
[6] Girvin, Ida—1948 South Eastern Athletic Conference Tournament Most Valuable Player
[7] Keith, Gwendolyn—1955 Southeastern Athletic Conference Tournament Most Valuable Player (Co-Most Valuable Player of the League in 1956)

Clark College
Atlanta, Georgia 30314

All Southern Intercollegiate Athletic Conference

Turmon, Roman, 1951–52, 1954
Bunn, Junius, 1954
Hubbard, Harold, 1954
Threatt, Reginald, 1954
Jones, Edwin, 1958
Clark, Henry, 1961
Smith, Charles, 1961–63
Simpson, Walter, 1962–63
Dickerson, Lowell, 1963
Norton, Theodis, 1964
Brown, Sam, 1965
Jackson, Ron, 1965–66
Walls, James, 1966–67
Epps, III, L.S., 1967
Floyd, Anthony, 1967
Mincey, Elder, 1982–83
Carter, Steven, 1983
Hunter, Marvin, 1983
Duffy, Alvin, 1984
Lee, Ernest, 1984, 1986–87

All-American (Division II)

Lee, Ernest, 1986–87

Fisk University
Nashville, Tennessee 37203

All Southern Intercollegiate Athletic Conference
Work, Fred, 1954–56
Drew, Weldon, 1955
Jobe, Ben, 1955–56
Gilliam, Robert, 1958–59
McAdoo, James, 1959
Washington, Alton, 1959–61
Glover, Renaldo, 1962–63, 1965
Lawson, Lamonte, 1963
Richardson, Lamar, 1965

Fort Valley State College
Fort Valley, Georgia 31030

Coaches of Varsity Teams
Craig, Richard, 1946–54
Hawkins, James E., 1962–63
Lomax, Leon J., 1963–69
Clemons, William, 1972–75
White, Calvin, 1975–79
Mells, Ronald, 1980–82
Patrick, James, 1982–93

Women's Basketball
Love, Flossie, 1960–72
Brown, Jessie, 1972–83
Bartley, Lonnie, 1984–93

All Southern Intercollegiate Athletic Conference
Wright, Rayfield, 1967

All-American (Black College)
Gilmore, Walter, 1969

Morris Brown College
Atlanta, Georgia 30314

All Southern Intercollegiate Athletic Conference
Benson, Ted, 1951
Andrews, James, 1951
Hannol, G.B., 1951
Glover, Frank, 1951–52
Williams, George, 1957
Glover, Howard, 1957
Bell, Curtis, 1957–59
Ross, Erwin, 1959–60
Scott, James, 1960

Alabama A&M University
Normal, Alabama 35762

All Southern Intercollegiate Athletic Conference
Phillips, Ed, 1968
Goston, John, 1975
Williams, Joe, 1975
Davis, Homer, 1975–77
Edwards, Jackie, 1975–77
Hill, Cornelius, 1979
Randle, Terry, 1980
Dixon, Dan, 1982–83
Hunter, Marvin, 1983
Thomas, Leafus, 1984
Reedus, Don, 1984

METRO CONFERENCE

1. University of Louisville
2. University of Southern Mississippi
3. Tulane University
4. Virginia Polytechnic Institute

University of Louisville
Louisville, Kentucky 40292

Coaches of Varsity Teams
Houston, Wade, (Assistant)
McCray, Carlton (Assistant), 1990–93

All Missouri Valley Conference
Unseld, Westley, 1966–68
Beard, Alfred "Butch," 1967–69
Price, Jim, 1971–72
Murphy, Allen, 1973–75
Bridgeman, Ulysses "Junior,"[3] 1973–75

All Metro Conference

Cox, Westley, 1977
Williams, Larry, 1977–79
Wilson, Rick,[3] 1978
Griffith, Darrell,[4] 1978–80
Turner, Robert, 1979
Smith, Derek,[5] 1981
McCray, Rodney,[6] 1981–83
Eaves, Jerry, 1982
Gordon, Lancaster, 1983–84
Wagner, Milt, 1983–84, 1986
Jones, Charles, 1984
Ellison, Pervis, 1988–89
Smith, LaBradford, 1990–91
Rozier, Clifford, 1993
Morton, Dwayne, 1993

All-American

Unseld, Westley, 1967–68
Murphy, Allen,[6] 1975
Bridgeman, Ulysses "Junior," 1975
Griffith, Darrell, 1980
Ellison, Pervis,[7] 1989

Other Outstanding Athletes

Bacon, Henry
Bond, Philip
Thomas, Ron
Branch, Tony
Gallon, Rick
Thompson, Billy
McCray, Scooter
Forrest, Manuel
Kimbro, Tony
Sullivan, Everick
Holden, Cornelius
Brewer, James
LeGree, Keith

[1] Bridgeman, Ulysses "Junior"—1974 and 1975 Missouri Valley Conference Player of the Year; Honorable Mention
[2] Wilson, Rick—1978 Metro Conference Co-Player of the Year
[3] Griffith, Darrell—1980 Metro Conference Player of the Year
[4] Smith, Derek—1981 Metro Conference Co-Player of the Year
[5] McCray, Rodney—1983 Metro Conference Player of the Year; member of the 1980 United States Olympic Basketball Team
[6] Murphy, Allen—Honorable Mention
[7] Ellison, Pervis—1986 NCAA Final Four Tournament Most Valuable Player; 1986 Metro Conference Freshman of the Year

University of Southern Mississippi
Hattiesburg, Mississippi 39406-3161

Coaches of Varsity Teams

Women's Basketball
Jones, Shirley (Assistant), 1983–84
Moore, Ralph (Assistant), 1984

All South Independent

Prince, John, 1977
Dawson, Joe, 1980–82

All Metro Conference

Green, Curtis, 1982
Siler, Ken, 1986–87
Weatherspoon, Clarence, 1991–92

All-American

Prince, John, 1977
Dawson, Joe, 1981–82

Other Outstanding Athletes

Whisby, Glen

Women's Basketball
Jones, Shirley
Lyons, Diane
Smith, Rose
Backstrom, Diane
Smith, Wilhelmina
Winston, Bridget

Tulane University
New Orleans, Louisiana 70118

Coaches of Varsity Teams

Lewis, James (Assistant), 1976–81
Saulny, Kirk (Assistant), 1981–93
Clark, Perry (Head), 1990–93

All Metro Conference

Thompson, Paul, 1980–81, 1983
Williams, John,[1] 1982–84
Reed, Anthony, 1992–93
Williams, Pointer, 1992–93

Other Outstanding Athletes

Lewis, Kim

[1] Williams, John—1984 Metro Conference Player of the Year

Virginia Polytechnic Institute
Blacksburg, Virginia 24061

Coaches of Varsity Teams

Allen, Frank (Assistant), 1975–92

All Metro Conference

Robinson, Wayne, 1979–80
Solomon, Dale,[1] 1979–82
Curry, Dell,[2] 1984–86

Young, Perry, 1985
Coles, Vernell "Bimbo," 1988–90

All-American

Curry, Dell, 1986

Other Outstanding Athletes

Pierre, Russell
Davis, Russell
Thorpe, Duke
Ashfold, Marshall
Hanson, Les
Lancaster, Wally

[1] Solomon, Dale—1979 Metro Conference Freshman of the [2] Curry, Dell—1986
Metro Conference Player of the Year

GREAT MIDWEST CONFERENCE

1. University of Cincinnati
2. Memphis State University
3. University of Alabama, Birmingham
4. Marquette University
5. University of Saint Louis
6. DePaul University

University of Cincinnati
Cincinnati, Ohio 45221-0021

Athletic Directors

Yates, Tony[1] (Associate Athletic Director), 1985–89
Purnell, Garnett (Assistant Athletic Director, Academic
   Counseling and Development), 1985

Coaches of Varsity Teams

Yates, Tony (Head), 1984–89
Turner, Ken (Assistant), 1984–89

All Missouri Valley Conference

Robertson, Oscar, 1959–60
Hogue, Paul, 1960–62
Thacker, Tom, 1961–63
Yates, Tony, 1963
Wilson, George, 1963–64
Roberson, Rick, 1967–68
Ard, Jim,[2] 1968–70

All Metro Conference

Miller, Robert, 1977–78
Lee, Eddie, 1979–80
Jones, Dwight, 1982–83
McMillan, Derrick, 1985
McClendon, Roger, 1986–87

All Great Midwest Conference

Jones, Herb, 1992
Buford, Anthony, 1992
Van Exel, Nick, 1993
Blount, Cory, 1993

All-American

Robertson, Oscar,[3] 1958–60
Hogue, Paul,[4] 1962
Thacker, Tom, 1963
Yates, Tony, 1963
Wilson, George,[5] 1963
Batts, Lloyd, 1973
Miller, Robert, 1978
McClendon, Roger, 1987
Van Exel, Nick, 1993

[1] Yates, Tony—1985 Metro Conference Coach of the Year
[2] Ard, Jim—1970 Missouri Valley Conference Player of the Year
[3] Robertson, Oscar—1958–60 United Press International College Player of the Year; 1959 and 1960 United States Basketball Writers' Associate College Player of the Year; member of the 1960 United States Olympic Basketball Team
[4] Hogue, Paul—1962 Helms Foundation Player of the Year
[5] Wilson, George—member of the 1964 United States Olympic Basketball Team

Memphis State University
Memphis, Tennessee 38152

Coaches of Varsity Teams

Finch, Larry (Head), 1986–93

All Missouri Valley Conference

Finch, Larry,[1] 1971–73
Robinson, Ron, 1971–73
Kenon, Larry,[2] 1973
Reed, Dexter, 1977
Wright, Alvin, 1978
Bradley, James, 1978–79
Lee, Keith,[3] 1982–84
Parks, Bobby, 1983
Haynes, Phillip, 1984
Bedford, William, 1986

All Great Midwest Conference

Vaughn, David, 1992
Hardaway, Anfernee, 1992–93

All-American

Finch, Larry, 1972–73
Kenon, Larry, 1972–73
Lee, Keith, 1982–84
Hardaway, Anfernee, 1993

Other Outstanding Athletes

Jones, Rich
Douglas, James
Hillard, Marion
Jackson, Otis
Gunn, John[4]
Phillips, Derrick
Turner, Andre
Lee, Rodney
Boyd, Dwight
Askew, Vincent
Perry, Elliott

Women's Basketball

Street, Regina

[1] Finch, Larry—1972 Missouri Valley Conference Player of the Year
[2] Kenon, Larry—1973 Missouri Valley Conference Player of the Year
[3] Lee, Keith—1982 Metro Conference Player of the Year; 1982 Metro Conference Freshman of the Year; 1982 John Gunn Outstanding Player Award recipient (Metro Conference Tournament Most Valuable Player)
[4] Gunn, John—died in 1976 of complications from Stevens-Johnson Syndrome. An award is given in his honor at the Metro Conference Tournament (John Gunn Outstanding Player Award)

University of Alabama, Birmingham
Birmingham, Alabama 35294

Coaches of Varsity Teams

Catlin, Oscar (Assistant)
Prince, John (Assistant)

All Sun Belt Conference

McCord, Keith, 1980
Robinson, Oliver,[1] 1981–82
Gilkes, Caris, 1981–82
Pruitt, Cliff, 1983
Mitchell, Steven, 1984–86
Mincy, Jerome, 1985–86
Rogers, Elbert, 1991

[1] Robinson, Oliver—1982 Sun Belt Conference Player of the Year

Marquette University
Milwaukee, Wisconsin 53233

Coaches of Varsity Teams

Cobb, Ulrich (Assistant), 1979–86
Ellis, Maurice (Assistant), 1992–93

All Great Midwest Conference

Key, Damon, 1992
Miller, Tony, 1993

All-American

Thompson, George, 1969
Meminger, Dean, 1970–71
Chones, Jim, 1972
Lackey, Robert, 1972
Lucas, Maurice, 1974

Ellis, Maurice, 1975–77
Walton, Lloyd, 1975–76
Tatum, Earl, 1976
Lee, Alfred,[1] 1977–78
Whitehead, Jerome, 1978
Worthen, Sam, 1979–80
Rivers, Glen, 1982–83

Other Outstanding Athletes

Washington, Marcus
Toone, Bernard
Lee, Oliver
Wilson, Michael
Downing, Walter

[1] Lee, Alfred—1978 James Naismith Award recipient; 1978 Adolph Rupp Award recipient

St. Louis University
St. Louis, Missouri 63108

Coaches of Varsity Teams

Coleman, Ron, 1977–78

All Missouri Valley Conference

Parks, Richard, 1966
Moore, Eugene, 1966
Wiley, Joe, 1970
Irving, Jim, 1971
Rogers, Harry, 1972–73
Leonard, Jesse, 1973

All Metro Conference

Johnson, Carol, 1977
Henderson, Kelvin, 1979
Burns, David, 1980–81

All Mid-Western Collegiate Conference

Burden, Luther, 1983–85

De Paul University
Chicago, Illinois 60614

All Great Midwest Conference

Booth, David, 1992
Howard, Stephen, 1992
Davis, Terry, 1992

All-American

Aguirre, Mark,[1] 1980–81
Cummings, Terry, 1982

Other Outstanding Athletes

Robinzine, Sr., Bill[2]
Robinzine, Jr., Bill
Garland, Gary
Bradshaw, Clyde
Patterson, Ken
Corbin, Tyrone
Comegys, Dallas
Dillard, Skip
Watkins, Curtis
Bryant, Emmette
Strickland, Rod
Nathan, Howard

[1] Aguirre, Mark—1980 United Press International and Associated Press Player of the Year; 1980 United States Basketball Writers Association Player of the Year; member of the 1980 United States Olympic Basketball Team
[2] Robinzine, Sr., Bill—played guard for DePaul, 1955–56

Great Midwest Conference Player of the Year

Year • Player • College • Position

1992 • Anfernee Hardaway • Memphis State University • G/F

METRO ATLANTIC CONFERENCE

1. Fordham University
2. La Salle University
3. St. Peter's College
4. College of the Holy Cross
5. Iona College

6. Manhattan College
7. Niagara University
8. Canisius College
9. Siena College

Fordham University
Bronx, New York 10458

All Metro Atlantic Athletic Conference

Tongal, Dud, 1982
Bona, Ed, 1982
Maxwell, David, 1982–83
Roberson, David, 1984
Samuels, Steven, 1984–85
McIntosh, Tony, 1984–85

All-American

Yelverton, Charles, 1971
Charles, Ken,[1] 1973
Maxwell, David,[2] 1983

Fordham University's Hall of Fame

Melvin, Robert
Yelverton, Charles
Charles, Ken

[1] Charles, Ken—Honorable Mention
[2] Maxwell, David—Honorable Mention

La Salle University
Philadelphia, Pennsylvania 19141

Coaches of Varsity Teams

Rines, Sam (Assistant, Part-Time), 1979

All East Coast Conference

Taylor, Bill,[1] 1975
Bryant, Joe,[2] 1975
Wise, Charles,[3] 1975–76
Brooks, Michael,[4] 1977–80
Lewis, Ralph,[5] 1983

All Metro Atlantic Athletic Conference

Simmons, Lionel, 1987–90
Overton, Doug, 1989–91
Woods, Randy, 1991–92

All-American

Durrett, Ken,[6] 1970–71
Brooks, Michael, 1979–80
Simmons, Lionel, 1989–90

Other Outstanding Athletes

Lewis, Alonzo[7]
Marshall, Hubie[8]
Williams, Bernie[9]
Moore, Jackie[10]

[1] Taylor, Bill—Big-Five Hall of Fame
[2] Bryant, Joe—Big-Five Hall of Fame
[3] Wise, Charles—1976 Robert Geasey Memorial Trophy recipient (given to the Big-Five Most Valuable Player); Big-Five Hall of Fame
[4] Brooks, Michael—1978–80 East Coast Conference Player of the Year; 1978–80 Robert Geasey Memorial Trophy recipient (given to the Big-Five Most Valuable Player); member of the 1980 United States Olympic Basketball Team; 1980 United States Basketball Writers Association Player of the Year; Member of the 1970–80 Eastern College Athletic Conference All-Decade Team
[5] Lewis, Ralph—1984 Robert Geasey Memorial Trophy recipient (given to the Big-Five Most Valuable Player)
[6] Durrett, Ken—1969–70 Robert Geasey Memorial Trophy co-recipient (given to the Big-Five Most Valuable Player); Robert Geasey Memorial Trophy recipient; Big-Five Hall of Fame
[7] Lewis, Alonzo—Big-Five Hall of Fame
[8] Marshall, Hubie—1966–67 All Big-Five; Big-Five Hall of Fame
[9] Williams, Bernie—1969 All Big-Five; Big-Five Hall of [10] Moore, Jackie—played on the 1952 National Invitational Tournament Championship Team

St. Peter's College
Jersey City, New Jersey 07306

All Metro Atlantic Athletic Conference

Brown, William,[1] 1982
Gibbs, Shelton, 1982–84

Jamison, Phil, 1983
Best, Tom, 1983–84
Hayes, Leonard, 1985
Haynes, Willie, 1987–89
Walker, Jasper, 1991
Walker, Tony, 1991

Women's Basketball
Berry, Amanda,[2] 1983–84

All-American
Webster, Elnardo,[3] 1969

St. Peter's College Hall of Fame
Lurie, Harry
Webster, Elnardo
Slappy, Ken

Other Outstanding Athletes
Anderson, Cliff
Richard, Steven
Brandon, Jim

[1] Brown, William—1982 Metro Atlantic Athletic Conference Player of the Year
[2] Berry, Amanda—1984 Metro Atlantic Athletic Conference Tournament Most Valuable Player
[3] Webster, Elnardo—Helms Foundation

College of the Holy Cross
Worcester, Massachusetts 01610

Coaches of Varsity Teams
Baker, Rodney J. (Assistant), 1978–80

All Metro Atlantic Athletic Conference
Floyd, Ernie,[1] 1984

Other Outstanding Athletes
Grayson, Stanley E.

[1] Floyd, Ernie—1980 Eastern College Athletic Conference Co-Rookie of the Year

Iona College
New Rochelle, New York 10801

Coaches of Varsity Teams
Brokaw, Gary (Head), 1986–90

All Metro Atlantic Athletic Conference
Burtt, Steven,[1] 1982–84
Springer, Gary, 1982–84
Hargraves, Tony, 1984
Grimes, Rory, 1985
Lott, Alvin, 1987
Simmons, Rich, 1988
Green, Sean, 1990–91
Canada, Derrick, 1992

All-American
Burtt, Steven, 1983–84

Other Outstanding Athletes
Simmons, Rich
Hart, Harold, 1990–93

[1] Burtt, Steven—1983 and 1984 Metro Atlantic Conference Player of the Year; Honorable Mention

Manhattan College
Riverdale, New York 10471-4098

Coaches of Varsity Teams
Solomon, Anthony (Assistant), 1992–93

All Metro Atlantic Athletic Conference
Wheeler, Billy, 1987–88
Bullock, Keith, 1991–93

Manhattan College Hall of Fame
Kellogg, Junius, 1950–53

Other Outstanding Athletes
Marsh, Eric, 1975–77
Rock, George, 1987–89
Williams, Russell, 1987–88, 1989–92
Grant, Steven, 1974–77
Lawson, Edward, 1983–88

Niagara University
Niagara University, New York 14109

Coaches of Varsity Teams
Walker, Andy (Assistant), 1984

All Eastern Collegiate Athletic Conference

Murphy, Calvin,[1] 1969–70
Phillips, Michael, 1982
Speaks, James, 1982

Women's Basketball

Williams, Cindy

All-American

Murphy, Calvin, 1969–70

Niagara University's Hall of Fame

Murphy, Calvin
Churchwell, Robert

Other Outstanding Athletes

Fleming, Ed

[1] Murphy, Calvin—1969 Eastern Collegiate Athletic Conference Player of the Year

Canisus College
Buffalo, New York 14208

Coaches of Varsity Teams

Seymore, Phil (Assistant), 1990–93

All North Atlantic Conference

Hall, Ray, 1984–85
Smith, Brian, 1987–88
Bailey, Marvin, 1988

All Metro Atlantic Conference

Wise, Craig, 1992

Other Outstanding Athletes

Fogle, Larry, 1973–75
Seymore, Phil, 1980–82
Becton, Ed, 1980–84
Brown, Mike, 1986–88
Hall, Ray, 1981–85

Siena College
Loudonville, New York 12211

Coaches of Varsity Teams

Beyer, Robert (Assistant), 1989–93

All North Atlantic Conference

Banks, Eric, 1986
Brown, Marc, 1988–89
Robinson, Jeffery, 1989

All Metro Atlantic Athletic Conference

Brown, Marc, 1990–91

All-American

Harrell, William "Billy," 1952

Metro Atlantic Athletic Conference Player of the Year Award

Year • Player • College • Position

1981–82 • William Brown • St. Peter's College • G
1982–83 • Steve Burtt • Iona College • G
1983–84 • Steve Burtt • Iona College • G
1985–86 • Tony George • Fairfield University • G
1987–88 • Lionel Simmons • LaSalle University • G/F
1988–89 • Lionel Simmons • LaSalle University • G/F
1989–90 • Lionel Simmons • LaSalle University • G/F
1990–91 • Marc Brown • Siena College • G
1991–92 • Randy Woods • LaSalle University • G

Metro Atlantic Conference Tournament Most Valuable Player Award

Year • Player • College • Position

1981–82 • Rory Grimes • Iona College • G
1983–84 • Steve Burtt • Iona College • G
1984–85 • Tony Hargraves • Iona College • G
1988–89 • Lionel Simmons • LaSalle University • G/F
1989–90 • Lionel Simmons • LaSalle University • G/F
1990–91 • Marvin Andrews • St. Peter's College • G
1991–92 • Randy Woods • LaSalle University • G

BIG SKY CONFERENCE

1. Idaho State University
2. Northern Arizona University
3. Eastern Washington University

Idaho State University
Pocatello, Idaho 83209

Coaches of Varsity Teams

Williams, Herb (Head), 1990–93

All Rocky Mountain Conference

Crump, Art, 1964
Frazier, Len "Buddy," 1966
Boone, Ron, 1967–68
Parks, Charles, 1967–68
Wilson, Ed, 1968
Simmons, O'Neal, 1969–70
Humes, Willie, 1970–71
Hicks, Edison, 1972–73
Griffin, Greg, 1976–77
Thompson, Ed, 1977
Butler, Lawrence, 1978–79
Fleury, Jackie, 1983
Williams, Michael, 1984

Northern Arizona University
Flagstaff, Arizona 86011

Coaches of Varsity Teams

Merritt, Harold (Head), 1990–93

All Big Sky Conference

Mannon, Walter, 1971–72
Payne, Nate, 1974–75
Allen, David, 1984

All-American

Nash, Willie, 1966
Mannon, Walt,[1] 1972

[1] Mannon, Walt—Honorable Mention

Eastern Washington University
Cheney, Washington 99004

Coaches of Varsity Teams

Wade, John (Head), 1990–93

OHIO VALLEY CONFERENCE

1. Eastern Kentucky University
2. Tennessee Technological University
3. Austin Peay State University
4. Middle Tennessee State University
5. Youngstown State University
6. Murray State University
7. Tennessee State University
8. Morehead State University

Eastern Kentucky University
Richmond, Kentucky 40475

Coaches of Varsity Teams

Washington, Robert, 1967–69
Smith, Garfield, 1968
Woods, Willie, 1970
Mitchell, Charles, 1972–73

Brown, Carl, 1974–76
Joiner, Lovell, 1978
Elliott, Ken, 1979
Tillman, James,[1] 1979–80
Jones, Bruce, 1979–80
Baker, Tom, 1981

[1] Tillman, James—1980 Ohio Valley Conference Player of the Year

Tennessee Technological University
Cookeville, Tennessee 38505

Coaches of Varsity Teams

Taylor, Steven (Assistant)

All Ohio Valley Conference

Jordan, Henry, 1966
Pack, Wayne, 1971–73
Lewis, Al, 1972
Stone, Rich, 1972
Jones, Frank, 1974–76
Porter, Robert, 1978
Troupe, Brian, 1979
Taylor, Steven, 1983
Kite, Stephen, 1984–86
Wise, Earl, 1990
Usher, Van, 1992

Austin Peay State University
Clarksville, Tennessee 37040

Coaches of Varsity Teams

Jackson, Howard (Head), 1984–86

All Ohio Valley Conference

Jackson, Howard, 1972–73
Williams, James,[1] 1973–74
Odums, Dan, 1974
Howard, Percy, 1975
Howard, Otis, 1976–78
Sanders, Roosevelt, 1980
Manning, Lenny, 1984
Mitchell, Lawrence, 1987

All-American

Williams, James, 1974

[1] Williams, James—1974 Ohio Valley Conference Player of the Year

Middle Tennessee State University
Murfreesboro, Tennessee 37132

Coaches of Varsity Teams

Crawford, Coleman (Assistant), 1982–84
Radford, Ralph, (Assistant), 1984–89

All Ohio Valley Conference

Brown, Willie, 1969–69
Riley, Ken, 1970–71
Sykes, Herman, 1972
Powell, James, 1973–74
Peeler, Steven, 1975
Sorrell, George,[1] 1975
Joyner, Gregory, 1977–79
Taylor, Claude, 1978
Coleman, Leroy, 1980
Beck, Jerry,[2] 1980–82
Washington, Duane, 1987
Kidd, Warren, 1991

Other Outstanding Athletes

Harris, Christopher

[1] Sorrell, George—1975 Ohio Valley Conference Player of the Year
[2] Beck, Jerry—1981–82 Ohio Valley Conference Player of the Year

Youngstown State University
Youngstown, Ohio 44555

All-American

Covington, Jeff, 1977–78

Murray State University
Murray, Kentucky 42071

All Ohio Valley Conference

Sleets, Lamont, 1984
Martin, Jeff, 1987–89
Jones, Ronald "Popeye", 1990–92
Allen, Frank, 1992–93

Tennessee State University
Nashville, Tennessee 37203

Coaches of Varsity Teams

Kean, Henry A., 1945–48
Matthews, Shelton, 1949
Kean, Henry A., 1950
Cash, Clarence, 1951–54
McLendon, John B.,[1] 1954–59
Hunter, Harold, 1959–68

Martin, Ed,[2] 1968–85
Meyers, Ed, 1985–86
Reid, Larry, 1986–89
Abernathy, Ron, 1989–91
Allen, Frank, 1991–93

Women's Basketball
Lawrence, Teresa Phillips, 1989–93

All Midwestern Conference

Wilson, Clarence, 1946–47, 1949
Taylor, Nathaniel, 1946–49
Grider, Joshua, 1947–49
Lewis, Frank, 1949
Brown, Sage, 1950
Gibson, Tommy, 1950
Landry, John, 1951
Reed, Willie, 1951–53
Nesbit, Remus, 1954
Thomas, Willis, 1954
McNeal, Vernon, 1955
Kean, Henry A., Jr., 1955
Jackson, Ben, 1955–56
Barnett, Richard, 1956–59
Hamilton, Ronald, 1957–58
Barnhill, John, 1958–59
Werts, Gene, 1960
Meriwether, Porter, 1961
Johnson, Rossie, 1961
McIntyre, Larry, 1962

All Ohio Valley Conference

Mason, Anthony, 1988

All-American (Black College)

Jackson, Ben, NAIA, 1955
Satterwhite, James, NAIA, 1957
Barnhill, John, NAIA, 1957–59
Barnett, Richard, NAIA, NCAA Little All-American, Associated
  Press, 1957–59
Werts, Gene, NAIA, 1960
Johnson, Rossie, NAIA, 1960
Merriwether, Porter, NAIA, United Press International, 1960–61
McClain, Ted, Division II, 1971
Neal, Lloyd, Division II, 1972
Robinson, Leonard, Division II, 1974

Tennessee State University's Hall of Fame

Coaches
McClendon, John B.

Players
Grider, Joshua
Buie, Boyd
Wilson, Clarence
Barnhill, John
Barnett, Richard
McClain, Theodore
Neal, Lloyd
Merriweather, Porter

The 1958–59 Men's Basketball Team; National NAIA Champions

McClendon, John B. (Head Coach)
Mack, Richard (Assistant)
Hunter, Harold (Assistant)
Clark, Robert
Barnhill, John
Johnson, Rossie
Werts, Gene
Satterwhite, James
Davis, Melvin
Barnett, Richard
Merriweather, Porter
Warley, Ben
Brown, Hillary

Tennessee State University Alumni in the National Basketball Association

Barnett, Richard, Syracuse Nationals, 1959–61;
  Los Angeles Lakers, 1962–64;
  New York Knicks, 1965–74
Meriwether, Porter, Syracuse Nationals, 1962–63
Walker, Dwight, Atlanta Hawks, 1968–69;
  A.B.A. Denver Nuggets, 1969–72
Buckhalter, Joe, Cincinnati Royals, 1961–63
Warley, Ben, Syracuse Nationals, 1962–63;
  A.B.A. Denver Nuggets, 1969–70
Robinson, Leonard, Washington Bullets, 1974–77;
  Phoenix Suns, 1978–82;
  New York Knickerbockers, 1982–85
Barnhill, John, Washington Bullets, 1966–69;
  A.B.A. Indiana Pacers, 1969–72;
  San Diego Rockets, 1967–58

McClain, Ted, A.B.A. New York Nets, 1975–76;
   Philadelphia 76ers, 1977–78;
   Buffalo Braves, 1977–78
A.B.A., American Basketball Association
Daniel, 1954
Howard, Clarence, 1955
Mitchell, Fay, 1955

[1] McLendon, John B.—1959 NAIA Coach of the Year; first black coach to serve
  on The United States Olympic Committee 1966
[2] Martin, Ed—1972 NCAA College Division Coach of the Year

Morehead State University
Morehead, Kentucky 40351

All Ohio Valley Conference

Harrison, Earl, 1984
McCann, Robert, 1985–87
Boyd, Elbert, 1990

Ohio Valley Conference Player of the Year Award

Year • Player • College • Position
1965 • Clem Haskins • Western Kentucky University • G

1966 • Clem Haskins • Western Kentucky University • G
1967 • Clem Haskins • Western Kentucky University • G
1970 • Jim McDaniels • Western Kentucky University • C
1971 • Jim McDaniels • Western Kentucky University • C
1974 • James Williams • Austin Peay University • G/F
1975 • George Sorrell • Middle Tennessee State University • F
1976 • Johnny Britt (Co-Winner) • Western Kentucky University •
   F
1977 • Otis Howard • Austin Peay University • F
1978 • Otis Howard • Austin Peay University • F
1979 • James Tillman • Eastern Kentucky University • G
1981 • Jerry Beck • Middle Tennessee State University • F
1982 • Jerry Beck • Middle Tennessee State University • F
1985 • Stephen Kite • Tennessee Tech University • F
1987 • Bob McCann • Morehead State University • F
1988 • Jeff Martin • Murray State University • F
1989 • Jeff Martin • Murray State University • F
1990 • Ronald "Popeye" Jones • Murray State University • F
1991 • Ronald "Popeye" Jones • Murray State University • F

Ohio Valley Conference Coach of the Year Award

Year • Coach • College
1981 • Clem Haskins • Western Kentucky University

INDEPENDENTS (BLACK COLLEGES)*

1. University of the District of Columbia
2. Lincoln University (Pennsylvania)
3. Kentucky State University

4. Cheyney University of Pennsylvania
5. Bishop College

* These schools did not submit information for this edition.

University of the District of Columbia
Washington, D.C. 20008

Coaches of Varsity Teams

Waters, Emory, 1977
Barnes, Dempsey, 1978–79
Jones, Wil,[1] 1979–87
Epps, Ed, 1990–93

Women's Basketball

Hall, Cynthia, 1977
Montgomery, Carolyn, 1978
Stockard, Bessie, 1979–81
McGriff, Windy, 1981–82

Stockard, Bessie, 1982–84
Cummings, Bertha, 1984–Present

All Eastern College Athletic Conference

Jones, Earl, 1981–84
Britt, Michael, 1982–83

All-American

Britt, Michael, 1981–82
Jones, Earl, 1982–83

University of the District of Columbia Alumni in the
National Basketball Association

Jones, Earl, Los Angeles Lakers (C, F), 1984–85
San Antonio Spurs (C, F), 1985–86

[1] Jones, Wil—won the 1982 NCAA Division II Men's Basketball Championship

Lincoln University
Lincoln University, Pennsylvania 19352

Coaches of Varsity Teams

Rivero, Manuel, 1946–47
Stackhouse, Chester R., 1947–49
Rivero, Manuel, 1951–52
Hunter, W., 1952–56
Smith, Robert, 1957–66
Laisure, Floyd, 1967–68
Laisure, W.F., 1970–74
Randolph, D., 1974–77
Jones, Melvin, 1977–86

Women's Basketball

Sloan, Clementine, 1971–75
Nolan, Joyce, 1975–76
Crittenden, Barbara J., 1976–86

All Tournament Team

Usry, James, 1946
Hall, William, 1946

All Delaware Valley Conference

Hall, David, 1963
Hall, Ken, 1968
Moon, Lawrence, 1968

PAIAW All Conference

Women's Basketball

Cooper, Sonia, 1979–81
Williams, Tonya, 1981
Clayton, Bernadete, 1983
Clark, Trina, 1983–84
Anderson, Julia, 1984

All-American (Black College)

Wright, Sterling "Tree,"[1] 1973
Gooden, George R.,[2] 1973

[1] Wright, Sterling "Tree"—Honorable Mention
[2] Gooden, George R.—Honorable Mention

Kentucky State University
Frankfort, Kentucky 40601

Coaches of Varsity Teams

Kean, Henry Arthur
Fletcher, Joseph G., 1946–56
Brown, James B., 1957–64
McClendon, John, 1964–66
Williams, Robert D., 1966–67
Mitchell, Lucius, 1967–75
Oliver, James V., 1975–78
Thread, Floyd, 1978–80
McKinnie, Silas, 1980–81
Mitchell, Ron, 1981–82
Lykins, John, 1982–83
Skaggs, Richard, 1983–86
Peck, Paul, 1986–1990
Graham, William, 1990–93

Women's Basketball

Russell, Corneith, 1963–81
Mitchell, Ron, 1981

All Mid-Western Conference

Gray, Grant, 1946
Robinson, Harold "Dribble," 1948
Dixon, Luther "Chest," 1947–49
Roberts, Richard, 1949
Stewart, Thomas L., 1958

All-American (NAIA)

Grant, Travis, 1970–72
Smith, Elmore, 1970–72
Sibert, Sam, 1972
Carmichael, Harvey, 1974
Cunningham, Gerald, 1975–77
Linder, Lewis, 1975
Bates, Billy Ray, 1977–78

Kentucky State Alumni in the National Basketball Association

Smith, Elmore, Buffalo Braves, (C) 1971–73;
  Milwaukee Bucks, (C), 1975–77;
  Cleveland Cavaliers, (C), 1977–81
Sibert, Sam, Kansas City Kings, (G), 1973
Grant, Travis, A.B.A., Indiana Pacers, (F), 1975–76
Theard, Floyd, A.B.A., Denver Nuggets (G), 1969–70
Bates, Billy Ray, Portland Trailblazers, (G), 1979–82;
  Washington Bullets, (G), 1982–83
A.B.A. American Basketball Association

University of Pennsylvania, at Cheyney
Cheyney, Pennsylvania 19319

Coaches of Varsity Teams

O'Shields, William, 1956–63
Blitman, Harold, 1964–68
Coma, Anthony S., 1969–71
Chaney, John, 1972–82
Johnson, Keith, 1990–93

Women's Basketball

Dudley, Mildred, 1965–66
Bembry, Joyce, 1967–68
Spencer, Deborah, 1969–70
Stringer, Vivian, 1971–82
Tunstall, Jackie, 1988–93

All Pennsylvania State College Conference

Washington, Tom, 1966
Booker, Harold, 1968
Fillmore, Greg,[1] 1968
Wilson, James, 1969
Eldridge, Leroy, 1971
Kirkland, Charles, 1972
Allen, William, 1973
Bell, Leon, 1973

All-American (Small College)

Kirkland, Charles, 1972
Fields, Andrew, 1979
Melton, George, 1981–82

Women's Basketball

Walker, Valerie, 1981–82
Laney, Yolanda, 1984

University of Pennsylvania at Cheyney Alumni in the National Basketball Association

Fillmore, Greg, New York Knicks (C), 1970–72

[1] Fillmore, Greg—New York Knicks, 1970–72

Bishop College
Dallas, Texas 75241

Coaches of Varsity Teams

Jones, Emanuel, 1965–69
Alexander, Charles, 1969–72
Allen, Roy-Fisher Dwight, 1973
Lilly, Sylvester "Ben," 1974–88

Women's Basketball

Robinson, Myrtle, 1978–82
Young, Abron, 1982–88

All Southwestern Athletic Conference

Fairfax, Ruben, 1952
Seabeery, Leland, 1953–55

All-District, All-Star (NAIA)

Prince, Edgar, 1966
Smith, Paul, 1966
Lee, Raymond, 1966
Carter, Curtis, 1971
Collins, Willie, 1973

All-American (NAIA)

Lilly, Sylvester, 1968
Perry, Leonard, 1968
Collins, Willie, 1973
Govan, Dwain, 1974
Lilly, Shannon, 1983
Wright, William, 1985

Women's Basketball

Shaw, Tina, 1984

West Virginia State College
Institute, West Virginia 25112

Coaches of Varsity Teams

Cardwell, Mark, 1946–64
Enty, Frank, 1964–67
Gray, Grant, 1968–69
Burris, Chester A., 1969–72
Price, Curtis, 1973–76

Women's Basketball
Walker, Bettie J., 1954–58
Clark, Barbara, 1959–74
Randall, Edgar, 1981–85

All Central Intercollegiate Athletic Association All Tournament

Clark, Clarence,[1] 1948–49
Wilson, Robert, 1948–50
Lloyd, Earl, 1948–50
Perry, Ervell, 1951
Morris, James,[2] 1951

All-American (Black College or NAIA)

Moore, Ron, 1987

All West Virginia Intercollegiate Athletic Conference

Women's Basketball
Gordon, Donna, 1985
Battle, Maria, 1985

West Virginia State Alumni in the National Basketball Association

Lloyd, Earl, Syracuse Nationals, 1952–58;
  Detroit Pistons, 1958–60

[1] Clark, Clarence—1948 Most Valuable Player of the CIAA Tournament
[2] Morriss, James—1951 Most Valuable Player of the CIAA Tournament

Langston University
Langston, Oklahoma 73050

All Southwestern Athletic Conference

Johnson, Jack, 1952
Holmes, Clint, 1953
Dixon, Jay, 1955

Index

259